EDMUND G. ROSS

✦✦✦

EDMUND G. ROSS

Soldier ✦ Senator ✦ Abolitionist

RICHARD A. RUDDY

University of New Mexico Press | Albuquerque

© 2013 by the University of New Mexico Press
All rights reserved. Published 2013
Printed in the United States of America

18 17 16 15 14 13   1 2 3 4 5 6

Library of Congress Cataloging-in-Publication Data
Ruddy, Richard A., 1939–
  Edmund G. Ross : soldier, senator, abolitionist / Richard A. Ruddy.
      pages cm
  Includes bibliographical references and index.
  ISBN 978-0-8263-5374-0 (cloth : alk. paper)
  ISBN 978-0-8263-5375-7 (electronic)
1. Ross, Edmund G. (Edmund Gibson), 1826–1907.
2. Legislators—United States—Biography.
3. United States. Congress. Senate—Biography.
4. Johnson, Andrew, 1808–1875—Impeachment.
5. Governors—New Mexico—Biography.
6. New Mexico—History—1848–
I. Title.
  E664.R74R83 2013
  978.9'04092—dc23
    [B]
                        2013015142

TO MY WIFE, MARY

✦✦✦

CONTENTS

✦✦✦

Illustrations follow page 165.

PREFACE

⌒ MY INTEREST IN EDMUND G. ROSS began in part with John F. Kennedy's *Profiles in Courage*. Even before knowing about the Ross chapter in Kennedy's book, I was introduced to a collection of photographs of the Ross family kept in the photo archive at the Albuquerque Museum, where I volunteered after retiring from a thirty-year career as a commercial photographer. I was surprised to learn that the Edmund G. Ross in the photographs, then a territorial governor of New Mexico, was the same person as the United States senator from Kansas featured in *Profiles in Courage*. I would soon discover that Ross played other roles in late-nineteenth-century America: first as a leader in the abolitionist movement in the years before the Civil War and then through his lifework as a newspaper editor and eloquent observer of the extraordinary times in which he lived.

In the spring of 2005 I used the museum images of Ross and his family, combined with additional research I had done, to give a talk to an audience of nearly two hundred people, including a number of Ross descendants. The response to my story of Ross's life was enthusiastic, with many questions and, most notably, the suggestion from several people that I write his biography. In late 2005 I found myself digging ever deeper into the life of this most interesting man.

Three previous biographies of Ross have been written. The first, *The Life of Edmund G. Ross* by Edward Bumgardner, was published in 1949. The book is based mainly on memoirs by Ross's daughter Lillian Ross Leis. It is a rather short account of Ross's life, mentioning almost nothing of his years in New Mexico. It is notable that Bumgardner realized the shortcomings of his book, and in the foreword he encouraged someone else to "unearth more material than has been accessible to me, and write an adequate biography of Senator Ross." In 1960 a fictional account of Ross's life was written by Loula Grace Erdman, told from the point of view of his wife Fannie. Because *Many a Voyage* is historical fiction, it is not the scholarly work that Bumgardner had in mind in recommending that someone else do the necessary research to write an adequate biography. In 1997 a very short and incomplete biography of Ross, *Edmund G. Ross: A Man of Courage*, was published by Ross's great-grandson Arthur Elliot Harrington. It was a noble effort by Harrington but very sparse. Yale historian Howard R. Lamar wrote a superb appraisal of Ross's tenure as territorial governor of New Mexico in a 1961 article for the *New Mexico Historical Review* and in 1966 wrote extensively about Ross in New Mexico for his history *The Far Southwest, 1846–1912*. In 1983 Karen Diane Shane wrote an excellent master's thesis about Ross's territorial administration, which I found very useful.

As I learned more about Ross, however, I found that in contrast to Kennedy's admiration for Ross, there were a few scholars who were not so sure about Ross's courage. What Kennedy and Ross's critics had in common was a very narrow look at Ross's life, for the most part confining their studies of Ross to the months surrounding the impeachment trial of President Andrew Johnson in 1868. While I was intrigued by all I had learned about Ross, I became more interested in uncovering the full story of his life and work.

I was fortunate to have a wealth of written material by Edmund Ross himself. He spent the bulk of his adult years as a newspaper editor and publisher, and virtually all of his journalistic writing is extant, nearly twenty years' worth of newspaper columns. Because he was frequently separated from his family, there is a reasonable collection of letters saved by Fannie, primarily during his Civil War years and his years in the United States Senate. Unfortunately, because Ross did not save personal letters, only a few of the letters she wrote to him are available. Ross's time in New Mexico as territorial governor is well documented with eight linear feet of documents and letters, mostly available on microfilm. Aspects of Ross's personal life are documented by Lillian Ross Leis, whose informal and unpublished memoir was done in three parts. Although Leis's recollections of her father are reliable and add richness to the Ross story, her historical references were at times not entirely accurate. I was therefore careful to find a second source for confirmation in these circumstances, or, failing that, to avoid using unsubstantiated information. Of course Ross, who was a controversial figure throughout much of his life, had his detractors and supporters, and there is an abundance of newspaper articles that both criticize and praise Ross. Care had to be taken with information derived from journalists who were strongly biased for or against him.

This book assumes that biography is history, that the recounting of the lives of individuals provides multiple ways of understanding the past. Edmund Ross's life reveals a great deal about who we were as Americans in the second half of the nineteenth century. Because Ross's life was a unique collection of experiences, his biography is a one-of-a-kind look at one of the most eventful periods in American history. The abolitionist movement and struggle to bring Kansas into the Union as a free state, the expansion of railroads west of the Mississippi, the Civil War, Reconstruction and the impeachment of Andrew Johnson, the Gilded Age with its greedy politicians and businessmen, as well as the rapid expansion of the United States into the isolated Southwest—Ross played important roles in all of these events. While he has been remembered as the senator who cast a crucial vote on May 16, 1868, there is more, much more, to be known of the life of Edmund G. Ross.

ACKNOWLEDGMENTS

⌒ THE YEARS OF RESEARCHING and writing this biography brought me in touch with many new friends and into a closer relationship with old friends. I will attempt to acknowledge the help I received from those who are so deserving of recognition and appreciation, and extend my sincere apologies to anyone I may have failed to mention.

As you might expect, my wife, Mary, is at the top of the list. Family members used to say she could be a great trial lawyer, and her careful reading of each chapter, followed by penetrating questions and comments, leaves me without a doubt this is true. She's been a wonderful partner and love for more than fifty years.

Ann Paden was my editor in the years before I was ready to submit the manuscript to the University of New Mexico Press, and more broadly speaking, she was a coach who advised and encouraged, making me believe I could do the work necessary to finish the Ross story. I have Denis Norlander, another good friend, to thank both for introducing me to Ann and for her belief that a definitive biography of Edmund G. Ross was needed. Ann Marlowe, copy editor extraordinaire, helped me through the final stage of polishing the manuscript.

Edmund and Fannie Ross's descendants must be recognized for their help. Foremost is Lillian Ross Leis (1849–1945) whose memoirs of her father were an invaluable source of information which I used extensively. Lillian longed for her father to be remembered and understood. Edmund Pitt "Ned" Ross and Elizabeth "Betsy" Ross Lackmann, Ross's great-grandchildren, helped with family stories and other recollections handed down through the generations. Betsy's daughter, Stephanie Padilla, the Ross family genealogist and archivist, generously devoted a huge amount of her time digging out facts, stories, documents, and photos. I am most grateful to Stephanie and hope I did not impose on her good-natured help too often. Two other descendants, Steven Edmund Ross (Ned's son) and Susan K. Woodward (granddaughter of Eddie Ross Cobb), gave up an evening to sort through boxes of family memorabilia at Steve's house.

I was privileged to have four superb educators commit to reading the manuscript in its early stages. Among them were three widely published authors from the University of New Mexico: David E. Stuart, Richard A. Melzer, and Vincent Barrett Price. Spencer Wilson, my friend from Historic Albuquerque, Inc., and emeritus professor of history at New Mexico Tech, likewise read the early manuscript and shared his comments.

The completed manuscript was read by two distinguished scholars for the University of New Mexico Press: David L. Caffey, a board member of the Historical Society of New Mexico, member of the New Mexico State Library Commission, and author of a number of books and articles on New Mexico history, and Mark Weitz, practicing attorney, author, and noted Civil War and constitutional law historian. The analysis and comments of all of these readers were superb and made me aware that there is a kind of kinship among historians who are willing to spend hours helping one another preserve history to meet the goal of "getting it right."

Friends from Historic Albuquerque, Inc., helped me as well. Diane Schaller, HAI president, devoted a great deal of time to retrieving nineteenth-century newspaper articles, for which I am most grateful. Ann Carson alerted me to a number of excellent sources about Vinnie Ream. I wish to also express my appreciation to other HAI members, particularly Mo Palmer, Deb Slaney, Glenn Fye, Dick Berg, Ray Shortridge, Joe Sabatini, and Richard Avery, all of whom encouraged me through the long process.

The librarians and archivists at various institutions were good listeners and retrievers. I had excellent help at the Kansas State Historical Society, the Center for Southwest Research at the University of New Mexico, the

New Mexico State Library and State Archives in Santa Fe, the Albuquerque/ Bernalillo County Library System, the Albuquerque Museum, and the Library of Congress in Washington, D.C.

As important as word processing is and as much as I appreciate its magical capabilities, inevitably technical problems arose that were beyond my limited skills. I could always count on one or the other of my two sons, Chris and Brian, to come to my rescue. My good friend Bob Tapscott carefully guided me through problems with endnotes and pagination.

Julie Dunleavy, another dear friend, read an account of Jim Lane's last days and helped me understand the demons that likely drove him to end his own life. I would also like to acknowledge friends of many years standing, Walter Haussamen and his wife Frances, both longtime students of New Mexico history. Walter's detailed notes on early Ross family photographs were particularly helpful.

Of course, the staff at the University of New Mexico Press patiently guided me through the complex process of book publication. In particular I want to express appreciation to W. Clark Whitehorn, Maya Allen-Gallegos, Elizabeth "Beth" Hadas, James Ayers, and Marie Landau.

Thanks also to Karen Mazur for the cover design and to my good friend Tom Antreasian who once again shared his graphic design ideas.

CHAPTER ONE

YOUNG MAN WORKING
AT THE CASE

In 1846 I attended the public high school, working at the case in the
Democratic Mirror printing office, mornings and evenings, to pay my way.
—Edmund G. Ross, quoted by Lillian Ross Leis

↶ JOSHUA GLOVER WAS A RUNAWAY slave from Missouri who, in 1854, made his way north to Racine, Wisconsin, a community known for its sizeable abolitionist population. He was able to secure employment at a mill and presumably was enjoying life until the night of March 10, 1854, when deputy federal marshals made a surprise raid on the shack he lived in. When he resisted arrest, he was knocked to the floor, beaten with a club, handcuffed, and dragged off to a jail in Milwaukee, where he was to be held until he could be returned to Missouri.[1]

Word of Glover's capture spread quickly throughout abolitionist circles and to the office of Sherman M. Booth, editor of the *Milwaukee Free Democrat*. Booth immediately began to organize a group of about one hundred men in Milwaukee who were joined by one hundred or so additional men from nearby Racine. Booth was said to have ridden up and down the streets of Milwaukee on a white horse yelling, "Freemen to the rescue." A crowd quickly grew to more than a thousand people, some of whom, including Edmund G. Ross and his brother William, stormed the jail where Glover was held, freed him, and helped him escape to Canada.[2]

It so happened that the Ross brothers worked for Sherman Booth. Lillian Ross, Edmund's eldest child, was just five years old on March 11, but she was old enough to remember part of the Glover story with the assistance of John Rastall, a family friend and participant in the Glover rescue. She writes about her father, her uncle William, and Sherman Booth's brother and about much excitement during a noon meal. When the three men left, Lillian's mother told her to take her doll and sit on the front porch, that she soon would see her father going by. After sitting there for a time she heard a rumbling sound that grew louder and louder "until there appeared a long column of men, two abreast and marching 'double quick' . . . then I saw my father and his brother, side by side, and he looked up at me and smiled while running."[3]

For Sherman Booth the Glover incident was a disaster. He was among the first slave rescuers to be charged and tried in court under the Fugitive Slave Act of 1850. His ordeal received national attention. Booth's contention that the law was unconstitutional eventually led to a Wisconsin Supreme Court ruling agreeing with Booth. The case, *Abelman v. Booth*, found its way to the U.S. Supreme Court, where a landmark decision found that the Wisconsin Supreme Court lacked the authority to find a federal law unconstitutional.[4] Booth's legal battle was complicated and lasted years, and in the end he lost. He lost his newspaper and was financially ruined.[5] The Ross brothers were fortunate to escape prosecution. Both Edmund and his brother William found jobs at the *Milwaukee Sentinel*, Edmund as foreman of the press and manager of the job office.[6]

The Glover rescue is the first time Edmund Ross, at the age of twenty-seven, was known to have participated publicly as an abolitionist, but his opposition to slavery reached back into his childhood. He and his siblings were raised to be abolitionists. He was born on December 7, 1826, in Ashland, Ohio, the third of fourteen children. Edmund was said to have been rather small when he was born. He also suffered through a serious bout of scarlet fever and may have been somewhat frail. Edmund's father, Sylvester Ross Sr., a former teacher turned farmer, must have been a loving man who paid close attention to his children, to their talents and limitations. For his eldest son, Sylvester Ross Jr., and Edmund, he arranged apprenticeships with Henry C. Grey, who owned the *Huron Commercial Advertiser*, a weekly newspaper. In particular, Edmund's father believed that life as a farmer was not suitable for Edmund because of his small size and delicate health. It appears that Edmund, while still a young boy, went to live with Mr. and Mrs. Grey to learn the trade of commercial printing. He and the Greys remained lifelong friends.[7] The printing trade would be a major way for Ross to earn his living throughout his life. Even when he was a newspaper owner, job printing was an important source of income supplementing the often marginal income produced by small-town newspapers.

In 1841 Edmund's brother Sylvester purchased the press owned by the Greys and moved it to Sandusky, Ohio, taking Edmund with him. Sylvester entered into a partnership with a man named Mills, forming the company Mills and Ross, publishers of the *Sandusky Mirror*, a newspaper later known as the *Democratic Mirror*. Edmund continued his apprenticeship at the *Mirror* while also attending high school, working mornings and evenings at the newspaper office. While living in Sandusky, Edmund attended the Congregational Church located next to the high school, where he sang in the church choir and in a quartet with Fannie Lathrop, a young woman who eventually became his wife.[8] The group of four, which also included Fannie's sister Esther and her boyfriend, sang together frequently at church and at picnics and other social gatherings. Throughout their married life, family singing and music would be a part of the Ross household.

Fannie's father was a prominent Universalist and temperance worker and a direct descendant of a Congregationalist pioneer.[9] Universalists and Congregationalists both were liberal denominations likely opposed to slavery, with at least some members involved in the Underground Railroad in Ohio. Sources say little about Ross's religious background, but we can presume it was liberal, given the abolitionist stand he and his siblings and parents shared.[10]

It is very likely that Ross was aware of the Underground Railroad, since Sandusky, a port community on Lake Erie, was a major terminus where runaway slaves would find transportation into Canada. The town was code named Hope, with at least a dozen safe houses.[11] Ross would also have known about Underground Railroad activities through his church or through his brother at the *Sandusky Mirror*. Whether he participated in assisting any runaway slaves in Sandusky is not known. He was still young when he and Sylvester arrived there in 1841, but he was clearly a devoted abolitionist as a teenager. Even at a young age Ross took an active part in the antislavery movement with his participation in the Liberty Party and later in the Free-Soil Democratic Party. His first vote was cast for Martin Van Buren in 1848.[12]

Leis records that her father had strong negative opinions about capital punishment, which he expressed at an 1846 high school assembly. Ross wrote about the assembly, a regular event at which students read their own compositions. Most students, according to Ross, read essays "representing the extreme religious ideas then prevailing." Without going into detail, Ross said that his paper represented an opposite point of view, one that did not go over well with the "so-called orthodox clergy" who were present. He was informed that he must cease, at once, presenting such essays or leave the school. He chose the latter course, ending his scholastic education.[13]

Leis tells us that after he left the school, Edmund went to Mills and Ross and printed the paper he had just presented, then distributed it among the students at the high school. The essay was also apparently printed in the *Democratic Mirror*. It is surprisingly well written for a teenager and uses quotes from the Bible to defend his position, probably rankling the orthodox clergy at the school. The incident foreshadowed the spring of 1868 when Ross would again be compelled to stand by his convictions.

A sample of Fannie Lathrop's writing from that period is also extant. Although the letter of December 10, 1846, to her brother George is only about family matters, it is well written and reveals a young woman who seems both happy and well educated. It is important only because it reveals the carefree period of extraordinary happiness she, and no doubt Edmund, was experiencing. She told her brother that it was "the common report around town that there is to be a wedding at the Lathrops before long." It seems that both Fannie and her sister would be married and that both sisters believed they would be moving from Sandusky. "I talk of going to Wisconsin and Esther, Oh! I forgot I must not tell where she is going."[14]

The fact is that only Fannie would leave town, and not until 1852; Esther never did. And although Fannie may have entertained the idea of an imminent marriage, that was probably not what Edmund had in mind. He was already by this time exploring the neighboring states, feeling the sense of freedom that young men yearn for in their late teens and early twenties. The letter also suggests that Edmund and Fannie had talked seriously about living in Wisconsin. By 1846 Edmund's parents and younger siblings had moved to a farm near Janesville, Wisconsin.

By the time he left high school, Edmund Ross already had seven years of experience as a typesetter and printer and was skilled enough to earn a living. Ross himself tells us that he spent a few years traveling throughout Ohio, Indiana, Michigan, Illinois, and Wisconsin as a "tramping" journeyman printer.[15] He would fill in on a temporary basis for people on vacation or absent from their jobs for various reasons. He traversed the distances between towns mostly by walking and in 1847 ended up in Janesville at the home of his parents. He spent the summer in Janesville and perhaps even discussed the idea of marriage to Fannie. During the year after his arrival back in Sandusky, Edmund and Fannie must have spent much time getting to know each other even better and planning their life together. On October 15, 1848, Edmund and Fannie were married. They would spend the next fifty-one years together until Fannie's death in Albuquerque, New Mexico, in November 1899.

There is a refreshing lightness conveyed by Ross's adventures "tramping" around neighboring states and Fannie's letter anticipating marriage. Seemingly there was an absence of worry, life without the weight of any tragedy in it. Even after their marriage, life for a time was carefree for Edmund and Fannie. Ross continued to work at the *Democratic Mirror* "at the case." In the nineteenth century this was a skilled job, typesetting every letter by hand and doing it with speed and confidence to meet deadlines. In addition to setting type for the newspaper, Ross was also a job printer, producing various forms, invoices, booklets, flyers, posters, and the like. Most likely this was a good job working for his brother and his brother's partner at Mills and Ross, but there was tragedy on the horizon that would corrupt this period of freedom from worry.

About six months after Edmund and Fannie married, the devastating Asiatic cholera epidemic of 1849 reached Sandusky. During the summer months of that year nearly four hundred residents of Sandusky died, including Sylvester, who was an early victim, and Fannie's father and two of her sisters, including Esther, who had yearned to leave Sandusky but never did. They died within a week of each other.[16] Leis tells us that Fannie's father and her sister Esther, by then married with two children, "were heroic in their efforts to aid others and paid the penalty."[17] During the epidemic, the population of Sandusky dropped from about five thousand to about one thousand as a result of the exodus from the scourge. It was a terrifying disease because it was so deadly and because its cause was unknown. Ross's uncle Elial J. Rice, his mother's younger brother, made a trip to Sandusky from Sullivan, Ohio, early in the epidemic to rescue family members. Rice took Edmund and Fannie, who was pregnant, back to Sullivan, where they remained until that fall when it was safe to return.

In the year after returning to Sandusky, Ross partially relived the epidemic when the printing firm, now without his brother, was hired to work with a Dr. Joel Roberts to produce a sixty-six-page book about the 1849 outbreak. The small book was a digest of theories by a number of "medical and other professional gentlemen" suggesting possible causes and methods of treatment. A father-and-son team came closest to understanding cholera when they observed through a microscope that "the animals found to exist in the atmosphere, and in the bodies of cholera patients, may be essentially concerned in the propagation of this frightful epidemic, or they may have nothing whatever to do in this way."[18] The "animals" were, of course, bacteria, and the specific source of cholera, contaminated water. The small book listed every Sandusky victim.

The horrors of 1849 were at least partially offset for Edmund and Fannie when their first child, Lillian, was born on October 14, 1849. As happy as Edmund and Fannie surely were about the birth, it must have been difficult for them to fill the void of four lost lives and to help Fannie's mother deal with the agony of a lost husband and two children. Thoughts of fleeing to another place with new distractions and new challenges certainly crossed their minds, and in 1852 Fannie, Edmund, Lillian, and Fannie's mother and brothers finally made the move to Wisconsin.

Much had changed in the eleven years since Edmund and his brother first arrived in Sandusky. Ross had learned some hard lessons in life and in surviving profound disappointment, from which he and Fannie gained strength of character. He also had acquired marketable skills in the printing trade and, more important, had honed his appreciation for and ability to use the written word. Certainly Ross would agree that the most important decision of his life was made during those Sandusky years, the decision to ask Fannie Lathrop to be his wife. Edmund Ross was able to count on Fannie for love and support through the full half century of their marriage—through numerous arduous household moves, through the death of a beloved child, through war and civil strife, and through periods of extreme financial hardship. She became his greatest source of strength when he faced fierce attacks on his character, especially during the years following the Andrew Johnson impeachment trial. But in 1852 the promise of a better life lay ahead in Milwaukee, with no hint of the hard times yet to come in Kansas.

CHAPTER TWO

THE ABOLITIONISTS

A Call to Action

We have not come here to be trampled upon or be made to toady to any power on earth . . . If we do not have to fight now we in all probability shall on or before the fourth of March, the time set for our legislature to meet and the Wheels of Government to commence turning.

—William Ross to Edmund Ross, Lawrence, Kansas,
January 10, 1856

⌐ LILLIAN ROSS LEIS, in recollections of her childhood, gives a glimpse into the life of her family in Milwaukee, no doubt with the help of stories passed on to her by her parents, aunts, uncles, and family friends. Although these may not be altogether her own clear memories, they are nonetheless valid. She writes about her mother referring to her father and her uncle William as "the boys" and describes the long cloaks with plaid linings the two men wore to their jobs at the newspaper and how they walked to work each day. She talks about the Barnum Circus setting up a large tent near their home and how her father took her there one evening to see Tom Thumb and the carriage given to him by Queen Victoria and how they saw a polar bear as well. She remembers concerts they attended as a family and Sunday afternoons singing together. It was a home with books: "Little Fearns," "Anderson's Tales," and "Auntie Wonderful" are storybooks she specifically mentions.[1]

Lillian particularly liked the house they lived in near the lake, a cozy nine-room cottage "painted salmon with a green latticed portico and porch." The living room was where they played and lived. She describes simple draperies and furnishings and a center table with books and an "astral lamp" that seemed fragile to her. There were two churches on the corner adjacent to their home, the Plymouth Church and a Presbyterian church. There was also an academy for girls on the corner where Edmund's sister Nancy went to school. Both Nancy and William lived with Edmund and Fannie and Lillian. We get a picture of a comfortable home in a well-established neighborhood with beautiful trees and green lawns.[2]

This description of life for the Ross family sounds almost too good to be true. It probably was not exactly as Leis remembered it, but it was a good life. Edmund and William had steady employment, and Edmund especially could be optimistic about his future as foreman of the press at the *Milwaukee Sentinel*, a daily paper. If life for the Ross family was comfortable, it was also in sharp contrast to what lay just ahead for them. The Joshua Glover episode foreshadowed the future. Life in America was changing rapidly, and these changes would profoundly affect the Ross family, given their willingness to be actively involved in the abolitionist movement.

The years leading to the Civil War included major legislative and judicial milestones. Among these was the Fugitive Slave Act of 1850, the law that Sherman Booth was charged with breaking. The law made it a particularly serious offense to assist runaway slaves. Law enforcement officers were required to arrest any runaway slave known to them or face a serious fine, and any person offering a runaway either food or shelter was subject to six months in jail or a $1,000 fine. Law enforcement officers were even rewarded with fees for capturing slaves.[3] The law was a significant appeasement to southern slaveholders. As John F. Kennedy pointed out, the Fugitive Slave Act to northerners was "the most bitterly hated measure—and until Prohibition, the most flagrantly disobeyed—ever passed by Congress."[4]

The Fugitive Slave Act was just one of five elements in the Great Compromise of 1850 engineered by the great compromiser, Henry Clay of Kentucky. The compromise was a means of keeping a balance between northern and southern states. In addition to the Fugitive Slave Act, the compromise admitted California into the Union as a free state. New Mexico and Utah were organized as territories without restrictions on slavery. Texas was entitled to compensation for territory ceded to New Mexico, and the slave trade was outlawed in the District of Columbia.[5]

A bigger milestone on the path to the Civil War was the Kansas-Nebraska Act of 1854. The Compromise of 1850 kept a balance between North and South, but as the country expanded into the West and Northwest, new territories were created, and an imbalance was inevitable. Lewis Cass, a presidential candidate in 1848 who lost to Zachary Taylor, is credited with the concept of popular sovereignty as a means of dealing with tensions between northern and southern states as new territories emerged. The idea was for residents of new territories to decide for themselves such issues as the legalization of slavery.[6] With the Compromise of 1850 Cass's popular sovereignty ideas were temporarily sidelined.

In January 1854 Senator Stephen A. Douglas of Illinois introduced a bill that called for the northern half of the Louisiana Purchase to be divided into two territories, Kansas and Nebraska. This bill was a modification of a bill introduced by Senator Augustus Dodge the year before.[7] Douglas included in his bill the right of the territorial residents to decide "yes or no" on the issue of slavery. This popular sovereignty approach automatically meant the repeal of the Missouri Compromise of 1820, once thought to be forever unchangeable. The Missouri Compromise allowed Maine into the Union as a free state and Missouri as a slave state, and established that after 1820 slavery would never be allowed north of the parallel 36°30', the southern boundary of Missouri, except within the proposed state of Missouri itself.

The thirty-four years between 1820 and 1854 saw major changes, as the North industrialized while the southern economy remained mainly agrarian. The abolitionist movement in the North also grew significantly and became more vocal. What was a reasonably acceptable compromise in 1820 to both North and South was no longer acceptable, especially to southern plantation owners who asserted that slavery was legal and that denying their right to take slavery into newly created territories was unconstitutional. The backlash in the North to the dissolution of the Missouri Compromise line set off more than mere vocal outrage. With the signing into law of the Kansas-Nebraska Act by President Franklin Pierce in May 1854, abolitionists and other free-staters began to move to Kansas in large numbers—but so did southerners, especially proslavery Missourians just across the border from Kansas.

The Ross family must have experienced the same outrage that other abolitionists experienced at the possibility of more states allowing slavery, but they also had responsibilities and distractions to deal with in their own lives. Edmund had a family to care for, and leaving Wisconsin to move to Kansas was not as simple an option as it would be for William. For William there was a major distraction, a very attractive French immigrant girl with large dark eyes. This led to marriage for William and the addition of another member to the Ross household in Milwaukee. Love and marriage also found their way to Edmund's sister Nancy Amelia, who married

S. P. Wemple. Leis gives no information about where the Wemples lived, but if it was in the Ross house, things must have gotten a bit crowded, especially since by this time Edmund and Fannie had their second child, Arthur Ross, born June 8, 1853.[8] In the midst of the happy events in the Ross family, there was certainly apprehension as they followed developments in Kansas.

If the tipping point between words and serious action for most abolitionists had not already been reached by May 1854, it certainly came in that important month. When the Kansas-Nebraska Act became a reality, abolitionists began to organize in groups with the intention of moving as many antislavery people as possible to Kansas. Through dispatches to the *Milwaukee Sentinel*, Edmund and William would have watched the development of such organizations as the New England Emigrant Aid Company, the brainchild of Eli Thayer. Thayer traveled throughout New England and New York lecturing about the company and its objectives. He enlisted other speakers including Edward Everett Hale, and because of their efforts the Emigrant Aid Company became a high-profile organization capturing the attention of Horace Greeley of the *New York Tribune*, William Cullen Bryant of the *New York Evening Post*, and Thurlow Weed of the *Albany Journal*.[9]

The Emigrant Aid Company was an inspiration to other groups and individuals including everyone in the Ross family. William and Nancy Amelia and their spouses, who did not have children yet, were relatively free to travel. They began their long trek to Kansas in the summer of 1855 accompanied by a third sibling, George Ross, who was not yet sixteen years old and still living on the farm at Janesville. Sylvester Ross Sr. sent George along to drive a few cattle in preparation for the Ross parents and other family members to make the same trip to Kansas in the near future.[10] Leis writes that William "had become imbued with the spirit then urging men to rally to the cause of the Negro and to make the Territory of Kansas a free state."[11] There was a big send-off for the newlyweds and George at the Ross farm in Janesville. Edmund and Fannie and their two children made the trip to the farm to say their farewells. It is a fair guess that Edmund and Fannie too would have been making the trip in 1855, except that Fannie was already pregnant with their third child.

Free-staters who made the move to Kansas did so for a variety of reasons, and not just because they were opposed to slavery. Many saw an opportunity to acquire land cheaply. Some were opposed to the expansion of the plantation system into the territories without simultaneously having much sympathy for slaves. Whatever complex reasons the Ross family had for leaving a comfortable home in Milwaukee to settle in Territorial Kansas, it is clear that the overriding reason was the abhorrence of slavery.

Details of the William Ross party's trip to Kansas are not known, but apparently their route took them through Missouri. This was partly documented by Sara Robinson, a resident of Lawrence who was among the first settlers to arrive under the sponsorship of the New England Emigrant Aid Society and whose book *Kansas: Its Interior and Exterior Life,* published in 1857, was a classic even at the time. Robinson writes that William Ross and company arrived on September 6, 1855, and that they were accompanied by two men hired in Missouri. One of these was a free black whose presence caused immediate problems when the man was confronted by a Dr. Wood, a disagreeable human being, whose reputation for causing trouble was well known. Wood demanded to see the man's papers proving that he was free, but even this did not satisfy him, and he threatened that "the negro should be thrown into the river unless he returned to Missouri."[12] The ensuing days brought even more trouble. A Hungarian immigrant named Schareff announced his intention to shoot the man and began his trek to the Ross property, which was located about two miles from Lawrence. Schareff had the bad luck to accept a wagon ride from a fellow named Evans who, as it turned out, was the freedman's good friend and the other man hired by William Ross in Missouri. Evans disarmed Schareff before he reached the Ross property.

On Sunday, September 9, a wagonload of men accompanied by others on horseback headed out for the Ross property to shoot the freedman or to otherwise rid the area of him. This caused enough commotion in town that few people showed up for Sunday services. When the mob arrived, the Rosses' black employee was out herding livestock and not nearby. William Ross, assisted by neighbors who saw the mob arriving, told the men that "[i]f they wished to fight him they could do so; but they could not have the Negro."[13] They left without provoking a fight but vowed to return with even more men.

The experience of William Ross and company is indicative of the extreme friction that existed at that time between pro- and antislavery factions in Kansas and even tensions that existed between some antislavery residents. It would soon enough escalate into bloody confrontations. In the early territorial years, free-state advocates tended to be rather passive. Until immigration from northern states picked up substantially, free-staters were overwhelmed by "border ruffians" from Missouri, a slave state, who were better armed and more aggressive in behavior.

The impractical side of popular sovereignty was readily apparent in the territorial election of legislators on March 30, 1855. Free-Soil voters were outnumbered and intimidated by proslavery voters, many, if not most, of whom did not actually reside in Kansas but had crossed the border from Missouri. Ballot-box stuffing and threats of violence were common. *Bleeding Kansas* author Nicole Etcheson, in her essay on popular sovereignty, cites a preelection Kansas census that recorded 2,905 legal voters in the territory; nonetheless, more than 6,000 votes were counted in the 1855 election, overwhelmingly in favor of candidates who favored slavery.[14]

Although the election was clearly fraudulent, the Franklin Pierce administration declared it valid. Free-staters were justifiably upset with the certification of the election, and the abolitionists among them were additionally appalled at the laws passed later in 1855 by the new proslavery legislative body in regard to slavery and the rights of blacks, whether free or slave. Edmund Ross cited a number of these laws in his essay "A Reminiscence of the Kansas Conflict." No black or mulatto person could be a witness against a white man in a lawsuit. Marriage between a white person and a mulatto was prohibited and punishable by fine and imprisonment. Schools were closed to blacks, free or slave. Assisting the escape of a slave was punishable by death or imprisonment for a minimum of ten years.

The unfolding of events in 1855–1856 became a matter of serious concern throughout the country. Kansas was the crucible where the fight over slavery began to play itself out. The concept of popular sovereignty was a way of appeasing southern slave owners, but there was no way factions on either side of the slavery issue in Kansas were going to meekly accept defeat. Free-staters could not and would not accept the authority of the territorial government, and in the summer of 1855 they began to organize a parallel Free-State government in defiance of the Pierce administration. A series of meetings for free-state advocates was held during July, August, and September, leading to the formation of the Free-State Party and the announcement of a Free-State constitutional convention for October 23, 1855. In addition, Free-Staters refused to participate in the October 1 election for a territorial representative to Congress, claiming that the territorial government had been fraudulently elected and therefore could not have been legally certified.

The site of the October 23 Free-State convention was Topeka. In effect, meeting as they did, the Free-Staters were effectively engaging in civil disobedience. Individuals defied the new territorial laws as well. The *Kansas Tribune*, published and edited by John Speer in Lawrence, openly flouted one of the new laws, which strictly prohibited the publication of anything that "denied the right of persons to hold slaves in the territory." Violation of the new law was punishable by "imprisonment and hard labor for a term of not less than five years." On September 15 Speer defiantly published a full-page condemnation of the law in bold type, saying, "and it is not only the right, but the bounden duty of every Freeman to spurn with contempt and trample under foot an enactment which thus basely violates the rights of Freemen."

William Ross, who had been in the Lawrence area for only eleven days when Speer published his declaration, probably was already well acquainted with Speer and soon became his partner. The earliest extant issue of the *Kansas Tribune* with William Ross's name on the editorial page is December 10, 1855. In that issue Speer and Ross announced the move of the newspaper from Lawrence to Topeka. Although not stated in the paper, the reason for moving to Topeka was probably its safer environment. Lawrence, being some thirty miles closer to Missouri, was more vulnerable to attack by border ruffians and in fact would be the primary target of proslavery ruffians for years to come. The *Kansas Tribune*, along with a few other antislavery papers, was thought to be a high-profile target of the ruffians. The fact that Lawrence had two other newspapers was an additional reason for the *Tribune*'s move to Topeka, where there was a potentially larger readership.

With the establishment of a Free-State constitution in December, the election of Free-State officers in January, and the first meeting of the Free-State legislature in March, the parallel and renegade Free-State government was complete, and proslavery residents cried "treason" loud enough to be heard throughout the United States. On January 10 William Ross wrote a letter to Edmund in which he refers to the election. He tells his brother that "[p]ro-slavery men attempted to take the ballot box from the people of Easton" and that elsewhere there was gunfire at polling places. William proclaimed that "our rights must be protected even at the cost of our heart's blood. . . . We have not come here to be trampled upon or be made to toady to any power on earth. . . . If we do not have to fight now we in all probability shall on or before the fourth of March." He expressed a dire need for guns and ammunition and asked Edmund for help in obtaining them. "If there is any way under Heaven of getting guns here I wish they could be sent for fight we must between this and Spring.[15]

The decision to make the move to Kansas could not have been an easy one for Edmund. By that January he was the father of three small children, and the decision to go had to include the feelings of his wife as well. Just how Fannie felt about uprooting a family that had security and a good life is not known, but it would not be surprising if she were unhappy about an arduous six-hundred-mile journey headed for pioneer life in a place known to be dangerous. In all likelihood Edmund and his father had thoroughly discussed the move to Kansas by late 1855 and had started preparations for a spring departure.

The move to Kansas included more than just the Ross family. Leadership in recruiting members for immigration to Territorial Kansas can be largely credited to Edward D. Holton, a Milwaukee banker. Holton also raised funds to assist those who needed it. In his honor the first settlement established by the Milwaukee group was named Holton, now a town north of Topeka. When Ross announced his intention to leave his job at the *Sentinel*, join the party from Milwaukee, and be its leader, the printers of Milwaukee honored him at a meeting and presented him with a rifle, handmade by a local gunsmith.[16] The *Sentinel* reported the departure of the wagon train on May 21, 1856. "The party of emigrants for Kansas, numbering about fifty persons, started yesterday on their journey over-land, the white tops of their wagons, as they passed through the streets, reminding one of the California caravans of a few years since. They will be joined on their route by other parties from this State and will form a welcome addition to the Army of Freedom in Kansas." [17]

At Janesville, Ross's mother and father and three more siblings joined the caravan along with five members of the Andrew Smith family and five members of the Lyme family. Edmund's father had loaded a farm wagon with all the belongings he could squeeze into it. His two youngest sons drove the wagon pulled by four oxen. A cow named Crump and a black filly named Meg were tied to the back of the wagon. In addition Sylvester rigged a two-seat surrey with a canvas top in which he and Edmund's mother and young sister would ride. Sylvester drove the surrey ahead of the caravan, scouting for resting places and overnight campsites.[18] Edmund Ross gave his own description of the wagon train. Edmund put the distance to Topeka at six hundred miles. When they started they had a dozen or so men on foot to serve as helpers in care of the teams, as aides at campsites, and as the principal fighting force should there be trouble. As the caravan moved along, they picked up additional wagons, until at Nebraska City the wagon train consisted of about one hundred wagons accompanied by some two hundred men, each with a weapon, on foot.[19]

In Leis's three-part reminiscences, the first part ends with nostalgic memories of the last year of the Ross family in Milwaukee. She remembered the river visible from the windows in the living room where she could see steamboats and railroad trains passing by. The lake was also nearby, and she loved to go there with her mother and father, sometimes just her father. She recalled the birth of the new baby, Pitt Ross, on December 8, 1855. She wrote of a maid and a seamstress who came on occasion to help her mother and to teach Lillian to speak German, a good indication of how well Edmund was doing at the *Sentinel* and the degree of sacrifice he would be making to take his family to Kansas. Concerning the last December in Milwaukee Lillian wrote: "That Christmas season was to be long remembered—and only a memory—not to be repeated for many years. Alas, for mother, the next year brought no seamstress, no maid. No pretty parlor, nor lovely living room."[20]

CHAPTER THREE

JOINING THE BATTLE FOR A FREE KANSAS

Most of us have come to this far-away land, with a mission in our hearts, a mission to the dark-browed race, and hoping here to stay the surging tide of slavery, to place the barrier which utters, in unmistakable language, "Thus far shalt thou go, and no farther." This unlocks our hearts to each other, and at once we recognize a friend actuated by like sympathies and hopes.

—Sara Robinson, *Kansas: Its Interior and Exterior Life*

⤳ THE ESSENTIAL REASON Free-Staters were able to stop the extension of slavery into the new territories of the West is embodied in the words of Sara Robinson: men and women deeply committed to ending the spread of slavery had a greater will to succeed than their proslavery counterparts. For abolitionists, the struggle for a Free Kansas was like a holy war. They had come over great distances from as far away as New England prepared to face the hardships of pioneer life in support of a cause. Sara and Charles Robinson came from Boston, traveling first by rail and by boat, then by wagon train, taking five weeks in all. Although a shorter distance, the trip from Milwaukee for Ross and company took more time and was more demanding, a journey of six hundred miles overland by wagon train, with many of the party walking the entire way.

Lillian Ross Leis wrote with a sense of pride in belonging to a caravan of pioneers led by her father as they crossed Iowa and a part of Nebraska and eventually into Kansas: "Before 'crossing the line' many other travelers joined the caravan for protection, driving along in the rear of our train, but not mingling in the encampments. They were like strangers and of various classes. I remember my mother holding me over the side of the wagon, that

I might look back toward the rear as the train rounded a curve. Someone remarked, 'It was a mile long.'"[1]

As Ross pointed out in his account of the journey, the train consisted of approximately one hundred wagons by the time they crossed the Kansas border. Even before Edmund Ross's wagon train left Milwaukee, it was known that any travel for Free-Staters though Missouri was dangerous. Fortunately for Ross and company, it was not greatly out of the way to cross Iowa and a corner of Nebraska, completely avoiding Missouri. By late 1855, and for years after, Free-State travelers from the eastern states were also compelled to take the northern route avoiding Missouri for their own safety. The route, known as the Jim Lane Road, had been suggested by James H. Lane, a Free-State activist. The route was no more than a suggestion. Wagon trains like Ross's made their own trails through uncharted terrain and mostly found their own ways of fording rivers and streams.

Ross took his caravan through Iowa City and Oskaloosa and eventually into Nebraska.[2] The time it took to complete the trip was eighty-three days, with arrival at Topeka on or about August 11.[3] For the men the days meant hard work, particularly dealing with river crossings and bad weather, while most of the women and children faced long, tedious hours as passengers. Ross had carefully packed his family wagon to leave a flat surface on which Fannie and the children could ride, which he covered with a carpet. He also built up the sides of the wagon with additional boards against which their featherbeds, used at night for sleeping, were placed during the day to make couches. Leis remembered her baby brother learning to crawl inside the wagon as it moved along. She could also see an older woman in an adjoining wagon sitting in a rocking chair and either sewing or reading.[4]

Packing for such a trip inevitably meant sacrificing prized possessions that may have been too large or too heavy. Ross would not sacrifice, in spite of the weight, his books, while Fannie, no doubt, shed tears for cherished pieces of furniture sold off in Milwaukee. Ross took histories, the works of Shakespeare and Milton, and medical journals.[5] Another of the books he had with him was a large, heavily bound portfolio of his best print work. It was filled with samples of stock certificates, letterheads, invoice forms, and posters, some printed in multiple colors, some dating back to Ross's days in Sandusky, and so well preserved that today they look new.[6]

Each evening was a relief from the daily boredom for the women, although it meant a time to work, cooking evening and morning meals.

Fannie had additional responsibilities beyond her family. She was the treasurer of common funds used for purchases of meat, milk, and other needed items available from local merchants.[7] For the children it was a time to run and play. The wagons were drawn into classic defensive circles, with the tongue of one wagon under the rear of the wagon in front of it. The oxen, two from each wagon, were kept outside the circle with the cattle. Their yokes were stored under the wagons. Most evenings families would gather to visit and often to sing. Leis tells of a man with a strong tenor voice who would sing with her "mother's high soprano voice above the rest, as they gathered on a knoll about sunset with song books, and never omitting Whittier's Hymn."[8]

Song of the Kansas Emigrants
—by John Greenleaf Whittier
We cross the prairie as of old
The fathers crossed the sea;
To make the West, as they the East,
The Homestead of the free.
We go to rear a wall of men
On Freedom's southern line,
And plant beside the cotton tree
The rugged northern pine.
Upbearing like the ark of old,
The Bible in our van,
We go to test the truth of God
Against the fraud of man.[9]

Near the place where the caravan crossed the border into Kansas, Ross was met by a party of men that included Samuel Clarke Pomeroy, James Henry Lane, and the infamous John Brown.[10] Although Ross's future contact with John Brown was minimal, both Lane and Pomeroy would profoundly affect Ross's life. Lane, Pomeroy, and Ross would be the first United States senators from Kansas, Lane and Pomeroy being the first elected senators and Ross replacing Lane upon his death in 1866. The three men shared the same fundamental goal of keeping slavery out of Kansas, but they were otherwise remarkably different from each other.

Ross was the most altruistic of the three; as an abolitionist who viewed slavery from a moral point of view, he and his siblings wanted an end to slavery in all states, wanted to live to see the day former slaves could enjoy equal freedom and equal opportunity under the law. While there may have been some motivation on the part of the Ross family to acquire land and establish a new and comfortable life as the years went by, their initial objective in moving to Kansas was the end of slavery. In the letter cited in chapter 2, in which William Ross was trying to entice Edmund to make the move to Kansas, there is no mention of potential wealth or other personal gain; the letter is all about the struggle to make Kansas free of slavery. "The God of battles is with us, truth and virtue are with us, and we'll never submit while a spark of life is within us."[11]

Pomeroy also was ostensibly an abolitionist, but he was equally motivated to accumulate wealth, a goal that consumed his political life and eventually led to his downfall. He was a coolheaded businessman and a key employee of the New England Emigrant Aid Company, but he made sure there was monetary gain in it for him. As the financial agent for the company, Pomeroy was paid $1,000 per year, plus 10 percent of profits from sales and rents, plus all travel expenses. He was possibly the best-paid member of the staff. In a 1938 paper by Edgar Langsdorf published in the *Kansas Historical Quarterly*, Pomeroy is said to have displayed "ardent Antislavery sentiment and keen interest in business opportunities, a combination which was to appear throughout his career." In applying for a position with the Emigrant Aid Company, he admitted to knowing little about the aims of the company, but what he knew he found "highly commendable." Langsdorf describes Pomeroy as a man who accumulated considerable wealth as a result of his association with the company.[12]

Jim Lane was the most enigmatic of the three. He moved to Kansas from Indiana to spearhead the establishment of the Democratic Party in Kansas. His goal was to be a senator, congressman, or governor of Kansas. His opportunities in Indiana were limited because of his support of the Kansas-Nebraska Act, which was not popular there. Both Lane and his father had been United States congressmen, and Lane himself had been lieutenant governor of Indiana. He had also served with distinction in the Mexican War as a regimental commander with the rank of colonel. Lane was an unlikely charismatic leader, an eloquent orator with wild-looking hair and a gaunt face. Although he had a severe look about him, he could inspire men as few others of his day could. Of a speech given by Lane in Chicago in 1866 it was said that "no man of his time possessed such magnetic power over a vast miscellaneous assembly of men as he. With two possible exceptions (Patrick Henry and S. S. Prentiss), no American orator ever equaled him in effective stump speaking, or in the irresistible power by which he held his audiences in absolute control."[13] He would regularly turn hostile listeners into allies. Perhaps the one time he failed at doing this was in trying to convince a meeting of Democrats in Kansas that their new party should be an antislavery party. With this failure Lane was left with the choice of remaining a Democrat in a Kansas party that was proslavery or joining those immigrants who opposed slavery but had yet to coalesce into a political organization. His choice was the latter. Lane became one of the founders of the Free-State Party in the fall of 1855, and he eventually became a Republican. Although an unabashed Free-Stater, Lane cared little about slavery beyond not wanting it to spread outside the southern states; in fact, he advocated "black laws" for Kansas that would prohibit blacks, whether slave or free, from taking up residence there. While he may have later equivocated his position on the issue, it is not likely it changed much. Nor was Lane's view on slavery and slaves different from the majority of Free-Staters'. It is significant that at the December 1855 Free-State constitutional referendum, when the issue of "exclusion of Negroes or mulattoes from the state" was voted upon, 1,287 voted in favor while only 453 voted against.[14]

An editor of the *Chicago Daily News*, in giving a talk about Lane to the Kansas State Historical Society in 1930, described him as "a Westerner, an Ohio River man; he chewed tobacco when he could borrow it; he was divorced; he didn't pay his debts; he took the name of his Lord God in vain—and in stride, he made no effort to halt the fabulous tales of what his contemporaries described as his 'worship at the shrine of Venus,' and he only laughed when he was branded as the father of political corruption west of the Mississippi River."[15]

Lane organized the Free-State Army in late 1855 when Lawrence was threatened by Missouri border ruffians during a crisis known as the Wakarusa War. The actual commander of the militia to protect Lawrence was Charles Robinson, with Lane second in command, but given Lane's military experience and Robinson's complete lack, it was logical for Lane to take day-to-day charge. The so-called war ended without casualties, but the core of Lane's Free-State Army, which was to play such an important role in the events of the following year, was formed.

Keeping Lane, and the even more radical John Brown, in check must have been a constant concern of Charles Robinson, who had been elected the Free-State governor in January 1856. Robinson, a medical doctor and husband of writer Sara Robinson, and one of the organizers of the New England Emigrant Aid Company, had brought the first Emigrant Aid colony to Kansas in 1854. Robinson believed that Free-Staters had a greater chance of achieving their goals with a nonviolent approach, while Jim Lane and John Brown were convinced that it would ultimately take some level of armed confrontation for the Free-State government to prevail. Under Robinson's leadership, the official position of the Topeka Free-State government was that Free-Staters had the moral and political right to form their own government; and while they most likely would be subjected to violence, they would not initiate any violence in resisting the federal government.[16] At the same time, proslavery citizens saw the Topeka Free-State government as nothing less than treasonous.

In the later months of 1855 and the early months of 1856 there were isolated serious confrontations and casualties, but Robinson managed to avert any situation from getting out of control. At the national level, the growing crisis in Kansas was increasingly debated in newspapers in both the North and South and in the Congress. In March, Democratic senator Stephen A. Douglas and his Committee on Territories accused the New England Emigrant Aid Company of being responsible for causing the problems in Kansas and charged that Free-Staters were revolutionaries whose intent was to overthrow the territorial government.[17] Free-State leaders persisted in their argument that the elections that resulted in the proslavery government of Kansas were fraudulent and did not represent the true will of the majority of Kansans. A congressional committee of three was created to investigate the legitimacy of the elections. The committee traveled to Kansas and carried out its investigations beginning on April 18 and continuing well into May during extremely heightened tensions that resulted in the Sacking of Lawrence.

Edmund Ross's wagon train left Milwaukee on May 20. The Sacking of Lawrence took place on May 21. During the weeks when the wagon train slowly moved toward Kansas, the bloody confrontations predicted by William Ross in his January letter came to pass. The Sacking of Lawrence resulted from repeated attempts by Sheriff Samuel Jones to arrest S. N. Wood of Lawrence, who was wanted for his role in an incident resulting in a casualty some months earlier.[18] On the first visit, April 19, Jones and his assistant were both disarmed by Lawrence citizens who also refused to hand over Wood. Jones made two more attempts to arrest Wood, first with a larger contingent of men and then with a group of U.S. Army dragoons. When the third attempt failed, Jones arrested six men who specifically refused to cooperate and marched them out of town. While Jones camped outside of Lawrence that night, someone shot him in the back, and although the wound was not fatal, proslavery citizens and Missourians were incensed.[19]

On May 5, Chief Justice Samuel D. Lecompte, reacting to the attempted killing of Jones, ordered the indictment of all Free-State officials and the closing of the two Lawrence newspapers and the Free State Hotel. Meanwhile the congressional committee investigating the elections of 1854 and 1855 was already finding clear evidence of voter fraud.[20] As the month of May progressed, proslavery forces slowly surrounded Lawrence, determined to destroy the town. Sara Robinson reported several instances of intimidation, including one near Benicia, a town only eight miles from Lawrence. On May 15 twenty-five Missourians surrounded a group of Free-State farmers who were working in a field. "They carried them into a neighboring cabin, and, with threats of instant death, ordered them to leave Kansas. 'G——d d——n you, if you are ever caught here again you shall be strung up! Go to Nebraska d——n you! You have no right in Kansas!' was the language of the ruffians. 'We are coming to Lawrence in a few days to wipe out the d——d abolition city, and to kill or drive off every one of the inhabitants,' was the finale of all their threats."[21] In another instance reported by Robinson, a young man named Jones, who had been to Lawrence to buy supplies, was later found dead near Blanton's Bridge. He was believed to have been shot to death by a marshal's posse.[22]

The U.S. marshal, J. B. Donaldson, charged with carrying out Justice Lecompte's orders, sent Sheriff Jones back to Lawrence, this time with a very large contingent of men. On May 21 Jones ordered the surrender of all weapons, and while Lawrence residents did not surrender their own private weapons, they did surrender their public arsenal and offered no resistance as Jones's men systematically shelled the hotel and then burned what was left of it. Jones's men also destroyed the newspaper printing presses and for several hours looted homes and burned a number of them, including the Robinson house. Fortunately no Lawrence residents were killed, but a posse member died when part of the Free State Hotel fell on him.[23]

The passivism of Lawrence residents during the sacking paid dividends when reported in northern newspapers. The aggressive, over-the-top action of Sheriff Jones and his men made the Free-State cause a most sympathetic one in the eyes of northern liberals. Nineteenth-century historian

A. T. Andreas described "the resolutions of public meetings" in the North and even "the voice of the Northern pulpit" as warlike. He cited in particular the charismatic preacher Henry Ward Beecher's advocacy of sending Sharps rifles, instead of Bibles, to Kansas. Beecher pledged that his famous Brooklyn church would provide its fair share.[24]

On May 19 and 20, Senator Charles Sumner of Massachusetts took up the cause of Kansas Free-Staters and spoke passionately on the floor of the Senate about the injustice of the "bogus" Kansas government and its support by Democrats, especially Stephen Douglas of Illinois and South Carolina senator Andrew Butler. Sumner's lengthy and florid oration claimed that Butler had "chosen a mistress to whom he has made his vows, and who, though ugly to others, is always lovely to him,—though polluted in the sight of the world, is chaste in his sight: I mean the harlot Slavery."[25] Enraged by Sumner's speech, Preston Brooks, a congressman and a relative of Senator Butler, attacked Sumner on May 22 on the Senate floor with his cane, severely injuring him, so badly that Sumner was unable to return to office for more than three years.

The caning of Sumner and especially the Sacking of Lawrence were "the last straws" for the emotional abolitionist John Brown and his sons. Late on the night of May 24 and into the early morning hours of May 25, Brown and his band of radicals viciously dragged five proslavery men from their homes along Pottawatomie Creek and murdered them either by shooting them or hacking them to death with swords.[26] Brown's murderous raid was exactly what Charles Robinson wanted to avoid, and although Robinson condemned the Pottawatomie killings, the murders precipitated a bloody summer and early fall of guerrilla warfare by both pro- and antislavery groups.

Travel throughout Kansas became extremely dangerous, and many residents slept with loaded weapons nearby. For the U.S. Army, keeping the peace was difficult to near impossible. Guerrilla bands would be dispersed by the army, only to regroup in short order. The summer of 1856 was the most dangerous time of all in the territorial years of Kansas. Sara Robinson reported many incidents of looting and burning of homes in July and early August and a number of instances of highway robbery including murder. The difficulty of getting supplies to various towns became critical, particularly at Lawrence with its two thousand inhabitants. There was serious scarity, and considerable danger attached to "send[ing] teams for provisions past the camps of ruffians."[27] Robinson also reported the approach of a large wagon train from the north, presumably Ross's. "There are over four hundred emigrants on the way. The train is more than a mile and quarter long. Such a body of men looked formidable to the spies of the enemy, and they returned to report large numbers."[28]

Among the many confrontations that summer, the Topeka Free-State legislature had planned its regular session for July 4, but territorial governor Wilson Shannon directed Colonel Edwin Sumner to disperse the assembly, which Shannon judged to be illegal. Sumner and a company of men carried out the order without resistance other than jeers from some of the legislators. The fact that Free-Staters did not resist once again paid dividends in the northern press, which characterized the incident as a suppression of the rights of free speech and assembly.[29]

Thirty miles north of Topeka, heavy rains seriously delayed the Ross wagon train. As the men constructed a temporary bridge to cross a swollen river, it also occurred to them that the area was an excellent site for a town. A sizeable number of people from the wagon train, including some members of the original Milwaukee group, decided they would stay there. Ross suggested they name the new community to honor Edward Holton, the Milwaukee banker who had helped fund the wagon train. As the remainder of Ross's group finally approached Topeka, two former Milwaukeeans came out to meet them. One was the familiar face of E. C. K. Garvey, a former acquaintance and newspaper editor, and the other the not-so-familiar face of William Ross, now "with a long beard, a belt around his waist, over his coat, and a revolver."[30] The town of Topeka itself was something of a disappointment. Lillian Leis remembered that there were "no walks, no trees, nor to my childish mind was there anything lovely or desirable."[31] Handsome town or not, the family must have found relief in finally reaching their goal and being reunited once again, but the reunion did not last long.

Ross recorded in a notebook, "My first occupation in Kansas, a few days after my arrival in Topeka, was as a volunteer in the Free State Army, carrying a musket as a private soldier in a hastily improvised army."[32] Ross does not go into much detail about his time in the Free-State Army, but good guesses can be made about some of the battles he participated in. For one thing, he did not remain a private, although this was a logical place for him to start, since he had no military experience. He clearly had leadership ability, and by the time he mustered out on October 1, 1856, he was a first lieutenant.[33] The commander of his regiment, the Second Kansas Volunteers, was Colonel Charles Whipple, alias Aaron D. Stevens, who was later hanged with John Brown at Harper's Ferry.[34] A skirmish that took place on August 12, known as the Second Battle of Franklin, may have been Edmund Ross's earliest action. This date suggests that the Ross-Milwaukee party could have arrived a few days earlier than August 11. The primary objectives of the Franklin battle were, first, to recapture a cannon and, second, to break up the ruffian gang quartered there.[35] The battle was successful, and the two sides suffered one casualty each.[36]

Another of Ross's probable early actions came in a raid on a proslavery mercantile store a short distance south of Topeka. The proprietor was believed to be a man who had tortured a northerner dying from a gunshot wound. The Free-State volunteers looted the store, taking poultry, pigs, and numerous other provisions, items badly needed by the people of Topeka. The proprietor had departed before the arrival of the volunteers, no doubt in fear for his life.[37]

Ross likely participated in the attack on Fort Titus on August 16 that resulted in the capture of thirty-four proslavery prisoners including Colonel Henry C. Titus. What must have been the bloodiest battle of the summer was at Osawatomie on the last day of August and the first day of September, where there were eight casualties.

It is certain that Ross participated in several battles, but he writes only of one, and he is vague at that. He describes the battle taking place in late summer, a few weeks after the arrival of the Milwaukee colony. The place was near the southeastern border of Kansas, and the adversary was "what was claimed by its friends to be a superior proslavery force" from Missouri. "They were met on the soil of Kansas by a force of Free State men composed in good part of the men of the colony I had led into Kansas a few weeks previously."[38] Ross went on to explain that the battle, such as it was, was fought in September and that it quickly became clear to the proslavery forces that their mission was futile. After two days of fighting, the Missourians retreated back across the border. There were no deaths and only a few wounded. This battle probably was the Battle at Hickory Point, fought on September 14 and 15. That was a battle that involved Colonel Whipple's men, and Ross surely was one of them.

The top-ranking Free-State man at Hickory Point, as in most confrontations, was General Jim Lane. A Free-State private in that battle was Samuel James Reader, who kept a diary throughout his life. His observations at Hickory Point were insightful and clear. His memoirs are now a valued treasure of the Kansas State Historical Society. He wrote about the occasion of shaking hands with Jim Lane, which he regarded as a great honor. He described Lane as "a man of medium size with a dark complexion, a black mustache and dark eyes. . . . On the whole he was a harsh-featured, severe looking man. He wore nothing to indicate his rank. . . . He was immensely popular with the free state boys; they made themselves hoarse hurrahing for him, and I might have done so myself, had I been of an excitable temperament."[39]

Edmund Ross, who was likely a lieutenant by this time and serving under Lane, received no mention in Reader's description of Hickory Point—not surprising, given the number of men there, and besides, Ross was not a man who called attention to himself. John Rastall, who came from Milwaukee with Ross and who was also at Hickory Point, had a very high regard for him: "My recollections of this man stamp him as one of character, firmness, courtesy and fair ability. He never touched intoxicating liquors, even at a banquet in his own honor. The rain had rather a charm for him than otherwise, for he passed bareheaded through every storm on the trip. Fear seemed not to enter his composition, for when approaching a deep and muddy stream in Iowa, which it was necessary to ford, he stepped from the bank without a moment's thought or preparation and found a spot suitable for our purpose, the shallowest being up to his armpits. 'Imperturbability' seems a word coined on purpose to express other characteristics. He never allowed himself to be much elated or depressed, and when he dropped a valuable revolver into the muddy Missouri, no exclamation of anger or regret passed his lips."[40]

While Lane was a flamboyant man of action, Ross was relatively quiet and unpretentious. He recognized that, while military action helped to hasten the day when Free-State citizens would prevail, persistence in establishing a workable government was where the real work still needed to be done, and that would take time and patience. Samuel Reader's observation from his memoirs ended with the insightful sentence "For it was ballots and not bullets that finally freed Kansas from the threatened curse of African Slavery."[41]

It is doubtful that Ross served from August 12 until October 1 as a full-time soldier. His daughter indicates that he was already writing editorials for the *Kansas Tribune*. It is more likely that Ross was a part-time soldier, standing by to be called upon at a moment's notice. In the day or so following his return from Hickory Point, Ross got word that U.S. Marshal Donaldson and a group of soldiers were on their way to Topeka to arrest a number of men known to be members of the Topeka Volunteers, including Ross. His family was startled one day when he rushed into their one-room house and, after a few minutes, emerged from behind chintz curtains with trimmed whiskers, wearing a broadcloth suit and silk hat. His children were ordered to ignore him on the street. He was able to evade capture by staying away from the *Tribune* office and, when asked if he knew where Ross was, replying that he had only just arrived in Topeka, a true statement.[42]

Ross's friend John Rastall was not so lucky. Marshal Donaldson arrested Rastall and about one hundred other Free-State men on a sweep of Free-State communities and took them to a prison camp at Lecompton without formal charges. Rastall escaped and returned to Topeka, where Ross advised him to leave the territory. With great difficulty Rastall took the same route back to Milwaukee. In later years he would write about his friendship with Ross, a friendship he regarded as one of the memorable experiences of his life.[43]

Names of events such as the Wakarusa War, the Sacking of Lawrence, the Pottawatomie Massacre, the Battle of Black Jack, the Battle of Franklin, the Battle of Fort Titus, the Battle of Osawatomie, and the Battle of Hickory Point, coupled with the name given to the era, Bleeding Kansas, would lead a reasonable person to conclude that the death toll must have been staggering. The truth is that in 1856, the bloodiest year, there were probably just thirty-eight deaths attributable to political confrontation. In all of territorial Kansas history from May 1854 until statehood in 1861, there may have been as few as fifty-six total deaths directly caused by the conflict over slavery.[44] Of course there were many more who were injured, and there were those who suffered property loss and those who left the territory, discouraged by the danger and the trials of pioneer life. With the arrival of a new territorial governor, John Geary, it became clear in the summer of 1856 that serious armed battles were soon to be over but the battle of words and political infighting was far from finished.

CHAPTER FOUR

FIGHTING SLAVERY WITH WORDS

The destiny of the entire domain of the United States west of the
Mississippi River hangs upon the decision of the question of slavery in Kansas.

　　　　　—Ross, editorial, *Kansas Tribune*, November 28, 1857

⌒ WHEN JOHN GEARY ARRIVED in Kansas in September 1856 to take on
the job of territorial governor, fighting between pro- and antislavery forces
had reached its peak; he was determined that it must end. More than his
predecessors, Geary quickly gained the respect of the U.S. Army in Kansas
and ordered the army to put a stop, once and for all, to the fighting that
raged between the two factions.[1] Not only did army officers respect Geary,
so did the likes of Edmund Ross, who had to assume a disguise to avoid
being taken prisoner after the Hickory Point confrontation. Ross also had
to watch his friend John Rastall and others march away under armed guard,
while Jim Lane was forced to flee to Iowa. Ross did not take these happen-
ings lightly and never returned to the Free-State Army after his discharge
on October 1.[2] He had the responsibility of a family, and, regardless of any
other inclinations, his first duty was clear to him. He had to pay attention
to earning a living.

　　Edmund and his brother William would now fight the antislavery
battle with words. Edmund purchased John Speer's interest in the *Kansas
Tribune*, making the Ross brothers the sole owners. On January 5, 1857,
the *Kansas Tribune* published its first issue with William and Edmund as
coeditors. Their paper featured poetry, reprinted from other sources, on

the front page of nearly every edition. Their editorials always dealt with Free-State issues and were very well written, often eloquent. It is hard to know whether Edmund was the principal editorial writer, since both brothers were named on the masthead. It may be that Edmund played a more dominant role as editor, but we have to guess that at least part of the time William was writing for the paper as well. The *Tribune* editorials never were specifically attributable to one or the other Ross brother. What surely is true is that they were of like mind.

Soon after Edmund became an owner of the *Tribune*, the brothers began construction on a new building. It was a stone building located on East Sixth Avenue in Topeka. Years later the building was expanded and was eventually "merged into the Topeka Capital." Lillian Leis tells us the building had "a pleasant commodious editorial room on the second floor with an outside stairway."[3]

The mission of the *Tribune* was to keep readers enthusiastic about the Free-State cause, to get people out to vote during elections and referendums, and to help readers stay focused on the issues. This was extraordinarily important during 1857 and the first half of 1858 when the conflict between pro- and antislavery forces changed for the most part from violent confrontations to a battle of will over whose proposed state constitution would prevail in the United States Congress and whose representatives would run the government. What the Ross brothers would accomplish during this crucial period was far more important than any battle in which they fought under Jim Lane. Free-State status ultimately would be won with debate, both in the public forum, as in the *Tribune*, and in legislative sessions. When a constitution finally was written barring slavery from Kansas, the Ross brothers could justifiably take a measure of the credit.

The Rosses certainly wrote about the various issues that arose during the complicated year and a half beginning in January 1857. However, it was their view, as abolitionists, that essentially there was only one issue. On August 1, the editorial in the *Tribune* dealt with the fact that the Proslavery Party in Kansas had changed its name to the National Democratic Party of Kansas. The *Tribune* saw this as nothing more than putting a new coat of paint on an already collapsing building. The Rosses made the point that until the matter of slavery was resolved, other issues mattered very little, and that Kansans should not allow themselves to be "deluded into ignoring it [the issue of slavery] by any attempt to create incidental issues by raising the standard of National Democracy, of Republicanism, of Know

Nothingism, or any other issue. It is with Kansas and her future, that we would confine the contest—for the establishment of unrestricted political freedom upon her soil we labor—That is the great issue."[4]

The *Kansas Tribune* was published in Topeka but was widely distributed throughout the territory. In a small article from February 1857 the Rosses boasted, "We think we can properly say that our circulation in Kansas is larger than any other paper printed within its borders, and continually increasing. We do not know of a town or neighborhood of any size where the Tribune is not circulated."[5] If you were an antislavery resident of Kansas in 1857, you were also likely to be a regular reader of the *Kansas Tribune*. The *Tribune* and the *Herald of Freedom* of Lawrence were known to carry the latest information on Free-State developments and the latest thinking of Free-State leaders.[6]

While southerners tended to see all Kansas residents as radical abolitionists, the truth was that even abolitionists were in the minority among Free-Staters. The majority of Free-State advocates were not inclined to welcome any blacks, whether slave or free, into Kansas. What happened elsewhere did not concern them. Edmund Ross and his brother, however, held a strong belief that slavery was inherently immoral and could not be justified for any reason. Another way of knowing what was in Ross's mind is to accept that his daughter's beliefs flowed from the father whom she deeply loved.

In her memoirs Leis tells us there were a number of times when her father helped runaway slaves, but she describes only one specific case. The incident probably happened in the late summer or early fall of 1857. One afternoon Lillian was caring for her two younger siblings while Fannie had "gone downtown" to meet Edmund at his office and to walk home with him. Lillian had taken her two brothers outside where she found the twilight to be less lonely. As she played with the children, "a mulatto" came from around the corner of the house and asked, "Dars Mr. Ross live here?" She took the man into their house and waited anxiously for her parents. "I was only eight years of age, but fully understood the penalty attached to helping the Negro if discovered. Later in the evening Col. Ritchie came and took the man away."[7]

That even his eight-year-old daughter understood the family commitment to assisting slaves is an indication of Ross's dedication to the abolitionist movement. The risks taken by anyone assisting runaways were quite real. In a November article in the *Tribune* titled "Slave Hunting," Ross detailed a raid on John Ritchie's home. Ritchie was a doctor who had a two-story home that was a safe house for runaways. A file of soldiers, slave catchers, and the deputy marshal marched up to the house with the intent of breaking down the door with an axe. Before the first blow was taken, the marshal and his men were "brought to a stand" by the click of sharpshooters' rifles. The marshal was there without a writ or any official documentation. When he later returned "no niggers were found." Ross further recounts how an identical raid was made on his house some three weeks before.[8]

As 1857 began, the pro- and antislavery factions each continued to maintain they were the legitimate representatives of the people of Kansas. The proslavery territorial government, which was recognized as the legal government by both the Franklin Pierce and then the James Buchanan administration, asserted its right to hold elections and pass laws and run the business of the territory. As we have seen, the Free-State government with its Topeka constitution took the position that the territorial government was in power only as a result of fraudulent elections. Both factions were optimistic about the future. Territorial governor Geary, who served from September 1856 to March 1857, was appointed by President Pierce. Governor Robert J. Walker, who served from May 1857 to December 1857, was a Buchanan appointee. Both urged the Free-State Party to participate in officially sanctioned territorial elections. In the view of Geary, then Walker, if the majority of people indeed supported the Free-State Party, it had nothing to fear. Free-Staters, however, did not believe the governor could guarantee fair elections. They feared a repeat of previous experiences at the polls. Moreover, Free-Staters believed that a vote in territorial elections amounted to recognition of the authority of the territorial government, which they regarded as bogus.

The issue that would come to dominate the political scene in Kansas by the fall of 1857 was the Lecompton constitution. Indeed, this constitution became the focal point of disagreement, which, when resolved, led essentially to the end of the proslavery movement in Kansas and became a significant contributing factor to the secession of southern states just a few years later. In January 1857 the territorial legislature passed a resolution to hold a constitutional convention in September, with the election of delegates to that convention to be held in June. In October there would also be an election for a delegate to Congress and new representatives to the state legislature. In March the Free-State Party held its annual meeting. Among the decisions taken at that gathering was a vote to boycott the June election, just as members had boycotted all territorial government elections since the spring of 1855. Even before the Free-State meeting in March, the *Kansas Tribune* had encouraged party members to vote against participation in the June election.

Congressmen, newspaper editors, and citizens throughout the United States carefully watched developments in Kansas. As early as May 9 the *Tribune* reported the impatience of northern newspapers with the Free-State policy of nonparticipation in territorial elections: "There are many papers in the North apparently friendly to the cause of Kansas who criticize with much warmth the line of policy adopted, and insist upon a trial of strength with our adversaries, at the ballot box." By midsummer this impatience among northern supporters became more apparent, and the rigid position of Free-Staters began to soften out of fear of losing important allies.

Ross reversed his advocacy of nonparticipation, but not until after the June election. He probably was influenced by Thomas Ewing Jr., the son of the well-known Ohio statesman and former senator, Thomas Ewing Sr., a man whose opinions carried significant weight well beyond the borders of Ohio. The elder Ewing, who clearly was not an abolitionist, responded to reports from Kansas sent by his son. He expressed his disapproval of the Free-State Party in Kansas in no uncertain terms and warned his son against having anything to do with it. His letter is worth quoting because it expresses the belief of many, if not most, northerners: "The movement of the Free State Party in Kansas is a strange compound of fraud and folly— Fraud on the part of the leaders out of the Territory, urging those in it to Treason and folly in those who suffer themselves to be led. . . . The free state party if successful effect a revolution—if beaten, they are guilty of Treason. . . . They had nothing to do but to take possession of the government in a legitimate manner & mould it according to their wishes, but this would not suit the Tribune[9] and others who choose to make capital out of their follies. . . . Enter not into their counsel. Your loving Father, T. Ewing."[10]

How such a letter affected Ross is a matter of speculation, but there is no doubt he had changed his mind about participation in territorial elections by the time of a Free-State meeting at Grasshopper Falls in August. Assuming Ross knew of the letter, the criticism of the abolitionist movement by such a powerful man had given him pause. In hindsight it is also clear that the elder Ewing was wrong about the Free-State cause. Had it not been for the stubborn and dramatic resistance of the Free-State Party and its leaders, including men like Ross and his brother, and their willingness to fight and even die for the cause, Kansas could have been admitted to the Union as a slave state.

While we do not know the actual extent of the Ewings' influence on Ross in 1857, we know that Ross later formed a strong bond with the younger Ewing during the Civil War, establishing a friendship that continued through the years that Ross served in the Senate. Although Ross retained his Radical Republican ties well into his term as a United States senator, Thomas Ewing Jr. played a major role in Ross's eventual shift to Moderate Republicanism and eventually to the Democratic Party.

The decision of the Free-State Party to boycott the June election of convention delegates of course resulted in the election of constitutional convention delegates who were exclusively proslavery. Meanwhile the strong pressure on Free-Staters exerted by northerners like Ewing Sr. led to a reversal of the Free-State Party policy of nonparticipation in territorial elections in at least one instance. October 5 was set as the date for the election of a territorial delegate to Congress and a territorial legislature. The lively debate in August at the Free-State meeting at Grasshopper Falls ended with a commitment to participate in the October election with the firm assurance by Governor Walker that voting would be fair and open. Edmund Ross along with C. K. Holliday and F. W. Giles drafted the official resolution to participate in the election. Free-Staters were also reassured by Governor Walker that the constitution drawn up at the September convention would be submitted to the people in a referendum for their approval. Walker had, or so he believed, the backing of President Buchanan for this promise.

The constitutional convention opened on September 5, 1857, at the territorial capital, Lecompton, but adjourned on September 11. The delegates said they preferred to continue their work after the October 5 election so they could use the time to campaign for proslavery candidates. The Ross brothers' commentary on the delay was rather tongue in cheek: "We consider this a wise and prudent move, as it will give the [proslavery] members an opportunity of working for the success of their party during the pending canvass which they would not otherwise have, and *which the party very much needs.*"[11] It was a comment designed to aggravate their opponents, saying in effect, "We don't think you stand a chance." The same issue of the *Tribune* carried the list of Free-State Party candidates for office and, at the head of the editorial column, a quote from Governor Walker promising a fair election.

October 5 was chilly and rainy, but turnout was heavy, so much so that in Lawrence a second day of voting was allowed. This time the voting was generally orderly, thanks to Walker's use of army troops at most polling places. Two locations were exceptional, Oxford and McGee, where the number of votes cast for proslavery candidates far outnumbered the population. It was later shown that names were simply copied from the Cincinnati directory onto the voting rolls at Oxford and McGee. Governor Walker disallowed the returns from those two communities, and the Free-State candidates easily won control of both houses of the legislature.[12] In the final tally Free-State candidates controlled 25 of 39 seats in the House of Representatives and 9 of 13 Council seats. Free-State candidate M. J. Parrott won the job of delegate to Congress by more than 4,000 votes.[13] Free-Staters were in control of the territorial government for the first time, but the question of slavery in Kansas was yet to be resolved.

When the Lecompton constitutional convention reconvened, the outcome—not surprisingly, given the composition of the delegation elected to the job the previous June—was a proslavery constitution. What made matters worse was the decision of the convention to submit the constitution directly to the United States Congress, bypassing the citizens of Kansas. The convention had the power to do this, but such an act would be in direct contravention of the promise Governor Walker had made with the backing he believed he had from President Buchanan. Anticipating the backlash that was sure to follow, the chairman of the convention, John Calhoun, negotiated a compromise that allowed the residents of Kansas to vote, but only on article 7, that portion of the constitution that allowed for future slave importation. Any slave ownership already in place would be legal and no amendments to this provision could be initiated for twenty years. The compromise was supported by Buchanan, who had even sent his own emissary to the convention in Kansas.[14] The date for the vote on the provision to either allow slavery in the state or to exclude slavery in the future was set for December 21. The reaction of the Ross brothers was predictable, and their editorial no doubt helped to express the alarm that soon was felt throughout the antislavery community. *Tribune* editorials were most likely read by Governor Walker and the territorial secretary of state, Frederick Stanton, the second in command. In the opinion of the Ross brothers, "That constitution in other parts, and in other ways, guarantees property in slaves, and recognizes the infamous decision of the Supreme Court in the Dred Scott case; which virtually forces slavery upon every State in the Union, and peremptorily, prohibits the Legislature and *the people* from interfering with Slavery in any way, for nearly twenty years to come."[15]

Walker was appalled by the action of the president, so appalled that he returned to Washington to confront Buchanan directly and to support the position of Free-Staters.[16] During Walker's absence, aroused Free-Staters insisted that Secretary Stanton, now the acting governor, call a special session of the newly elected legislature, which was not scheduled to meet until January. Jim Lane traveled throughout Kansas giving highly emotional speeches calling for the special session. The Ross brothers, for their part, wrote strongly worded editorials throughout the month of November. Their sense that the conflict between pro- and antislavery factions had reached its most crucial stage was certainly correct, as history would show. If Free-Staters were to prevail in their goal of ending slavery in Kansas, the time had come to stand firm. A *Tribune*-printed editorial on the last weekend of November even hinted at the possibility of armed conflict with proslavery citizens. "If ever there was a time in the history of Kansas when unity of action and firmness of purpose, in an eminent degree, were required at the hands of the people, to thwart the most hellish machinations that human depravity could conceive, that time is NOW. The most imminent crisis in our affairs is rapidly approaching. . . . It is not Kansas alone which is at stake in this game of political chicanery which the Administration and its tools in this Territory are playing. The destiny of the entire domain of the United States west of the Mississippi River hangs upon the decision of the question of slavery in Kansas. Let opposition come in whatever shape it chooses, either of diplomatic finesse or of hostile bayonets, we must meet it hand to hand and shoulder to shoulder; like men who know how to prize the boon for which we battle, and we shall not be long in doubt as to the result."[17]

In the emotionally charged atmosphere of the territory, a meeting of Free-State leaders at Leavenworth called on Stanton to authorize the special session of the legislature. Fearing what might happen if he failed to meet their demands, and not seeing any serious harm in the legislature meeting, Stanton approved the special session and set December 7 as the date for the session to begin. It was a fateful decision for Stanton. When the president learned what he had done, Stanton was immediately fired. But it was too late.

The legislature, now controlled by antislavery members, authorized a second vote on the Lecompton constitution—this time on the entire document—and set January 4 as the date for the vote.[18] Free-State Party members once again were unwilling to vote with their proslavery counterparts on just one part of the constitution. Predictably, the result on December 21 was the acceptance of article 7 by a vote of 6,226 to 569.[19]

With the putative passage of Lecompton there was another problem for the Free-State Party. The election of statewide officials to serve under the new constitution was set for January 4. These newly elected officials would be ready to serve in the new Kansas state government as soon as Congress approved Lecompton and declared statehood for Kansas. The election would take place on the same day the territorial legislature had planned the referendum on the entire Lecompton constitution. On December 23 the Free-State Party met in an emergency session in Lawrence to decide whether to participate in the election. It was an emotionally charged meeting, with Jim Lane and John Brown pushing hard to encourage the boycotting of the election and claiming there was already newly erupted violence by pro- and antislavery factions in southern Kansas, an exaggeration at best and probably a complete fabrication. In spite of a strong argument in favor of participation by moderate member Thomas Ewing Jr., the meeting voted 75 to 64 in favor of a boycott.[20] The moderates, like Ewing and Charles Robinson, were not about to give up and called for another meeting that night. Once again Jim Lane followers disrupted the meeting, which ended in several fistfights, but moderates persisted and scheduled a Christmas Eve meeting in the basement of the *Herald of Freedom* in Lawrence to nominate a slate of Free-State Party members to run in the January 4 election.[21]

Between Christmas and New Year's Day, Ewing poured all of his energy, time, and even personal money into persuading party members to vote. George Brown of the *Herald of Freedom* produced an issue of the paper claiming that a majority of Free-Staters were going to vote in both January 4 elections, and Ewing personally paid for its distribution throughout the territory.[22] Among the many party members who were persuaded were the Ross brothers, who joined the moderates in favor of participation and, in an editorial, encouraged others to vote.[23] This was the second time within six months that Ross, probably influenced by Ewing, had decided to vote with moderates in an election. Ewing had convincingly made the argument that acceptance by the United States Congress of the Lecompton constitution, a good possibility, would mean proslavery statehood for Kansas. By participating and electing antislavery officials on January 4, the new state legislature could rewrite or at least have some measure of control over the constitution.

Meanwhile the January 4 referendum, with Free-State Party members voting on the entire Lecompton constitution, was a complete reversal of the December 21 vote: 10,226 Free-State votes were cast against the entire Lecompton constitution, while only 138 agreed to accept it as written.[24]

The January 4 election of state officials was chaotic, but Ewing, who had anticipated illegal voting and intimidation in several key communities, had persuaded the new territorial governor, James Denver, to provide troops at polling places that were likely to be a problem. Meanwhile Ewing himself, with thirty Free-State men, kept an eye on voting at Kickapoo, where there had been problems in the past. After the election, a monthlong investigation of voting irregularities by a commission headed by Ewing showed so much fraud that Governor Denver wrote to the president to inform him that, in his opinion, the Free-State candidates were easily victorious and that civil war could result from Kansas achieving statehood under Lecompton if the proslavery candidates were certified winners.[25]

The United States Congress was now faced with a dilemma: considering the Lecompton constitution with slavery as submitted after the December 21 vote while at the same time knowing from the January 4 votes that most residents of Kansas were not in favor of a proslavery constitution. Republican opposition to Lecompton in Congress was pretty much a given. Additional support came from Democratic senator Stephen Douglas of Illinois, a champion of popular sovereignty, who led strong opposition to Lecompton by northern Democrats, while southern Democrats, of course, strongly favored Lecompton. Douglas's stand was in direct opposition to President Buchanan, a fellow Democrat, who pushed hard to get acceptance of the proslavery constitution.

Buchanan was faced with serious pressure from southern states, some already threatening to secede if Lecompton was not accepted. Buchanan believed that Free-Staters in Kansas had been given their fair chance to participate in the writing of the constitution and to vote on at least a partial ban on slavery on December 21. With good reason Buchanan was concerned about the secession of southern states if Congress did not accept the Lecompton constitution. If Buchanan had his way, Congress would accept Lecompton and Kansas would enter the Union as a slave state. Once in the Union, Buchanan believed, the people of Kansas could then change their constitution if they desired. To abolitionists like the Rosses, not voting in the December referendum was a matter of principle; they did not want slavery in any form. In 1857 there were approximately 450 slaves in Kansas, almost none working on a plantation.[26] Had the Free-State Party participated in the December 21 referendum and approved Lecompton without

future slavery, the likelihood of slavery in Kansas ever growing to any significant size was small, and the likelihood of Kansas achieving statehood in
1858 was large. To abolitionists, however, slavery was a moral issue and its
existence in Kansas, or anywhere else in the country, was just not acceptable. In a March editorial titled "Will Kansas Enslave Herself?" the Ross
brothers blasted the absurdity of Kansas entering the Union as a slave state
with the idea of changing the constitution later. "The amendment tacitly
admits what is claimed, that Lecompton is not what the people want—is,
in short, something that they will not have; otherwise what need of any
change. . . . It is resolved into the simply absurd proposition that wrong
must be done that a wrong may be undone. Although an utterly barren victory, the Administration has signified its readiness to accept it."[27]

Even Free-State governor Charles Robinson had grown so weary of
fighting the Lecompton battle that he was willing to support the president
and go along with Kansas becoming a slave state, if only temporarily.[28] To
the credit of the Rosses, the *Tribune* stood firm.

The debate on Lecompton continued through the spring of 1858 and at
one point met with a vote of acceptance in the Senate (33 to 25) but not in
the House of Representatives.[29] There was even another constitution written at Leavenworth, Kansas, in March, but it was widely criticized for being
far too liberal in extending rights to freed slaves. The *Kansas Tribune* stood
squarely behind the new Leavenworth constitution, the Ross brothers both
having actively participated in its creation. The new constitution was never
given serious consideration.

The so-called English compromise eventually was arrived at in April.
It was a bill in the United States Congress that called for still another referendum on Lecompton, but this time it was tied to a land grant to Kansas of
5.5 million acres to be used for public buildings, educational facilities, and
other public purposes. The compromise also allowed Kansas to be a state
even though it had not achieved the required population of 93,000 people.[30]
The terms of the compromise bill were acceptable to both northern and
southern members of Congress. In effect the compromise amounted to a
bribe to get Kansans to vote for the proslavery constitution. Using an alle-
gorical reference to the devil tempting Jesus, a *Tribune* editorial described
the English compromise: "In other words, the proposition is—take the
Lecompton constitution, with slavery, and you shall have all this [land],
and your settlers shall have their own time in which to pay for their claims,
and you may come into the Union now though you may have but forty or

fifty thousand inhabitants; but reject that constitution and you shall have no land—your claims shall be sold from under you and you shall stay out of the Union until you can prove that you have a population of 93,000. We think the people of Kansas will not be long in deciding between these propositions. They will not be caught in the snare, well laid though it be."[31] The *Tribune* prediction was correct. The actual final vote on Lecompton in Kansas took place on August 2. Lecompton was resoundingly defeated for good by a vote of 11,300 to 1,788.

Although another constitution had to be written and voted upon, the August 2 vote was effectively the end of any hope that southern slaveholders had of the extension of slavery into the western territories. After the rejection of Lecompton, it would not take much more to cause southern states to secede, primarily the election of Abraham Lincoln and the admission of Kansas to the Union as a free state. In a real sense, civil war had already begun in Kansas years before. For the Ross brothers, their finest hours were spent in Topeka on the second floor of their stone building on Sixth Avenue. Looking back more than a century and a half, it's hard to judge just how influential the Rosses were, but there is no question their role in territorial Kansas history was important.

During that summer of 1858 an unexpected event took place: the *Kansas Tribune* went out of business. It seems likely that the reason for the end to this important territorial paper was economic. The Ross brothers probably were not making a living. A number of Kansas newspapers of that day were short lived; one can only guess that it was because expenses exceeded income. Even if income slightly exceeded expenses, the work of producing a daily, or even weekly, paper was relentless and labor intensive. It was far from an easy way to earn a living. Indeed, the other long-running territorial paper, the *Herald of Freedom*, ended publication in December 1859.[32] That Edmund and William struggled in spite of editorial success seems evident. A tactfully written notice in 1857 asked their advertisers to please pay their bills, noting that the newspaper was a business and their livelihood dependent on prompt collection of debts.[33]

Leis recalled that her father sold the house they had lived in for less than a year in the spring of 1858. The sale probably took place somewhat later, since the *Tribune* likely was still in operation until sometime in late summer, although the last extant issue was dated May 29. That May issue gave no indication that publication was about to be suspended. What is seen in the paper is an article noting that the government was announcing the sale of land on the fifth and tenth of July. The article says the land "will be sold at the office in Lecompton, unless taken up by preemption."[34] Leis explains that both her father and his brother preempted government claims in Wabaunsee County, land that was near their father's house. It was their intention to become farmers. Edmund built a log cabin on the property near a stream and a forest. The cabin had three rooms with a porch running the entire length. It was intended to be temporary until Edmund could build a house of stone farther up the hill from the cabin.[35]

One would think that the person who suffered most from this was Fannie. It could not have been more than a year since Edmund finished building the new house in Topeka for his family. Before that, as we have seen, the family lived in one room divided by a curtain. During the year that they lived in the new house, life tended to have some resemblance to the life they knew in Milwaukee. Leis tells us her parents belonged to a literary club called the Philomathic and that there were many people "of refinement and culture, a social element that greatly mitigated the hardships of pioneer life and a bond of sympathy created by their mutual need."[36] We get a feeling for the closeness of the community by reading the *Kansas Tribune*; the newspaper frequently reported on social events in churches, at the Philomathic Society, and at other venues.

Lillian Leis, as an eight-year-old, took both dancing and singing lessons in the building next to her father's office. She tells how her father would come to the dance classes in the evening to watch his daughter or would stand outside the building to hear her sing. She went to school in a two-story building probably run by the Episcopal Church. Leis writes especially fondly of the house they lived in for such a short time. She tells of a frame house in front of which her father transplanted a small tree from near the river and recalls that later, in 1900, she visited with Judge John Martin, who then owned the house. He told her that when he first moved in, he could put his arms around the tree. Now, he could only put his arms halfway around. She wrote, "I was grieved when that tree had to be cut down."[37]

If life in Topeka could be described as "pioneer life," as Leis put it, then life on the new farm located thirty miles west of town was even more difficult. Leis writes that the summer was beautiful, but the winter was severe. They had cows to milk and poultry to protect. The Ross home was probably little different from most farmhouses of the day: "too small for the family . . . lacking in sanitary conditions, and . . . infested with insect pests of various kinds. Homes were isolated from neighbors, adding to the loneliness of women."[38] For Leis, still a child, the acceptance of hardship was somehow easier. Mostly life simply was the way it was. As an adult her perceptions would have been different. She remembered evenings on the farm being filled with music and singing, and her father often reading until late at night "with a green silk shade over his eyes." Ironically, given his own distant future, a favorite book of his was *Thirty Years' View,* Thomas Hart Benton's memoir of his five terms as a senator from Missouri.[39]

For William Ross early autumn brought double tragedies. In October, William's wife died after giving birth to a second child, and within a few weeks the child also died. Grief-stricken, William "became a rambler for a time," in Leis's words. About this same time, Edmund and Fannie became parents for the fourth time. In November their third son, Flynt, named after Fannie's father, was born.

Leis's fondest memories of that first winter appear to be trips to her grandparents' home, where they stayed all night. There was a large fireplace with a "huge back-log. White curtains in the windows and a red carpet—cozy and bright." Her father would take his bass viol, while her uncles George and Charles would play their violins. Grandfather Sylvester and Lillian's youngest uncle, Walter, took down their flutes, and everyone else would sing. The following summer was a mix of pleasant memories and recollections of hardship:

> On the hillside above the cabin, on the broken sod were immense melons, squashes and pumpkins. And in another field green corn which the young men hoed on moonlight nights, lounging and reading in the shade of the porch on warm afternoons. The center table with the Astral lamp, for which there was no oil, graced the living room. A bookcase, a couch, which could be drawn out and converted into a bed, and the dining room table always with a snowy linen cloth—for mother was fastidious—and silver spoons dropped by children, were often carried off by rats, lurking beneath the floor, which stood rather high from the ground.
>
> There was plenty of water from the stream nearby and lovely clear springs. But water had to be carried to the house.

Leis writes about an incident that took place on the Fourth of July in 1859 when her father was away on an extended trip. Fannie had prepared a chicken dinner for herself and the three eldest children while the new baby slept in a crib in the adjoining room. As they ate their meal, Arthur yelled, "There's a snake." It was a rattlesnake gliding toward the room where the baby slept. Arthur ran for a stick, which Fannie used to beat the snake to death, after which she collapsed for a time, Lillian caring for baby Flynt. "There were times when my mother thought she was alone, I would find her weeping. But she displayed great fortitude with others. She had my lessons also—I was required to read aloud every day, for there was no school near. The children's interests were never neglected.[40]

What were Fannie's thoughts and feelings about this isolated life? That she cried when no one was looking, had rats to deal with, water to carry from a stream, no school for her children, and the presence of rattlesnakes, had to weigh heavily on her. And Edmund was not always there. Her thoughts must have gone back to the house and life they had in Milwaukee, or at least to the house and life they knew for just a short time in Topeka.

Ross certainly saw that his own year on the farm was a mistake. He was a skilled writer and an intelligent, levelheaded man. He had spent a number of intense years devoted to the abolition of slavery and to the shaping of public opinion through his newspaper. This dedication to a cause probably took him away from his family more than he wanted, and he may have believed that farming would keep his family close together, but what this did to him personally could not have been good. Writing and involvement with the critical issues facing Kansas and the United States had to dominate his thoughts. Given the quality of his writing and the soundness of his reasoning, especially for such a young man, it is hard to imagine him withdrawing to farm life. He must have felt compelled to return to his life in Topeka. He was not nearly as much a farmer as he was a journalist and an abolitionist.

In early June 1859 Ross was elected as a delegate from Wabaunsee County to the Wyandotte constitutional convention. Ross joined thirty-four other Republicans and seventeen Democrats charged with drawing up yet another constitution. Because Republicans dominated the convention, Kansas easily was made "free" for the first time, pending the approval of voters. Among other features of the constitution, state boundaries were defined. An attempt to give women the right to vote in state elections was advanced by Ross's fellow abolitionist John Ritchie. Although there was some support for the idea, in the end only white males who were twenty-one or older were sanctioned to vote. A majority of the delegates remained unwilling to grant the right to black and Native American residents, but a compromise of sorts with respect to women was realized when women were enfranchised to vote in school elections and were granted the right to own property.[41] With the Lecompton, Leavenworth, and Topeka constitutions now dead and gone, this new antislavery constitution was the one finally accepted by the United States Congress.

As a delegate Ross must have renewed old acquaintances and found himself once again steeped in the admixture of politics and friendship. As an added incentive, William returned from his "ramblings" and was ready to renew their former activities on Sixth Avenue. On October 1, 1859, they published their first edition of the *Kansas State Record*, and although it had a different name, it was really just a continuation of the old *Kansas Tribune*.[42] Even the masthead looked pretty much the same, but now Edmund's name was listed first.

CHAPTER FIVE

Ross, the Record, and the Railroads

The construction of a railroad from the Missouri River to this point, would secure to Topeka this entire commerce sufficient of itself to build up a city on these plains, surpassing in wealth and greatness the aggregate of all the towns and cities now in existence west of the Missouri River.

—Ross, editorial, *Kansas State Record*, November 5, 1859

⌐ THE RETURN TO TOPEKA in the fall of 1859 was a new beginning for the Edmund G. Ross family. For a time they lived in a rented house until Ross purchased half a block of property on Sixth Avenue, where he built a stone cottage with the interior finished in black walnut. This may sound like an imposing house on a huge lot, but it was more likely a fairly modest residence. It would be the family home until 1864, although Ross himself would live in it only a couple of those years.[1] Assuming he could produce enough income to provide for his family, he was right where he wanted to be in life. He could ask for nothing more and was willing to tolerate the lean years that he expected were inevitable.

With the defeat of the Lecompton constitution, the Free-State Party could be assured that slavery in Kansas was no longer an issue, so the party dissolved and the Kansas Republican Party was established to replace it. Likewise the *Kansas State Record* became the voice of Republicanism. While the *Tribune* had been a shared project between William and Edmund, the *Record* was Edmund's. With farming now ruled out as a career, making a go of the newspaper business was about the only option left to Edmund— not that he would have wanted anything else. Newspaper publishing and job printing was always Edmund's first choice. Making it pay was another matter. Edmund would be a soldier, a senator, and a governor for relatively short periods during the forty-eight years that lay ahead of him, but newspaper publishing and printing were the skills he would always return to. The same was not true for William, who was more like a key employee at the *Record*. Early in 1861 William moved on to become an Indian agent for the Pottawatomie tribe and never returned to the newspaper business. The fact was, it may have been very difficult for a newspaper in a town the size of Topeka to produce a living wage for more than one man with a family. William's name would disappear from the *Record* on April 13, 1861.

The *Kansas State Record* had a simple declaration under the banner: *We render equal and exact justice to all, and submit to wrong from none.* In the first issue of the *Record*, dated October 1, 1859, Ross stated the intention of the paper was "to make the *State Record* a reflex of the aims and principles of the Republican party." The most pressing of these aims was approval of the Wyandotte constitution—which, of course, Ross favored, having been a delegate to the convention—in a referendum scheduled for October 4. Wyandotte, as we have seen, made slavery illegal in Kansas, gave women the right to vote in school elections, and made black immigration into Kansas legal.[2] Some voters, particularly Democrats, feared that a lack of restrictions on black immigration would cause Kansas to be overrun with blacks fleeing the South. Nevertheless, Wyandotte was approved by a vote of 10,421 to 5,530.[3] Statehood was another matter. It took until January of 1861 for Congress to accept Wyandotte and officially declare Kansas a state.

The *Kansas State Record* relentlessly continued to seek an end to slavery. Seemingly every issue of the paper contained either articles or commentary on various aspects of the slavery question. It is remarkable how Ross could repeat his outrage at slavery and slaveholders in issue after issue of both the *Tribune* and the *Record* and find a new way of doing it each time. He often did this by reporting events that related to slavery, and then adding his own commentary. When reporting on John Brown's raid on Harper's Ferry, for example, Ross, who did not approve of Brown's tactics, nevertheless found a way to be critical of slaveholders. "The raid at Harper's Ferry is, of course, a reprehensible affair, not to be justified on any grounds. . . . We are no apologists for treason or servile insurrections, but when slaveholders at the South, and their toadies at the North, seek to brand John Brown as a bad man—as a bloodthirsty monster, we say to them: Behold the work of your own hands. Stop the mouths of your own bloodhounds which you have let loose upon the territories—raze your own gibbets which you have erected for all who have the manhood to oppose the machinations of the God of slavery, and there will be no more John Browns to disturb your slumbers, or apply the brand to the seething volcano which now sleeps beneath your feet."[4]

While it was true that Ross continued to fight for an end to slavery, he also began a new crusade that often took precedence over other issues. As early as 1857 the Ross brothers were promoting railroad lines through Kansas. In the *Record* this became an all-out push, with practically every issue devoting some space to railroad promotion. Edmund was not alone in this campaign. Other territorial leaders advocated rail lines that would connect Kansas with Chicago and the East Coast as well as western lines to California and New Mexico. The New Mexico line would approximate the same route as the Santa Fe Trail, connecting Kansas to lucrative trade with Old Mexico, and Ross wrote often about it in the *Kansas State Record*. A December issue of the paper cited statistics on Santa Fe trade and encouraged civic leaders to find a way of extending rail service from the Missouri River to Topeka. "Do our people realize that there is constantly passing and repassing, not more than twenty miles south of us, a trade involving millions of dollars annually—compared to which the famed caravans of the African deserts were but a retail affair."[5] Ross cited figures from a source identified as the *Kansas Press*, which in turn reported statistics supplied by the firm of S. M. Hayes and Co. The article reported that during the summer months some 2,440 men, 1,827 wagons, 429 horses, 15,714 oxen, 5,316 mules, and 67 carriages passed through Kansas, transporting 9,608 tons of freight.[6]

Ross recognized that the railroad itself was a form of industry and that an industrial base was necessary to create the kind of job opportunities that were sorely needed in Kansas. Furthermore, the railroad would make Kansas attractive to other forms of industry and facilitate increased mercantile trade and expanded agriculture. Without industry, the principal means of generating income were agriculture and ranching—not the kinds of enterprises that would produce widespread wealth without railroads to carry harvested crops and livestock. For families relying on subsistence farming, life was difficult at best, as Ross found out in Wabaunsee County, and in drought years, when rainfall was inadequate, farming could be a disaster. Such was the case in the growing season of 1860. Throughout the decade of the fifties, poor rainfall, high winds, and scorching temperatures well over a hundred degrees frustrated farmers, but the worst year of the era was 1860, when drought conditions equaled famine conditions for some.[7] The severity of the 1860 drought was widely reported by newspapers throughout Kansas, including the *Kansas State Record.*

By the fall of 1860 it was becoming clear that organized relief was needed to mitigate the suffering that many Kansas residents were experiencing. A Territorial Relief Convention was organized for mid-November at Lawrence. A group of seven civic and religious leaders, including Edmund Ross, prepared the business agenda of the convention. The convention sought help in the form of money, guaranteed loans, food, clothing, and other necessities of life. A group of five men was appointed to prepare an address to the people of the United States to seek relief. Another group of fourteen men headed by S. C. Pomeroy, all unpaid volunteers, would oversee relief, while a distinguished group of men including the territorial governor and the chief justice of the Supreme Court of Kansas were responsible for inspecting and auditing the accounts of the relief committee.[8] That the drought was real and that people were suffering, there is no doubt, but some people did not believe in the severity of the situation. Samuel J. Crawford, a longtime resident of Kansas and one of its state governors in the 1860s, claimed that the seriousness of the drought was greatly exaggerated. Writing more than forty years later, he expressed the belief that the whole scheme of relief was a fraud designed to line the pockets of its leaders.[9]

Edmund Ross's participation in the relief effort was mostly restricted to the original organizational convention, but through his newspaper he strongly supported the relief committee and may have been involved to some extent with the distribution of donated items in the Topeka area. Ross continued to support the relief committee with frequent news articles and editorials and was especially supportive of S. C. Pomeroy. Even when Pomeroy came under attack for poor accountability of collected funds, Ross continued to support him, refusing to believe there was anything unethical about Pomeroy or the relief committee. The truth of any graft in connection with the 1860 relief effort on the part of Pomeroy, or any of the other organizers, was never proven, but Pomeroy's reputation for less than honorable dealings would surface again later in the 1860s, and his eventual downfall would start with a particularly strong editorial attack by Edmund Ross in 1872. In 1860, however, Ross had a decidedly different take on Pomeroy when he wrote, "As far as General Pomeroy is concerned, we repeat what we have stated before, we do not believe that a man could have been found in the Territory of Kansas, who would bring to this business, a clearer judgment, or a higher degree of fidelity, or could give more perfect satisfaction in the discharge of the onerous duties thus imposed upon him."[10]

Until the summer of 1862 Ross continued to be a strong supporter of Pomeroy. Together they would work, with other prominent men of Kansas, to organize the Atchison, Topeka and Santa Fe Railroad, and after the Civil War they would serve together as United States senators from Kansas. The man credited with founding the Atchison and Topeka Railroad Company (forerunner of the AT&SF) was Cyrus K. Holliday of Topeka, a good friend of Edmund Ross. Holliday apparently was the sole writer of the charter for the new company incorporated by an act of the territorial legislature in January and February 1859. Ross's name was not listed as an incorporator, but at the first meeting of the new organization on September 15, 1859, he was listed as a member of the board of directors.[11] Undoubtedly Ross was picked because of his long-standing and high-profile endorsements of railroads in both the *Kansas Tribune* and the *Kansas State Record* and because of his friendship with Holliday.

That first organizational meeting took place in Atchison at the office of Luther Challiss. Ross, Holliday, Major Joel Huntoon, and Judge Jacob Safford traveled together from Topeka to attend the meeting in Atchison. These were not men of wealth, with Ross probably being the poorest of the four. What they had was great determination to make the initial phase of the rail line between Atchison and Topeka a reality. To keep their expenses down, the men packed three days of rations. For his part, Ross took "a stuffed boiled beef heart, and the others made up the cuisine in bread, pickles & etc."[12] Ross reported that Judge Safford provided a spring wagon and a set of horses. River crossings were not difficult, because the drought conditions allowed easy fording. The nights were warm enough that the men could sleep outside, saving the cost of hotel bills en route. In Atchison they were treated to free hotel accommodations.[13]

The *Kansas State Record* reported the formation of the corporation that September and listed thirteen men on the board of directors including Ross. Holliday was elected president, with P. T. Abel as secretary and M. C. Dickey as collector and treasurer.[14] Ross's 1882 recollection also reported a pledge by each of the directors of $4,000 initially to fund the company. It is difficult to imagine Ross coming up with $4,000 to help finance the company unless from a bank loan, perhaps using his property as security. The money was to be used to do a study and plan a proposed route.[15] A major reason for having the meeting in Atchison was to catch the ear of Thaddeus Hyatt, known to be a generous philanthropist, and while they no doubt talked to him about participating, they came away empty-handed.

In 1860 Ross increased the frequency of articles about railroads in the *Record*. In addition to promoting the rail line between Atchison and Topeka, Ross proposed a railroad convention to be held on October 17, 1860. This territory-wide meeting, with delegates coming from every county, was designed to create a comprehensive plan for rail service throughout Kansas and to appeal to the United States Congress for assistance in making the rail lines a reality. Kansas needed rights of way on property for the proposed track system and thus needed Congress to provide land grants, a practice that already had precedents in the United States. Although Ross earned a reputation for being a pioneer in helping with the formation of what would become the Atchison, Topeka and Santa Fe, perhaps an equally important contribution was his role in involving the entire territory in a conference called to support the building of railroads in Kansas.

When the gavel sounded in Museum Hall in Topeka for the opening of the convention, 120 enthusiastic delegates from nineteen Kansas counties were present. S. C. Pomeroy began the program with a few short remarks and then nominated Edmund G. Ross to be the temporary president of the convention.[16] It was an honorary title meant to pay tribute to the man who proposed the convention and who tirelessly promoted it through his newspaper. It is probable that Ross was only willing to serve as a temporary president. He likely preferred to simply cover the convention for the *Record* and let higher-profile leaders take the stage.

In the end, the convention proposed five rail lines connecting in a pattern that reached most of the territory of Kansas. The lines were the Kansas Central Railroad, the Atchison, Topeka and Santa Fe, the Jefferson City and Neoshe Valley Railroad, the Lawrence and Fort Gibson Railroad, and the Atchison and Pike's Peak Railroad. A committee of five men representing the five proposed lines was established to write the memorials necessary to communicate the needs of the various railroads to the president of the United States and to Congress. When it came to appointing a permanent executive committee, Ross was one of five men appointed including Samuel C. Pomeroy.[17]

As enthusiastic as the founders of the Atchison and Topeka Railroad Company were, the $52,000 raised may not have been spent. The drought and accompanying famine of 1860 was serious enough that the planning of the rail line was postponed. By the following year the Civil War further delayed the beginning of work. With Ross then an active participant in the war, he was not available to continue to serve on the board when planning began in earnest. Ross may have been allowed to withdraw his $4,000 from the company. C. K. Holliday and others from the board began to actively pursue a land grant from the United States Congress. On March 3, 1863, the grant became a reality, and a new company with a new name—Atchison, Topeka and Santa Fe Railroad—was founded with a board of directors that did not include Ross. S. C. Pomeroy was named president. The state of Kansas was given rights of way on sections of land along the proposed route with the understanding that construction would be complete within ten years. The land was then given to the AT&SF. Money for construction was raised by the sale of stock to eastern capitalists, but the actual construction of the railroad did not begin until October 1868.[18]

The Atchison, Topeka and Santa Fe would, of course, become one of the great railroads in United States history. The inability of Edmund Ross to participate as a member of its board must have been one of the great disappointments of his life. It certainly was his best chance to become financially comfortable if not wealthy. In later years, after his time in the United States Senate, this disappointment would deepen as he watched his colleague Samuel Pomeroy become one of the wealthiest men in the Senate.

Just four days before the railroad convention, a short, unusual article appeared in the *Record*. It was unusual because it was about the struggle Ross was having in keeping the newspaper in business, a subject not mentioned in previous editions. It was extremely rare for Ross to put anything personal in his paper. The date selected for the article was the first anniversary of the newspaper. Ross eloquently repeated the objectives of the paper and thanked his readers for their support, but explained that the cost of producing the paper far exceeded income. On the other hand, they were determined to succeed. Ross placed the blame for the losses they were experiencing on the lack of population in Kansas and the poor economic conditions but promised that "no abatement will be suffered in the energy with which we have labored." What followed was an apology for having to cut delinquent subscribers from circulation but with a hope for the speedy inauguration of better times.[19]

William would leave the paper for good within a few months, while Edmund Ross remained dedicated to making the *Kansas State Record* a success. The paper was his life, and that he might not be a wealthy man did not matter to him. If he could somehow hold out for better times and an increased population base, and thus increased readership, he would be satisfied that a comfortable life for his family was in the future. Being a newspaper editor-publisher suited Ross perfectly. Given his rather quiet personality, he could still be an important civic leader from the semi-solitude of his office. He could let politicians pursue their high-profile lives and be satisfied that he was every bit as influential in his own way. Newspapers, particularly in the West, where libraries and other channels of information were hard to come by, were the media outlets of their day.

Edmund continued to publish his paper with a staff of several young men. That these young men greatly admired him and looked to him for leadership was evident. In the late spring of 1861, when the Civil War had just begun, Ross's employees and the women of Topeka presented Ross with a twenty-four-by-thirteen-foot American flag made of French merino. The flag was presented at a ceremony at the Congregational Church held in conjunction with a festival. A young woman named Mollie Campbell made the formal presentation and a speech. "This flag has been associated with everything that is good and great in our nation's history. It is the banner beneath which Washington led forth our victorious armies in the memorable struggle for American Liberty. The same bright ensign of the Free that has floated in the breeze from the dome of our Nation's Capitol—cheered the hearts of our soldiers in war, and made the hearts of patriots rejoice with exultant pride ever since we were known as the Independent United States of America . . . I wish you to receive this Banner of the Free. In behalf of the Ladies of Topeka and the Compositors of the State Record Office I present you with this, the noble Flag of the Union."[20]

Two men of Topeka named Emerson and Hall made and erected a flagpole in front of the *Record* office on which the flag was raised. Ross listed fifteen names of employees who honored him that night as well as the names of the women of Topeka. Whether all of the employees named worked for him at the time is doubtful, but they all had been with him in the past. Ross responded to the presentation in his paper: "Stimulated by their approving smiles, and cordial cooperation, we hope to continue worthy of their high confidence, as a journalist and as a man."[21]

Kansas had officially become a state on January 29, 1861. Perhaps at another time in history or even a different time of year, celebrations would have spilled into the streets of towns throughout Kansas, but that particular January was bitter cold and the mood of the country about as despondent as it could be. A month earlier South Carolina had seceded from the

Union, and the act of declaring Kansas a free state by the United States Congress moved the country even closer to civil war. In just a matter of weeks Abraham Lincoln would be inaugurated, and it was becoming clear that more states would secede.

Ross observed these events, as most every American no doubt did, with a sense of dread but with a degree of hope as well. In February a national Peace Convention was held in Washington to find a solution to the differences that separated the states. The convention, initiated by the congressional delegation from Virginia, included delegates from every state. While Ross realistically doubted that any good would come of the meeting, he nevertheless believed that "there are measures of compromise which we have every reason to believe would be satisfactory to the great body of the people of the South." The slave states of Maryland, Virginia, Tennessee, Kentucky, and Missouri could be reasoned with, he believed, and even if the same could not be said of deep southern states, he held out hope that the border states could somehow keep the Union together.[22] They did not. By the time of the firing on Fort Sumter on April 12, a total of seven states had left the Union. After April 12 four more states seceded.

If Congress and the Peace Convention could not find a solution, Ross hoped that President Lincoln would provide the leadership necessary to restore unity among the states. Two days before Lincoln's inaugural, Ross wrote a column expressing his hope that Lincoln might bring "relief from impending calamity, the shadow of which has for months past darkened the prospects of our country. . . . History has demonstrated the Proverb that the Hour will always produce its Man."[23]

Ross's perception of Abraham Lincoln was insightful at a time when many were uncertain just who this new president was or how he might carry out his awesome duties. What Ross could not see was the horrible bloodbath that would overwhelm the country for the next four years. He could surely see that some fighting was inevitable, but there was an optimistic sense in Ross's writing, almost a yearning that somehow things would get better and that life in Topeka would go on without affecting his ability to publish a newspaper of the highest quality or interfering with his family's happiness.

Throughout the summer Ross's hopes were dashed as reports came in of horrendous losses at places like Bull Run and of losses closer to home in Missouri, losses that included Kansans, people he knew. Inevitably, he was forced to see reality along with the rest of the country. By October 12 his editorials took on a much more ominous tone. When it became clear that more men would need to volunteer, Ross knew that he would be one of them. An editorial he wrote seems almost to be a letter to his wife, as if he could not bear to tell her directly what was needed of him. He was thirty-five years old, and there were others his age who avoided military service. Although he must have been tempted to use the argument that he had a family to care for and a business to run and nobody could blame him for staying in Topeka, he would still have himself to deal with the rest of his life. "Enlistment has become the duty of every man who is capable of bearing arms. The young man who has his health and strength is squandering his energies by following peaceful pursuits in such a time as this. His government owns his sinews, *and calls for them now.* The man of family has a double duty to perform now. His duty to his wife and little ones requires him to meet the enemy *far off,* and keep them from his door, while gratitude to his government for past protection, in the rearing of his household Gods, demands the cheerful yielding of his life, if need be, in her defense."[24]

His enlistment didn't happen overnight, but there was really no doubt that he would volunteer. He had his business to think about first. If he was forced to give up the newspaper, he no doubt wanted to find a buyer rather than just shutting the door, and Fannie, who was pregnant again, surely had her opinion about her husband leaving her with a family to care for.

The early months of 1862 brought joy mixed with profound sadness. On February 15, Fannie gave birth to a baby girl whom the parents named Edmundie after her father, although the much easier nickname Eddie was the only name the family, or anyone else, ever used.[25] The joy of a new child in the Ross family was quickly followed by the tragic death of Flynt, who at three and one-half years succumbed to diphtheria on March 7. The effect of their son's death on Edmund and Fannie was devastating, but Edmund had the more difficult time dealing with it. Lillian Leis writes that her father was "completely broken hearted." Flynt was buried on top of a hill east of Topeka. In writing about the burial in the 1930s, Leis remarked that the grave was the only one on the lot and that it was still there, designated by a granite marker.[26] The four sons of Fannie and Edmund are buried in four different states, but the lone grave of a toddler is the most profoundly sad of the four. The memory of a tiny child, buried alone, must have haunted the Rosses for the remainder of their lives.

With the war going poorly, the president issued a call for 300,000 additional volunteers in July 1862. For Kansas this meant three additional

CHAPTER SIX

THE CIVIL WAR AND THE KANSAS VOLUNTEERS

I shall be glad indeed when it is over and we can all go home again. I do not think I shall occasion again to leave you or the little ones. My fireside has too many attractions to me to ever again leave it, except upon the most urgent necessity. This time I felt the necessity of the country demanded the sacrifice from every man that could possibly make it.

—Edmund Ross to Fannie, December 12, 1862

↶ HENRY C. LINDSEY was a twelve-year-old boy when he went to Kansas with his father in 1856. Elza Lindsey was a stonemason and a widower who no doubt believed Kansas offered a better future for himself and his young son, but it is safe to assume that their life was no better in Kansas than it had been in Iowa. By his mid-teens Henry appears to be living totally on his own and working on a farm northwest of Topeka.[1]

Perhaps because of drought conditions, when he was about sixteen years old Henry Lindsey lost his farm job and found himself homeless in Topeka. Of the two suits of clothes he owned, he sold the better suit for cash to live on and did his best to survive in a town where employment was hard to come by. An acquaintance named Jimmy Conwell who worked at the *Kansas State Record* as a printer's devil, an apprentice, offered to introduce Lindsey to Edmund Ross, a man Lindsey greatly admired. Ross, who likely already knew something about the boy and his "street" reputation, offered to hire him if he promised to stop cursing. Lindsey essentially had no choice and accepted the job for one dollar per week plus room and board, a satisfactory situation for a boy who had no experience. Ross, impressed with Lindsey's advancement, raised his salary to $1.50 per week within a few months. In time he became a true father figure to the boy.[2]

With Lincoln's call for 300,000 more troops in July 1862, the War Department sought three regiments of men from Kansas. Thomas Ewing Jr., then the chief justice of the Kansas Supreme Court, was enlisted to lead one of the regiments. Each of the regiments consisted of ten companies of about one hundred men each. From the Topeka area Ewing asked Edmund Ross to raise one of the companies. Ross was able to recruit sixty-seven men from Topeka, and in early September he rendezvoused with his company at a place called Camp Lyon, which Ross and others preferred to call Camp Ewing, near Leavenworth. The remainder of the men needed for Ross's company came from the recruits of Preston B. Plumb, who brought more than 130 men with him from Emporia, including John Kitts, who had previously worked for Ross.[3] Like Ross, Plumb was a newspaper editor and publisher.

One of the men transferred from Plumb's company to Ross's was Kitts, and among the men Ross brought with him were three who worked for him at the *Record*: Nathan P. Gregg, Jim Conwell, and Henry Lindsey. Ross had also recruited his brother George. Henry Lindsey, not yet eighteen and too young to be a soldier, was made a drummer boy instead. In time Lindsey proved to be a fine soldier, and at the age of nineteen he achieved the rank of second lieutenant.[4]

Ross was given command of Company E, with the rank of captain. Charles Drake was elected first lieutenant and Nathan Gregg was made second lieutenant. In addition to Ewing as commander of the Eleventh Regiment, Thomas Moonlight was made lieutenant colonel and Preston Plumb was made major. When completely mustered in by September 14, there were ten companies in the Eleventh Kansas Volunteers, the entire regiment an infantry unit.[5]

The new recruits faced several problems. They were, first of all, untrained. Even Colonel Ewing had no military experience. However, Ewing had grown up in a family of privilege where he was expected to assume leadership roles as an adult. His sister Ellen's husband, who literally was raised as a member of the Ewing family, was William Tecumseh Sherman. Although Ewing was unschooled in warfare, he learned quickly and earned the respect of his men. Second, they were expected to be ready for battle within weeks. General James G. Blunt, under whose command they would fall, wanted the regiment to be ready to march by early October. Third, they were poorly equipped. They had expected to go into battle with state-of-the-art Enfield rifles, but these did not arrive before they were ready to leave Camp Lyon. Instead they were given ancient Prussian muskets made in 1818, rifles that were at least one-quarter heavier than the Enfields and had a much more limited range of effectiveness. Fourth, the advance pay the men were promised had not arrived, and many had families to provide for, so Colonel Ewing had to arrange with a Leavenworth bank to let the men have loans.[6]

The first march of the Eleventh Regiment began on October 4. It was a difficult march of 125 miles to Fort Scott in southeastern Kansas—difficult because the men were still not fully conditioned for such a distance and because their inexperienced commander, Colonel Ewing, believed 30 miles per day was not unreasonable. Before he left camp, Ross wrote to Fannie about the dangers that lay ahead and the preparations he had in place should he not return. "I think I have made arrangements by which you will be entirely protected in case of my death. William [brother] and Holliday [good friend] were in Leavenworth yesterday and will see that my business is arranged as speedily as possible. That done I shall have no good reason for hesitancy on the battlefield in the employment of my utmost energy."[7]

The regiment managed to complete the march to Fort Scott in five days, although scattered out over many miles near the end of the march and thoroughly exhausted. At Fort Scott the men were able to rest for five days as they awaited an ammunition supply train. On October 15 they were assigned to escort the train to the area of Pea Ridge in northwest Arkansas, the site of the recent battle between the forces of Union general Samuel R. Curtis and Confederate generals Sterling Price and Earl Van Dorn.

After reaching Pea Ridge, and with only one day to rest, on two successive nights the Eleventh was force-marched to the vicinity of Fort Wayne in the Indian territories west of Arkansas. The objective was to take part in a battle with the 3,000-man army of Confederate general Douglas Cooper, who was believed to be preparing for an assault on Fort Scott to the north. By this time the Eleventh had marched about 250 miles in two weeks. General Blunt used his cavalry in an October 22 morning raid with the intention of following up with infantry troops, including the Eleventh, still en route. The cavalry, under the leadership of Captain Samuel Crawford of the Second Kansas, was so successful in routing the Confederates that there was really no need for the infantry. The men of the Eleventh, in their determination to be on hand for the battle, abandoned their overcoats to make better time and ran nearly three miles in less than half an hour, but they arrived only in time to see the rebel army in retreat, hotly pursued by Crawford's cavalry.[8] Among the men in Crawford's company was Charles Ross, another of

Edmund's brothers.[9] Cooper's men were apparently regrouping when the Eleventh entered the battle. In Ross's words, "they could not stand the sight of our fixed bayonets in heavy column, coming over the hill on a full run and immediately broke and ran like the devil."[10]

The same incident reported in the biography of Preston Plumb gives a slightly different interpretation of the fight, with a comic reference to the ancient rifles the Eleventh carried, rather than their bayonets, being the cause of the rebels' retreat. "It is jestingly said that when the Confederate troops saw the Eleventh Kansas, long drawn out in columns of twos, descending the winding road with their ancient brass-mounted muskets glittering in the morning sun, they were seized with panic and precipitately fled, believing the whole Federal army armed with diabolic contrivances was upon them."[11]

The first serious battle in which Ross and the Eleventh Regiment were participants was a confrontation with Confederate forces under the command of Colonel J. T. Marmaduke. Marmaduke, with a force of some 8,000 cavalry, had been ordered by his commander, General Thomas C. Hindman, to take control of the town of Cane Hill, Arkansas. General Blunt, aware of the movements of both Marmaduke and Hindman, was bivouacked with his army of 5,000 men some thirty miles north of Cane Hill and was impatiently awaiting supplies. On November 26 the supplies finally arrived, and each man was issued four days' rations and eighty rounds of ammunition. Fearful that Hindman would soon join Marmaduke with an even larger army, Blunt ordered the troops at his command to engage Marmaduke's men immediately. What resulted was a forced march of twenty-seven hours over thirty-eight miles of rough terrain. Ross reported that he went into battle with sixty-seven men and three officers. In the end all he could muster were twenty-six. "The sight of a battlefield is very sickening. All along the road, during the pursuit were scattered dead and wounded men and horses, marking spots that were hotly contested."[12]

Ross's company suffered no losses in the battle. His thin ranks at the end of the day were the result of exhaustion, men simply being unable to keep up. The success of the Union Army, in spite of fewer men, can probably be attributed to motivation. Many of the Confederate soldiers were conscripts and some reportedly were deserting as they had the chance. The Union men, especially the men from Kansas, saw these battles as a defense of their homeland. By keeping rebels out of Kansas they were protecting their families. Most of the men of the Eleventh were family men, and of those who were not already husbands and fathers, some were looking forward to being married in the near future. Ross reported at the end of that November: "I have a book which Lieut Gregg obtained here and which he proposes to present to Lillie when he gets back. Her name and presentation are already written in it."[13]

With the successful routing of Marmaduke's army, the men of the Eleventh occupied the town of Cane Hill and once again had a few days of rest. In a letter to Fannie, Ross reported that he had found an abandoned printing office and proposed to print a regimental newspaper.[14] Although the press had been damaged and the thousands of pieces of type scattered in and around the small cabin that housed the press, the find to men in the printing business was exciting. In particular Ross and Plumb saw this as a diversion to what might be a long and boring stay for their men, some of whom were skilled printers. The job of assessing whether or not a paper could be produced fell to Private Kitts, who sorted through the almost hopelessly scattered pieces of lead type. Although there is no credit in the single edition of the paper ultimately printed, certainly Nathan Gregg, James Conwell, and Henry Lindsey also were involved.[15]

Ross's intention of publishing multiple editions appealed to General Blunt, who thought the press could be carried by wagon to other battle sites. Ross had previously worked with Blunt; both men had been delegates to the Wyandotte constitutional convention, and there was a friendly rapport between them. Nevertheless, the idea of a regimental newspaper came to an abrupt end when Brigadier General John Schofield, the new commander of the Army of the Frontier, decided otherwise. The first side of the paper reported on the brief history of the Kansas Eleventh from its beginnings at Fort Lyon and Cane Hill, and included an article by Major Plumb about the destruction of civilian property. The second side of the paper was not printed until after the Battle of Prairie Grove and featured an account of that battle and the earlier Cane Hill confrontation. The paper, which was called the *Buck and Ball*, is certainly important for the firsthand information it contains, but it has historical significance beyond that. The paper is a curiosity that has caught the attention of historians. The only known extant copies of this first and only edition are in the collections of the Kansas State Historical Society.[16] Printed under the *Buck and Ball* title was the motto "Calibre 72, gives the rebels h—l." The number 72 was the caliber of the Prussian muskets used by the Eleventh.[17]

The largest and most important battle in the Eleventh's first year was essentially a follow-up to the Cane Hill fight. Colonel Marmaduke had retreated south over the Boston Mountains and regrouped to fight again with General Hindman's other units of artillery, infantry, and cavalry. In an early dispatch to Fort Leavenworth, General Blunt estimated the size of Hindman's army to be about 25,000. In anticipation of another attack, Blunt possibly estimated the number on the high side to emphasize the urgency of the situation. Later, he more accurately reported 10,000 men under Hindman, even at that an army much larger than the one Blunt commanded.[18] The war in the west had not gone well for the rebel forces, and Hindman saw a chance of striking a serious blow by attacking General Blunt's division, including the Eleventh, still bivouacked in northwestern Arkansas and numbering only about 5,000. Blunt's nearest reinforcements were some one hundred miles to the north in Missouri. This meant reinforcements would have to cover twice the distance Hindman had to travel to engage Blunt. Unfortunately for Hindman, he did not move his troops quickly enough, and he had to deal with crossing the Boston Mountains. On December 6, as Hindman moved north along the Fayetteville Road, his Confederate troops were met by General Francis J. Herron and his two divisions coming to the aid of General Blunt.

The confrontation that resulted was the Battle of Prairie Grove, fought throughout the day and into darkness on December 7. At ten o'clock on the morning of the seventh, Blunt marched his troops from Cane Hill to join in the battle with Herron, arriving by midafternoon. Captain Ross's Company E was assigned to support the Second Indiana Battery situated just opposite the center of the Confederate line, where rebel firepower was heaviest. Ross described the field of battle as being about a mile and a half wide and some three to four miles long with gently ascending timbered hills on either side.[19] Although the fighting was intense, Ross's men fired from a prone position with the Indiana cannons firing over them. Historian William Shea quoted from a letter written by Ireneus Myers to his brother: "When I think of the time we were engaged and the way the balls flew around us, it looks almost like a merricle that we were not cut to pieces. All that saved us was laying flat on the ground and they shot over us."[20] The battle that day was mostly a standoff, with the Eleventh forced to retreat a short distance late in the day.[21] By nightfall fighting ceased, but the Union generals, assuming the fighting would continue the next day, ordered intense preparations that night.

At first light in the morning there was little, if any, activity behind the Confederate lines, and to the surprise of General Herron, Generals Hindman and Marmaduke crossed the battlefield under a flag of truce to request a meeting of the generals of both sides. The Confederate generals requested a delay in fighting so they could clear the battlefield of their injured and dead. Their ulterior purpose, it soon became apparent, was to buy time. The damage inflicted by the Union forces the day before apparently was more serious than first supposed, and the rebels had secretly been in full retreat since the night before. Samuel Crawford, whose account is firsthand, describes Generals Marmaduke and Hindman leaving the armistice conference and riding back through the field of battle "where their dead were lying all around and their wounded suffering and begging for water and medical treatment, without stopping to make any provision for them."[22]

Union casualties, killed and wounded, were about 1,200, while Eleventh Regiment history placed Confederate casualties at about 2,500 men. All the dead and two-thirds of the Confederate wounded fell into Union hands. About 3,000 Confederate soldiers deserted.[23] Ross reported to Fannie that nearly every house in the area for miles around was turned into a hospital, "the dead and dying and wounded covering the floor of every room and all the sheets and bedding of the owners taken for use."[24] Colonel Ewing's Eleventh Kansas suffered 7 killed and 31 wounded. It is interesting to note that during the armistice conference the generals took the time to agree on "Battle of Prairie Grove" as an official name.

In Ross's letter to Fannie after the Battle of Prairie Grove there is a decided hint of melancholy and a need for him to express again his reason for not being with his family, as if Fannie still needed to be convinced that there was good reason for the sacrifices they both were making. "I do not think I shall occasion again to leave you or the little ones. My fireside has too many attractions to me to ever again leave it, except upon the most urgent necessity. This time I felt the necessity of the country demanded the sacrifice from every man that could possibly make it."[25]

In the same letter Ross expressed his admiration for Colonel Ewing, who he hoped would soon be promoted to general. Ross told Fannie to expect a letter from Mrs. Ewing. The colonel had written to his wife and, among other things, asked her to write to Fannie Ross to assure her that Edmund was all right and had survived the battle at Prairie Grove. Ross encouraged Fannie to write back to Mrs. Ewing. The friendship between Ross and Ewing could not be described as intimate, but it was strong and would become important when Ross became Senator Ross. Ironically, Ewing wanted to become one of the two senators from the new state of Kansas and had run unsuccessfully for the office in 1861.

Many, if not most, of the casualties suffered by the Kansas Eleventh did not come from direct combat. The entire story that these men lived through would not be understood without knowing something of the hardships the company faced between battles. On December 27, 1862, the forces under Blunt departed for points fifty or so miles south of Cane Hill in the vicinity of Van Buren on the Arkansas River. They marched, meaning they hiked and climbed and waded their way though difficult terrain, each man carrying blankets and six days' rations. Through the Boston Mountains they forded swift-running streams some forty times in very cold temperatures, sometimes being swept away or losing rations and equipment and sometimes pushing on at night. Some died of exposure. When they reached the Arkansas, they were surprised to find that Hindman had left a regiment of men on the north side of the Arkansas, which Blunt and his army had surprised and easily defeated. Four steamboats loaded with supplies and rebel sick and wounded were captured, and the ships then destroyed.[26]

Sometime in January the divisions that fought in Arkansas were ordered to fall back to a place near Springfield, Missouri, and to remain there until spring. The roads north were very bad, made worse by snow and rain and bitterly cold temperatures. The task of crossing the high and swift-running White River was particularly difficult, but a contingent of men from the Eleventh found wood and a cable at a local mill and built a ferryboat that safely carried the entire army across. At a camp thirty miles south of Springfield a measles outbreak spread quickly and, together with other illness, took many lives. The place soon came to be known as the Valley of the Shadow of Death. As many as three hundred men of the Eleventh sadly were gone by this time.[27]

Fannie and the children had the support of Edmund's father, who kept them supplied with food and other items, making regular trips from the farm. He also took them to the farm for visits, which Leis describes with some ambivalence, half enjoying the visits but finding them sad at the same time, with Edmund and George and Charles all fighting. Leis also mentions that William was in the militia. It is unclear what this means, because Edmund in his letters home often reminded Fannie that she could always count on William, suggesting that he was in Topeka or nearby. What Edmund's family looked forward to more than anything was the sound of a horn announcing that a stagecoach was in town and sending Lillian's two brothers out the door to the post office to see if there was a letter from their dad. Apparently Ross wrote home often, but the number of extant letters today is small by comparison.

On March 17, 1863, General Schofield ordered the Eleventh back to Fort Scott and then declared a one-month furlough. Ross returned to Topeka with a large group of men, who were entertained at a festival put on by the women of the town. The celebration was, of course, complete with food and dancing. During that month Edmund also took the family to Wabaunsee County to see his parents, a joyous reunion especially for Edmund's mother, who could see firsthand that at least two of her sons were healthy and happy.

March 1863 was also a big month for Colonel Ewing, who received a promotion to general and who would by June 15 assume command of the District of the Border, a vast area that included all of Kansas and a sizeable part of western Missouri. It was also during this period that the Eleventh Regiment was converted from infantry duty to a cavalry regiment and was at last given Enfield rifles. Ewing would now have a total of 102 officers plus 2,346 men, essentially two regiments including the Eleventh. It was a small force to cover and protect nearly six thousand square miles including the Indian frontier.[28] The various companies of the regiments at Ewing's command were given widely scattered assignments rather than working as one large unit. For Ross, the assignment for Company E and one other newly created company appeared to be a plum assignment. Ross took the two companies to Fort Riley, west of Topeka, with the expectation they would be stationed there for an extended period. Fannie and the children could then join him and live in a house adjacent to those of other officers' families. Moreover, they would have the convenience of being only three miles from Junction City.

Ross certainly knew by mid-1863, and his family must have learned, that military life is unpredictable, so they should have been prepared for General Ewing's "request" that Ross take one of the companies at Fort Riley and station it outside Lawrence, nearly one hundred miles to the east. Just how long Ross was able to enjoy life with his family at Fort Riley is unclear, but it wasn't long, perhaps not more than a couple of weeks, before he had to leave for his new assignment. Since it was to be temporary duty, Fannie and the children remained at Fort Riley hoping for Edmund's return, which didn't happen. It wasn't all bad, however. Leis described the summer at Fort Riley as cool and breezy, with visits to Junction City. If Lillian and a family friend from Topeka, who stayed with Fannie and the children, wished to ride, "Captain Adams would issue an order, which the boys would carry [out], and horses would be at the door when we wanted them."[29]

While his family was at Fort Riley, Captain Ross and his men were charged with providing protection for the town of Lawrence, which potentially was a major target of rebel guerrillas and in due time would be an actual one. Lawrence was not a strategic target for the Confederate Army, but with its abolitionist history it was certainly on the top of the list for any rebels seeking vengeance, particularly the renegade bands of which General Ewing's men were attempting to rid his district. Ross stationed his company outside the town to the west.

It is easy to imagine that the men of Company E could be noisy and at times rowdy, no doubt encouraged by visits to Lawrence saloons. They were in the hurry-up-and-wait business and were bored much of the time. Hindsight would later tell the residents of Lawrence that the presence of Company E was a more than fair trade-off for their protection, but the value of hindsight has been abundantly demonstrated countless times in history. As the weeks wore on, the nerves of some Lawrence residents wore thin; with the boisterousness of Ross's men, push came to shove, and some of the people of Lawrence wanted Company E gone. As far as they were concerned, the Civil War was somewhere else, not anywhere near Lawrence. So they circulated a petition, according to Lillian Leis, asking General Ewing to remove the troops, and Ewing complied by having Company E moved to a new assignment patrolling the Missouri-Kansas border.[30] The *Lawrence Tribune* of August 13 describes Ross's company as passing through town "last Monday morning on their way to Kansas City. As they went down Massachusetts Street they sang 'John Brown,' and it takes the Kansas boys to sing that song."[31] Only a week later William C. Quantrill began his march on Lawrence with a force of 448 men. The story as told by Lillian Leis is somewhat different from another account, which has Ross arriving there in late July as requested by Mayor George Colamore, who had heard rumors of an imminent attack by Quantrill. In this version, Ewing apparently did not believe the source to be credible and, when there was no attack by August 10, had Ross and his men prepare to withdraw. The August 10 date of Ross's departure is about the same as in the newspaper article and probably correct.[32]

Accounts of Quantrill's raid on Lawrence are not lacking. It was one of the darkest events of the Civil War and has been written about extensively. One doesn't need many words to describe William C. Quantrill. He was a despicable human being. His followers were renegade guerrilla thieves and desperados, not members of the regular Confederate Army. However, Quantrill at just twenty-six years of age was given the rank of captain by the Confederate government and encouraged to dispense havoc and death wherever he could. Quantrill boldly planned the raid against Lawrence with the specific goal of killing every male citizen capable of carrying a gun, not just men actually carrying guns. If male residents appeared to have the strength to reasonably carry and use a weapon, even if they were just large children, it was Quantrill's intention to annihilate them. The one exception was Senator Jim Lane. Lane, who was known to be in town, was to be taken back to Missouri as a prisoner to be "semi-publicly" executed.[33]

From Blackwater Creek in Johnson County, Missouri, Quantrill set out for Lawrence, a distance of more than seventy miles, on August 19. In order to make the trip in two days, his men were literally strapped to their saddles on the second day, to enable them to sleep while still moving.[34] Quantrill knew the town well. He had lived there in 1860 under the name Charley Hart. During his time in Lawrence, Quantrill posed as an abolitionist supposedly assisting with Underground Railroad activities. He had the job of taking runaway slaves north to other safe havens, but instead he took them back to slave owners in return for rewards. Because he knew Lawrence, he carefully planned assignments for the men under him.[35] Some sources believe Quantrill had intelligence from allies within Lawrence on the days before the raid. Knowing precisely where some men would be found and knowing that Jim Lane was there, and perhaps having the knowledge that Company E had just departed, suggests this is true.

On the morning of August 21 the Quantrill raiders entered Lawrence from the southeast while people were just beginning their daily activities. The first to die was the Reverend S. S. Snyder, who had spent some time in the Second Kansas Colored Infantry. Snyder was milking a cow. Seventeen recruits of the Kansas 14th Cavalry were next.[36] Some of the recruits were gunned down as they "emerged from their blankets." The slaughter continued for three hours, interspersed with rounds of drinks from the saloons. Some men, running for their lives on foot, were gunned down by men on horseback. Others were dragged from their homes and shot in front of their families. Others, remaining in their homes, were burned to death as their houses went up in flames. Few men survived, but among them was Jim Lane, who, with John Speer of the *Kansas Tribune*, managed to escape into a cornfield. In the end at least 150 and perhaps as many as 180 men were killed.[37] When Quantrill left the town at about nine that morning, most of the buildings of Lawrence were burning. It is sad to note, and perhaps telling about the regard for black residents, that the *Kansas State Journal* some weeks later gave a list of the dead by name with a single sentence added to the end: "Besides the above, twenty-nine Negroes were killed."[38]

It is unclear when Ross returned to Lawrence, but a letter dated September 17, 1863, indicates Company E was back there by that date and that Fannie and the children were still at Fort Riley. In this letter Ross says nothing about the raid by Quantrill but reveals the degree of financial sacrifice the war had cost him. Returning to the life he had before the war already seemed unlikely anytime soon, and his degree of melancholy seemed even deeper with this letter. "I had some talk with Vernon before I left Riley about letting me have a thousand dollars to pay for our house in Topeka. I wish you would see him immediately and see whether he can let me have it. I want it for three years at ten percent, he taking a mortgage on the place for security. If I have to lose that place, I think I shall leave Topeka and perhaps Kansas although I should dislike very much to do so and commencing anew somewhere else. I expect to lose the printing office building also, so that I shall not have much left to stay there for. However I hope to come out right yet. I shall endeavor to the last to save what we have."[39]

Leis's "Memoirs" place the returning Company E outside Lawrence to the east, at a spot where a Friends Church was later erected. "Tents were fortified against the cold—my father putting up a small frame building for his office, with a stove in it."[40]

The increased control of his troops in the fall of 1863 was most important, given the tragedy of the August 21 raid. In respect for the shroud of sadness that must have been present in Lawrence, frivolity would have been totally inappropriate. With this in mind and the town under martial law, Ross asked the saloon owners not to serve his men any liquor. As the months passed from fall into late winter, the saloon owners found ways of getting around Ross's rules, and Ross, who was now the military commandant of the area and vested with supreme authority, simply closed all the saloons. In time, owners pleaded with him to allow them to reopen. Lillian Leis, who was on a visit to Lawrence with her mother and siblings, tells how one morning she came down to the lobby of the hotel where they were staying and found her father reading a newspaper. As she sat with him, two owners of saloons, influential men of Lawrence, approached him and asked if he would not reconsider his order. Leis said her father was pleasant to the men but unwilling to change his mind.[41]

One Sunday morning Ross's brother George, a sergeant, was on patrol duty. When he checked the door of a saloon to be sure it was locked, a woman came from around the back of building and, not recognizing him as Captain Ross's brother, invited him through the back door to where men of the company were drinking and playing pool. The next day Ross showed up in town with a detail of men and systematically took whatever kegs he could find and broke them open in the streets using sledgehammers. As a reward for having "made liquor flow in the streets of Lawrence," Ross was presented with an album of photographs of the women of the town. The inscription inside the cover reads: "To Captain E. Ross. By the Ladies of Lawrence. For his manly defense of Temperance while in command of the Post."[42] The album is now in the possession of the Kansas State Historical Society. The *Kansas Tribune* reported Ross's raid on Lawrence saloons in a fairly lengthy editorial claiming that many, if not most, of the men causing problems in saloons were troops passing through town.[43]

Another important newspaper article from the *Kansas Tribune* reported early in 1864 that General Ewing had decided to leave "the gallant Captain" and his forces in Lawrence for an extended period. "We are happy to have such news in our city. Three cheers for Captain Ross."[44] This was a stroke of good luck for Ross as well. With the danger of losing both his home and his business building in Topeka, Edmund was already thinking about starting life anew somewhere other than Topeka. Being allowed to remain in Lawrence for a relatively long time, while still in the military, gave Ross the chance to adjust to a new place, to see long-term possibilities there, and to renew his acquaintance with John Speer, editor of the *Kansas Tribune*.

During the spring of 1864 Ross also recruited enough men in the Lawrence area to fill out another company for the Kansas Eleventh Volunteer Regiment, plus an additional fifty men to replace losses in other companies. The new company was mustered in as Company M, with Lieutenant Nathan Gregg as the captain and Sergeant Lindsey as a lieutenant. With the company now at full strength, Moonlight was promoted to colonel and Plumb to lieutenant colonel, while Ross of Company E, N. A. Adams of Company G, and Martin Anderson of Company B were raised to the rank of major.[45]

Occasional visits by Fannie and the children gave them the opportunity to experience life in Lawrence also. In the spring of 1864, Fannie received an exceptionally good offer on their house in Topeka, which they could not refuse. It was hard to leave the house they loved so much. It was difficult for the entire family, with each member having to leave behind special memories, but perhaps hardest of all for Fannie and Edmund to leave the grave on the hill, to have to say good-bye to a child all over again. The Ross family lived in a rental house in Lawrence until the early fall of 1864, when they bought a house that Edmund could not have lived in very long before he was gone again.

The mission of the District of the Border Command changed in September 1864 from dealing with border insurgents to preparing for the threat of a large Confederate force of 12,000 men under the command of General Sterling Price coming north from Arkansas. On October 15, at Hickman Mills, Missouri, the Second Brigade was organized. It consisted mainly of ten companies from the Kansas Eleventh, two companies from the Kansas Fifth, and two from the Kansas Sixteenth. In addition, Ross's Company E was assigned four mountain howitzers. Colonel Thomas Moonlight commanded the Second Brigade, which joined with the First Brigade, both of them under General Blunt, as General Ewing had been reassigned to the Federal District of St. Louis.

General Price initially met resistance at Pilot Knob, the site of Fort Davidson in eastern Missouri. Price's objective was to take St. Louis and Jefferson City, and although he was successful in defeating the much smaller force at Fort Davidson under General Ewing's command, he thought twice about attacking St. Louis and instead directed his forces westward toward Jefferson City and Kansas City. His intent was to cross into Kansas and take Fort Leavenworth, Lawrence, Topeka, and Fort Scott on his way back south.[46] The plan was ambitious and ultimately unrealistic. Price had 9,000 veteran soldiers and perhaps as many as 3,000 recruits and bushwhackers, while General Blunt, who was amassing his forces to the west, had only 4,000 experienced men but counted on an additional 15,000 men of the Kansas militia who had been called into emergency service.[47]

While General Blunt badly needed the militia to deal with Price's advancing army, a dispute between Kansas governor Thomas Carney and Senator Jim Lane kept the militia in Kansas. Carney believed that Lane wanted the militia in Missouri so they would not be available to vote in the national and local elections in Kansas. Lane was a supporter of Abraham Lincoln, while Carney was not. Carney believed most of the men of the militia would vote against Lincoln and therefore wanted them to stay in Kansas. Meanwhile the militia and General Blunt's division were under the command of General Curtis, with whom Carney also disagreed, in this case over which of them had the authority to order the militia into battle.[48] Carney believed that the presence of General Price and his army in Missouri, and marching toward Kansas, was just a story concocted by Jim Lane. Even on the day, October 21, when General Blunt was forming his troops to fight at the Little Blue River, Governor Carney was preparing a proclamation to disband the militia.[49] Fortunately Carney did not disband the militia, and at least some of those forces were deployed to Missouri. General Curtis, who was old and not the most competent of commanders, failed to move the militia quickly to the front, leaving Blunt and his relatively small army to deal with Price.

While General Blunt was doing his best to slow Price's advance, General Alfred Pleasanton and his army coming from the east were "slashing" Price "right and left in the rear."[50] For Blunt's far-outnumbered men, the best they could do with Price was slow him down by fighting for a time and then retreating and fighting again. At times the cavalry would simply make a brief stand firing from their horses but obviously much preferring to take cover behind obstructions. At a substantial creek called the Sni, a detachment of forty men led by Henry Lindsey, the former drummer boy who was now a lieutenant and adjutant to Ross, burned a covered bridge just after men of the Second Brigade passed through it and just before Confederate general Joe Shelby's regiment approached.[51]

Perhaps the most noteworthy stand by the Second Brigade took place at the river known as the Little Blue. Once again, Blunt's men burned a major bridge behind them. Fighting from the west bank of the river, they held Price's troops in check for half a day. When the fighting men of the Second Brigade temporarily ran out of ammunition, they began to cheer, leaving the Confederate forces baffled.[52] Samuel Crawford's account of the Battle at Little Blue reported on the superb stand of the Second Brigade from the west bank of river, where he believed the men could have easily held on for another half day or more. Unfortunately, in Crawford's judgment, General Curtis ordered their retreat well before he needed to.[53] During the fighting of October 21, Ross is reported to have had two horses shot out from under him.[54] It was probably on this day that Colonel Samuel Crawford observed Ross's heroics. When Governor Samuel Crawford appointed Ross to the United States Senate less than than two years later, it was most likely October 21 that came to his mind: "I had seen him on the field of battle amid shot and shell that tried men's souls, and I knew he could be trusted."[55]

The story of Price's eventual defeat and retreat from Missouri is complex, and a detailed account is beyond the scope of this biography. It is important to know that Price's army was turned back at the Battle of Westport not far south of Kansas City. The retreat of the Confederates, demoralized and depleted, was agonizing. In desperate need of supplies, Price hoped somehow to successfully attack Fort Scott, not to regain the ability to mount another military attack, but mainly to acquire the necessary supplies to survive the retreat back into Arkansas. The Second Brigade engaged in a number of skirmishes with Price, including the successful defense of Mound City. Suspecting that Price was headed for Fort Scott, General Blunt ordered the Second Brigade to press on south and hold Fort Scott at all costs. Pleasanton's army followed relentlessly and once again attacked Price's army at the Battle of Mine Creek a short distance north of Fort Scott. In just twenty minutes several hundred of Price's men were killed or wounded, and nine hundred prisoners were taken, including two generals and four colonels.[56] There was nothing for Price to do but simply continue south, with Union forces that included the Second Brigade in pursuit. Colonel Moonlight reported that "nothing of importance transpired during the balance of the pursuit via Cassville, Keetsville, Elkhorn, Bentonville, Elm Springs, Fayetteville, Prairie Grove, Cane Hill, Dutchtown, and to the Arkansas River."[57] For the Confederates the march was a living hell, with little or no food for the men or their horses. Once across the Arkansas River, as Crawford put it, Price's army scattered "like chaff before the wind."

The chase by Union forces was relentless and only marginally easier for them, the men sometimes getting no more than coffee and hardtack to sustain them. The return of the Second Brigade to Kansas, as described by Preston Plumb's biographer, was done in the midst of "much rain and wet snow. . . . The country had been stripped by the Confederates on their retreat. . . . Horses died on the road, thus constantly augmenting the column marching on foot."[58] Leis described Ross's return to Lawrence. "Toward evening, one grey day, walking—and leading his horse, a very boney one with dropping head—not the dashing black one on which he rode away— Billy (the horse) was left on the battlefield. And my father with his handsome uniform ruined—a long blue overcoat—his wide hat drooping. And a white linen handkerchief tied over his head and under his chin. He had left the command three days before, to arrive home earlier, both himself and horse exhausted. The horse he gave to me. A dark bay."[59]

It appears Ross remained in Lawrence into the spring of 1865. On an inspection trip back to the town of Paola, Ross took his daughter Lillian with him. They traveled in a carriage with Ross's orderly and "a colored driver." They stayed in camps and forded streams, one deep enough that Lillian had to stand on the back seat holding her suitcase above her head. It rained part of the time and there were "annoyances and discomforts," but Leis described her father as "never gloomy or irritable. Just the same, even-tempered—considerate and humorous, making the best of everything disagreeable."[60] At Paola, on a Sunday, there was a review, probably in celebration of the end of the war. Several regiments paraded. Leis records that her father "was on a beautiful black horse, slender and graceful . . . looked very handsome riding up and down the lines." But a terrible pall was cast over the day when it was learned that President Lincoln had been assassinated. In the hotel and throughout the city the president's death was the only topic of conversation.[61]

For Ross, there was no option about service in the Civil War, but Edmund Ross never could have been a career soldier. A couple of years after the war, when Senator Edmund Ross was in his office in Washington, D.C., he was paid a visit by his former printer's devil turned drummer boy turned lieutenant, Henry Lindsey. The Civil War for Lindsey was the high point of his life, and he thought a military career might be just the thing for him. What he needed was the endorsement of a United States senator to be accepted in the regular army. For Lindsey, what could be easier? His former boss and commander was now a United States senator. But the meeting didn't go quite the way Lindsey expected. Ross was delighted to see him, of course. This was a young man he loved like one of his sons. Yet the requested endorsement was not what Ross was willing to give. Ross essentially told him that peacetime military life was one of idleness, card playing, and drinking. He saw more in life for Lindsey than that. In spite of Ross's refusal, Lindsey did go on to make the army his career, eventually commanding a regiment and achieving the rank of colonel, never forgetting Edmund Ross.[62]

Leis's comments about Ross's return home when finally discharged in August 1865 are short: "When the war came to a close, he was mustered out in Leavenworth, changed to a civilian suit—was shaved and came home. Not having seen him with a smooth face for years, I failed to recognize him, until he smiled—he had a wonderful smile."[63]

CHAPTER SEVEN

MAJOR ROSS

Return to Civilian Life

The only hope of a thorough reconstruction of those states, is to couple amnesty with suffrage—put the Negro in a political position, which he has merited by his loyalty and services, in which he can protect himself if the government will not protect him.
—Ross, editorial, *Kansas Tribune*, January 4, 1866

AT THE END OF THE Civil War Edmund Ross had simple goals, the same goals he had before the war: to be with his family, to operate a printing business, and, better yet, to once again publish his own newspaper. In a letter to Fannie a few months before he mustered out of the army, Ross wrote about what lay ahead for him and his wife. The letter expressed his anxiety and concern for how they might get by. "The pay of all officers in this department is stopped. . . . So it will not be long before I shall be at home again as a citizen, and have to go to work. . . . I am afraid we shall have to sell our horses in order to pay for the house as it will probably be several months before I shall get any more pay. In the meantime I must raise money the best way I can. You had better see Johnson and tell him how it is and tell him you will sell the mares if you can, for it will be impossible otherwise to pay him as soon as I promised him. I agreed to pay him two hundred dollars this month but I do not now expect to draw any more pay until sometime after I am mustered out, as it will take perhaps several months to settle up my accounts."[1]

The sacrifices made during the war by veterans like Ross were considerable, and at the end of the war there were new problems. In addition to financial difficulties, Ross was not exactly coming home. Although he had spent some months in or near Lawrence during the war, Lawrence really was a new town for him. He was not resuming a role in a hometown business atmosphere where he knew everyone; in Lawrence he was something of a stranger in business circles and unemployed. The businessmen of Lawrence, who did not go off to war, no doubt had compassion for returning veterans, but they could not appreciate the sacrifices in the same way that fellow veterans could. The bond between those who had served was special, and the way in which this bond would change Ross's life within the next year would surprise many, not least Ross himself.

For three months after mustering out in August 1865, Ross must have gone through a period of readjustment, learning to be a father, a husband, and a civilian again and worrying about how to survive financially. When Ross signed up with the army, he knew well that he was committing to at least three years of service, unless the war should end sooner. Of course it did not, and for three years Ross was away from his family except for a few intervals that were mostly short. The winter of 1865 was difficult also because Ross's eldest son Arthur had pneumonia and suffered through a long and worrisome recovery. Ross had practically no money and just barely had a home he could call his own. What he did have going for him was his reputation in the newspaper business.

Probably soon after becoming a civilian again, Ross reacquainted himself with John Speer, the same John Speer who had sold the *Kansas Tribune* to William and Edmund ten years before. Sometime after William and Edmund stopped publication of the *Tribune* in Topeka, Speer began publishing it again, this time in Lawrence, where Speer had originally founded the paper in 1854. When Ross again became associated with the *Tribune*, Speer was running it as both a daily and a weekly paper with a staff of at least ten printers. It was decidedly a Republican paper, which would have been essential for Ross, and possibly had the largest circulation of any paper in Kansas.

Speer was a complex man, an abolitionist not afraid to speak his mind. He had courageously defied the gag laws of the "bogus" territorial legislature when in September 1855 he printed, in bold "circus type," a full front-page declaration that "persons have not the right to hold slaves in the territory . . . and we will emblazon it upon our banner in letters so large and in language so plain . . . that the corrupt and ignorant Legislature itself, may understand it."[2] The declaration was a clear defiance of the law prohibiting such printed statements, among other odious statutes of the fraudulent Kansas territorial government. Speer was indicted for violating the statute but was never tried. Without a doubt the most horrific day for Speer was August 21, 1863, when Speer lost two sons in the Quantrill raid. Quantrill also burned Speer's newspaper office to the ground and set fire to Speer's house.

Ross struck a deal with Speer whereby Ross went to work for Speer as his editor. It is unclear whether Ross had a financial interest in the paper. He certainly had little or no money, but Lillian Leis suggests that he may have worked out some kind of contract with Speer that would allow him to acquire part ownership eventually. She also suggests that he wasn't entirely pleased with the arrangement but that it was his only option at the time.[3] Speer not only owned the newspaper but was also involved in other business activities in Lawrence, was the United States collector of internal revenue, and was serving as a member of the state legislature. He was clearly an important man in the town. Although Speer's name continued to appear as an editor with Ross, it was Ross who ran the paper and who wrote the editorials, freeing up Speer to pursue both commercial and political interests. Speer did not entirely ignore the *Tribune* and surely continued to confer with Ross about the position the paper would take on certain issues, and most likely wrote some articles; but Ross was the principal writer and director of daily activities.

Speer took advantage of Ross's reputation as a newspaper editor and a soldier whose army company had once been placed near Lawrence for its defense. The November 11, 1865, edition of the *Tribune* ran a short article about the change in editors:

> Our readers will observe that Major Ross has been associated with us in the publication of the Daily, Weekly and Tri-Weekly Tribune, as a full partner in interest. It would be superfluous to say anything in regard to our new partner. As a soldier and an editor all Kansans know him. He is a vigorous writer, true Republican and an upright man.
>
> We trust that under the new firm, we shall not only retain our old friends and patrons, but add hosts of new ones. Major Ross will devote his whole time to the paper and that is the best guaranty that it will be worthy of patronage.[4]

How long the working arrangement between Speer and Ross would have continued without intervening events is hard to say, but Ross would not have been content with a subordinate position to Speer for too many years. That Speer had a domineering personality is clear in a story told by Lillian Ross Leis. On a return trip from Glen Ross, where Edmund's parents lived in the spring of 1866, the family stopped to rest in Topeka and while there paid a visit to Colonel Cyrus Holliday. John Speer discovered them there and proposed that he should go back to Lawrence with the Ross family instead of taking the stagecoach. Edmund explained that they had no room; he was, after all, carrying his entire family in a single carriage with their luggage. Speer insisted, and Ross appears to have been unable to say no. The trip was slow and very crowded and required Speer to walk alongside the carriage for some of the time. One would guess that Ross spent part of the trip walking as well.[5]

The opinions of the two men about the future of former slaves was about the same. In August Speer was the probable writer of an article called "The Negro Question," which was critical of any plan for former slaves that did not include full rights of citizenship. "We can refuse to do this [extend voting rights to former slaves], but we cannot evade the responsibility of such a refusal. Future generations would ask, What manner of men were those who in their hour of extremity called to their assistance this race of people, and, when their country was saved, lacked the courage and generosity to grant them the rights their blood paid for?"[6]

One of Edmund Ross's early editorials at his new job in Lawrence was a commentary on the report of General Carl Schurz, whom President Johnson had dispatched to the South to assess the progress of his policies. Johnson simultaneously sent Ulysses Grant to do the same thing on a different circuit through the South. While Grant's report was generally positive, Schurz's was not. In his editorial on the Schurz report, Ross noted "the rapid return to power and influence of so many of those who but recently were engaged in a bitter war against the union. . . . Prominent among them is the Legislature of Alabama, which, while it affects to comply with the amendment of the constitution abolishing slavery, yet enacts in its vagrant and apprentice laws, a more terrible and barbarous slave code than was ever known in the United States before."[7] Ross especially advocated suffrage for freedmen as their most important weapon of self-defense. "Continued action like this must soon convince the Nation that the only hope of a thorough reconstruction of those states, is to couple amnesty with suffrage—put the Negro in a political position, which he has merited by his loyalty and services, in which he can protect himself if the government will not protect him, and let the rebels take whatever alternative they choose—to be treated as rebels still, or listen to the dictates of humanity and reason."[8]

Political differences did not cause much friction between Ross and Speer. To a certain extent there were personality differences, but it was Ross's attack on Senator Jim Lane, Speer's good friend, in the spring of 1866 that would lead to a serious problem in the Ross-Speer partnership. It is not likely that Ross and Speer had openly different opinions about Lane when they began working together. As an employee Ross would have been cautious about saying anything negative about Lane in front of Speer, even if he had such thoughts. Ross had, in fact, been a supporter of Jim Lane when he ran for the United States Senate in 1861.[9] Lane was opposed to slavery, at least in Kansas. However, Lane was less than sympathetic to the plight of slaves, having also led a sizeable faction of delegates to the Free-State convention in October 1855 who were in favor of laws that would exclude blacks, whether slave or free, from the state.[10] In addition, Lane had tended toward an aggressive, even militant, approach in opposing proslavery advocates during the territorial years. He had been known widely throughout Kansas and Missouri as the Grim Chieftain, and his name, along with that of the infamous John Brown, had struck terror in the minds of proslavery Kansans of the late 1850s. Ross and Lane knew each other but were not close, especially since Ross had lived in Topeka while Lane had always lived in Lawrence. Their paths certainly crossed from time to time at both Free-State and Republican meetings, and of course Ross had served under Lane in the Free-State Army for a short time in 1856. Ross could admire Lane's many accomplishments and support him as a Republican ally, but Ross's support was not without question.

At the close of 1865 it is safe to assume that Ross and Speer had a reasonable working relationship. Ross was relatively satisfied with his life for the time being and had good reason to hope for a bright future. It may be that he hoped to become the sole owner of the *Tribune* again sometime in the future. Speer was ten years older than Ross and had other business interests, and the fact that Speer hired Ross to edit the paper suggests he was tired of the work himself. Ross was again with his family, something he had thought often about during the seemingly endless months of the war. Like most editors around the country, Ross and Speer observed what was happening in Washington from a distance and devoted much space and commentary to the deepening chasm between President Andrew Johnson and Congress. What neither of them could have predicted was the series of tragic events that would destroy both their partnership and their friendship in a few short months.

CHAPTER EIGHT

SOUTHERN PRESIDENT, RADICAL CONGRESS

If we were wise and discreet, we should reanimate the [southern] States and get their governments in successful operation, with order prevailing and the Union re-established, before Congress came together in December.

—Gideon Welles, paraphrasing President Lincoln

⌐ IN 1896, WHEN EDMUND ROSS was seventy years old, he wrote *The History of the Impeachment of Andrew Johnson*, the first book-length account of the impeachment trial of 1868, and the only one written by a participant in the trial. Ross introduces the account with known information about Abraham Lincoln's plans for Reconstruction. He cites Secretary of the Navy Gideon Welles's account of a meeting of the cabinet just before Lincoln's death. At the meeting there was a discussion of the restoration of southern states to their previous status as states of the Union. According to Welles, Lincoln believed it important to take executive action while Congress was in recess until December. "If we were wise and discreet, we should reanimate the States and get their governments in successful operation, with order prevailing and the Union re-established, *before Congress came together in December.*" This Lincoln thought important. "We could do better, accomplish more than with them."[1]

Lincoln was not trying to dictate to Congress or to usurp its authority; he was doing what he could to provide badly needed leadership. He hoped to be able to establish his own ideas about restoration before Congress reconvened in December, "in order that he might be able then to show palpable results, and induce Congress to accept and follow up a humane, peaceful and satisfactory system of reconstruction."[2] An assassin's bullet on April 14 put an end to Lincoln initiating such leadership, and it was left to his vice president to carry on. Historian Eric L. McKitrick suggests that the solutions to the problems of restoration of seceded states to their former status ranged from a lenient "southern theory" to a severe Radical Republican "conquered provinces" approach. There were complex constitutional questions to be considered, and issues of policy that were equally difficult.[3] With no precedent for dealing with these problems, Lincoln was attempting to provide a starting point. Basic to the Lincoln plan was the assumption that seceded states, as a consequence of losing the war, had not been successful in leaving the Union and that after they agreed to certain conditions, their former constitutional rights as states could be restored. Radical Republicans in the legislature believed that not only did the southern states successfully secede, but at the end of the war they had reverted to, at the very most, territorial status.

On May 29 President Johnson issued two proclamations drawn from plans discussed in the Lincoln cabinet in the days just before and after the assassination and mostly supported by Lincoln. Johnson declared rebel authority null and void and granted blanket amnesty to the vast majority of Confederates who would swear allegiance to the United States and whose property, excluding slaves, was worth less than $20,000. Amnesty for those with property worth more than $20,000 was possible only by presidential pardon. Radicals in Congress were encouraged by the $20,000 rule, believing that Johnson was taking a sterner hand with Reconstruction than Lincoln would likely have done. But Johnson was liberal with pardons to wealthy landowners and former Confederate leaders. Historian Eric Foner notes that not all in Congress agreed in the assessment of Johnson's motives. Some members saw these pardons as Johnson's tool to acquire needed southern support for his own future political plans.[4]

His second proclamation called for North Carolina to form a new state government with a provisional governor appointed by the president. North Carolina was to be a model for establishing governance in other Confederate states. The new governor would hold elections for delegates to a constitutional convention. Voters in the election were those who were eligible when the state first seceded, which excluded freedmen. All officeholders in the Confederate government were to be excluded from holding office in the restored states, and constitutional changes outlawing slavery were required. The appointed governor was to remain in place until orderly government had been secured.[5] Radical Republicans had expected a harder line from Johnson. Historian Brooks Simpson observes that in the days following the assassination, Johnson had promised that traitors would be punished and blacks would be given the vote. Radicals could be suspicious of Johnson's true motives just weeks into his presidency.[6]

In his message to Congress on December 6, 1865, President Johnson tried to demonstrate the wisdom of the program he had started since the Congress last met and was thereby hoping to induce members to legislate programs consistent with his policies. In particular he pointed out the importance and wisdom of the United States Constitution as it defined states' rights. He also tried to show the negative side of continuing military rule in the South, indicating that the far healthier course was to restore the "rightful energy of the General Government and of the States."[7]

The difficulties Johnson had with Congress in 1866 and 1867 can be traced in large measure to his unwillingness to compromise. Certainly Lincoln would have found some common ground with the House and Senate; he was skilled at working behind the scenes, and he abhorred the institution of slavery. Johnson, on the contrary, was stubborn and difficult and believed that blacks were better off as slaves and were inferior to whites. He was a strict constructionist whose knowledge of the Constitution was superb, and he was inflexible in its interpretation. Moreover, Johnson was both a southerner and a Democrat. He had become Lincoln's running mate in 1864 because he was the only southern senator who had opposed secession and because, with his party affiliation, he was expected to attract Democratic votes that Lincoln believed he badly needed.

Just as Johnson had warned his southern colleagues, the secession of southern states created a strong bias in favor of Republican control in Congress. Most southern senators and representatives were Democrats, and without their presence in the House and Senate, Republicans came near having the votes needed to override presidential vetoes; after the fall elections of 1866, they did indeed acquire such power. For Johnson to fail to compromise with Congress was to invite disaster. If Johnson was uncompromising and bullheaded, so were Radical Republicans who, on the other end of the scale, sought retribution from the southern states that included confiscation of plantations to be divided up among former slaves. Moderate Republicans were more willing to compromise with the president, but by the spring of 1866, Johnson's uncompromising nature drove even most Moderates away.

In March 1865, while Lincoln was still in office, Congress had created the Bureau of Refugees, Freedmen, and Abandoned Lands, commonly referred to as the Freedmen's Bureau. Managed by the War Department, the bureau was intended to help freed slaves and other refugees cope with such problems of post–Civil War life as finding food, work, land, adequate shelter, legal aid, and medical care and to assist in the establishment of schools. In effect the Freedmen's Bureau was a temporary welfare system, but it was authorized for only one year. In February 1866 Congress granted the bureau a new charter, this time of indefinite duration. Introduced by Senator Lyman Trumbull of Illinois and endorsed by Senator William Pitt Fessenden, it expanded the role of the bureau, creating an enlarged bureaucracy with a complex set of laws and the authority to enforce them. In effect, the new rules usurped the authority of the civil governments set up under Johnson's Reconstruction program.

Johnson vetoed the new bill, believing it violated the rights of state governments and courts, especially since the country was no longer at war. He also failed to see any further need for the Freedmen's Bureau and regarded it as too expensive. Radical Republicans found the veto outrageous, but Moderates were willing to compromise, and Johnson's veto was sustained in the Senate.[8] While Johnson believed he was right to veto the bill, he offered no alternative for handling the serious problems facing freed slaves, even though he said he sympathized with their circumstances. Ross, as expected, sided with the Radicals: "It is unfortunate for the President, and for the country, that he has chosen to defeat, so far as his action can, this important measure. . . . It is possible that the President has a matured plan for the accomplishment, in a different way, for the objects aimed at by this bill; but if so, he has thus far, during the long discussion thereon, failed to indicate it. Indeed the tone of the message itself suggests that he has none, and that he proposes to leave the freedmen where they substantially are; subject to the tender mercies of the rebel populace and rebel militia of the South."[9]

Johnson failed to see that it was not enough that the Thirteenth Amendment ended slavery. What the country sorely needed was a focused effort by the president and Congress to assist former slaves. The future of four million or so freed slaves cried out for strong and compassionate presidential leadership. The difference that such leadership would have made cannot be known, but what Lincoln would have done surely would have been significant, while Johnson did less than nothing, constantly opposing legislation offered on behalf of freedmen and offering no alternatives.

Congress passed an altered version of the Freedmen's Bureau bill in early July 1866, and although it was again vetoed by Johnson, the revised bill became law in mid-July when the Johnson veto was not sustained.

The real split between Johnson and the majority of Republicans came in early spring when Congress passed the Civil Rights Act of 1866, which guaranteed citizenship to all persons born in the United States, except Native Americans who did not pay tax. Citizenship would be guaranteed regardless of race or color or previous condition of slavery or servitude. The act specifically ensured the right "to make and enforce contracts, to sue, to be parties, and give evidence, to inherit, purchase, lease, sell, hold and convey real and personal property."[10] Again, President Johnson vetoed the bill because he believed it violated the rights of states to decide citizenship. He failed to use his influence as president and as a southerner to promote any alternatives. On April 8, 1866, the Senate voted to override Johnson's veto of the Civil Rights Act. What surprised many Kansans, if not most, was Senator Jim Lane's vote to sustain the veto. Lane must have realized that in his state, with so many politically active abolitionists, he would experience a serious backlash. Certainly Edmund Ross would not remain silent about Lane.

If there was not any stress between Ross and John Speer in early April, there probably was after Jim Lane's vote on the Civil Rights Act. Speer was torn between his close friendship with Lane and his principles as an abolitionist. It is likely that Speer and Ross discussed Lane's vote and possibly collaborated on the editorial that expressed the official position of the *Kansas Tribune*. If Ross was the sole writer, his words were minced; they failed to express his true feelings about Lane's vote. Yet he would have been obliged to write a statement that struck a compromise between his position and Speer's. "It is useless to disguise the fact that the vote of Gen. Lane to sustain the veto, meets with opposition by his truest friends in Kansas; but that opposition ought not to be—and we trust will not be—of such a character that it will prejudge him before his reasons for his action are given to the public. We know that he deprecates any disagreement between the President and the Republican members, and that he had the most implicit faith in the honesty and integrity of President Johnson."[11]

If Ross could not write what he truly believed in the *Tribune*, his action away from the newspaper was significantly different. A sizeable number of Lawrence men organized a Saturday night meeting to discuss the issue. That day's *Tribune* contained a notice of the meeting inviting people to attend. The meeting may have been set before Lane's vote, to discuss a wide range of issues, but it was Lane's vote that came to dominate the gathering. The meeting was endorsed by seventy-six men, and at the top of the list was E. G. Ross. John Speer's name was not included.[12]

The gathering was at Miller's Hall, presided over by Lawrence mayor Gordon Grovenor. The proceedings were rather formal, with Grovenor acting as president and others acting as vice presidents and secretaries. On a motion by Edmund Ross, a committee on resolutions, consisting of three men led by Ross, was selected. The committee adjourned to a separate room to draw up its resolutions while the remainder of the audience heard a number of men, including John Speer, express their favorable opinions, presumably about Jim Lane and his vote.

When the committee returned, Ross read the resolutions to the audience. Given the careful wording of the document, supposedly written by the committee, one would guess that Ross had already prepared a draft before the meeting. It ran about three hundred words in five paragraphs. It essentially condemned the policies of Andrew Johnson in regard to Reconstruction and specifically his veto of the Civil Rights Act. The third resolution dealt with Jim Lane's vote to sustain the veto: "*Resolved*, That occupying as has the State of Kansas, a position of intense, radical loyalty, during the terrible contest of arms that has just closed, we feel humiliated by the recent vote in the United States Senate, of our Senator, James H. Lane, in opposition to the Civil Rights bill, and in endorsement of the pernicious doctrines with which the President returned and endeavored to defeat that eminently just and proper measure."[13]

The resolutions were voted on and accepted. Speaking against the Lane resolution were a Colonel Adams and John Speer. The meeting was certainly critical of Lane but, at the same time, the forum was a dispassionate and reasonable way to express deeply held views about the course of progress of Reconstruction and a clear way of letting Jim Lane know how a significant number of his constituents regarded his vote.

At the same meeting John Speer offered an additional resolution, which was considered and tabled. His resolution expressed his abolitionist views of when and how southern states should be readmitted into the Union. The tabling of Speer's resolution and the censuring of his good friend Lane by such a large gathering, with Ross in a leadership role, must have caused some serious friction between Ross and Speer. But whatever ill feelings there were that evening, they were minor compared to what was coming.

The reaction to Lane by his fellow Republicans in Kansas was, to a degree, a reflection of what was going on in Congress. There was not necessarily a uniformity of opinion about any given issue among Republicans. Republicans could hold rather conservative points of view that were not greatly different from the Democrats', and some Republicans were often much at odds with their Radical Republican colleagues. For Lane to vote with Johnson was not altogether surprising, and for Ross to react as he did to Lane's vote also was not surprising. The viewpoints of the two men in regard to the Civil Rights bill were completely consistent with their individual histories in Kansas. Though both Republicans, they were different men in nearly every other way. Lane had always been a high-profile, charismatic leader and a natural politician, while Ross was a quiet, undemonstrative man who was not inclined to be a politician.[14] When it came to slavery, Ross was unequivocally opposed to the practice on moral grounds and expressed compassion for the plight of slaves. Lane, it would seem, held views on Reconstruction that did not include much sympathy for former slaves, and in this regard Lane was not much different from Johnson.

For Ross to speak up and lead a group of people in censuring Lane was not at all out of character. He had always been the kind of man who believed that if an individual was not actively part of the solution to a problem, then he was most definitely a part of the problem. It was this mindset that prompted him to lead a wagon train to Kansas in support of the abolitionist movement, to spearhead a drive to help distressed farmers during a serious drought, and to volunteer for full-time service in the Civil War. Speaking out against Lane was, in Ross's mind, a position he had to take to the public forum without regard to personal consequences. By speaking up as he did, he was risking his job and the security of his family. What mattered most to him, however, was that he should do the right thing. In just two years this same mindset would lead to the most crucial public decision he would ever face—a decision that would dramatically affect his life and perhaps the history of the country.

CHAPTER NINE

A Surprising Death, an
Unexpected Appointment

Ross himself, had recommended the appointment of another man,
but I knew him to be an honest, straightforward soldier of sterling worth and unflinching courage; and on that account he was
appointed. I had seen him on the field of battle amid shot and shell
that tried men's souls, and I knew he could be trusted.

—Samuel Crawford, *Kansas in the Sixties*

᠊᠊ᢣ JUNE AND JULY 1866 were crucial months both in Washington and
in Kansas. On June 13 the extraordinary Fourteenth Amendment to the
Constitution was passed and sent to all states, including all seceded states,
for ratification. It secured the right of citizenship, both state and national,
to all persons either born in the United States or legally naturalized; it guaranteed the right of all citizens to life, liberty, and property; it guaranteed all
citizens the right of due process and equal protection under the law. While
amendments to the Constitution are strictly a matter between the United
States Congress and the states, Andrew Johnson nonetheless expressed his
disapproval of the Fourteenth Amendment. Citing diminished power of
states, Johnson's objection to the amendment likely contributed to a delay
in ratification and further deepened the chasm between the president and
the Republican delegations in Congress.

In Kansas, with its heavy concentration of Radical Republicans, the
impeachment of Johnson had started to be a topic of conversation along
with the disapproval of Senator Jim Lane's support of the president's veto
of the Civil Rights bill. The Lawrence meeting led by Edmund Ross may
have been the most prominent of meetings censuring Lane, since Lawrence
was Lane's hometown, but openly expressed disappointment in Lane's vote

was heard throughout Kansas. To deal with the growing negative sentiment, Lane returned to Kansas on June 16, 1866.[1] He gave a speech in the state capital on June 18 and began his trip back to Washington on June 20. Given the difficulty involved in traveling so far, Lane's stay was oddly short. Moreover, he was making the trip to Kansas against the advice of physicians. He had complained of dizziness and numbness for several months. When he reached St. Louis on his return trip on June 22, his condition worsened, and a doctor was summoned to the Lindell Hotel to examine him. The St. Louis Post Dispatch reported that the doctor "found him in bed complaining of dizziness, extreme depression of spirits, sinking sensations, numbness of the limbs after sleeping, intense nervousness and loss of sleep. The patient was also timid, and expressed himself as afraid to be alone." Lane, in fact, would not permit himself to be left alone, and his private secretary, Captain Williams, stayed with him constantly.[2]

Lane's wife, herself ill in Lawrence and unable to travel to St. Louis to be with him, asked that Lane be brought back to Lawrence. For the return trip Lane insisted that the doctor accompany him and Williams. On the trip Lane complained that he was losing his mind and asked to be taken to an insane asylum. He complained about the bitter denunciations from his former friends who did not understand him. When they reached Leavenworth, Lane was met by a group of his supporters but was unable or unwilling to talk to them. His brother-in-law, General McCall, brought a carriage to take Lane to his home two miles from town. The doctor reported that Lane was melancholic and that he had related the story of how his brother in Florida had some years before committed suicide.[3]

On July 1 Lane and McCall took a carriage ride, probably part of Lane's convalescent routine. When they reached the gate of the farmhouse on their return, McCall stepped down to open the gate. He turned when he heard Lane—who apparently had jumped from the carriage—say goodbye. Before McCall could react, Jim Lane shot himself.[4] He remained alive for ten days. One report had it that Lane shot himself in the mouth, but a report by John Speer, who visited with his friend on July 8, had Lane in grave condition but also eating with relish and both recognizing and responding to visitors.[5] On July 10 Speer reported that Lane's room was crowded with friends. The same report expressed disgust with a story sent to the New York Tribune from Washington on July 2 that Speer believed misrepresented the facts leading to Lane's suicide attempt. Speer certainly hated the story that made Lane appear to be friendless. Ross, too, could not have been pleased by the implications of the story, because he was the highest-profile critic of Lane. Nevertheless, the article was reprinted in the *Kansas Tribune*. The report certainly was over the top, badly written and intended to sensationalize the suicide attempt, beginning with a report of Lane's return to Lawrence in June. "His first appearance on the streets of Lawrence shocked him with a sense of terrible error. In a town where he had once walked a Monarch, no man spoke to him. Old friends passed him on the sidewalk without recognition."[6]

The story was meant to suggest that the entire reason for Lane taking his own life was total rejection by friends and constituents. Censure by his fellow Kansans may have been a trigger, but the underlying cause of his suicide was either seriously deep, clinical depression or possibly something biological such as tumor. Biographer Lloyd Lewis believed that "with the end of the Civil War, he saw his whole world gone, his era dead, his age vanished."[7] Lane's adult life had been defined by military campaigns. He had fought in the Mexican War, organized and commanded the Free-State Army in Kansas, and been made a general in the Civil War by Abraham Lincoln, with whom he shared a close relationship. Lane had even convinced Lincoln that he should have a company of men stationed in the White House for his protection and organized the Frontier Guard, a contingent of men from Kansas who literally occupied the East Room of the White House to protect the president. As leader of the Frontier Guard, Lane had frequent close contact with Lincoln, and no doubt Lincoln's assassination also contributed to Lane's depressed state of mind.

Lane's family wanted people to know that friends had not abandoned him, that he had many friends who were devoted to him and stood by him without question. However, at the very least, there undoubtedly were some Kansans who read the *New York Tribune* dispatch and believed without question that it was rejection by people like Ross that caused Lane to take his own life. There were others who read it and had their doubts about its veracity but perhaps wondered if it held a degree of truth. In Lawrence, where Lane had so many close friends, Ross must have been castigated by some who believed he contributed to Lane's despondency and death.

As for the relationship between Ross and Speer, it must have been decidedly cool. Just as Lane was drawn to the power Lincoln had as president, so too was Speer drawn to Lane for his magnetic personality and status as a United States senator. Lane could charm people in a way that few people could and often was compared to Lincoln as a persuasive speaker.

Lewis says that "he had what all great artists have—the power to make the thing they imagine and conceive pass out from themselves and possess other minds. Again and again it is recorded that Jim Lane's enemies feared to meet him lest they be charmed out of their principles."[8] It seems likely that Speer reveled in his friendship with the powerful Lane and could not help but place some of the blame for his death on Edmund Ross. At the same time, another part of him reveled in the thought that he would be the one to replace Lane in Washington—especially when, after Lane's death, Mrs. Lane asked the governor to name Speer as her husband's replacement.[9]

The day following the *New York Tribune* article reprint, July 11, 1866, Lane died at his brother-in-law's farm near Leavenworth with family members and friends, including John Speer, nearby. An editorial, almost certainly written by Ross and preceded by the text of Speer's wire from Leavenworth, justifiably lauded Lane's career. There had been no more widely recognized leader in Kansas since its earliest days as a territory. Lane was a natural leader highly regarded even by his strongest critics, including Ross, whose thoughts must have gone back to that day ten years before when Lane met Ross's wagon train as it crossed into the Kansas Territory. "It was but natural that he should have evoked criticisms and antagonisms peculiar to the stirring times during which he occupied his most exalted position, but we believe his bitterest enemies are with general accord ready to lay aside their animosities, and bury them in the grave of the distinguished Senator."[10]

With Jim Lane's death, it fell to Governor Samuel Crawford to appoint a replacement. This was no small problem for Crawford, who would be seeking another term as governor and facing a state Republican Party convention within a few months. In selecting a replacement for Lane he had to avoid, as much as possible, offending the diverse factions within the party. An article in the *Kansas Historical Quarterly* in 1962 superbly explores the dilemma for Crawford. In addition to a number of unlikely candidates, there were four prominent men seeking the job: James G. Blunt, who was Crawford's army commander; Jim Lane's friend, and Ross's partner, John Speer; the Reverend H. D. Fisher, a highly regarded pioneer Kansas preacher and politician; and former governor Thomas Carney. On July 17 Crawford apparently discussed the appointment with John Speer and Speer's son-in-law C. W. Adams and, without making an immediate commitment, may have led them to believe that Speer would be his choice when the announcement was made within days.[11] The governor also asked Ross to come to Topeka on July 19. Ross, according to Lillian Leis, was "thinking that as

Mr. Speer's associate in the newspaper, the Governor wished to question him in regard to the Speer appointment."[12] Leis agreed that Mrs. Lane had recommended John Speer to replace her husband. It is not hard to imagine that Ross and Speer discussed, in advance, Ross's trip to the capital. Ross and Speer were close in their political views, and other than their disagreement about censuring Lane in April, they may have still been on reasonable terms, especially since Speer would now really need Ross to run the *Tribune* while he was off to Washington. When Ross reached the governor's office in Topeka, he "began at once to advance Speer's interest," but, as the governor years later told Leis, her father "apparently had no idea I wanted him and not Speer."[13]

The selection of Ross made political sense for Crawford, since nearly all Kansans who knew him thought he was a good choice. Historian Mark Plummer pointed out that Ross was acceptable to Radical Republicans because he was a high-profile critic of President Johnson; his fellow senator Samuel Pomeroy and his supporters did not perceive Ross to be a threat to them; newspaper editors saw Ross as one of their own; and since he was a popular veteran of the war, he was acceptable to veterans.[14]

In his autobiography Crawford tells the same story but does not mention Speer by name. He also explains exactly why he selected Ross: "Ross himself, had recommended the appointment of another man, but I knew him to be an honest, straightforward soldier of sterling worth and unflinching courage; and on that account he was appointed. I had seen him on the field of battle amid shot and shell that tried men's souls, and I knew he could be trusted." The appointment of Ross was well received by the people generally and especially by Kansas soldiers who had served with him in the field and those who had known him before the war. Nevertheless, his appointment did not please all the "statesmen" who had remained at home during the war and had been playing politics for their own personal benefit.[15]

Crawford's comments are telling. He was not impressed with pretenders whose egos and personal goals often got in the way of true public service. He even put quotation marks around the word "statesmen," making it a point that they were the ones who "had remained at home during the war." In Crawford's mind, all things being equal, he would give the job to a veteran who had sacrificed dearly for his country and state. It was a bond that was formed over a period of three years that saw fellow soldiers die in battle or of pneumonia or cholera or the measles. It was a bond forged by hundreds of miles of marching in the cold, at night, when it rained or snowed and when there was little to eat. "Statesmen" who were the important movers and shakers of their communities would not understand the bond.

Word of Ross's appointment was staggering news to Speer, who must have been quite sure the appointment was his. Lillian Leis tells how "Mr. Speer walked the street in Topeka that night, until the train (only the Union Pacific) came by—and the next morning had my father's name struck from off of his paper as an editor. There was never any settlement. Also—from that time—Mr. Speer was very bitter towards him."[16]

Just as Leis recalled, on July 21, 1866, the *Kansas Daily Tribune* was published as usual, but on the top of the front page that had always listed Speer and Ross as editors, only the name Speer appeared. The same was true at the top of the editorial page. The lead comment on the editorial page was a single sentence: "Maj. E. G. Ross, of this city, was on Thursday night, appointed by the Governor to the vacancy occasioned in the United States Senate by the death of General Lane."[17]

Speer mentions nothing about Ross's editorship of the newspaper or their partnership. There were no congratulations, only the coldest possible acknowledgement. It was not, however, the only thing Speer had to say on the subject. A long editorial immediately below the announcement lashed out at Governor Crawford, never mentioning Ross by name. The tone of Speer's commentary was bitter and emotional, referring to Crawford as a man with a "poor, weak, vacillating mind." He condemned Crawford for selecting a man who was no friend of Lane's, saying that in selecting a replacement for Lane he had deliberately insulted Lane's family, and using terms such as "ingrate" and "imbecile" to describe the governor.[18]

The next day Speer's harangue continued with another editorial, this time on the front page, beginning with the statement "The public will bear us out that selfishness has not been our characteristic." Speer was indignant that a good friend of Lane's was not selected by Crawford. Speer simply could not accept that he had been excluded from the honor he felt was his, to be a member of that most "exclusive of men's clubs." Perhaps the selection of anyone but himself would have been a crushing blow to Speer, but to have his own partner, who had never really expressed an interest in politics, be moved all the way to the front from out of nowhere was too much for him to bear.

Leis confirms that Mrs. Lane would not see Ross before he departed for Washington but attributes her refusal to exhaustion from mental and physical strain and makes the point that afterwards they were good friends.[19]

As Speer continued his editorial campaign against Crawford, Ross was en route to Washington to present his credentials to the United States Senate, which was due to adjourn within days. He left with ambivalent feelings, since Fannie was very late in pregnancy again; indeed, Ross was probably in Washington when his fourth son, Kay, was born on August 6. Leis ends her notes about that summer with a couple of sentences that express sadness about this remarkable appointment. "At the close of the war, we had thought we would not be left alone again—we had but one winter together— but we could not be with him. The children must be in school, and the home cared for. So mother still watched over her boys alone."[20]

If there was loneliness and a degree of disappointment for Fannie, there was apprehension and at least some bewilderment for Edmund, who had no idea what to expect in Washington, D.C. Getting off the train and flagging one of the dozens of hacks in front of the railroad station was unlike anything he had experienced in the remoteness of Kansas. As he moved along Pennsylvania Avenue, lined with a myriad of businesses and hotels and the sidewalks thick with pedestrians dressed in unfamiliar styles, Ross must have felt like a stranger in a foreign country. His first look at the Capitol Building, visible from anywhere in Washington, was surely intimidating, and if not, walking through the rotunda rising more than 180 feet from the floor, with its frescoed walls and statue of Alexander Hamilton in the center, surely would have prompted some fear in one who never imagined himself in such a place.

Samuel Pomeroy, Ross's fellow senator and fellow Radical Republican, was there to help him and give him confidence. So was Ross's former commander there, Thomas Ewing Jr., a lawyer, a Democrat, and a sometime advisor to the president. Between the two he would hear conflicting points of view in the coming months. Ross also had the good fortune to have a friend, Robert Ream, living in Washington in a large enough home to rent Ross a room while Congress was in session. And then there was Perry Fuller, a Lawrence businessman now living in Washington and married to Mary Ream, a daughter of Robert Ream. If Ross did not already know Fuller, the two men would become friends before the year was out. Each member of this unusual admixture of acquaintances would play an important role in Ross's life in the coming years.

CHAPTER TEN

RECONSTRUCTION

The Lines Are Drawn

We have with us the widowed and orphaned ones of this war. We have with us an army of maimed heroes who are condemned, but wrecks of their former selves, to walk the earth in sadness and sorrow all their after lives. We remember that it was by this great affliction that the country was saved—that they unflinchingly stood in the breach between the Republic and her foes, and we will be true to them.

—Ross, speech to the United States Senate, December 20, 1866

⌐ THE PROBLEMS OF RECONSTRUCTION were unprecedented in United States history. There was no model to follow, and the solutions, in general, of Radical Republicans and the southern-born Democratic president differed greatly. By the middle of 1866 Radicals generally believed that seceded states should at least ratify the Fourteenth Amendment and extend full rights of citizenship to former slaves, including the right to vote, and that confiscated plantations should be subdivided into farms for freedmen. Radicals were not inclined to be magnanimous with southern rebels: their approach to Reconstruction could sound a lot like revenge.

Edmund Ross's December 20 speech, his first as a senator, expressed the sentiments of those Republicans who were not willing to accept southern representation in the Senate without specific concessions. Ross, who was one of few senators who actually had experienced combat in the war, spoke on behalf of Civil War veterans. "We who have stood shoulder to shoulder in the battle's red front, where the fires of carnage lighted the souls of brave comrades to death and immortality, will not now insult the cherished names of the dead; will not falsify the issues upon which we have fought and conquered in this war; will not now blacken the record of devotion to our country and to liberty which has been signalized upon a thousand battle-fields by honoring treason and exalting traitors."[1]

Ross also gave credit to Unionist southerners who had resisted seces-sion and had, in fact, served their country well under difficult circum-stances. He expressed the grief that many people still felt over the loss of President Lincoln at the hands of an assassin who was widely viewed as an agent of southern rebels. "We have not forgotten our murdered President—we have not forgotten our martyred comrades, starved in the loathsome pens of Libby, of Andersonville, of Saulsbury, and of Belle Isle. We have not forgotten those faithful spirits who piloted our escaped prisoners through dreary nights of wandering in southern swamps and forests, who fed and secreted them from their blood-hound pursuers, and then paid the penalty with their lives. We have not forgotten those unconquerable southern loyal-ists who braved persecution and death to signalize their love for the old flag and their faith in the ultimate triumph of the cause which it symbolized."[2]

Andrew Johnson was a rigid Jacksonian Democrat, not the compro-miser his predecessor had been. At the same time, the Radical wing of the Republican Party was just as inflexible and difficult. The just society that white supremacist Johnson knew included blacks who were subservient. In 1865, in a conversation with Senator John Conness of California, he offered the opinion that he had never been opposed to slavery, and that, in fact, he believed blacks to be happier as slaves or in some similar role and that it was important that only white men manage the South.[3] After a contentious meeting in the White House with Frederick Douglass and several other black leaders, the angry president blurted: "Those d——d sons of b——s thought they had me in a trap! I know that d——d Douglass; he's just like any other nigger, and he would sooner cut a white man's throat than not."[4] It would seem that Johnson came to accept the end of slavery only with reluctance. Radical Republicans, on the other hand, wanted immediate fundamental change in the South. Slavery was now dead, but that was not nearly enough for Radicals who, it would seem, could not see that changing fundamental attitudes and traditional ways of life was going to take genera-tions, nor that this was not going to happen simply by changing laws or even amending the Constitution.

Johnson's 1866 message to Congress, the equivalent of the modern State of the Union address, was sent in written form and then read aloud in both houses. Johnson used the lion's share of his message to scold Congress for its failure to accept the elected delegates from ten southern states. All the seceded states had amended their constitutions, declared ordinances and laws of secession null and void, repudiated all war debts, and enacted "measures for the protection and amelioration of the condition of the colored race."[5]

With those few fundamental conditions nothing else was necessary, in Johnson's opinion, to justify southern representation in Congress, but there was simply no way Congress was going to seat the ten southern states that so far had refused, with Johnson's encouragement, to ratify the Fourteenth Amendment. Without trying, Johnson had managed to unify Radical and Moderate Republicans. As a result Johnson lost support not only among nearly all Republicans in the Congress but among much of the electorate in the North as well. The congressional elections of 1866 were a disaster for Johnson in spite of the fact that he went on an extended speaking campaign through northern states, commonly referred to as the Swing Around the Circle, to generate support for fellow Democrats running for office. Listeners at his various whistle stops were shocked to hear Johnson use abrasive language in dealing with hecklers. It was an unheard-of way for a president to act, and syndicated reports of his behavior further damaged his reputation.[6] In the final election tally Republicans easily surpassed the two-thirds majority mark in both houses, carrying all northern states except Delaware, Maryland, and Kentucky.[7] With so much Republican power established in the Congress, and with Moderates following the lead of Radicals, Congress could, in a very real sense, dictate to the president.

Johnson's soft policy toward the South probably encouraged the vindictiveness of some southerners toward former slaves and those who had opposed the rebellion in the South. Taking advantage of Johnson's leniency, many former Confederates found their way back into elected positions of power. There resulted the enactment of "black codes," which effectively returned former slaves to serfdom. Violence toward blacks was common. In his message to Congress Johnson did not propose any legislation to deal with conditions in the South, and he never mentioned the pending Fourteenth Amendment. While Johnson claimed to be sympathetic to former slaves, his actions, or lack of action, said just the opposite. His policies on Reconstruction were rapidly returning the South to the way it was before the war. Certainly the Thirteenth Amendment had been ratified and southern state constitutions rewritten to abolish slavery, but although slaves were now "free," their lives were no better and perhaps worse.

The Ross speech was interesting and important from several points of view. In a sense he had only been a senator for a matter of days. When he arrived in Washington with his credentials at the end of July 1866, Congress was about to adjourn until December. In December there were few significant highlights in the Senate; among the most notable events were the reading of the president's message to Congress and perhaps Ross's maiden speech just before the Christmas break. The Ross speech was eloquent because he was a skilled writer and an abolitionist who had been writing about slavery issues since 1856. It was an important speech because it was made to persuade the Senate to support Ross's resolution to ask the Joint Committee on Reconstruction essentially to wrest control of Reconstruction from the president. The resolution passed unanimously.[8] In effect Ross was initiating the course of action the Senate would take after the Christmas break in establishing the controversial Reconstruction Act.[9]

Before Ross was recognized by the president pro tempore, remarks were delivered by Senator William Pitt Fessenden of Maine, a Moderate Republican and the chairman of the Joint Committee on Reconstruction, encouraging the president pro tempore to allow Ross to speak before the Senate adjourned for the Christmas break. The assumption is that Fessenden wanted to hear for himself what this new guy had to say, especially because Ross would speak about issues facing Fessenden's own Reconstruction committee. Ross must have been flattered to have such a distinguished member stand up for him, and the fact that he was able to give this important speech gave Ross a high profile for such a junior senator.

Fessenden was an important man in the Senate. He was a fierce debater and always highly respected. He was levelheaded and not easily moved by emotional rhetoric. He had served in both the House and the Senate and for a time was secretary of the treasury under Abraham Lincoln. He once said, "Did I know that the opinions of every one of my constituents differed from my own, if I acted at all I would act according to my own honest convictions of right were it directly in their teeth. I would never violate the dictates of my own conscience. I am willing to be the servant of the people, but I will never be their slave."[10] It is not known if Ross ever heard Fessenden directly express these thoughts, but Ross came to admire Fessenden perhaps more than any other member of the Senate. There is no evidence of the two men having a close relationship, but the time was not far off when Ross and Fessenden would find themselves voting side by side in the extraordinary impeachment trial of Andrew Johnson. Both would have to act according to their "own honest convictions of right" even though directly "in the teeth" of their constituents.[11]

The Ross speech is also interesting for what it appears to say and what it actually says. Ross was discovering that there was a difference between writing about issues in a newspaper in Kansas and having to deal with the same issues as a United States senator. As a journalist he was an unabashed Radical Republican, but as a senator he was moderating his points of view even in his first weeks on the job. In a five-page, handwritten document from about 1895, Ross identified himself as having been "elected as a representative of the Radical element of the Republican Party," the implication being that he was specifically confirmed by the Kansas Legislature with the understanding that he would represent Radical views in Washington and that he would vote accordingly.[12] This expectation by his constituents was well understood by Ross from his first day as a senator. Because the December 20 speech was his first, Ross had to project the appearance of being a Radical even if on close examination it can be seen that his thoughts were already beginning to sound Moderate.

When Ross spoke about voting rights for freedmen, he was not only eloquent; his words, if they had been spoken by a giant of American history, would have been memorable. The statement is important to understanding what Ross believed.

> Sir, what is kindness? Is it simply the doling out of a few crumbs, or perchance a pleasant word, to one whose manhood or womanhood we are daily and hourly grinding out of them under the heel of oppression? Or is it a confession and fostering of that manhood, and a concession of those God-given rights which it carries, the right to live, the right to work, the right to be peers in the Commonwealth, the right to own ourselves and be ourselves? That, sir, is kindness, that is justice. . . .
>
> For one, sir, I confess I do not share the fear expressed by some gentlemen, of the effect of precipitating a mass of ignorance, as it is styled, upon the ballot-box. The black man's aspiration for liberty has always been as fervent and enduring as the white man's. . . .
>
> Where will you draw a line of demarcation which will rule out such men as these? Shall the fact that a man is able to make a scratch with a pen and call it his written name, or read his A, B,

C, alone entitle him to the almost sacred right of suffrage? By no means. There is a test infinitely above these by which they should be judged—a test established by God himself when He set his seal upon his finished work and saw that it was good. That test is manhood, and by no other can we safely abridge that right which was an outgrowth and has become a characteristic of this western world.[13]

These beliefs about slavery were instilled in Ross when he was just a child, and the superbly crafted words of the entire speech suggest that he saw this as a landmark event in his life, which it certainly was. Ross, in one way or another, had dedicated his adult life to the abolition of slavery, and to speak in the United States Senate was undoubtedly a heady experience. But Ross could already see that significant southern change would be many years in the making and involve much more give and take. He was a realist as a senator; he knew that the country, and especially the South, could not change abruptly. In spite of his eloquent and apparently Radical appeal for black enfranchisement as a journalist, the next paragraph of his speech said, in so many words, that he knew voting rights for former slaves should not be made a condition for the readmission of seceded states, although he was hopeful that this sacred right to vote would not be far behind.[14] In Kansas Ross had been an unflinching advocate of the right of former slaves to vote without delay.

As a senator Ross believed, as Abraham Lincoln did, that it was best not to press the issue of voting rights for former slaves. In his last public speech Lincoln said, "Grant that he [the colored man] desires the elective franchise, will he not attain it sooner by saving the already advanced steps towards it, than by running backward over them?"[15] Commenting on Lincoln's statement, Ross wrote in 1896: "If Mr. Lincoln's views had been seconded by Congress, the enfranchisement of the negro would have been, though delayed, as certain of accomplishment, and on a vastly higher and more satisfactory plane—and the country saved the years of friction and disgraceful public disorder that characterized the enforcement of the Congressional plan afterwards adopted."[16]

Ross believed, along with other Moderate Republicans, that the passage of the Fourteenth Amendment was the basic requirement for a seceded state to qualify for readmission. The amendment was remarkable for the major changes it initiated in constitutional history. It was written in four sections and established a set of conditions that would permanently change southern states in particular. The first section established the right of the federal government to define citizenship, superseding the right of states, and by definition overruling the Dred Scott decision. The first section also contained the oft-cited due process clause ensuring equal protection under the law for all citizens. With several million former slaves recognized as citizens, the southern states could have seen an increase of fifteen seats in the House of Representatives. The second part of the Fourteenth Amendment dealt with this issue by allowing only those citizens who could vote to be counted in determining representation in the House of Representatives. Thus ex-slaves must be allowed the franchise or not be counted. The Fourteenth Amendment failed to grant suffrage to blacks outright; it took the Fifteenth Amendment in 1870 to guarantee that right, and even with that amendment, denial of suffrage was still common. Section 3 of the Fourteenth disqualified anyone who had previously refused to uphold the Constitution and had participated in rebellion from holding any office civil or military and either state or federal. A two-thirds vote of Congress could override this provision on a case-by-case basis. The objective of the section was to control the thousands of pardons being freely given by the president. Section 4 made all debts of the Confederacy illegal and void.[17]

Two major issues unified the Republican members of Congress in drawing up its own Reconstruction approach. First, President Johnson discouraged southern states from passing the Fourteenth Amendment; consequently, even the few states that might have been inclined to pass the amendment were not doing so. Second, the increasing number of reports of atrocities against ex-slaves and southern Unionists was alarming. Direct intervention in southern government seemed to be the only answer, even to Moderates.

Ross's resolution that the Joint Committee on Reconstruction tackle the problems of bringing Congressional control to the South and securing the safety of southern loyalists and former slaves was taken up immediately after Congress reconvened on January 3, 1867. Ross, however, would not be in Washington for the first critical month of debate on Reconstruction. He was occupied during that time in Kansas formally running for the United States Senate, his position until then being merely provisional. Meanwhile, the matter of congressional Reconstruction dominated the work of both houses of Congress for two months.

While Fessenden was chairman of the joint committee, the most vocal member was Thaddeus Stevens, a representative from Pennsylvania and one of the most powerful members of the House. Stevens was an outspoken defender of minorities and would later lead the House of Representatives in its impeachment proceedings against Andrew Johnson. As Stevens and other Radicals saw it, the seceded states had not just left the Union as a form of protest, with the hope of resuming their previous status after the war, but had severed all ties, voluntarily forming an entirely new Confederate government.[18] The Confederate states had forfeited all their rights as states, had no legal state governments, and, especially with their refusal to ratify the Fourteenth Amendment, could not be accepted into the Congress. As spokesman for the Radicals, Stevens believed the only course of action was to establish military rule in the South, to exclude all former Confederates from citizenship for five years, and to grant former slaves the right to vote.[19] As Stevens saw it, military rule was entirely justified, given reports from the South; he believed action was needed as soon as possible: "Now, Mr. Speaker, unless Congress proceeds at once to do something to protect these people [southern Unionists and freed slaves] from the barbarians who are now daily murdering them; who are murdering the loyal whites daily and daily putting into secret graves not only hundreds but thousands of the colored people of that country; unless Congress proceeds at once to adopt some means for their protection, I ask you and every man who loves liberty whether we will not be liable to the just censure of the world for our negligence or our cowardice or our want of ability to do so."[20]

Recognition by both Radicals and Moderates of the widespread violence in the South resulted in a mutually held opinion that some sort of military occupation of the South was necessary. After weeks of debate and political infighting, the First Reconstruction Act was passed on March 2, 1867, the last day of the Thirty-ninth Congress. To further control the president, Congress also passed a military appropriations act that required all orders to the military from the executive branch to pass through the General of the Army, whose headquarters was to be in Washington and who could not be reassigned without approval of the Senate. There were so many questions raised by the First Reconstruction Act that a second act, a supplement to the first, was passed on March 23 to provide clarification and to instruct military commanders on how to take the initiative with constitutional conventions.[21] In vetoing these acts, President Johnson complained about the usurpation of his power. Congress ignored his objections and used its power to override the vetoes. In July the Third Reconstruction Act was passed to further clarify and control, "thus piling up an accumulated mass of supplemental, explanatory, and interpretative legislation that only a Philadelphia lawyer could grasp."[22]

The Reconstruction Act divided the South into five military districts. Civilian governments established under Johnson's plan continued to exist but were merely provisional. The military commanders of the five districts were all generals and had supreme power to overrule anything enacted by locally elected southern governments. They were "empowered to make arrests, conduct trials by military commissions. . . . Elections for state constitutional conventions were to be held in which persons of color were authorized to vote. . . . Negro suffrage and disqualification of ex-Confederate leaders must be permanently written into the newly formed state constitutions."[23]

It is not known how Ross felt about the Reconstruction Acts at the time of their passage, but his hindsight opinion of the acts that resulted from his December 19, 1866, resolution was decidedly negative. Ross played only a minor role in the debate on Reconstruction. He was not a member of the Joint Committee on Reconstruction and did not formally suggest any amendments to their plans. Probably no plan could have satisfied all the parties involved. Under the best of circumstances it would be impossible to quickly change generations-old, traditional southern values—even if Johnson's plan were not so insensitive to the needs of southern minorities and Johnson himself so unwilling to work with Congress to effect compromises. Moreover, in practice, the bureaucratic structure of the military districts set up to enact Reconstruction encouraged opportunistic carpetbaggers and various other forms of corruption. The process of passage and enactment of the Reconstruction Acts must have been frustrating and disappointing for Edmund Ross as he saw his hopes for a country free of slavery and human servitude compromised by rancor and corruption while the sacrifices made by so many Civil War veterans hoping for real change in the South remained as yet unrewarded.

CHAPTER ELEVEN

THE 1867 ELECTION

Pomeroy and Ross

A condition of rottenness will be proven to the world to exist, and
to have existed for years in this State, far beyond the apprehensions
of large portions of our people, and fully equal to the most damaging suspicions that any have entertained of us.

—*Ross's Paper*, March 1, 1872

⌐ EDMUND ROSS'S APPOINTMENT to the Senate by Governor Crawford
after the death of Senator Lane was official but temporary. At the first meeting of the Kansas State Legislature following his appointment, Ross had to
stand for election. Ross was running to fill out the remainder of Jim Lane's
term, four years. As it happened, Samuel Pomeroy had served six years in
the United States Senate and was required to run for a second term at the
same legislative session with Ross in January 1867. There were other candidates for the Senate seats held by Ross and Pomeroy, so election to those
seats was not mere formality. Had the two men been elected without much
opposition, the legislative session might not be worth mentioning, but there
was more to the story: five years after the election of Ross and Pomeroy,
both were accused of bribery in securing their seats.

After Ross gave his December 20 speech to convince his fellow senators of the wisdom of Congress in establishing its own Reconstruction
plan and policies, he remained in Washington during the Christmas break
and was still there on January 3 when Congress reconvened. It appears that
Ross remained in Washington until about January 10, when he returned to
Kansas to run for his Senate seat at the annual legislative session in Topeka.[1]
It was not practical that he return home for Christmas, given the number

of days he would have spent traveling to and from Kansas only to turn right around and repeat the entire trip.

Previous biographies of Ross say nothing about bribery at the 1867 session of the Kansas Legislature, simply referring to Ross and Pomeroy as having been elected by the joint session with not much additional detail. Edward Bumgardner's biography of Ross indicates that it was the "adroit strategy" of state senator R. A. Riggs that secured the election for Ross but makes no mention of any possible wrongdoing.[2] The rumors of bribery that eventually surfaced were centered on a man of dubious reputation named Perry Fuller. The 1867 legislative session was not controversial until 1872, after Ross was out of office. In February 1872 a joint committee of the legislature met to investigate reports of bribery in both the 1867 and 1871 senatorial elections. What the committee heard from some of the people who were subpoenaed was that bribery was so widespread that a candidate for United States Senate could not be elected without buying votes. Bribery was particularly blatant in 1871, triggering the call in 1872 for an investigation of Kansas election practices. A lawyer named Wilson Shannon Jr., in testifying about the 1871 election, stated that Sidney Clarke, the incumbent representative to Congress and a candidate for Ross's seat, "told me he had from forty to fifty thousand dollars to secure his election, and that he could get all the money that was necessary from his friends east; I understood at that time it was from Washington. He told me that he was satisfied that the Senatorial election was a question of dollars and cents and the man that had the most money was going to win."[3] Governor Crawford, who was also persuaded to run for Ross's seat in 1871, and who had firsthand experience with the process of the election of senators, claims in his memoirs that the 1871 senatorial election was the first "where money was openly and notoriously used in the bribing of members."[4] It may have been the first where bribery was "open," but it is also probable that bribery was alive and well in 1867, just hidden a little better. Others claimed that bribery was common and transparent even in 1867.

During the 1872 hearings I. S. Kalloch testified about the 1867 election and reported that although he had no firsthand knowledge of bribery, he was told by Perry Fuller that he, Fuller, "came here to put somebody there for the Senate—came here prepared to do it." When asked whose interest Fuller was working for, Kalloch answered, "For Mr. Ross. At the time of the conversation he had with me, he was not working for anyone, but afterward he supported Mr. Ross."[5] The testimony of William Spriggs was more specific:

Q. Were you here during the Senatorial election of 1867?
A. Yes.

Q. Do you know of any money or other corrupt influences being used to secure votes of the members of the Legislature for candidates for the United States Senate?
A. Not of my own knowledge.

Q. What have you heard in regard to such influences being then used?
A. The only thing direct was from Perry Fuller. He told me the evening after the election of United States Senator, that Pomeroy and Ross' election had cost him forty-two thousand dollars. He told me he considered that he made fifty-eight thousand dollars; that he had set apart one hundred thousand dollars. He said he had left Kansas and established himself in New York City in business, and his object was to control the entire Indian trade of the West; that if Tom Carney was elected with such a house as he had at the door of the Indians, he would at least divide the trade with him. He said the trade was worth a half million dollars annually.[6]

If Fuller did indeed spend $42,000 to secure the elections of Ross and Pomeroy, there is no indication of how the sum was apportioned between the two men. Also the testimony implying that Ross and Pomeroy had allowed Perry Fuller to buy votes for them was weak, because whatever bribery may have taken place was not witnessed firsthand by anyone willing to come forward. Moreover, the testimony relied on witnesses' ability to recall events that happened five years before. Fuller himself could no longer be subpoenaed in 1872; he died of a heart attack in 1871. The exact truth of what happened in 1867 is uncertain, and it would be risky to presume to judge Ross on the basis only of hearsay accounts. However, in a factual biography it is important to know what we can. For sure, Ross was acquainted with Fuller and in June 1868 Senator Ross did write to President Johnson recommending the appointment of Fuller as commissioner of internal revenue.[7]

This in itself is not enough to prove any corrupt activity on Ross's part, but it raises serious questions.

Perry Fuller is described in a number of sources as a mysterious person, and indeed the relationship between Ross and Fuller is something of a mystery and a vexing problem for anyone trying to understand what may have motivated Edmund Ross. A fair amount actually is known about Fuller, but there are also frustrating holes in the story. Orphaned when his parents died from cholera in about 1833, Fuller was taken in by a Dr. Chandler of Chandlerville, Illinois, who raised him and provided him with a good education. In 1846 he was married for the first time and emigrated with his new bride to Atchison County, Missouri. He moved to Westport (now Kansas City) in 1849.[8] With the opening of the Kansas Territory he moved himself and his wife to Franklin County, Kansas, where, with several other men, he established the town of Centropolis. He opened what amounted to a trading post dealing with the nearby tribes and made a handsome living. His dream for Centropolis was for it to become the capital of the territory.[9]

On February 10, 1863, it appears that Fuller purchased land in the town known today as Baldwin City, not far from Centropolis, and built a lavish home there.[10] He was by that time supposedly a millionaire from his trade with the Sac and Fox tribes and with other tribes in Oklahoma, Kansas, and New Mexico. What became of his wife is unrecorded, but in 1865 Fuller was married to Mary Ream, the sister of Lavinia "Vinnie" Ream. Vinnie would gain fame as a sculptress and a peripheral figure in the impeachment trial of Andrew Johnson.[11] In this connection she would become an important figure in Ross's life in Washington. During Ross's term in the Senate he boarded with the Ream family and undoubtedly had contact with Fuller, who was living in Washington at the time of the impeachment trial. It is also important to know that Fuller was a friend and business associate of Thomas Ewing Jr., Ross's former commander in the wartime Kansas Volunteers.[12]

Fuller's reputation in some circles was poor. In the late 1850s when Fuller lived in Centropolis, the agent representing the interests of the Sac and Fox tribes, Francis Tymany, complained bitterly to the Indian Office about Fuller, who he believed was taking unfair advantage of tribal members; indeed, said Tymany, Fuller was thoroughly dishonest. Fuller in turn used his influence with tribal chiefs to discredit Tymany. Tymany reported that many Sacs and Foxes were dying from what appeared to be poisoned liquor acquired from Centropolis, which Tymany believed was liquor laced with strychnine. Additionally, Tymany charged, Fuller was stealing timber from tribal lands and milling it in Centropolis. After about a year, Tymany was replaced by Fuller as the official Indian agent for the Sac and Fox tribes. Fuller's connection through one of various Indian "rings" apparently was overwhelming.[13]

While it is not possible to know what precisely happened behind the scenes at the meeting of the State Legislature in January 1867, it is important to at least explore the possibilities. The first possibility is that Governor Crawford was right, that the first time bribery was a factor in senatorial elections in Kansas was 1871. It would be naïve to believe this. On the other hand, Crawford, who was a seasoned politician and a lot closer to the events, believed that was the case. Another possibility is that Ross believed Fuller was using his influence to secure votes for him without money being involved, that all Fuller expected from Ross in return for his lobbying efforts was for Ross to return a favor or two if he were elected. Although that seems unlikely, it is possible. By far the most believable scenario, but not one that can be accepted without reservation, is that Ross did indeed agree to let Fuller buy votes for him and Pomeroy with the promise of return in the form of future favors. Ross's endorsement of Fuller for the position of commissioner of internal revenue certainly would lead a reasonable person to believe this was an attempted payoff. If money were passing from Fuller to legislators in 1867, it is hard to believe that Ross would not have known.

When the investigative committee released its findings, Ross was already out of office and publishing a weekly newspaper in the town of Coffeyville, Kansas. Although it appears he was embarrassed, Ross was obliged to print the findings the week following the release of the report. The conclusion of the committee in regard to the 1867 election stated that "[a]t the Senatorial election of 1867, a large sum of money was used and attempted to be used in bribing and attempting to bribe and influence the members of the Legislature to secure the election of S. C. Pomeroy, E. G. Ross and Thomas Carney, by Pomeroy, Thomas Carney, Perry Fuller and others in their employ."[14] Note that although Ross's name was linked to the scandal, he was not specifically named as a probable guilty party.

On the day that his paper published the findings, Ross was, perhaps conveniently, out of town. Ross did not admit to participation in the bribery of 1867, but in the same edition there was an article almost certainly written by Ross himself that comes close to an admission. "If the testimony taken by the Committee, and not yet printed, shall sustain the representations of the Committee, and we have no reason to doubt that it will, it is most scathing and terrible. A condition of rottenness will be proven to the world to exist,

Pomeroy. Do you believe these stories they told about your paying money to Finn and others?
Ross. No, I don't believe anything of the sort, of course.

Pomeroy. Nor do I.
Ross. I never heard that I did.

Pomeroy. Or anybody for you?
Ross. I heard that Perry Fuller had paid him [Finn] money for you and me.

Pomeroy. Do you believe it?
Ross. I do; I believe Perry Fuller paid him money and I believe Carney paid him money. Whether you [to Mr. Pomeroy] paid him money I have not as good testimony as I have of them; that is, not what I consider as absolute.

Pomeroy. Do you think I paid him any at all?
Ross. I strongly suspect that you did. It is well understood that he went for money, and was going the rounds for it.

Senator Logan further questioned Ross about the possibility that he had directly bribed legislators and also asked whether he had any knowledge "whatever that anybody was to use money to procure your election?" Ross's response was "No sir, none whatever."

Pomeroy was not suspended or censured by the Senate. In effect the Committee on Privileges and Elections did not support the Kansas investigating committee, instead determining there was no conclusive evidence of corruption by Pomeroy or, by implication, Ross.[17]

Like Pomeroy, it would have been hard for Ross to be found guilty of bribery based upon the testimony of men who were called before the Kansas investigating committee or the men called before the Senate Committee on Privileges and Elections. Conclusive evidence of wrongdoing did not surface, and some key participants, including Perry Fuller, were now dead. What can be said is that there were a number of people who had heard that Ross, Pomeroy, and others had paid legislators to vote for them or had arranged for Perry Fuller to do so on their behalf. A reasonable person would conclude that bribery was alive and well in Kansas. Indeed, the senator who replaced Ross at the 1871 election, Alexander Caldwell, was ejected from the United States Senate for failure to be duly elected in Kansas. It was a kind way for United States senators to declare their belief that he had bribed his way into the Senate. He was forced out of office after serving for less than one year.[18] It is impossible to know the behind-the-scenes complexities of the senatorial election process in Kansas in 1867. It is just as impossible for a modern objective observer to know the true nature of Ross's relationship with Pomeroy, Fuller, and others.

Edmund Ross was not enamored of power, nor was it his ambition to be a politician. His appointment to the Senate was a complete surprise to him. As an abolitionist and an influential journalist, he had persevered over a period of many years in his goal of helping bring an end to slavery. As a United States senator, however, he was able to do far more than just write about the complex issues surrounding slavery, as was seen in his speech of December 20 on the floor of the Senate and the unanimously adopted resolution that set in motion a debate that led to Congress wresting control of Reconstruction away from the president. In these circumstances, it would have been difficult for Ross to surrender the influence he might command.

If others whose judgment he then trusted—Samuel Pomeroy, for example—told him it might be necessary to let Fuller buy a few votes, he could well have been tempted. Ross had been an admirer of Pomeroy, and although eventually this changed, he may still have placed a great deal of trust in Pomeroy at the time of the 1867 legislative session. He no doubt saw how the game was played, particularly in Kansas, and even if it was distasteful to him, he may have realized there was no other way to assure election to a full term in the Senate.

Certainly the road to power for some senators in other states must have involved the same distasteful decisions. The eventual passage of the Seventeenth Amendment, making the direct election of senators by the citizens of each state the law of the land, was at least partially motivated by the corruption in state legislatures in regard to senatorial elections. Even with passage of the Seventeenth Amendment, money would still buy power; it just wasn't purchased the same way.

The Perry Fuller story would not be complete without a few more details. Ross's support of the nomination of Fuller for commissioner of internal revenue in 1868 was a lukewarm recommendation. Ross was requesting his appointment all right, but his letter was not an enthusiastic endorsement;

it was more like Ross was helping the president, who knew Fuller, and was advising him on when to send Fuller's name to the Senate.[19] Ross clearly was testing the waters, so to speak, trying to gauge the best time to submit Fuller's name. In the letter he mentions that Fuller had personal friends in the Senate who "have been exerting themselves very actively in his behalf," suggesting perhaps that he was not one of them. In fact, Fuller was not confirmed in that job by the Senate, but he eventually was named collector of the Port of New Orleans.

Two negative stories about Fuller appeared in the *New York Times* in September 1869. The first reported that Fuller had a claim of $10,000 against him by the First National Bank in Washington and that a shipment of goods had been seized by a sheriff to satisfy the claim.[20] The second story charged Fuller, the collector of New Orleans, with failure to collect duties on large quantities of sugar and coffee, the implication being that he received kickbacks.[21]

The charge against Fuller was serious and adds to the mystery. It gives one pause to think that Fuller may have been just telling a story to William Spriggs in January 1867 about putting up $42,000 for Ross and Pomeroy, a way of inflating the possible myth that he was a millionaire. After all, the only testimony that the 1872 committee had was hearsay to the effect that Fuller bragged he had bought votes for Ross and Pomeroy. A reasonable person would be inclined to think that Fuller did purchase votes for Ross and Pomeroy, or claimed he had, but whether he spent $42,000 is questionable. If Fuller ever had the vast fortune he was reported to possess, he squandered it very quickly. A note in cursive inserted into the Harold E. Miner letter of 1954 to F. H. Blackburn of the Kansas Historical Society indicates that "after Fuller's death [January 1871] his 'supposed' wealth was found to have vanished and his widow left dependent on relatives."[22]

In the writing of a biography of a political figure who lived generations ago, not everything is clear and explainable. Possibly, if not probably, Ross tarnished his otherwise superb reputation, but we should take care in trying to understand him even if we cannot excuse him. Clearly Ross sought a favor from Andrew Johnson in 1868 for Perry Fuller, but politicians sought favors of the president all the time. What can be said of Ross categorically is that beyond his salary he never personally benefited financially from his job as a senator nor from his job as territorial governor later in life. To the end of his life Ross always struggled to make ends meet and at times lived in virtual poverty. It is also important to realize that Ross was an idealist, at

CHAPTER TWELVE

CONGRESS DECLARES WAR ON THE PRESIDENT

The Constitution commands that a republican form of government shall be guaranteed to all the States; that no person shall be
deprived of life, liberty, or property without due process of law,
arrested without a judicial warrant, or punished without a fair trial
before an impartial jury.

> —Andrew Johnson, Annual Message to Congress,
> December 3, 1867

⌁ THE RECONSTRUCTION ACTS were the most important measures
enacted by Congress in 1867. Passed on March 2, March 23, and July 23,
these far-reaching statutes reflected the extreme frustration felt in the
House and Senate with President Johnson's anemic Reconstruction policies
and his seemingly proactive efforts to restore the South's pre–Civil War
power structure. As 1867 began, Congressmen had two courses of action
open: they could wrest control of Reconstruction from Johnson with legislation that amounted to a kind of military occupation of the South, or they
could find a way to impeach the president and remove him from office. They
chose to pursue both.

When the First Reconstruction Act became law on March 2, 1867,
another bill became law on the same date: the Tenure of Office Act, a statute that became the key to the successful impeachment of Andrew Johnson
the following year. Senator George H. Williams of Oregon first introduced
the Tenure of Office bill on December 3, 1866.[1] The bill was designed to
give Congress greater control over the patronage activities of the president.
Johnson openly admitted that he used his power of appointment of federal officeholders to strengthen his plan to revitalize the National Union
Party with himself as the leader.[2] To illustrate the depth of Johnson's use

of patronage, historian Michael Les Benedict cites Johnson's exercise of power with postal employees: During the half year between December 1865 and June 1866, Johnson removed a total of 52 postmasters. In July 1866, the single month following the creation of the Fourteenth Amendment in Congress, Johnson removed 56. During the four-month recess of Congress from August 1866 until the beginning of the second session of the Fortieth Congress in December, Johnson removed a total 1,664 postmasters, 1,283 of whom were removed for strictly political reasons.[3]

The Senate Committee on Retrenchment was assigned the task of debating and refining Williams's Tenure of Office bill and making its recommendations to the full Senate. In effect the bill stated that the president could not remove from office any person who had been appointed to that office and confirmed by the Senate without the approval of the Senate. The original bill, as it read when sent to the House, exempted cabinet officers from the provisions of the bill.[4]

The House approved the tenure bill and returned it to the Senate with the important stipulation that cabinet officers should be included in its provisions, thus further limiting the discretionary powers of the executive. Once again the Senate debated the issue, and once again it arrived at the conclusion that cabinet officers should be excluded. The vote, taken on February 6, was 28 to 17 in favor of exempting cabinet officers. Edmund Ross, who had just returned from Kansas with fellow senator Samuel Pomeroy, voted with the minority in favor of inclusion of cabinet members within the terms of the Tenure of Office Act.[5] Given Ross's vote in the impeachment trial the following year, he may have been among the senators who personally favored cabinet exclusion but understood that his Radical constituents, men who had just voted to retain him in office, certainly would have favored the requirement of Senate approval to remove a cabinet member from office.

A joint committee of the two houses was formed and negotiated a compromise of sorts, namely, that cabinet officers "shall hold their offices respectively for and during the term of the President by whom they may have been appointed, and for one month thereafter, subject to the removal by and with the advice and consent of the Senate." Essentially the House had won the battle. Johnson, in a lengthy message, vetoed the bill, saying: "If the Constitution has invested all executive power with the President, I return to assert that the Legislature has no right to diminish or modify his executive authority."[6]

Ross voted in favor of the final modified Tenure of Office Act, along with a majority of his colleagues including the other six senators who would vote to acquit Andrew Johnson in May 1868.[7] The vote was 35 to 11. But was Ross really convinced of the legality of the new law? Just one year later, in early 1868, there would be indications that he believed the Tenure Act was unconstitutional. We have to assume he accepted its legality at the time of its passage but had lingering doubts. Eventually Ross would take a very strong stand against the Tenure of Office Act. On March 24, 1869, Ross gave one of his rare speeches on the Senate floor. He spoke in favor of a House bill to repeal the law, stating: "At the time of its enactment I supported it simply as a temporary political necessity, but, I confess, with some misgivings as to its propriety, and also some doubts as to its practical utility."[8]

In vetoing the Tenure of Office Act in April 1867, Johnson had sought the advice of his cabinet, all of whom believed the act unconstitutional, including Edwin M. Stanton, the secretary of war. Stanton's vigorous support of the veto is ironic, given the events that would unfold during the summer and fall of that year. For legal opinions Johnson relied most heavily, of course, upon his attorney general, Henry Stanbery, and on Stanton, who had been attorney general during the Buchanan administration and secretary of war in Lincoln's administration. Stanton was particularly adamant that the president should veto the bill, which he viewed as a deep infringement of presidential rights protected by the Constitution. The veto message to Congress may have been partially or even wholly written by Stanton.[9] However, the Tenure of Office Act appears to have been one of very few issues on which the two agreed. Stanton had long been opposed to slavery, a friend of Radical Republicans, and seriously at odds with Johnson regarding Reconstruction policy. He was a constant thorn in Johnson's side, and why Johnson had tolerated Stanton in his cabinet as long as he did is hard to understand.

There was some urgency to the enforcement of the Reconstruction Acts as the spring of 1867 turned into summer. The Civil War had been over for two years, and Johnson's lenient policies prevailed in the South. Congress now was intent upon imposing its will once and for all, and it did so with the passage of the Republican-sponsored Reconstruction Acts. The South was under military rule, with civil governments relegated to diminished status. The five regional generals were given broad authority to overrule civilian policies. General Philip Sheridan, a Radical sympathizer who was in command in Louisiana and Texas, used what he believed was his authority in May to remove a judge, a mayor, and even the governor of Louisiana. With other generals threatening to take similar actions in their regions,

Attorney General Stanbery prepared a brief for the president defining what he believed the five generals could legally do. The brief led to a June 20 set of written orders transmitted by Johnson to the generals. Among other provisions, they were instructed not to take action against anyone who committed an offense before passage of the Reconstruction Acts nor to investigate what they believed were violations of loyalty oaths. They were not allowed to remove anyone from a provisional government office. Johnson was doing all he could to obstruct enforcement of congressional Reconstruction policies.[10]

Under the circumstances a July emergency session of Congress was convened, which began with disagreement between Radicals and Moderates. Radicals believed they should not adjourn again until impeachment was given serious consideration, as they saw no hope for Reconstruction to become effective unless or until Andrew Johnson was removed from office, but the Moderates prevailed, insisting that Congress should pass new legislation only to override Johnson's June 20 directives. Johnson, thoroughly convinced that his way was the right way, waited until Congress adjourned and continued to undermine congressional Reconstruction. Secretary Stanton, the presidential counselor who constantly sided with congressional Radicals, finally pushed Johnson to the breaking point. On August 5 Johnson asked Stanton to resign as secretary of war. Stanton refused, saying, "In reply I have the honor to say that public considerations of a high character, which alone have induced me to continue at the head of this Department, constrain me not to resign the office of Secretary of War before the next meeting of Congress."[11]

Johnson was left with no choice but to fire Stanton—something he would have been wiser to do before the Tenure Act became law. If he had, there might never have been reasonable grounds to impeach. Johnson perhaps hoped to avoid problems with Senate approval by appointing the very popular general Ulysses Grant, a Republican, to replace Stanton ad interim. Grant, who disagreed with Johnson about the Fourteenth Amendment and Reconstruction and even the Tenure Act, was reluctant to accept the job but found himself saying yes to the president. With Grant in place as the temporary secretary of war, Johnson, against the advice of his entire cabinet, fired two of the Reconstruction district commanders, Sheridan and General Daniel Sickles. In addition, Johnson issued a proclamation pardoning nearly all Confederates who were not already pardoned.[12]

A majority of northerners probably favored impeachment, but Johnson continued to believe that the American people eventually would support his

Reconstruction policies and that his strict interpretation of the Constitution would be shown to be right. Johnson was encouraged by the strong showing of Democrats in the off-season local elections held throughout the North in the fall of 1867. He also contended that Republicans were hypocritical in insisting on imposing black suffrage on the South when there was so little black suffrage in the North and no real will to establish it. His perception was shown to be right when black suffrage referendums were defeated in Ohio and Minnesota and, of all places, Kansas with its high population of abolitionists.[13]

Johnson sent his third annual message to the House and Senate when they reconvened in December 1867. He reiterated his previous contention that southern states should be properly recognized in Congress and argued eloquently against the Reconstruction Acts.[14] Given the establishment of military occupation of the South more than two years after the end of the Civil War, Johnson's objections to the Reconstruction Acts certainly could be interpreted as legally sound.

Johnson was uncompromising and brash in his public opposition to congressional policy toward the South, and in such an official and public forum as his annual message to Congress, Johnson was also unabashed in expressing his white supremacist points of view in regard to black suffrage: "The subjugation of the States to Negro domination would be worse than the military despotism under which they are now suffering. It was believed beforehand that the people would endure any amount of military oppression for any length of time rather than degrade themselves by subjection to the Negro race. . . . But if anything can be proved by known facts, if all reasoning upon evidence is not abandoned, it must be acknowledged that in the progress of nations Negroes have shown less capacity for government than any other race of people. No independent government of any form has ever been successful in their hands. On the contrary, wherever they have been left to their own devices they have shown a constant tendency to relapse into barbarism."[15]

The House of Representatives kept the real possibility of impeachment hanging over Johnson's head for nearly the whole of 1867. It had begun on January 7 with an impeachment resolution introduced by the Radical congressman James M. Ashley of Ohio—a fanatic who was convinced that Johnson had been a coconspirator in the assassination of Lincoln and guilty of other crimes as well. The House Judiciary Committee had the job of investigating the charges.

The Judiciary Committee began its investigation in February, an exhaustive investigation that was not completed until late in the year. The committee's inquiries included the possibility of collusion between Johnson and former Confederate president Jefferson Davis and the possibility of Johnson's connection to the Lincoln assassins. In addition, the committee looked at a wide variety of subjects to show corruption by Johnson in carrying out his duties as president.[16] Ross states that a total of eighty-nine witnesses were called, some for a second and third time, and that the testimony filled "more than twelve hundred octavo pages of print."[17] As 1867 progressed, Radicals struggled to keep impeachment alive, but it became clear to most observers that Ashley's charges were unsubstantiated. Johnson may have been a considerable thorn in the side of Republicans and his policies and actions a sad attempt to return to the status quo antebellum South, but he clearly was not guilty of any impeachable offenses as long as these were defined as "treason, bribery, or other high crimes and misdemeanors." Nevertheless, the disturbing possibility of impeachment continued to haunt the country and would remain unresolved until the December 1867 session of Congress.

In the second regular session of the Fortieth Congress beginning December 3, the House at long last took up the issue of impeachment as initiated by James Ashley eleven months before. No one expected that the Judiciary Committee would support impeachment after its extended hearings, but Johnson's brash defiance of the Reconstruction Acts may have precipitated the surprise recommendation for impeachment by a narrow vote of 5 to 4 in the committee. Perhaps even more surprising, given the mood of Congress, on December 7 the House voted by the wide margin of 108 to 57 not to impeach Johnson.[18] But if Radical Republicans were discouraged over the failure of the House to impeach the president, they didn't have to wait long to initiate another attempt.

On December 12 the president sent his message to the Senate, as required by the Tenure of Office Act, giving his reasons for suspending Edwin Stanton and seeking Senate approval of his decision. His argument was, "The mutual confidence and general accord which should exist in such a relation had ceased to exist."[19] Johnson's detailed message filled ten pages of the *Senate Executive Journal*. As with his other written arguments, his logic and eloquence were strong. The Senate referred his message to the Committee on Military Affairs and Militia. Johnson failed to argue in his message that the Tenure of Office Act did not cover Stanton.[20] If that had been a key part of Johnson's argument, it might have caused the constitutionality of the law to be taken up by the Supreme Court, and likely would have strengthened arguments against Johnson's removal during the impeachment trial the following spring. As it was, his message requesting Senate approval for removal of Stanton implied that he did not disagree with the legality of the Tenure of Office Act.

The Military Affairs Committee did not respond to Johnson's message until after the Christmas break. On January 10 the Senate considered the recommendations of the committee, presented as a formal resolution: "Resolved, That having considered the evidence and reasons given by the President in his report of the 12th of December, 1867, for the suspension from the office of Secretary of War of Edwin M. Stanton, the Senate do not concur in such suspension."[21]

On the following day Senator James Rood Doolittle, a Johnson conservative, offered an amendment that restated the resolution: "Resolved that the Senate advise and consent to the removal of Edwin M. Stanton."[22] The Doolittle resolution stated the same issue using the precise words of the Tenure of Office Act. The question remained the same, but the wording from the Military Affairs Committee possibly implied that the president was guilty. Doolittle's wording suggested nothing more than a yes-or-no vote. Of the thirty-nine senators voting on Doolittle's amendment, only eight senators, four Democrats and four Republicans, including Ross, voted to revise the wording. This may not be particularly noteworthy except that when the final vote on the resolution took place, Ross chose not to vote, suggesting that he had seen merit in the president's arguments and/or that he had serious doubts about the validity of the tenure law. The vote to reinstate Stanton using the original wording of the Military Affairs Committee was a resounding 35 to 6.[23]

The situation for Grant, who was still serving as the secretary of war ad interim, was awkward at best. He could remain at his post until he was forced to leave, as Johnson preferred, but he ran the chance of being labeled a Johnson supporter. For this immensely popular man, who was already a frontrunner to be the next Republican candidate for president, this was less than a good idea. He could resign and, in effect, give the keys to his office back to the president. This would have been acceptable to Johnson, although not what he preferred. The third option was to acknowledge the correctness of the Senate vote to restore Stanton to his old office and to give the keys directly to Stanton. Although Grant did not support Stanton, he chose this last option, exacerbating a serious breach between himself and Johnson, with the president charging Grant with insubordination.[24]

Johnson was determined, or so his defense attorneys would later argue, to have the Tenure of Office Act tested in the courts and was confident he would prevail. His plan was to once again suspend Stanton, who now literally occupied the office of the secretary of war, taking his meals and sleeping in his office at the War Department.[25] To carry out his plan, it was necessary for Johnson to find another qualified person willing to serve as secretary of war ad interim. His first choice was General Sherman, who could not have been more adamant in his refusal to accept the post. Several others refused as well, and in spite of sound advice from the likes of Thomas Ewing Sr. that he simply accept Stanton back into his cabinet, Johnson insisted on testing the law. General Lorenzo Thomas, who was elderly and who had never advanced in his career as he thought he should, was more than willing to be the pawn in Johnson's scheme. On Friday, February 21, 1868, Johnson informed Stanton that he was once again relieved of his post and was to turn over his office to General Thomas, the new ad interim secretary of war.[26]

The events in the days that followed were frenzied and often lacking in dispassionate consideration by responsible minds. After presenting his credentials to Stanton, who refused to recognize them and who refused to leave his office, General Thomas left the War Department and later attended a masked ball the same night. As he drank far more than he should have, he boasted that the next day he would forcibly oust Stanton. Stanton meanwhile had an arrest warrant sworn out for Thomas, who was brought before a federal judge the next day. After making bail and reporting back to Johnson, Thomas was ordered by the president to return to the War Department office and to again remove Stanton. Thomas not only failed to do this but ended up sharing a belt of whiskey with Stanton before breakfast.[27] Thomas never truly held the post of secretary of war.

Meanwhile when the Senate received Johnson's message that he was appointing General Thomas secretary of war ad interim, members immediately debated the wording of a resolution in response, settling on: "Resolved, by the Senate of the United States, That, under the Constitution and laws of the United States, the President has no power to remove the Secretary of War and designate any other officer to perform the duties of that office ad interim."[28]

The vote on the resolution was taken on the same day Johnson informed the Senate of his actions, with 28 voting for and only 6 against. Twenty senators did not vote, including Moderates like William Pitt Fessenden. Ross was listed as voting with the majority, but he later claimed that this was a mistake made in the *Senate Executive Journal*. "My distinct recollection is, that though present, I declined to vote."[29] According to Ross, there was extreme pressure both from within and from outside the Senate to establish that the president had indeed broken the law. With the passage of the resolution, the House of Representatives then had a clear reason to proceed with impeachment. It is significant to note that twenty (twenty-one if Ross is counted) senators chose not to vote on such an important issue, suggesting that more than a third of the senators present were reluctant to feed the frenzy that prevailed.[30]

If some senators were impulsive on February 21, the House seemed to be overcome with a kind of craziness.[31] On Monday, February 24, when the vote finally came, it was overwhelmingly in favor of impeachment. According to historian Eric McKitrick, in the weeks that followed "matters had reached such a pass that many men were quite willing to stretch their principles all out of shape, to seize upon any form at all that was plausible, and to face their consciences later."[32]

If his constituents had not detected Ross's move toward the center of the party at the time the Senate voted on the impeachment resolution on February 21, by March 4 this inclination had been detected. An article in the *Kansas State Record*, a newspaper once owned by Ross, indicated that some Kansans were worried about him. It was as if Ross had been accused of a crime that was suspected but yet to be proven. There is a kind of sorrow to the article suggesting a latent doubt by an editor pleading the equivalent of "say it isn't so." It seems as if the writer, by composing the article, is discovering a truth that he doesn't want to believe, that Edmund Ross was changing, that his politics were tending toward the Moderate, and that Thomas Ewing Jr.'s friendship was indeed influencing him. Telegrams from Washington indicated that Ross had recently been seen with Ewing. The *Record* editor rationalized the reports by saying it was only natural for Civil War friends to be seen together. "That there is harmony of feeling between these gentlemen politically we do not believe. . . . When impeachment means [so much], no man who knows E. G. Ross doubts on which side he will be."[33]

When the impeachment trial of Andrew Johnson began in March, Edmund Ross had been an active senator for a mere fifteen months.[34] The 1867 year had been a time to absorb the routine and protocol of the Senate and, at the request of William Tecumseh Sherman, to participate (although not a voting member) in the massive Medicine Lodge Treaty in Kansas with the leaders of the Kiowas, Comanches, Apaches, Cheyennes, and Arapahoes. Most important, Ross became a witness to history as President Andrew Johnson and the Republican Congress struggled to dominate one another.

It is true that Ross spent time with his old commander, Thomas Ewing Jr., a member of the revived National Union Party, who was practicing law in Washington. Thomas Ewing Sr. was an advisor to Andrew Johnson and, in fact, one of the men who had turned down the job of secretary of war when Grant resigned. It would be extraordinary if Ross and Thomas Ewing Jr. had not discussed politics; in fact, a reasonable person could feel confident that they had. The Ewings, as lawyers and conservatives, would have had a bias for Johnson's strict constitutional views, and Thomas Ewing Jr. would not have been hesitant to argue from this same point of view. To what extent Ewing might have influenced Ross is unimportant. To Ross's credit, he had an open mind and was not averse to change. Although Ross was not about to leave the Republican Party in the spring of 1868, he was disappointed in the irrational way that many of his fellow party members behaved and at the same time impressed with the rational arguments of his former commander and others whose emotions were detached from the issues at hand. Ross was not a politician who simply followed the dictates of party leaders. As time went on, Ross would find that he could not reconcile party loyalty with sound reasoning, and it would frustrate him as nothing else ever had.[35]

CHAPTER THIRTEEN

THE IMPEACHMENT TRIAL OF ANDREW JOHNSON

[I] weighed the cause as the Constitution and laws and my oath
demanded.
—Ross, speech to the United States Senate, May 27, 1868

ﾍ ALTHOUGH THE 1868 MOVE to impeach Andrew Johnson became tied
to Johnson's defiance of the Tenure of Office Act, the impeachment always
was more about politics than it was about a violation of law. It was inextrica-
bly linked to the Reconstruction Acts and Johnson's obstructionist policies.

The first effort to impeach, in December 1867, had failed when the
House was unable to find charges against Johnson substantial enough to
warrant his removal. No president had ever been impeached, and so no
precedent existed for removal from office. The House, in the 1867 effort, had
by implication made "high crimes and misdemeanors" sufficient justification for impeachment. So as the impeachment trial of 1868 began, the question before the House, as prosecutor, and the Senate, as jurists, became to
decide whether Andrew Johnson had violated a valid law and, if so, whether
that was an impeachable offense.

The 1867 Tenure of Office Act made it illegal for the president to remove
any government officer appointed by the president and confirmed by the
Senate unless and until the Senate confirmed a replacement. The law covered
officeholders from cabinet members right down to postmasters in the small-
est towns in the United States. An exception in the law allowed the president

to remove an official when the Senate was in adjournment, but the Senate had the right of review upon reconvening. Clearly Johnson was in violation, or attempting to be in violation, of the Tenure of Office Act with the appointment of General Lorenzo Thomas to replace Edwin Stanton in February 1868 while the Senate was in session. In the eyes of the Radical leaders in Congress, this was all that was needed to seek the removal of Johnson. So eager were the Radicals in the House of Representatives that their vote on impeachment was taken even before they had drawn up articles.

The leader of the House delegation that formally notified the Senate of its intentions was Thaddeus Stevens of Pennsylvania. Stevens's health was so poor that two black servants regularly carried him around in a chair. In appearing before the bar of the Senate on February 25, Stevens was able to stand for the short time it took to advise the Senate of the House's intentions to impeach and to announce that the House would have articles of impeachment ready within days. On March 2 the so-called House managers, the designated prosecutors, returned to read the eleven articles at the bar of the Senate. While Stevens would have preferred to read the articles himself, he was obliged to allow Representative John A. Bingham to do the reading. In addition to very poor general health, Stevens was cursed with the pain of a clubfoot. Of the seven impeachment managers, six stood during the reading while Stevens remained seated.

The first eight articles of impeachment were legalistic variations accusing Johnson of firing Stanton and attempting to replace him with General Thomas in violation of the Tenure of Office Act. The first article was the linchpin holding the next seven in place. The ninth article involved the alleged attempt by Johnson to circumvent the bill passed by Congress to confine Johnson to issuing orders to the military only through the general of the army. The basis for that article was the testimony of General William H. Emory, commander of the Washington Garrison, that in conversation the president had told him that the law was unconstitutional, that it deprived him of his constitutional rights as commander-in-chief, and suggested that he intended to find some way to ignore it.[1] Article 10 was written by Representative Benjamin F. Butler at the urging of Thaddeus Stevens, who believed the articles needed more "vigor." It was a weak article that alleged that Johnson had publicly ridiculed Congress with the intent to "set aside the rightful authorities and powers of Congress."[2] Article 11 was essentially a vague summation of the other articles in a strongly worded attempt to characterize Johnson as guilty of "a high misdemeanor in office."[3]

The proceedings in the newly expanded and remodeled Capitol Building were both a serious undertaking and a public spectacle. The impeachment trial was easily the biggest show in town. To limit the size of the gallery in the Senate chamber, one thousand tickets were issued. Women were there each day in their finest clothing, arriving well before proceedings began to have the best view and the most conspicuous seat possible. Each senator was allowed four tickets; forty went to Washington diplomats, four to the chief justice, and two each to cabinet members. Sixty were set aside for press members, while the members of the House and government officials shared the remainder.[4]

As provided in the Constitution, the chief justice of the United States presided over the trial. The Honorable Salmon P. Chase had a distinguished career as governor of Ohio, as a United States senator from Ohio, as secretary of the treasury under Lincoln, and finally as chief justice of the Supreme Court. He favored black suffrage and the Radical approach to Reconstruction. Chase's power was unlike that of a judge in a civil trial. The Republican-controlled Senate carefully drew up the procedures that Chase was required to follow. The chief justice was allowed to rule on routine matters of law, but if any senator objected to his ruling, a vote of all senators present was required to decide the issue, including the admissibility of testimony or evidence.[5] This makes it possible to track Edmund Ross's position on various issues.

President Johnson was ordered to appear before the Senate on March 13 to answer the charges. Johnson did not appear in person but sent a team of defense lawyers that included Henry Stanbery of Kentucky, a Republican who until days before was the attorney general; Benjamin R. Curtis of Massachusetts, a Republican and a former justice of the U.S. Supreme Court who had dissented in the Dred Scott case; Thomas A. R. Nelson, a Democrat from Tennessee; William M. Evarts of New York, a longtime Republican who would become Johnson's attorney general following the impeachment trial; and William G. Groesbeck of Ohio, the only Democrat besides Nelson to defend Johnson. It was a highly prestigious team of lawyers, and the fact that the team was dominated by Republicans was no accident. Together they asked for a forty-day delay to properly prepare their defense, but they were granted only ten days.

Besides Thaddeus Stevens of Pennsylvania, the members of the prosecution team, the so-called House managers, included Bingham of Ohio; George S. Boutwell of Massachusetts; James F. Wilson, a talented young representative from Iowa who would eventually turn down offers for cabinet positions but would become a United States senator; John A. Logan of Illinois, who had resigned his earlier congressional seat to serve in the Civil War; Thomas F. Williams of Pennsylvania; and Butler of Massachusetts, a Radical Republican who had an illustrious career as a Union general and was appointed lead prosecutor of the impeachment team. Butler was difficult and uncompromising, with about as bad a reputation in the South as a former Union general could have. He was widely known in Louisiana, where he had served much of his Civil War time, as the Beast Butler or as the Butcher of New Orleans.

As the trial progressed, the Radical leadership must have grown uneasy about Ross and six other Republicans whose votes on various issues were out of step with the majority. Just as Democrats were expected to acquit Johnson, so too did the Republican leadership expect a guilty vote from all of its members, especially from the likes of a very junior senator like Ross. Ross was expected to "toe the line." He was, after all, a Radical—or so they thought.

In his own book about the Johnson impeachment, Ross discussed the testimonial phase of the trial, the phase that lasted the better part of April. Ross believed that much of the testimony was unimportant in the long run, but he selected thirty instances when the Senate was required to vote on issues that were important. Ross reported on the proceedings with comprehensive quotes from the *Congressional Globe* and provided complete documentation of the voting. Most of the votes involved challenges to the admissibility of testimony. Ross's votes show a decided willingness to allow evidence to be given, regardless of what side was challenging. Of the twenty-eight votes on admissibility of testimony or evidence, twenty-one challenges were by the prosecution and seven by the defense. Of the twenty-eight votes, Ross voted twenty-seven times for admissibility and only once for rejection.[6]

During the trial the voting by Ross and the six other Republicans who eventually voted for acquittal, and who became known as "the recusants," was consistent. Senators Joseph S. Fowler and Peter G. Van Winkle each voted twenty-six times with Ross. Senators William Pitt Fessenden, Lyman Trumbull, and James W. Grimes each voted twenty-four times with Ross. Senator John B. Henderson voted nineteen times with Ross, and this number would likely have been larger had Henderson not been absent or abstained for eight votes. The preponderance of votes by the twelve

Democratic senators amounted to agreement with Ross twenty-three times. By comparison, Ross's fellow Republican senator from Kansas, the Radical senator Samuel C. Pomeroy, voted only seven times with Ross. So while Ross was displaying open-mindedness in allowing evidence and testimony, if one paid close attention, he was also demonstrating a shift away from Radicalism at least on the issue of impeachment.

Two of the issues involving testimony that directly related to the president's defense are worth noting. On April 11 General William T. Sherman was called upon for testimony regarding Johnson's attempt to appoint him as secretary of war ad interim. What the defense was trying to show was that the president intended this appointment and the second firing of Stanton to be tested in the Supreme Court and that Sherman could confirm that this was the president's intention. The counsel for the defense pursued Sherman's testimony with a number of questions. Each time, the prosecution objected on the grounds that the question was either leading or incompetent. The questions included the following:

> At the first interview at which the tender of the duties of the Secretary of War ad interim was made to you by the President did anything further pass between you and the President in reference to the tender or your acceptance of it?

> In either of these conversations did the President say to you that his object in appointing you was that he might thus get the question of Stanton's right to the office before the Supreme Court?

> Was anything said at either of those interviews by the President as to any purpose of getting the question of Mr. Stanton's right to the office before the courts?

> Did the President, in tendering you the appointment of Secretary of War ad interim, express the object or purpose of so doing?[7]

In voting on each of these questions, Ross was for the admittance of the testimony. However, because Republicans had an overwhelming number of votes, they were able to block Sherman's answers to the questions. This impaired Johnson's ability to prove a deliberate intention to test the constitutionality of the Tenure of Office Act. The House managers contended that he never mentioned a Supreme Court test until after he was impeached. To a degree, they were right. In December, when Johnson submitted his reasons for suspending Stanton for the first time in August 1867, he seemed to be tacitly accepting the Tenure Act as a valid law; he did not mention a belief that the law was unconstitutional. The Radical leadership in late February and early March argued that a Supreme Court test was just an excuse by Johnson and not his actual plan of action. Sherman's testimony might have supported the president's contention, but that testimony was never heard.

The other issue worth noting came during the testimony of Gideon Welles, the secretary of the navy in Johnson's cabinet. The defense was trying to show that in February 1867, when the cabinet met to discuss the Tenure Act before it became law, they were unanimous in the opinion that members appointed by Lincoln, and who continued to serve in Johnson's cabinet, were not covered by the provisions of the Tenure of Office Act. This kind of authoritative support lent credence to Johnson's contention that Stanton was not covered by the law. Welles could have confirmed that Johnson had the full support of the cabinet and was not just acting without good counsel, but the Republican majority again prevailed in rejecting Welles's testimony, while Ross and five of the other recusant senators (Henderson apparently was absent) voted unsuccessfully in favor of Welles testifying.[8]

When the testimonial phase of the trial ended, a caucus of senators was planned for May 11. While it was widely believed that Johnson was sure to be found guilty, Ross states that comparatively few senators actually had declared how they would vote on the articles, and informal polling before the eleventh revealed unexpected weakness in the Senate ranks. At the May 11 session two influential Republican senators, John Sherman of Ohio and Timothy Howe of Wisconsin, both of whom had been involved in drafting the Tenure of Office Act, declared their lack of support for the first article, stating that they did not believe that Edwin Stanton was covered by the tenure law. This quickly made it clear that article 1, charging Johnson with the blatant attempt to remove Stanton while the Senate was in session, in violation of the tenure law, would fail. Not only that, eight of the articles would fail, and Johnson stood a chance of being found guilty only of the second, third, and/or eleventh articles.[9] Articles 2 and 3 could only be considered possibilities by the slimmest of margins, given that article 1, closely related to the next two, was destined to fail. Article 2 charged Johnson with writing a letter authorizing Lorenzo Thomas to act as ad interim secretary of war. Article 3 alleged that Johnson's unlawful appointment of Thomas was a deliberate attempt to violate the Constitution. Article 11 had the best chance to succeed, because a guilty vote allowed senators to hide behind the hodgepodge of charges.

It was not a surprise that only three senators declared their intention to vote guilty on all eleven articles: Charles Sumner, Thomas W. Tipton, and Ross's fellow senator from Kansas, Samuel Pomeroy, all Radical Republicans. Six of the recusant senators—Fessenden, Fowler, Grimes, Henderson, Trumbull, and Van Winkle—stated that they did not support any of the charges. Ross, the seventh recusant, either refused to say how he would vote or was vague about his stand on several of the articles, allowing the Republican leadership to believe they might still count on him to vote with the majority. The popular history of the impeachment has Ross as the only senator who refused to say how he would vote. That may have been true in the days just before May 16, the day set aside for the first formal vote, but in early May there were a significant number of uncommitted senators, according to Ross.[10] With assurance of conviction in danger, the Radical leadership applied pressure to all Republicans who were either uncertain or sure of voting for acquittal. Because Ross was a junior senator, and because he was ostensibly a Radical, the pressure on him was particularly strong. How could he, a Radical Republican from Kansas, refuse to vote guilty on at least one article?

All the recusants were relentlessly stalked and warned that their future was grim if they did not vote to convict. Ross was aware that the people in heavily Republican, and often Radical, Kansas would not hesitate to end his career. Ross's intentions were unknown to anyone but himself, and because he refused to say what he would do, Republican leaders were persistently stubborn in trying to induce him to announce that he would vote "guilty" on at least a couple of the articles. Ross likely knew he would vote to acquit on all articles but preferred to keep his intentions secret, hoping to have the vote postponed until July 1.[11] If the vote could be postponed, new developments could possibly save him from having to reveal his true convictions. The closer to May 16, the more pressure there was on Ross. In an interview for the *Kansas City Star* in 1903 Ross told the reporter, "I was aware at the time that I stood in personal danger. . . . I was given a friendly intimation that I stood in danger of assassination. One man voluntarily acknowledged to me after the trial that he had been connected with a plot to kidnap and take me to New York city."[12]

Historian David Dewitt described Ross as "the target of every eye; his rooms beset by his Radical constituents, associates and friends wild to gain some satisfactory inkling of his mind. His outgoings and incomings, his companions and his convivialities, his breakfast, his dinner, his lodgings, were marked and set down in note-books."[13]

The Radical leadership of the Senate later claimed that Ross had committed to vote guilty on several of the articles. Ross, in fact, later said he had indicated a possibility of voting guilty on article 1 and perhaps 11, but he claimed never to have made a firm commitment to anyone on the other nine articles. Had the Republican leadership been certain of Ross's commitment, there would have been no need to continue pursuing him as they did. Clearly they must have detected hesitancy. Senator Pomeroy, the team leader in confronting Ross, cornered him several times in the days before the May 16 vote. On Tuesday the twelfth or Wednesday the thirteenth, according to a report by Pomeroy, the two men met in the room of the sergeant at arms, where Pomeroy claimed to have Ross's firm commitment on articles 1, 2, 3, and 11. Ross reported that the meeting had actually taken place on the afternoon of the fourteenth and that he told Pomeroy he was a certain "yes" on article 1, but that he should be listed as uncertain on the rest except number 8, which he absolutely did not support.[14]

If Ross had committed only to the first article, as he claimed, Pomeroy would have seen through Ross's plan. Ross could easily vote yes on number 1 because it was clear from the caucuses that there was not enough support for article 1 to pass. Thus Ross could say he was for conviction, to satisfy his constituents that he was indeed in favor of putting an end to Johnson's career. Had article 1 ever been voted on, Ross could possibly have voted yes. Ross claims that until May 14 he made no promises to vote for any of the articles. After the May 14 meeting Pomeroy continued to hound Ross right up to the final minutes before the Senate convened to begin voting, which suggests that Pomeroy was not convinced that Ross would vote "yes" for any article with the possible exception of number 1.

Pomeroy said he met by chance with Ross at the National Hotel in the room of Senator Van Winkle on Thursday night, the fourteenth. Ross was meeting with Senators Trumbull, Henderson, W. T. Willey, and Van Winkle, who obviously were discussing the votes they would cast in little more than thirty-six hours. Van Winkle and Willey were Senate colleagues from West Virginia. They had arrived at the conclusion that, if needed, both would vote for acquittal, but if only one vote were needed, only Van Winkle, who was the more certain of the two about acquitting the president, would vote "not guilty."[15] Years later Henderson would also report that at that meeting the plan was made for Senators William Sprague and Willey to cast "not guilty" votes if one of the recusants before them failed to do so, but only if necessary.[16] In joining the conversation, Pomeroy claimed to all in the room that there were enough "guilty" votes to achieve conviction, 36 to 18. Henderson disagreed and said enough senators would vote "not guilty" to cause the conviction to fail by 4 votes. When he heard Pomeroy say that there were 36 "guilty" votes, Ross asked if he were counting him in that number, and Pomeroy said yes. Ross then said that he could not be counted on for any of the articles and that if anyone asked Pomeroy how Ross was going to vote, he should say he didn't know. Ross reiterated that he preferred to have the voting postponed.[17]

While Ross may have been hesitant to tell Pomeroy how he was going to vote, it is almost a certainty he told the others in the room of his plans to acquit. In his May 27 speech to the Senate, Ross revealed that he shared his "not guilty" intentions for the first time on May 14.[18] The decision on how to vote must have been agonizing to Ross; he hoped for some easy way out, because he knew the consequences of voting his true conscience. The next meeting between Ross and Pomeroy took place the following night, May 15, the eve of the formal vote. Pomeroy had received a telegram from Daniel R. Anthony of Kansas addressed to both senators. Anthony claimed to represent "1,000 others" and said: "Kansas has heard the evidence and demands the conviction of the President."

In order to ensure that Ross saw the message, Pomeroy invited Ross to his home for dinner. According to Pomeroy, they had a pleasant dinner with the Pomeroy family at which they discussed how the voting might go the next day. Pomeroy remembers Ross saying that the eleventh article was the strongest and that he felt freer to vote for that article than any other but that he preferred there be a postponement, and he asked Pomeroy to support him. However, Ross's recollection of the evening was slightly different. Ross said they had dinner without discussing the impeachment and that the only time it was discussed was on the front porch of the Pomeroy residence as Ross waited for a streetcar. It was at that time that Ross asked for his colleague's support for a postponement and again refused to commit himself on the eleventh article.[19]

Ross's whereabouts until breakfast the next morning are uncertain. One source suggests that Ross was later seen at a Washington restaurant with Henderson and Van Winkle and that Thomas Ewing Jr. met Ross around midnight at the Ream house and they departed together for the Western Union office to allow Ross to respond to the Anthony telegram.[20]

Pomeroy was not the only Republican working overtime to make sure Ross voted "the right way." One last desperate attempt to secure Ross's cooperation was made by General Dan Sickles. Sickles had commanded the congressional Reconstruction program in the Carolinas, a job from which he was fired by President Johnson the previous summer. His attempt to "reach" Ross involved a daughter of Ross's landlord, Robert L. Ream. Vinnie Ream was a young and beautiful sculptress who at the age of eighteen was commissioned to do a statue of Abraham Lincoln. During the impeachment Vinnie worked daily on the project in the basement of the Capitol. Vinnie's father, a surveyor, had advised Ross on the purchase of property in Wabaunsee County in 1857, and their friendship continued through the years. In 1868 the Reams kept a home in Washington, D.C., and rented Senator Ross a room while Congress was in session.

Vinnie was an extraordinary talent who, as a teenager, had gone to the White House virtually every day to sketch President Lincoln as he hurried down a hallway on his way to lunch. When Lincoln finally took notice of her presence and learned she was a sculptress, he invited her into his office during his periods of rest. The extraordinary and regular access to the president that Vinnie enjoyed allowed her to create a medallion and at least two early busts of Lincoln. Because of her proven talent and competence and her familiarity with Lincoln, she was given the impressive commission of $10,000 by Congress to undertake the full-length statue of Lincoln in July 1866, at just the time that Ross was selected to replace Jim Lane.[21]

With Vinnie working in the Capitol and Radicals doing all they could to win over Ross, it was inevitable that Vinnie would be approached to use her influence with Ross. She was frequently interrupted in her basement studio, but the boldest approach came in the very early hours of May 16, just hours before the final vote. General Sickles knocked on the door of the Ream house shortly after midnight. He apparently had difficulty finding the house but, seeing lights on inside, decided he would press on with his mission. On crutches (he had lost a leg at Gettysburg) he pushed his way into the house when Vinnie answered the door and announced that he was looking for Ross. When Vinnie said he wasn't there, Sickles insisted on waiting until he came home. He tried again to persuade Vinnie to help Ross see what a dear price he would pay if he voted "not guilty." As the minutes turned into hours, Sickles even persuaded Vinnie—who, in addition to her reputation as a sculptress, was known for her beautiful voice—to sing for him. Hearing footfalls upstairs, coupled with occasional trips by Vinnie to the parlor door to talk to someone he could not see, Sickles was convinced that Ross truly was there. It may well have been Vinnie's mother at the door. The wait continued until 4 a.m., by which time Vinnie was in tears from dealing with Sickles and finally asked him to leave, telling him she was sure that Ross was going to vote for acquittal.[22] Vinnie's assertion that Ross was not home actually may have been true. If Ross were there, it seems logical that he would confront Sickles, even if he preferred not to, just to get rid of him and not burden Vinnie with entertaining Sickles for nearly four hours in the middle of the night. It is quite possible that Ross spent the night at the home of Perry Fuller, a neighbor whose wife was Vinnie's sister. It is known that both Ross and Senator Henderson had breakfast on the morning of the sixteenth at Fuller's house.

Knowledge of the connection between Vinnie Ream and Edmund Ross had also reached members of the press in early May. In a 1985 article, Mark A. Plummer cites a printed remark by an 1868 Kansas editor named Sol Miller who "hinted that Ross took his pleasures, not by the quart as drunkards do, but rather by the Ream."[23] There may not have been bolder references to Ream in the press, but there certainly were others. Such remarks were cheap and probably hurtful to Fannie, but there is no evidence to suspect Ross and Ream of anything improper.

Either the night before with Thomas Ewing Jr. or after breakfast at the Fullers', Ross wired his response to D. R. Anthony and others: "I do not recognize your right to demand that I shall vote either for or against conviction. I have taken an oath to do impartial justice according to the Constitution and laws, and trust that I shall have the courage and the honesty to vote according to the dictates of my judgment and for the highest good of the country."[24]

The oath that Ross referred to in the telegram had been administered by the chief justice to each senator, individually, before the trial began. This would have been a solemn promise in Ross's mind, not one that he would take lightly.

The closing arguments of Thaddeus Stevens for the prosecution and Henry Stanbery for the defense summarized the issues facing all senators, especially those senators who understood the importance of voting without prejudice.[25] Stevens's arguments were given at a time when he was extremely weak. He did his best to stand but eventually had to sit down; halfway through, he had to give his prewritten summation to Benjamin Butler, who read the remainder of his arguments. Stevens argued that "the only question to be considered is, is the respondent violating the law?" Specifically, Stevens argued, "When Andrew Johnson took upon himself the duties of his high office he swore to obey the Constitution and take care that the laws be faithfully executed. That, indeed, is and has always been the chief duty of the President of the United States. The duties of legislation and adjudicating the laws of his country fall in no way to his lot. To obey the commands of the sovereign power of the nation, and to see that others should obey them, was his whole duty—a duty which he could not escape, and any attempt to do so would be in direct violation of his official oath."[26]

Among the counterarguments of the defense was the important assertion by Stanbery that the president was held to a different standard than an ordinary citizen, since he was the head of one of three coordinated branches of government:

... the President is not a ministerial office. His function is not merely to execute laws, but to construe them as well. The Constitution makes this too clear for question. It does not, it is true, vest him with judicial power, which always implies the exercise of discretion. It vests him with the executive power, but, nevertheless, with a discretion as to the mode of its execution. The Constitution contemplates that, in the exercise of that executive power, he may be involved in doubt and perplexity as to the manner of its exercise, and, therefore, gives him the privilege of resorting to his Cabinet officers for advice. The Constitution binds him by an oath not only faithfully to execute his office, not merely to carry into execution laws of Congress, but also, to the best of his ability, to preserve, protect, and defend the Constitution itself. . . .

When, therefore, this tenure-of-office act came to be considered by the President in reference to his purpose to remove Mr. Stanton from office, he had a right and it was his duty to decide for himself whether the proposed removal of Mr. Stanton was or was not forbidden by the act. As yet that act had received no construction by the judicial department, nor had the President any authority to send the act to the Supreme Court, and require the judgment of that court upon its true meaning. The Constitution gave him no right to resort to the judges for advice.[27]

The only avenue for the president to test the validity of the Tenure Act was to defy the law and have his actions become a judicial matter leading to an opinion in the Supreme Court. In effect, the president had as much authority to question the constitutionality of a law as Congress did to enact it. The vast majority of Congress was not interested in going to court except the court of impeachment. This was an opportunity to rid themselves of the man who stood in the way of congressional Reconstruction. Even the recusant senators were apprehensive about the president seeking revenge and interfering even more with Reconstruction if he remained in office. Senators Fessenden and Grimes insisted on some assurance from Johnson that he would not interfere with Reconstruction.

On Friday, May 4, Ross went even further than Fessenden and Grimes when he asked the president, through acting attorney general Orville H. Browning, to show his good intentions by sending the new constitutions of Arkansas and South Carolina to Congress for approval. These were the first of the new state constitutions drawn up under the provisions of congressional Reconstruction. Although Secretary Welles encouraged Johnson not to send them to Congress, Browning and defense counsel Stanbery assured him it was essential to secure Ross's vote.[28] Johnson submitted the constitutions the next day. On June 22 Arkansas would become the first southern state to be accepted back into Congress since Tennessee and the first whose constitution conformed to the provisions of the congressional Reconstruction Acts. In the days following, South Carolina and four other southern states likewise rejoined the Union with similar constitutions. Ross's request of the president was significant because it was, in effect, his promise to acquit if the president submitted the Arkansas and South Carolina constitutions. Since these constitutions included acceptance of the Fourteenth Amendment, which Johnson opposed, Johnson was giving in to save his presidency. Ross had clearly made up his mind by May 4 in favor of acquittal based upon his belief that the House managers had not proved their case. By withholding public declaration of his intentions, Ross was leveraging the strength of his vote to help achieve the ends of congressional Reconstruction. Of course, what Ross really preferred was a lengthy postponement of the trial vote and possibly never having to vote at all.

At the time of the impeachment there were fifty-four senators representing twenty-seven states. Of these, twelve were Democrats, and their votes for acquittal were assured. Of the forty-two Republicans, only thirty-six were needed for conviction, but by the time of the vote on May 16, it was certain that six Republicans would vote for acquittal. If any other senator voted to acquit, the ouster of Johnson would fail. Ross had still not firmly revealed his intentions, but by that morning it was reasonably certain he would vote "not guilty," with the probable exception of article 1.

A special dispatch to the *New York Times* on May 16 described the drama and outcome of the first article to be considered, article 11. This was the catchall article that was believed to have the best chance of finding the president guilty. While John F. Kennedy chose to use Ross's own words to describe the events of that day,[29] the words of the *Times* correspondent give a somewhat broader, more objective description. Should Ross's words in any way be found self-serving, the same cannot be said of the *Times* article.

The morning opened with the most agreeable atmosphere we have yet had in this cold, chilly month of May. Possessors of tickets started early for the Capitol, and before 11 o'clock the best seats were all taken. Senators made their appearance very slowly. At 11:30 o'clock when the Senate was called to order scarce a quorum was present. They dropped in one by one, seeming loath to step up to the task. The friends of conviction were heavy-hearted, for they also knew the last condition of Ross. . . .

At 12 o'clock the galleries were crowded. Every ticket was in use. The diplomatic box overflowed as it rarely does. The reporters' gallery was as usual, inundated by the friends of easy natured Mr. Wade, representing unheard of advocates of his aspirations. [As president pro tempore of the Senate, Benjamin Wade, a Radical, was next in line for the presidency.] The day was propitious for fine toilettes, and the dramatic effect was brilliant outside. Thousands lingered in the corridors or strolled in the beautiful grounds, inhaling the fresh odor of new-mown hay, waiting to catch the first vibration of the result. Down on the streets many more thousands waited in groups and in crowds, to hear the first note from the Capitol. . . . Everywhere and everything, and everybody but time, waited on impeachment.

Twelve o'clock rang out from the city bells, and the black-robed Chief Justice assumed the chair, while Ben Wade assumed his Senatorial seat with a determination fully aroused to vote or die. The sick Senators had begun to arrive. Conkling, pale, but straight and firm and dignified, as he always is, sat erect in his chair. Morton was also there, determined and sincere, promising to be the statesman of the Senate. Howard was brought in leaning on the arms of friends, walking very feebly, and tottering into his chair with a heavy shawl thrown around him. Mr. Grimes was brought in by four men in an invalid's chair, and allowed to recline on his side without taking his seat. . . . On the floor were Sickles, Gen. Holt, Anthony Trollope, and a score more of notables.

. . .

The eleventh article is now read. The Clerk calls "Mr. Anthony." Mr. Anthony rises in his seat, and the Chief Justice says, "Mr. Senator Anthony—How say you, is Andrew Johnson, President of the United States, guilty or not guilty of a high misdemeanor, as charged in this article?" Mr. Anthony, with the poise of self-possession and the demeanor of an elegant gentleman, answers in clear, decided tones, "Guilty."[30]

The *Times* description carries on with details of many of the votes, including those of Fessenden, Fowler, and Grimes, who was so ill he had to give his "not guilty" vote from a reclining position.[31] Each senator was asked the same question: "How say you, is Andrew Johnson, president of the United States, guilty or not guilty of a high misdemeanor?" The *Times* reporter continued through the alphabet:

Then, came the President's son-in-law, Mr. Patterson, of Tennessee, quickly and with evident pleasure responded "not guilty." After him, Pomeroy and Ramsey, prompt and positive "guilty." Then a thousand pair of eyes shot into the very heart of the modest, quiet little man who rises, at the call of the name Ross. Nervously and quickly he responds, "not guilty." A suppressed condemnation is heard on all hands, and the fate of impeachment is sealed. The remaining votes cannot save it.[32]

Ross's description of the voting comes from his *Scribner's* article of 1892. In part it says, "Conscious that I was at that moment the focus of all eyes, and conscious also of the far-reaching effect, especially upon myself, of the vote I was about to give, it is something more than a simile to say that I almost literally looked down into my open grave. Friends, position, fortune, everything that makes life desirable to an ambitious man were about to be swept away by the breath of my mouth, perhaps forever."[33]

If there were other senators who were inclined to vote for acquittal, and there apparently were a few, they were not heard from; if they existed, those senators chose to protect their own interests rather than vote their consciences.[34] It was Ross's vote that allowed Johnson to escape, along with the votes of the other six recusants. It was courageous of all seven senators to cast "not guilty" votes, and in varying degrees they all paid for it.

On entering the Senate chamber on the morning of May 16, Ross had been met by Pomeroy, who in the presence of Thaddeus Stevens, supposedly by coincidence passing by, warned Ross that if he voted for acquittal it meant his political death and that bribery and corruption charges in the House were certain to follow as well.[35] Pomeroy later confirmed the story in somewhat softer terms, but what followed in the days immediately after the vote substantiates Ross's interpretation of the Pomeroy prediction.[36]

As soon as the voting on the eleventh article was completed, the chief justice ordered the reading and vote on the first article; but before the reading, Senator George Williams of Oregon moved for an adjournment of ten days until May 26. The postponement was a move to buy time, to find some way of inducing one of the recusants to reconsider on the ensuing votes. When the Senate recessed, the House of Representatives met immediately to vote on a proposal to investigate charges of bribery and corruption that may have influenced the voting on the eleventh article. The move was blatant intimidation against the seven renegade Republican senators in the hope that one of them had something to fear and might change his vote on one of the remaining articles to avoid an embarrassing public revelation. On May 19 Navy Secretary Gideon Welles made this notation in his frequently quoted diary: "Ross is abused most. He is to be investigated by the House, or his acts are, and the Senate will submit to the indignity."[37]

Historian David Dewitt reported that "[h]is colleague [Pomeroy], his constituents, his fellow-senators, swore to his previous statements favourable to conviction. His Indian office connection [possibly Fuller]; his visits to the studio of Vinnie Ream; his lodging at her mother's; his association with advocates of the President;—were exploited: the menace that, unless he redeemed himself from his corrupt apostasy, a chain of circumstantial evidence would be fastened about him and he himself pilloried before the nation, flashing like a drawn sword in the background."[38]

May 26 came, but before the vote was taken, a motion by Senator Lot M. Morrill of Maine was made to again delay the vote until June 23. Ross then moved that the date be pushed back to September 1. Fifteen senators voted yes to the Ross amendment, including five of the recusant senators, but the motion failed. Morrill's motion to wait until June 23 was then voted upon, with all the recusants voting "yes" except Ross, who surprised the others with a "no" vote that gave a glimmer of hope to the majority that he had been won over.[39] However, when the vote was taken on the second and third articles, the result of May 16 was identical. There was no sense in continuing a process that would simply repeat the same results, and the House managers gave up the fight to depose the president.

Two years had passed since Ross led his Saturday night attack on Jim Lane condemning Lane's support of Johnson's veto of the Civil Rights bill. Now Ross had come full circle and felt the wrath of his fellow Kansans far worse than Lane ever had. A newspaper editorial in the *Leavenworth Conservative*, one of many such editorials in Kansas, was merciless: "It was left for the State whose noblest citizen was John Brown, the State whose soil is hallowed all over with the blood of men, women, and children, the State which has only four words on its banner, 'Equal rights for all,' to be betrayed and outraged by this creature Ross. He is dead—dead to honor, dead to liberty, dead to Kansas. Let him go his own way. A half-civilized bushwhacker would spit in poor Ross's face if he should dare to speak to him about honor. Every man in the United States has read the news from Washington and instinctively felt that Ross from Kansas was a coward and a sneak. Wherever Ross lives or travels that record will follow him!"[40]

The same newspaper also ran the text of telegraphic responses sent to Ross on May 16. One was from D. R. Anthony, who had sent the "demand" telegram to Ross and Pomeroy the day before and to whom Ross had responded with his "I do not recognize your right to demand" telegram: "Your telegram received. Your vote is dictated by Tom Ewing, not your oath. Your motives are Indian contracts and greenbacks. Kansas repudiates you as she does all perjurers and skunks." A second telegram was from a Kansas

Supreme Court justice, L. D. Bailey: "Probably the rope with which Judas hanged himself is lost, but the pistol with which Jim Lane committed suicide is at your service."[41]

In Topeka a group of former Eleventh Regiment soldiers hanged Ross in effigy in the square between Kansas Avenue and Sixth, not far from the place where the citizens of the town had once honored Ross with an American flag and flagpole installed in front of his newspaper office. The effigy incident was reported all over the country and identified the men as Ross's own soldiers. Henry Lindsey, the boy whom Ross had hired on the condition that he stop cursing, went to Lawrence to see Fannie Ross to assure her that the men of Company E had nothing to do with it. Lindsey had been there and said, "A lot of us were gathered on the corner, watching and feeling greatly puzzled. One of the boys said, let's go tear it down, but the others decided to let them alone since it might make more trouble." Lillian Leis commented that Lindsey "seemed to feel very deeply the avalanche of abuse heaped on father, also at a loss to understand the reason."[42]

Surely for Ross the saddest aspect of 1868 was the effect his votes had on his family. Leis wrote that they were as much in the dark about his position on impeachment as anyone. Even his brother William, who was in Washington at the time and who corresponded with Fannie and her children, did not know how his brother would vote. Perhaps the first correspondence from Ross to his family after the vote on the eleventh article was dated May 22. Leis described the day the letter arrived. "The boys coming from the Post Office one morning rushed in. Arthur with the letter in his hand—the letter which has since been widely published—and mother standing in the parlor very tense." The letter read: "Don't be discouraged, dear wife, it's all coming out all right. This storm of passion will soon pass away, and the people, the whole people, will thank and bless me for having saved the country by my single vote from the greatest peril through which it has ever passed, though none but God can ever know the struggle it has cost me. Millions of men are cursing me today, but they will bless me tomorrow. But few knew of the precipice upon which we all stood on Saturday morning last. Your aff Hus."[43]

Together the family all wrote back to him with letters of encouragement, but Fannie's letter must have been the one that touched him the most. It is not known what she wrote, but later the family learned from Mrs. Ream, Vinnie's mother, that when he read the letter, apparently as he sat with the Reams for dinner, he broke down and had to leave the table. Leis wrote, "I have not found it [the letter] among his papers. I think he always destroyed the family mail."[44] Leis's remark explains why so few of Fannie's letters are extant.

At the end of May 1868 there was nothing to suggest that Ross's participation in the impeachment trial of the president was anything other than honorable, with the exception of the speculation of bribery by Ross's bitter Republican colleagues. Ross did not give a written explanation for his vote at the time of the impeachment trial as the other recusants did, but he did explain his vote in two speeches he made before the Senate, on May 27 and July 27:

> In this spirit I discharged my duty as a member of the court of impeachment. I voted to admit all the evidence offered by both the prosecution and the defense, so that the Senate, sitting as a court and jury, as judges of law and fact, might sift it all and determine the cause with no fact shut out by technical rule which bore on the guilt or innocence of the accused; and when I voted on the several articles of impeachment I cast out of the scale, as far as I was able, all mere party considerations, and weighed the cause as the Constitution and laws and my oath demanded.[45]

> But I saw, or thought I saw, in the conviction and removal of the president upon inadequate testimony, and upon accusations mainly of a partisan character, the establishment of a precedent which would render every future President liable to successful impeachment whenever he found himself in a minority in Congress. . . .
> Viewing the question thus I felt that it would be cowardly to act otherwise; that I should be untrue to the principles of justice, untrue to my party, untrue to myself, and untrue to my country, if I permitted my judgment to be overborne by party clamor or a dread of party indignation.
> It will not do to say that it was my duty to subordinate my individual views to those so earnestly and so clearly entertained by the great mass of the party on so grave a question as this. In the first place, I was sworn to act according to the law and the testimony in the case, while my constituents were not. My own judgment was

worth more to me than that of those who were thousands of miles away, and could by no possibility be as thoroughly informed of the facts as I was expected and ought to be.

In the second place, I was sent here to vote on all questions according to my own best judgment, and not to follow the lead of any one, or any number of peers, however learned or distinguished they might be. My convictions are my own, and whenever I shall not have the courage and the honesty to follow them I will vacate my seat, and give the people I represent an opportunity to fill it with one who has. Confident that I am right, and that history will vindicate my act, I can well afford to await the calm and unimpassioned judgment of time. . . .

. . . Impeachment cannot in any sense be said to be properly a party cause. Articles of impeachment may originate in partisan considerations, may be preferred for the accomplishment of important partisan ends, but when they come to the Senate for trial they are at once divested of all such aspects. The highest judicial officer of the Government presides, and each Senator is sworn by a special oath of an entirely different import from that under which he discharges his legislative duties.

When sworn as members of the court of impeachment we took an oath to impartially try the President. Now, what did "impartiality" mean in this connection? Did it mean to decide the case according to the desire and expectation of the Republican Party? Did it mean to decide it according to our own individual preconceived opinions? By no means. It meant simply what it said, that we would hear and determine the cause "impartially," without bias from any cause or source whatever, without reference to our own political sentiments and predilections, and without reference to the political sentiments of our constituents, fairly and candidly, on its merits, "according to the Constitution and Laws." . . .

To deliberately trample upon law and established forms was the only way in which impeachment could have been carried as a party measure, and that no party, however strong, can afford to do. When we depart from those forms of law by which we seek the ends of justice we at once inaugurate confusion and anarchy, and we substantially do that when we subordinate the issue of a trial, largely judicial in its nature, to the behests of party will.[46]

The impeachment process had been devoid of objectivity and fueled by the emotions of an electorate that did not have to pay heed to legalities. The Constitution didn't matter; getting rid of Johnson was all that mattered. The constant threats and badgering that Ross and the others experienced was disgraceful. Certainly there was some leeway for political lobbying to apply pressure to the recusants, unlike the absolute prohibition of intimidating juries in United States courts, but the line surely was crossed with various threats including bribery investigations, political ostracism, false rumors harmful to reputations, and even threats of physical harm. Looking at the process objectively in later years, when tempers and emotions subsided, it was clear that the recusant seven were the wiser of those men who participated in the impeachment in the spring of 1868. Had the Radicals in Congress been successful, Johnson would have been put out of office for purely political reasons. The impeachment trial itself would have been a mockery, and in fact it was pure theater to the majority of participants whose minds were made up before the trial began. As David Dewitt pointed out, why bother with a trial if the outcome was already known? Just take a vote, and if half the House and two thirds of the Senate agreed, the president could be deposed; a trial would be superfluous.[47]

The abuse that Ross felt from his Senate colleagues, his constituents, and Kansas newspapers in late May must have left him with a muddle of thoughts and emotions and wondering why he ever agreed to assume Jim Lane's Senate seat. It would not be surprising if his thoughts went to that day twelve years before when he crossed into Kansas leading a wagon train of pioneers, and there to meet him were Jim Lane and Samuel Pomeroy. These were men he would come to greatly admire, and yet Lane was now tragically dead and Ross was about to declare war on Pomeroy.

CHAPTER FOURTEEN

EMPTY ACCUSATIONS

Ross Fights Back

If there be on this floor a Senator who had received or offered, or agreed to take a bribe of any nature whatever to convict or acquit the President, let him be proven guilty before a committee of his peers and expelled.

—Ross, speech to the United States Senate, May 27, 1868

⌐ EDMUND ROSS GAVE A SPEECH before the Senate on May 27, 1868, the day following the collapse of the impeachment trial; it was a speech that began a new phase in his political life. He was no longer a quiet, low-profile member of the Senate. Now Ross was an angry and outspoken fighter who took the charges of bribery and corruption leveled at him very personally. Ross spoke in favor of a resolution introduced by Senator Garrett Davis, a Democrat from Kentucky, that a three-member Senate committee be formed to look into the possibility that "threats and intimidation, and other unlawful and improper means" were used to influence the way senators voted in the impeachment trial. This committee would conduct its investigation separately from the House inquiry. After some debate on the wording of the resolution, the president pro tempore recognized Senator Ross. Ross made it clear that such an investigation should look at possible illegal or unethical activities by all members of the Senate. It was not a long speech, but it was eloquent and charged with anger: "If there be on this floor a Senator who has received or offered, or agreed to take a bribe of any nature whatever to convict or acquit the President, let him be proven guilty before a committee of his peers and expelled. If there be one who has yielded his convictions to threats, let us expose the coward to the merited contempt and scorn of a courageous people. If there be one who attempted to bully or bribe a fellow Senator, let us know the fact, and determine whether he is a fit associate for us in this high council chamber."[1]

Ross was beginning to fight back against colleagues whose intent it was to do him harm because of his acquittal vote. With this speech he was putting them on notice that he would no longer sit idly by while his reputation was impugned. "I have borne in silence until now assaults on my character and motives as a member of the court, such as few, if any, of my associates have endured. . . . But the trial is now ended, and I have something to say in vindication of my conduct during it, which it is both my right and my duty to say."[2]

Ross was specific about the way he thought the proposed Senate investigation should be handled. He abhorred the secret inquiry in the House. He demanded that any Senate inquiries be both open and thorough. In addition he insisted that the Senate "call on the House for copies of all the testimony . . . , so that if any evidence of corrupt practices by or toward any Senator, whether he be one of those voting for or against conviction, be in possession of the board, it may not fail to be brought to the attention of the Senate."[3] Ross invited any man or board to bring evidence against him, confident that no legitimate charges could be filed. Ross spoke with clarity and to the point. He had discovered a far different political world in Washington from what he had imagined. He disliked it, and, in no uncertain terms, he shared his anger at what this political system was doing to him. "Mr. President, I feel that this charge is heralded over the land and evidence ostentatiously sought to sustain it to make me a scapegoat for the egregious blunders, weaknesses, and hates which have characterized this whole impeachment movement; itself a stupendous blunder from its inception to the present time."[4]

Ross was unhappy with a number of fellow senators, but none more than his Kansas colleague Samuel Pomeroy. It was, after all, Pomeroy who had promised him that charges of bribery would be brought against him. In the aftermath of the May 16 vote, charges of outright bribery involving Ross and the president were rampant throughout Kansas and much of the country. Virtually every Republican newspaper in Kansas condemned Ross, and most assumed he had sold his vote for "greenbacks."[5] It was difficult for Republicans, especially Radical Kansans, to believe that a Kansas senator could vote any way other than "guilty"; if he did, he could only have done so for money. When, in the days following the vote on article 11, Ross was seen entering the White House—as a committee chair Ross was often responsible for taking bills to the White House for the president's signature—Congressman James G. Blaine was reported to have said, "There goes the rascal to get his pay." Years later Blaine would apologize for the remark and attest to Ross's good character.[6]

While Edmund Ross likely had many opportunities to enrich himself by yielding to temptations offered through the power of either his pen or his political position, the fact is that he lived in very modest circumstances. That he would accept a bribe of money is not likely, and equally unlikely that such would be offered by a president who was already in enough trouble. However, money is not the only currency of bribery. During June and July of 1868 there unfolded a scenario involving political patronage that suggested Ross might have traded his vote for political favors. That possibility cannot be overlooked, but it must also be recognized how the political patronage of 1868 differed from patronage as we know it in twenty-first-century America.

Political favoritism and patronage was the accepted practice in the nineteenth century, particularly when a congressman or senator was of the same party as the president. Government jobs, especially the higher level jobs, were routinely doled out to help secure votes at election time and thus strengthen the party. All it took was a request from a senator or congressman of similar political persuasion for the president to take under consideration the recommended appointments. Abraham Lincoln detested the system, which took inordinate amounts of his time, especially in the months following his first election. Dreading the new onslaught of requests for government service postings after his second inaugural, he asked Senator Daniel Clark of New Hampshire, "Can't you and others start a public sentiment in favor of making no changes except for good and sufficient cause?"[7] Control of patronage was important: after all, the Tenure of Office Act was passed for the specific purpose of giving Congress more control over President Johnson's appointments.

Although Edmund Ross and Andrew Johnson were from different parties, Ross, who was a Moderate in reality, was politically somewhat closer to Johnson than either Senator Pomeroy or Congressman Sidney Clarke, the other two members of the Kansas delegation. Any request from Ross was likely to be looked upon with greater favor than requests from Pomeroy or Clarke, particularly after Ross's acquittal vote. Nonetheless, given the tone and frequency of favors requested of the president by Ross in June and July, it is reasonable to wonder if Ross may have been approached before May 16 by an intermediary promising political favors in return for voting "the right way" in the impeachment trial. Johnson, who must have been aware of Ross's drift away from Radical Republicanism, was known to have given Ross's patronage requests serious consideration both before and after the impeachment trial while ignoring requests from either Pomeroy or Clarke.[8]

The relationship between Ross and Pomeroy changed dramatically after May 16. In Pomeroy's words, his association with Ross was on as "cordial and intimate terms as any two colleagues, perhaps, in the Senate" until the fateful impeachment vote.[9] That vote, however, made it clear to Pomeroy that he did not control Ross and badly damaged any continued friendship between the two men. Congressman Clarke also despised Ross for his vote; but Clarke wanted Ross's job, a job he was unlikely to get unless he could defeat Ross in the next senatorial election.[10] A major key to being elected and, for that matter, staying in office, was the control of patronage. It was to Pomeroy's and Clarke's advantage that Johnson be convicted and that Ben Wade, the president pro tempore of the Senate and so next in line for the presidency, should become President Wade. With the very radical Wade of Ohio in the White House, key presidential appointments could be made to favor Pomeroy and Clarke, who in turn could overwhelm the patronage standing that Ross enjoyed.[11] In short, Pomeroy and Clarke wanted to put an end to Ross's senatorial career.[12]

A story appearing in the *Burlington (Kansas) Patriot* on June 20, 1868, suggests that Ross's recognition of a Pomeroy-Clarke conspiracy against him could have been a major reason for his acquittal vote.[13] While it is true that a guilty vote by Ross would have the effect of handing control of presidential patronage in Kansas to Pomeroy and Clarke, this outcome would have been the least of Ross's considerations. Clearly Ross anticipated the outrage with which an acquittal vote would be met in Kansas; he certainly knew that any political advantage he might gain from a "not guilty" vote would be far offset by the negative and lasting consequences he would face at home. Ross also ran the risk that any presidential appointees whose names originated with him would be rejected by an equally vengeful Senate.[14] No matter how Ross voted on May 16, he knowingly placed himself in serious danger of being a single-term senator, and it was for this reason that he sought to have the impeachment vote postponed as long as possible.

If Pomeroy and Clarke could not take advantage of presidential appointments because of Johnson's acquittal, Ross, because of his vote, certainly could and did. On June 6, Ross wrote the first of four letters to President Johnson seeking appointments. This first letter, marked "private," reveals Ross's motives and frame of mind more than the others. It also reveals that Ross had personally talked to the president some time earlier than June 6 about the appointment of Ross's friend Newton Robinson to replace a Mr. Wortham as southern superintendent of Indian affairs. He wrote: "I am very reluctant indeed to ask you to do an act which would disoblige or embarrass a gentleman whom I suppose to be an old personal friend of yours, but this appointment is one of such vital importance to me in the effort that I am called upon to make for my maintenance in consequence of my action on the impeachment, that I feel constrained to ask for the change at once." Ross went on to explain his plans to seek the defeat of Sidney Clarke at the polls in October. The letter reveals the depth of Ross's anger. "The possession of this superintendency in the hands of my friends will enable me at once to make war against Clarke, and the election being so near at hand, it is important that I should be able to commence the organization of my plans at once. Every day's delay is a loss of valuable time."[15]

The letter raises at least one important question: Could the June 6 reference to "our last interview" suggest that an arrangement between Ross and the president had been made before May 16? Such a meeting would seem to have been neither necessary nor likely for the reasons earlier cited: Johnson was already in enough trouble without risking a charge of bribery and, moreover, Ross had already promised, on May 4, to vote "not guilty" if the president submitted the constitutions of Arkansas and South Carolina, which Johnson did within twenty-four hours. The president therefore had Ross's word on May 4 and would not have had reason to doubt Ross's vote or to risk any further arrangement with him. Most likely, the request that Newton Robinson be appointed to the job of southern superintendent of Indian affairs was a matter of Ross taking advantage of the president's favorable opinion of him; and if such an appointment could mean the defeat of Sidney Clarke, a vocal opponent of Johnson, so much the better as far as the president was concerned.

The next extant letter from Ross to Johnson, dated June 23, again indicated that the two had discussed the matter of an appointment in advance of the actual request. This time Ross was requesting the appointment of Perry Fuller as commissioner of internal revenue. The letter does not tell us what position he was requesting for Fuller; it was simply understood. This would seem to be Ross's payoff to Fuller for his help, financial or otherwise, with the Kansas Legislature in January 1867. Ross writes, "My judgment is that now is the time to make the appointment if at all, and therefore I respectively request that if consistent with your own view his name be sent in tomorrow. . . . some very radical gentlemen who are his personal friends have been exerting themselves very actively in his behalf."[16] In using the phrase "if at all" Ross seems to be uncertain about the wisdom of the appointment, and he further gives the president an out by saying "if consistent with your own view." Ross also mentions Fuller's personal friends "exerting themselves very actively in his behalf," suggesting perhaps that Ross was not one of them. It is also true that Fuller was the son-in-law of Robert Ream, Ross's landlord and friend, so Ross may have been acceding to a request from Ream.

The president did comply with Ross's request, but Gideon Welles, the secretary of the navy, whose diaries as a cabinet member provide a wealth of information for historians, was unimpressed with Johnson's nomination of Fuller. In a June 25 entry he writes, "Perry Fuller, an improper selection for such a place, is nominated Commissioner of Internal Revenue." In the next sentence Welles goes on to record that Johnson "has hopes of renomination," a hope that Welles frankly thought was delusional and "beyond the bounds of probability."[17] Johnson likely hoped for Ross's support for a second term and therefore had an additional reason, besides his appreciation for Ross's acquittal vote, to comply with his requests. Fuller's nomination was not confirmed in the Senate, but he was later named as the collector of customs in New Orleans.[18]

The third request letter from Ross came on July 1 and had nothing to do with solidifying Ross's position with his Kansas constituents. Ross was using his influence as a senator to get the job of "special mail agent" for his brother William in Florida. William Ross had applied for the job with A. W. Randall, the postmaster general, who was willing to comply with the request but needed the approval of the president before making the appointment. In his letter Ross assured the president that William had lived in Florida for a year and a half and intended to make Florida his permanent home. The letter was short and to the point.[19]

On July 10 Ross sought appointments for three friends who, he assured the president, were gentlemen who "all stand high in the confidence of the people of the state [Kansas] to whom they are all well known as men of high moral character and first class business capacity." The men were N. A. Adams, who had served in the war with Ross and for whom Ross was asking an appointment as surveyor general in Kansas, R. W. Jenkins to be the agent of the Kiowa and Comanche Indians, and William H. Dodge to be agent for the Pottawatomie Indians. Ross left no doubt that these appointments would directly benefit him politically: "I am aware that I am asking a good deal of you, but I feel constrained to do so by the persistent efforts that are being made for my destruction and I also feel warranted in doing so by the warm assurances of kindly personal regard that I received from you."[20]

The Ross letters to Johnson do not answer the question of whether Ross had a prearranged deal with Johnson to vote "not guilty." What appears to be true is that by May 5, at the very latest, Ross had already decided to vote "not guilty." Based on his voting record during the impeachment trial, Ross certainly believed that Johnson was not guilty of the impeachment charges, but Johnson could not be sure of this. Ross was in a strong position to warn Johnson that he must cooperate with Congress on Reconstruction.[21] It was an astute bit of political maneuvering on Ross's part.

It is not surprising that the House managers who prosecuted the president were the same men who conducted the investigation of bribery and other illegal activities involving Ross and the other recusants. The irony was that they could find no illegal activities on the part of any of the seven Republican men who voted against conviction, but the same prosecutors could easily have found, if they had a mind to, much that was illegal and/or unethical about persons trying to influence a guilty vote. While the House managers failed to show any bribery connected to Edmund Ross, Benjamin Butler, leader of the House managers, was reported to have said early in May, referring to Ross, "There is a bushel of money; how much does the damned scoundrel want?"[22]

A story with a reasonable level of credibility involved the testimony of a post office agent for Kansas and New Mexico named Legate, who was called before the House committee specifically to testify about the activities of Ross and his friends. His testimony proved nothing damaging to Ross but did implicate Senator Pomeroy and his brother-in-law in an offer to sell Pomeroy's vote and the votes of two other senators for $40,000. The story, according to David Dewitt's 1903 book on the impeachment, involved a letter written by Pomeroy to Legate. Legate, who got his job as a result of Pomeroy's influence, showed the letter, dated April 16, 1867, to the postmaster general. In the letter Pomeroy promised that if the postmaster general or the president were ever in trouble, even if impeached, they could count on Pomeroy to "aid in getting them out, by word and vote." The postmaster general testified to the authenticity of the letter and even produced a photographic copy of it. A point of interest is the date of the letter, sent at the time the first impeachment investigation was just beginning, and more than a year before the House investigation of corruption related to the impeachment votes.[23] Pomeroy denied ever writing such a letter, and its authenticity could not be proven absolutely.

Without doubt, Ross's reputation was seriously damaged on May 16. If no grounds for charges of bribery were found—and none were—the accusations were inexcusable and illegal, exposing the ugliest side of politics: "Vote the way we want you to vote or we will ruin your reputation!" Without real evidence to the contrary, it is possible and reasonable to see Ross's motivation in the impeachment vote for what it likely was: an honest belief that the prosecutors had not proved their case. Some scholars, who looked at Ross's vote in the years following John Kennedy's profile of Ross, believe the help Ross sought from Johnson in June and July was the payoff for his vote or, at the very least, not what should be expected of an honorable senator. The truth is, there is no evidence that the patronage help Ross sought was arranged before the May 16 or even the May 26 vote. Ross's requests for Johnson's help with patronage were a common and acceptable aspect of political life at that time. Moreover, these requests were a far cry from the disgraceful conduct of those among Ross's colleagues who did try to influence his votes with threats and money.

If Ross was to continue as a senator, he had to learn to deal with the system both in Kansas and in Washington and use it in a manner as consistent as possible with his own ethical code. If that meant controlling patronage in his state by seeking the assistance of the president, so be it. Ross was prepared to fight for his place in the Senate rather than meekly serve out his term and then return to some semblance of his previous life in Lawrence. In essence he was willing, if reluctantly, to play the game of politics as it was understood in 1868. He was willing to forge ahead as best he could, doing what he had to do, and that probably meant manipulating patronage for some votes and the hope of honest judgment by at least some Kansas legislators.

The congressional spring session dragged on until July 27, with Ross ending the session with a blistering attack on the Senate. He started with a commentary on the Senate committee that was supposed to be investigating bribery and corruption. He would not have been surprised that the committee had accomplished nothing. Certainly there was much that was embarrassing to be uncovered in the investigation involving many senators, and for that reason, if no other, the investigation just never got started. "I had hoped that we would long since have been furnished with a complete report of the operations of this committee, with nothing held back. . . . Up to this time, however, now at the close of the session, no such report has been given us."[24]

Ross commented at some length on the secret House investigation as well. The final report of that committee was delivered just days before Ross's speech. Although the report found nothing conclusive to charge Ross or any other recusants with, the House committee was not spared Ross's wrath. He protested that "the testimony contained in this report was all taken in secret. No information was afforded me as to the charges that were to be investigated, what witnesses or whether any were to be called, no opportunity given for replication or explanation of circumstances that might otherwise be misconstrued. . . . Certainly I may claim it to be due to a Senator that he at least be allowed to know something of a proceeding designed to blacken his character, and degrade him from his high and honorable position, if not to face his accusers and their witnesses. The meanest criminal is guarantied this by the most sacred and obligatory of our laws."[25]

The House investigation sought whatever evidence it could to bring charges of bribery against the senators who voted against conviction, in particular Ross; but as Ross pointed out about the report, "[N]ot one word is said of the efforts made and persisted in during the entire trial, and even after the vote on the eleventh article, to improperly influence the court for conviction."[26] Ross taunted the Senate: "In regard to the promise of patronage for the defeat of the impeachment, if true, there may be two sides to that also. Was it, or was it not, true that the forty thousand offices of the country were farmed out, from the cabinet down to the cross-roads post office, in the interest of a cabal which had predetermined that one set of men should go out of office simply that another set might go in."[27] Just five years later the number of patronage jobs was estimated to be fifty thousand, this number significantly higher with all eleven secessionist states restored to the Union.[28]

And it wasn't just seven senators who were intimidated by the House committee. For her association with Edmund Ross, Vinnie Ream was threatened with eviction from her Capitol studio in late May. A lawyer named Charles W. Woolley, who had earned a good deal of money betting on the outcome of the trial, was detained by the House managers for contempt of Congress when he refused to answer all questions put to him. In seeking a place to detain him, the suggestion was made to remove Ream from her studio and confine Woolley there. Moving the life-sized clay sculpture would have destroyed it, and Vinnie pleaded her case to members of the House, urging them not to make such a foolish move. Ream's biographer Glenn Sherwood cited Horace Greeley's *New York Tribune* as saying that Woolley was being subjected to "'cruel and unusual punishment' by being locked up with Vinnie's Lincoln statue."[29] Benjamin Butler's comment on May 30 showed his callous nature with the comment "It is very clear that these rooms ought to be cleared out, and at once; because, without saying a word about the woman, whom, I believe, I never saw, she ought not to be left in rooms in this Capitol, where she is exposed to such suspicion. Let her and everybody else who visits her there be cleared out, and if the statue of Mr. Lincoln, which she is supposed to be making, is spoilt in so doing, as one of his friends I shall be very glad of it, for, from what I hear of it, I think it is a thing that will do neither him nor the country credit."[30]

Oddly, it was Thaddeus Stevens who came to Vinnie's rescue. Vinnie had done a bust of Stevens that he liked very much. Unlike Butler, Stevens believed Ream to be a rare talent and insisted that she be allowed to continue her work in the same room. This act of kindness toward Ream was among Stevens's last; he died on August 11, 1868. Stevens, for all his impassioned championing of civil rights for ex-slaves, probably did more harm for black civil rights by coalescing southern whites behind a defiant Democratic Party in the South. And even though Ross was Stevens's enemy during the trial, Ross would have admired Stevens for both his choice of burial site and his epitaph: "I repose in this quiet and secluded spot, not from any natural preference for solitude, but finding other cemeteries limited by charter rules as to race, I have chosen this that I might illustrate in my death the principles which I advocated through a long life, equality of man before his Creator."[31]

As for Congressman Clarke, Ross was not successful in unseating him in the October congressional election in Kansas, but two years later Clarke would be defeated, much to the satisfaction of Edmund Ross. Probably with some urging from Clarke, the Kansas State Legislature on January 18, 1869, considered a resolution asking for Ross to resign because of the impeachment vote. In a letter to Ross dated January 19, a Kansas legislator named C. C. Whitney reported that a group friendly to Ross had succeeded in defeating the resolution. Whitney cited the efforts of a gentleman named

Fitzpatrick in leading the defense of Ross and added, "Without wishing to seem importunate, I wish to say that Fitzpatrick ought to be remembered as soon as possible. Could not the Pattowatomie Agency be secured for him?"[32] Patronage was alive and well.

The years that Ross spent in the Senate were in a sense reminiscent of his years in the Civil War. He was serving his country as best he could, at times under difficult circumstances, which included lengthy separations from his home and family. When the prolonged spring session of Congress ended on July 27, exactly two years had passed since Ross arrived with his credentials from Kansas, and he probably had not seen his family since Christmas. Leis wrote movingly about his homecoming: "The session was a long one, and it was rather late when father returned. On the morning we expected him home, mother sent for a carriage to take us over the river to the station. Someone remarked to the driver of the carriage, loud enough so that my brothers heard—for it was a livery team, our carriage and horses having been sold—'You'll get that carriage spoiled. They are going to rotten egg him when he arrives.' We drove the span up to the station, mother remaining at home, so as to be there when father arrived. There was no appearance of any demonstration, and he failed to arrive, someone having persuaded him to stop over a train in Leavenworth. And he was not afraid—the time for caution had passed by. At evening we drove over again, and this time brought him home—very quietly. There really were no citizens of Lawrence who would lift a hand to injure him—the threats and abuse were entirely political. So after a long absence, we were again united."[33]

CHAPTER FIFTEEN

THE LAST TWO YEARS

A Working Senator

The Constitution intentionally made the office of the President one
with great powers, and such is the perfect balance and blending of
the functions of all the coordinated branches of the Government . . .
—Ross, speech to the United States Senate, March 24, 1869

⌁ EDMUND ROSS CONTINUED to have difficulty with his fellow senators
and fellow Kansans in the fall of 1868, but a strong, albeit smaller, base of
Kansans still admired him. The months between May and October seemed to
heal some of the wounds brought about by the impeachment and trial. While
some, if not most, of his Senate colleagues averted their eyes when passing
him in the Capitol, Ross had to feel honored when he received an invitation
to be the guest of honor at the groundbreaking for the Atchison, Topeka and
Santa Fe Railroad in Topeka in October. General C. K. Holliday, president
of the AT&SF and a longtime friend, had not forgotten Ross's strong advocacy of a rail system to serve all of Kansas, in particular his vision of a rail
line that would mimic the Santa Fe Trail. Although Ross was on the original
board of directors of the AT&SF, his tenure on the board and participation
in the development of the Santa Fe line was interrupted by his decision to
serve with the Kansas Volunteers during the Civil War. But he did not lose
his interest in railroad development. In a December 1862 letter to Fannie
he was excited to have news of the long-awaited line from Leavenworth to
Topeka: "I have learned that the railroad from Leavenworth to Topeka has
commenced which gratifies me very much. I think I will take a trip over it to
Leavenworth when I get home. The children shall all go too."[1]

The complications of getting the AT&SF on the ground, however, were protracted, involving the securing of adequate financial backing, rights-of-way across Indian land, and federal land grants—all further delayed by the years lost during the Civil War. Ross was not active in any of these stages of development. Still, in large measure it was his inspiration that got the Santa Fe started, and it was appropriate that he should be the dignitary to turn the first shovel of dirt. The ceremony took place on Washington Street in Topeka on October 30, 1868. The *Topeka Leader* reported (with some inaccuracies regarding Ross's years in the army and the Senate) that "after an absence of four years in the Army of the Union, and three years in the United States Senate, our friend Ross returns to Topeka in time to take up the shovel and throw the first earth upon the grading of this same railroad that ten years ago he helped organize. . . . [I]n speaking of these years of strife and turmoil, and reverting to his old established company, Col. Huntoon being present, Major Ross felt happy that he had been instrumental in helping to form a company that would in a few years, at most, be of so much consequence to the state."[2]

The best news for Ross involved his family. Ross's youngest and fifth living child, Kay, who turned two in August, was old enough to travel, making it possible for Ross to take his family with him to Washington that fall. Edmund and Fannie shared a three-room suite on the second floor of the Ream house with their daughters Lillian and Eddie and baby son Kay while the two older boys, Arthur and Pitt, lived across the street on the third floor of a rooming house. The two boys, now fifteen and thirteen, were enrolled in a business college and took dancing lessons from a Professor Maim, one would presume with some reluctance.[3]

Leis described the parlor of the Ream house as being more like a salon where there was "seldom an evening without several callers coming or going." Vinnie, talented not just as a sculptress, would often sing for guests. "She was bright, vivacious, ready to play an accompaniment for some singer. Or seated on a low chair, the harp beside her, ever ready with some song at request." With the Ross family living room directly above the Ream parlor, Vinnie's sweet voice could be heard, a pleasing experience for the Ross family and a strong memory for Leis.[4]

Probably on more than one occasion during the fall and winter of 1868–1869, the Ross family visited the Capitol Building. It was, after all, the principal attraction in the city. James Dabney McCabe, under the pseudonym Edward Winslow Martin, wrote in 1873 that it was "indescribably grand. The pure white marble glitters and shines in the sunlight, and the huge structure towers above one like one of the famed palaces of old romance."[5] A walk through the rotunda with its spectacular frescoed dome, eight vast canvases depicting pivotal events in American history, and the marble statue of Alexander Hamilton in the center would have been unlike anything ever seen by Ross's wife and children. Although there was a lot to see and remember, Lillian Leis's only recorded recollection was visiting Vinnie Ream in her studio in the basement of the Capitol. The clay model of Lincoln was in a corner, and Vinnie would climb "nimbly up the ladder chiseling here and there and keeping a chatter all the while." Leis told of people coming and going all day, curious to see how the statue was coming, and of Vinnie's patience with interruptions.[6]

Ross's family also had the opportunity to see the Senate in session and perhaps even Edmund Ross himself in action. But they did not see Ross give one of his most important speeches, as it was given late on the night of February 8, 1869, probably near eleven o'clock. The matter under consideration was a House resolution that ultimately established the Fifteenth Amendment to the Constitution with its two simple declarative sentences: "The right of citizens of the United States to vote shall not be denied or abridged by the United States or by any State on account of race, color, or previous condition of servitude" and "The Congress shall have power to enforce this article by appropriate legislation." As simply worded as the amendment is, the debate to arrive at its final form, and even its existence, consumed the better part of February in both houses of Congress and in a joint committee. The night of the Ross speech was particularly dramatic, with the somewhat subdued gaslight illuminating the Senate chamber. Ross cited three parts of the Constitution that he believed gave Congress the authority to simply enact a law that former slaves had a right to vote in all states, a law that could not be overruled by any state. However, most senators believed a constitutional amendment was necessary to override the long-held belief that only states decided voting qualifications. A congressional enactment would be the speediest course, in Ross's view. "But if gentlemen prefer the other . . . remedy—an amendment of the Constitution—let us have that."[7]

There was a simple justice to the amendment. It reflected a concept that Ross had so often articulated in his newspaper career and that compelled him to speak, but he did so hesitantly. Ross believed he was not the good debater that many of his legally trained colleagues were—men he admired like William Pitt Fessenden, James Grimes, and Lyman Trumbull—so he simply didn't debate. But being a skilled writer, Ross was a good orator whose speeches were clear and well reasoned. His February 8 speech began almost apologetically: "Mr. President, conscious of my inability to handle instructively a subject of such magnitude as the one under consideration, I had determined to remain a listener, and to cast a silent vote for the proposed amendment."[8] Ross's compassion for former slaves was evident:

> For it will not be denied that the negro has the same interests at stake; that he is under the same obligations and responsibilities for the preservation of the public peace, for the conservation of the public good and the advancement of the public weal in all respects as ourselves. He is endowed with the same aspirations for improvement, for a higher and better life, and with the same instincts which are common to us all. He is susceptible to the same motives which move us all, capable of the same degree of cultivation and the same ambition to achieve it. . . .
>
> . . . Slavery is not dead, however, until all its supports are removed. It will never die until the negro is placed in a position of political equality. . . . Without the ballot he is the slave of public prejudice and public caprice—the foot-ball of public scorn.[9]

Ross felt strongly about a related issue debated that February: states' rights versus power centralized within the federal government. Among the senators who opposed passage of the Fifteenth Amendment was fellow recusant Lyman Trumbull, who believed it was the right of states to decide voting qualifications; but when the voting outcome became evident, even Trumbull voted for the amendment.[10] Ross's position was unequivocal from the beginning:

> I am not a friend of the principle of decentralization, as it is termed—I call it disintegration—which for many years characterized our form of government. One of the inevitable sequences of our great civil war was the demonstration of the necessity for a strong, centralized Government, such as we never had, and such as Washington, and Hamilton, and many of the fathers contended for—a Government able to act promptly and effectively when assailed from within or without; a Government able to protect

itself against all contingencies, near or remote, liable to threaten its existence or embarrassment. . . .

. . . Who is to stand as the champion of the individual and enforce the guarantees of the Constitution in his behalf as against the so-called sovereignty of the States? Clearly no power but that of the central Government is or can be competent for their adjustment, and it is equally clear that unless the power may be enforced by the central Government, that Government fails of the object of its institution and develops within itself the seeds of its own disintegration; for when the Government fails to protect the individual in any of his rights, it forfeits to the degree of that failure its claim upon his allegiance and support.[11]

The February 8 speech was important because it publicly reiterated beliefs that to a large extent had motivated Ross's life choices and the goal of social equality to which he remained committed. In March and April he would speak about other issues that mattered greatly to him, but achieving freedom and justice for black Americans was the most important of all. When Ross finished speaking near midnight, Senator Thomas Hendricks moved for an adjournment. Except for a dinner break, the Senate had been in session since noon. When Hendricks's motion was put to a vote, an overwhelming number of senators voted to continue. The debate lasted another twelve hours, adjourning at noon on February 9. The Fifteenth Amendment would be ratified by the states just one year later.

Passage of the Fifteenth Amendment by both houses of Congress on February 26, 1869, was a significant accomplishment, but the wording did not assure all the safeguards Ross had hoped for. Although former slaves were protected at the ballot box in regard to race, color, and former condition of servitude, the intent of the amendment could be easily circumvented—and was in the years and decades to come—on such grounds as literacy, property ownership, and other contrived means.

Slavery and its related issues had been a part of Ross's life since he was in his teens, but the impeachment of the president was the issue that dominated his senatorial career. At the core of the impeachment trial was the Tenure of Office Act. Ross had originally voted in favor of the law, but in the course of the trial he came to realize that it enhanced the power of the legislative branch at the expense of the executive. When a bill to abolish the tenure law was introduced in the House of Representatives, Ross delivered a speech in favor of repeal. He had nothing personal to gain by pursuing the end of the Tenure Act. Andrew Johnson was out of office by that time, so there was no political favor at stake. Ross understood that the law fundamentally was unconstitutional. Although he apologized for being "unlearned in the law," his argument on March 24 was clear and sound. "The balance between the coördinate branches is seriously disturbed, if not destroyed. The measure of power which is lost to the executive is absorbed by the legislative department. Power is always aggressive, and its tendency is to accumulate to itself, no matter in whose hands it is placed."[12] Even though there were a fair number of senators and representatives willing to vote for the abolition of the Tenure of Office Act, it would be another eighteen years before that actually happened.

When it was convenient, Ross took one or more of his children with him on various errands, even on official business. On one occasion he took his six-year-old daughter Eddie with him to the White House, where Eddie met President Johnson. The president graciously gave Eddie a bouquet of flowers from his desk and asked for a kiss in return. He knelt down for the kiss that Eddie gladly gave.[13] It was odd that Ross enjoyed a cordial relationship with Johnson but not with Ulysses Grant, Johnson's successor. Odd but probably not unexpected. Ross's perceived disloyalty to his party during the impeachment proceeding was not easily forgotten nor forgiven, even though a "guilty" vote by Ross would have meant that Benjamin Wade, not Grant, became president.

Given the accidental way Ross had become a senator and given the remoteness of Kansas, both geographically and politically, nothing could have prepared him for the experience of arriving in the imposing Capitol. Any idealistic notion he may have held of how things should be in Washington were shaken. Soon enough he was exposed to the far less than idealistic way that work was accomplished. The control that party leaders insisted on enforcing, with serious sanctions for not conforming, was disturbing to him. As the pseudonymous Edward Winslow Martin noted in 1873, "Men who are not fit, either by reason of intellectual gifts, or the admiration and confidence of the people, to represent the great States of the Union, have found their way into the Senate, and the high standard of fitness for the position once set up by that body has been effectually, and most unfortunately lowered."[14] Although Ross did not have the legal training that Fessenden, Trumbull, Thomas Ewing Jr., and many others had, his knowledge of the foundation of the American system of government was excellent and in some ways not different from Andrew Johnson's background and understanding. Each man had an almost reverential respect for the United States Constitution. To that extent it is not surprising that Johnson and Ross were at least cordial and perhaps even experienced a degree of friendship in spite of political differences. Ross respected Johnson far more than he respected Benjamin Butler and Samuel Pomeroy and others who were supposed to be his allies but who, instead, despised him for not following their dictates.

Although Ross did his loyal Republican best to campaign for Grant, it was Senator Pomeroy and Congressman Sydney Clarke who had the new president's ear. Within his first month in office Grant was already supporting sweeping patronage changes in Kansas and most other states. Ross could, and perhaps should, have expected Grant to favor the other two members of the Kansas delegation, but he nonetheless made an appointment to confront Grant directly. Ross was hurt not only because he had been a supporter of General Grant but because Grant seemed not to recognize him as a fellow Civil War veteran, one of the very few serving in the Senate. Accounts differ about the meeting between Ross and Grant, but certainly it did not include smiles and handshakes. Leis gave us her account of the confrontation. "Finally he called on the President—and I think he was not received very graciously, but he stated his case—The President said—'Mr. Ross, I do not propose to be criticized.' Father replied—'Mr. President, I propose to criticize you.' And asked—'Am I to understand then, that this will continue to be your course'? 'You may,' was the answer. Father withdrew, went to the Senate, and began his opposition to Mr. Grant."[15]

In reaction to a story in the *New York Herald* published on April 13, 1869, reporting on the confrontation between Ross and Grant, Ross asked for the floor of the Senate to condemn the account which, the paper stated, had Ross "boiling over with rage." Ross quoted the story as claiming that President Grant had said sharply, "I have no intention to be dictated to, sir," and that, "muttering between his teeth," he had said, "I must decline to be annoyed any further on the subject," adding his "desire the interview should terminate." Ross reportedly replied, "You and your desires can go to hell."[16]

Ross claimed that even more outrageous versions of the meeting were dispatched throughout the country, and especially to Kansas, by "parties interested in manufacturing public opinion against myself, who were witnesses to that interview, and knew that those statements were false."[17] Ross also felt compelled to give his version as a courtesy to the president. "I feel it my duty to say that on the occasion referred to, no words inconsistent with the strictest rules of propriety and decorum, found utterance from either of the parties to that interview."[18] One of the few individuals to witness the exchange, according to the *New York Herald*, was Senator Zachariah Chandler, a Radical Republican from Michigan.[19] Senatorial propriety would not have allowed Ross to specify who else was in the room at the time, but having the news article read into the record with Chandler's name attached allowed Ross to politely identify Chandler as the one who falsely reported on the Grant-Ross exchange. Chandler had a history of denouncing non-Radicals. In a speech before the Senate on July 20, 1867, Chandler attacked Republican conservatives, in particular William Pitt Fessenden of Maine, calling them "perverts" and declaiming, "Sir, the path of conservative republicanism is as clearly marked by tombstones as the great highway to California by the carcasses and bones of dead mules. No man can mistake its path, because the tombstones are scattered thick all along the route. Here lies the body of a recusant: a man who could not be trusted by the people."[20] Chandler would have savored the chance to witness the Ross-Grant exchange and to make the most of it and could possibly have been in the room with Ross and Grant by design. For Ross to have told the president to "go to hell" is not consistent with his long record as a levelheaded, rational person who detested any form of cursing, but it nevertheless may have been true. The meeting between Ross and Grant was a turning point for Ross. If he had entertained any hope of retaining his seat in the Senate, it surely was clear after their meeting that the hope was minimal at best. The truth of what happened at the confrontation is probably somewhere between the unreliable newspaper account and Lillian Leis's biased story. The sense of Ross's April 20 speech is one of frustration, perhaps even frustration that took him beyond the bounds of propriety with the president. Ross's frustration was not only with Grant but with a political system that favored the likes of Pomeroy and Clarke.

Ross found it offensive that capable men were replaced with others who were less than qualified, for strictly political reasons. He was offended in particular that Civil War veterans were replaced by "skulkers" and "men notoriously unfit for any public trust." He cited several examples: "In one instance a gallant soldier, eminently qualified for the position he held, and who will go a cripple to his grave, is displaced by a man who not only enjoyed the security of his fireside during the war, but is known to have been a proslavery sympathizer during the border ruffian disturbances of the then

Territory." He also emphasized that nearly all new appointments were men who defamed him and who were personally hostile to him. "A combination of my colleagues from Kansas in Congress has been formed to drive me from political life because I have dared to defy the dictation of party when I believed that other objects than the country's good were sought to be subserved thereby, and I fear the President has been deceived into giving that combination his powerful aid. Hence the sweeping and unjust removals of officeholders, chiefly Republicans and soldiers, . . . and as an important part of that party machinery which is being used for my destruction."[21]

Ross had not been hesitant to use patronage to his own advantage; he really had no choice but to go with the system. He claimed he did not favor the removal of anyone from office unless for "good and sufficient cause," as Lincoln had once suggested.[22] If Ross can be believed, there was more than a fine line between his "ethical" patronage and Grant's "reckless appointments," but it was patronage in both cases.

It was about the time of Ross's April speech that his family returned to Kansas. The end of the special session of the Forty-first Congress came just two days after the Ross speech, but Ross, like many of his fellow senators, remained in Washington for some weeks to clear up unfinished business. In a June 2 letter to Fannie, Ross said he still wasn't able to fix the time for returning home, but he hoped it would be very soon. He was following up on matters involving both railroad and Indian legislation. "The Secretary of War talks very kindly, and I feel sure is ready to do what I ask, but is taking time to deliberate a little too long, I think. I want to wait here until both these matters are finally settled, as if I go away before that, I fear they will be greatly delayed."[23] This was a sad and lonely time for Ross. His family was gone, his prospects for remaining in office extraordinarily thin, his friendships limited. One can easily imagine him preferring the pressures of the impeachment trial; at least then he was not ignored.

The Ross family was probably reunited by mid-June in Lawrence. Little is known about Ross's activities that summer except that Lillian Leis remembers it as a pleasant time, with Edmund and Fannie having a lot of time together. Leis records that the two traveled often but doesn't say where they went. There is some indication that Ross gave a patriotic speech at a Fourth of July gathering in Lawrence. He remained away from Washington until the beginning of the second session of the Forty-first Congress. That probably means Ross was back in Washington before the end of November of 1869, with the actual start date for the session the first Monday in

December. This time Fannie and the children remained in Lawrence. Leis records that life for Fannie and the children was more comfortable at home, and she says there were financial reasons. She indicates that there was gossip, as "a great many people concerned themselves over our arrangements, commenting and criticizing, as many will do."[24]

That there were financial reasons for the family to remain in Lawrence is clear from the letters Ross wrote to Fannie. There was another reason unmentioned by Leis: Fannie was pregnant again and probably unwilling to travel. What is also clear in the letters is Ross's loneliness without his family, the continued frustrations with his job and dealing with colleagues and members of the press. Detecting Ross's feelings in his June 2 letter is just that, detection, a reading between the lines, but in his letter home of December 15, the loneliness and frustration of his circumstances are plainly stated. "I have not heard from you since I left home. What is the matter? Surely some of the children can get time to write. . . . I am strongly tempted sometimes to give up and try to get into some business which will permit me to be at home. I begin to feel that even a morning paper is preferable to this kind of life."[25]

On December 29 Ross wrote to Fannie and included a check for forty dollars. Most of Ross's letters included money for Fannie to manage the household. Usually his checks were in the range of twenty to one hundred dollars. He also told her about a loan he was arranging that he expected to be firmed up quite soon. He was apparently going to use that money to pay a note owed to a man named Read. Without the loan money he was only able to make a partial payment, but he was confident he would clear matters up within a week or two. Ross's monthly income as a senator was slightly more than $400, out of which he had to pay for room and board in Washington, make a mortgage payment, and supply Fannie with household money, in addition to miscellaneous expenses.

The bulk of the December 29 letter dealt with a news article in which a correspondent had interviewed a man named Cornelius Wendell who, it was claimed, had knowledge of Ross, Fowler, Henderson, and Van Winkle having received money from friends of Johnson for their acquittal votes. Ross reported to Fannie that he had talked to Wendell that day and that Wendell denied ever saying any such thing to the correspondent and intended to seek a retraction. What Wendell did tell Ross, and probably the reporter, was that he knew of one of Ross's intimate friends having been approached to intercede with Ross to take a money bribe, but that Ross's friend had told the briber it would be useless to try it. The "intimate friend" is not identified in the letter. Ross told Fannie, "I am satisfied that it is all a concerted plan to keep me down and prevent my reelection." Ross at this point still hoped that he could somehow be returned to office.[26] It is interesting to note that at about the time Fannie received Edmund's letter, the *Kansas State Record* ran a lengthy article that reported on the Wendell interview with the correspondent. The reporter turned out to be from the *New York Sun*, and nowhere in the interview does Wendell talk about Ross, Fowler, Henderson, or Van Winkle. Wendell admits to having firsthand knowledge of attempted bribery on the part of friends of the president, but he states that Johnson had no knowledge of what was happening and would not have approved if he had.[27]

Another letter dated March 6, 1870, reveals more about the financial problems Ross was dealing with. He tells Fannie that he received her letter of February 27 and that he had also received a letter from Lillian, who was away at school.[28] Ross explains to Fannie that he had a draft for thirty dollars ready to send home, but he decided to send it to Lillian, who needed to make arrangements to travel back to Lawrence. To Fannie he writes, "I enclose $5 in this which is all I have in my pocket now and send it, thinking it may be of some use to you and will send some more within a day or two." Ross then goes on to say that he has "made arrangements for a loan of a few thousand dollars. And this time I feel sure of getting it, and in the course of a couple of weeks at farthest you can then get a sewing machine."[29] The loan he expected in December apparently did not materialize.

Ross's thoughts during this period are centered on the idea of having a nicer home in Lawrence, suggesting that he was comfortable with the idea of not serving a second term: "I think it would be a good plan to buy the house on Tennessee Street, which you speak of, if you can sell the one where we live. Judge Hendry has the sale of it and the owner is now here [Washington]. I will see him about it the first time I meet him and see how it can be bought." An even longer-range plan for Edmund and Fannie was to build a home on two lots they owned in Lawrence. Having a nice home is a recurring theme with Ross. He finishes the letter by saying that he had another picture made of himself, which he thinks Fannie will like a lot.[30]

The very next day, Ross wrote to Fannie to tell her he had seen Colonel Bowler, who owned the house she spoke of. The house was under a court order to be sold. An attorney named Riggs (probably Ross's good friend) in Lawrence was handling the sale for Bowler, and Ross advised Fannie to see him immediately.[31] On March 28 Ross wrote again about the house and wanted to know if Fannie had made any headway. He clearly was very eager to own the house and wanted Fannie to do her best to buy it. This time he also enclosed a draft for one hundred dollars.[32]

On April 4 Ross sent Fannie another draft for one hundred dollars and a rambling kind of letter covering a number of diverse subjects. He reported that he was well but life was "very lonely and dull." Ross was also disappointed that Fannie did not like his latest photograph. "I thought it was very good and I had it put in the gallery of photographs of the Senate which [Mathew] Brady has been putting up. I am getting so fleshy that I thought I looked better without a beard." Ross also tells of a report being circulated that "I am drinking very hard. Have you heard anything of it?" He also mentions that a man named Bob Wilson was supposed to plant trees on their property. He had arranged for it the previous summer and forgot, until this letter, to tell Fannie. He closed by asking if she knew any more about the house on Tennessee.[33]

A letter on April 19 was short and again included a draft for one hundred dollars. There is no mention of the house on Tennessee Street. It appears that the sale did not take place. He says that he is doing well, but "I am beginning to feel as though I did not care if I came back here or not. . . . I shall never come back here to stay unless I can bring my family with me."[34]

Although Ross's letters home do not say much about his senatorial life, and although in later life he would write, "The record of my five years of membership of the Senate was practically devoid of public interest except in the matter of the impeachment and trial of President Andrew Johnson,"[35] the truth was that he did accomplish a fair amount. In looking at just the Forty-first Congress, Ross sponsored at least forty bills or resolutions, some of which are notable, some routine, but all important to his state and in some cases beyond Kansas. For example, he sponsored a bill instructing the secretary of the interior to look into the possibility that money and provisions were due the Shawnee Indian tribe (March 30, 1870). Ross also sponsored a resolution to ensure that children of deceased Indian men who had served in the army and who were entitled to pensions, back pay, and other benefits would receive any uncollected money or compensation due their fathers (March 18, 1869). He sponsored several bills to encourage the forestation of Kansas, including a bill that would allow homesteaders to have an additional one-quarter section (160 acres) of land as long as the settler planted twenty of those acres in trees and proved that the trees' health and density conformed, in ensuing years, to standards specified in the bill (January 13, 1870). A year later he sponsored a bill to donate the land of

Fort Harker to the state of Kansas for use in developing an experimental tree farm and school for the study of related subjects (January 14, 1871). During that Forty-first Congress, Ross sponsored a number of bills to aid in the construction of rail lines through Kansas, including bills that would help with acquisition of property needed for the construction of the Union Pacific, the St. Louis, Lawrence and Denver line, and the Atchison, Topeka and Santa Fe. He also submitted a bill to incorporate the AT&SF for interstate expansion (May 24, 1870). He sponsored a bill to aid Civil War veterans who had been deprived of war benefits by unscrupulous attorneys, a bill that applied to all veterans regardless of the state in which they lived (June 20, 1870).

Note the date of the last bill, June 20, 1870. That was just one week after the birth of the Rosses' newest child, a girl born on June 13 and named Fannie after her mother at the insistence of Edmund even though his wife preferred another name. Given the travel time back to Washington, Ross would have had to leave no later than five days after his new daughter's birth. Assuming he stayed until the end of the session, Ross would not have returned home until July 16 at the earliest.

There appears to have been considerable ambivalence in Ross's mind during the two years following the impeachment trial. He had both a desire to make the United States Senate his career and a conflicting desire for a simpler life with his family in a nice home in Lawrence. As it turned out, he had no choice but to make the latter his dream for the future, a dream that would always be elusive. Ross put considerable energy into his last two years in the Senate, perhaps with hopes that people back home would somehow take note of his diligence. Even in the modern world of mass communication, e-mail postings, and regular airline travel, it is not easy for constituents in a home district to know what their representatives in Congress are doing on a daily basis. In 1870 that would have been nearly impossible. News then often came only belatedly and only in the form of newspaper accounts, which could be unreliable at best. Moreover, much of the Radical Republican Kansas press now chose to ignore Edmund Ross. Theoretically, reelection based on merit would have been easier for members of the Senate who were not popularly elected but chosen by the state legislature. In practice, however, that process, as Ross had seen, was fraught with the potential for corruption, and was one in which Ross would never again participate. When Congress adjourned in the summer of 1870, Edmund Ross's senatorial career was practically at an end.

Fannie Lathrop Ross, circa 1848, probably at the time of her marriage to
Edmund G. Ross. Cobb Studio. Courtesy of the Albuquerque Museum of Art
and History, PA 1990.13.357.

Edmund G. Ross, circa 1848, probably at the time of his marriage to
Fannie Lathrop. Courtesy of Stephanie Padilla.

Captain Edmund G. Ross, Civil War, circa 1862. Cobb Memorial
Photography Collection, Center for Southwest Research,
University Libraries, University of New Mexico, 000–119–0241.

General Thomas Ewing Jr., Edmund Ross's commander (and later his friend when Ross was serving in the United States Senate), circa 1863. Mathew Brady photo. Library of Congress, LC-B813–2054 A.

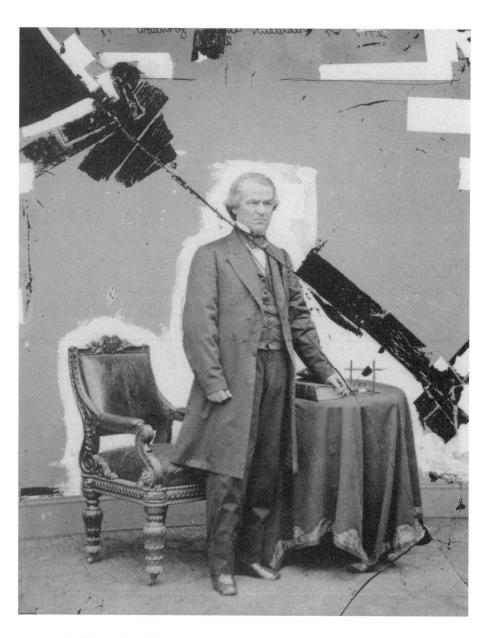

President Andrew Johnson, circa 1865. Mathew Brady photo. Library of Congress, LC-BH832–2417.

Senator Samuel C. Pomeroy of Kansas, Edmund Ross's colleague and archenemy, circa 1866. Mathew Brady photo. Library of Congress, LC-BH82–4652.

Senator James H. Lane of Kansas, whose death in office resulted in
Edmund Ross being named as his replacement, circa 1865. Mathew Brady
photo. Library of Commerce, LC-BH8266–1640.

Lavinia "Vinnie" Ream, daughter of Edmund Ross's friend and
Washington, D.C., landlord. Vinnie was a talented young lady
who at age eighteen was commissioned by Congress to sculpt a
life-size statue of President Lincoln. Library of Congress, BIOG
File—Hoxie, Vinnie Ream. 1847–1914.

Senator Edmund G. Ross, circa 1866. Mathew Brady photo.
Courtesy of Stephanie Padilla.

Fannie Lathrop Ross, circa 1886, standing in the doorway of a small home, which Fannie referred to as their "shanty," on Ross property acquired through the Homestead Act and located about four miles south of New Town Albuquerque. Cobb Studio. Courtesy of the Albuquerque Museum of Art and History, PA 1990.13.209.

Fannie Lathrop Ross, circa 1885. Albright Studio, Albuquerque.
Courtesy of Stephanie Padilla.

New Mexico governor Edmund G. Ross, circa 1885. Albright Studio,
Albuquerque, copied/modified by Cobb Studio.
Courtesy of Stephanie Padilla.

Five of Edmund and Fannie's six children: *left to right*, Arthur, Eddie,
Kay, Pitt, and Lillian, circa 1891. Cobb Photo, Albuquerque.
Courtesy of Stephanie Padilla.

Edmund G. Ross, circa 1902. Cobb Studio. Courtesy of the
Albuquerque Museum of Art and History, PA 1990.13.375.

Edmund G. Ross and daughter Lillian Ross Leis, circa 1905.
Cobb Studio. Courtesy of the Albuquerque Museum of Art and
History, PA 1990.13.380.

Edmund G. Ross at Pitt and Clemie Ross's home on Barelas Road in
Albuquerque, circa 1905. Cobb Studio. Courtesy of the Albuquerque
Museum of Art and History, PA 1990.13.376.

Hugh Cameron, the Kansas Hermit, March 1907. Cobb Memorial
Photography Collection, Center for Southwest Research, University
Libraries, University of New Mexico, 000–119–0257.

Edmund G. Ross and Hugh Cameron (back seat) with unidentified driver and Albuquerque businessman Robert Putney (front seat) during the March 1907 visit of Hugh Cameron. Courtesy of Stephanie Padilla.

CHAPTER SIXTEEN

THE CAMPAIGN TO EXPOSE POMEROY

When he demands money in consideration of his support of given measures, over which he has a power by virtue of the position the people in their trustfulness have given him, he is a blackmailer and a bribe-taker. . . . His name is Pomeroy.

—*Ross's Paper* editorial, December 22, 1871

⌁ EDMUND ROSS ARRIVED in Washington for the third session of the Forty-first Congress in December 1870, a little more than one month before the Kansas Legislature would meet to either return him to office for another term or select a new senator to replace him. Ross was under no illusion about what it would take to keep his seat and probably did not go back to Kansas to campaign. Had he returned, he would have been keenly aware of widespread vote buying by several candidates seeking his seat in the United States Senate. Without even trying, Ross did receive eight votes on the January 24 initial ballot, but none on the final ballot the following day; sixty-two votes were needed for election. By this time Ross would have been formulating plans in his own mind to return to private life, probably hoping to reestablish himself as a newspaper publisher and editor. He would remain in office in Washington until early March when the new senator would report for the first time.

The 1871 Kansas election for senator was, in fact, so corrupt that it became, in time, a matter for discussion at the national level and for investigation by the United States Senate. As Robert S. LaForte pointed out in his essay "Gilded Age Senator," given the manner in which United States senators were chosen, policy issues were unimportant. "Personality, friendships, residence, factional relationships within the party, potential appointments to office, money, and the likes were much more significant."[1] There were essentially four candidates for Ross's seat. The true heavyweight in terms of wealth was Alexander Caldwell of Leavenworth, who made his fortune through a number of enterprises but mainly in the freighting business, where he at one point employed thousands of men and as many wagons. Caldwell was not a politician and got into the race for senator only a few months before the balloting. Former Kansas governor Thomas Carney, who had sought the same Senate seat in the past, was a solid candidate for the position but would later confess to stepping aside and taking $15,000 from Caldwell for doing so, while Sidney Clarke, Ross's old archenemy, who had lost his House seat the previous fall, would find it difficult to outspend Caldwell and also confessed to taking a bribe of $15,000 to pull out of the race.[2] Finally there was Samuel Crawford, the former governor who had appointed Ross in 1866. Crawford was a so-called "purifier" who would not bribe anyone for his vote and, sadly, would not rally enough support to defeat Caldwell, who easily won with 87 votes to Crawford's 34.[3]

On March 8, 1871, with the new Congress in session and Senator Caldwell now seated, Ross wrote to his son Pitt telling him he didn't know how soon he would be able to wrap up his affairs in Washington but encouraging him and Arthur to take the first good job offers they could get, "for I fear you will need it."[4] Ross was already bracing his family for hard times. On March 12 he wrote to Fannie saying that he hoped he could get Jim Walker's business into shape soon. While this matter is unclear, it appears Ross was acting as a sort of lobbyist on behalf of Walker. Ross was apparently charging a fee for this work, which would have been an important source of income, given that he had no ready means of supporting his family otherwise. In the letter he also reminded Fannie about an assortment of seeds he had sent home and told her to have Arthur start a garden on the lots they owned. "A good garden there would help us out very much in our living expenses for the summer. He and I can, I think, make a profitable garden of it when I get home."[5] Ross dreaded the possibility that he would have to sell a few of the six tracts of land they owned to make ends meet. On March 17 he wrote to Fannie saying he anticipated being in Washington for a while longer. His business with Jim Walker involved getting a bill through the Senate successfully, which he had accomplished, but getting it through the House was his next problem. He then shared his thinking about a plan for a newspaper and printing business that would involve himself and his children, noting that "Lillie" would keep the books, Pitt would take care of distribution, and Arthur would be given "some place where he can learn to oversee the other business of the office." He added, "Of one thing I feel quite sure—that I will never again go into public life with nothing but my salary to live on."[6]

Much to the disappointment of the Ross family, Edmund was still in Washington in late July. In a letter home dated July 24 he explained that Jim Walker's business was still keeping him there and that Walker wanted him to stay for a few more weeks. Although Ross was not happy about it, he reminded Fannie that at least he was being paid for his work. He also asked again if Arthur and Pitt had been able to find work. "It is necessary that they get into something soon for I may not be able to get into business for sometime after returning home. . . . If I should have to go to work at the case as I fear I shall, at least for a while, it will be difficult to earn enough to support the family comfortably unless the boys can earn something also. This is hard, but it is honest and may after all be the best thing that could happen to me."[7] Ross returned to his family by mid-August.

In preparation for their father's return, Lillian and Pitt attended a business college. Leis remarked that it kept them busy and helped to encourage their father.[8] Once back in Lawrence, Ross reported that all avenues to employment in the newspaper business were closed to him and that he had "some months of idleness" as a result. There is an additional side to the story. When Ross applied for a job as a printer with a Lawrence newspaper/printing company, he was told that he would have to join a union (the "L.T.U.") and "take his chances." Ross was furious; he was, after all, highly qualified and with a long reputation in the newspaper and printing business in Kansas. "So, in as temperate a mood as we could command, and the occasion would permit, we advised the L.T.U. to proceed summarily to a place somewhat distinguished for its great abundance of charcoal and sulphur."[9] What Ross settled on was the publication of *Ross's Paper* in the small southern Kansas town of Coffeyville. "Our first object in coming here was to earn a living for our self and family—the next to pay our debts—the next to 'open out' on speculating and bribe-taking politicians, political cowards, L.T.U.'s and all such vermin."[10] In *Ross's Paper* there was an edge to Ross's commentary, an irascibility that appeared for the first time in his long editorial-writing career.

Ross told an interviewer that he borrowed several hundred dollars to finance the project.[11] What he borrowed must have been combined with some money he had put aside, perhaps money he had earned in Washington after his term was completed in March or perhaps from the sale of one or more of his lots in Lawrence. The railroad had just reached Coffeyville, and the future there seemed bright to Ross. Initially the paper, a weekly, was housed in a rented building. The first issue appeared on December 1, 1871. *Ross's Paper* was a departure from the typical newspaper. The bold nameplate on the front page of nearly all papers was replaced with a small headline (perhaps a quarter inch high) that simply stated, "Ross's Paper, Coffeyville, Kansas," plus the date. Pages were numbered consecutively from issue to issue so that the January 12 issue, for example, began with page number 25. Beside stories originating with Ross, he also featured articles from other Kansas papers as well as papers from other states, often with his own commentary following. Subject matter varied, but campaigning against corruption was the major theme, with Senator Samuel Pomeroy a particular target.

Ross was constrained as a senator from speaking frankly and openly about other senators, but as a journalist he felt free to say precisely what he thought without mincing words. As a colleague, Ross knew Pomeroy better than he knew any other senator. He had been to Pomeroy's lavish house in Washington, perhaps to his 5,000-acre ranch in Kansas, and knew of his other home in Boston. In his first editorial dealing with Pomeroy, Ross does not make it clear how he knew of Pomeroy's business dealings or holdings, but he is not hesitant with his allegations. The first detailed exposé came on December 22, 1871: "Eleven years ago he [Pomeroy] went into the Senate, still comparatively poor. Today he is reliably reported to be worth three millions of money. He has vast possessions of lands, Bank stock, Railroad stock, State Bonds and County Bonds." Ross was willing to grant that the accumulation of wealth by a senator was not in itself wrong, but he submitted that Pomeroy had done so dishonorably. He gives several examples, including Pomeroy's speculation in gold during the war when a defeat of Union forces would perhaps double the price of his gold. Ross accused him of demanding money from interested parties for voting the right way on legislation. He wrote of how Pomeroy had promoted an Atlantic Cable scheme in Congress for years and then, once the legislation passed both houses, sold out his own personal shares for "half a million of gold."[12]

Ross made it clear that Pomeroy may have been the most egregious of self-serving congressmen, but he was by no means the only one; there were, said Ross, many more in the Senate and the House of Representatives.

Certainly his attack on Pomeroy was personal, but it was not only Ross speaking out. Pomeroy was widely known in the national press as Subsidy Pom or Old Subsidy. The *New York Tribune* said of Pomeroy, "From his first entry into public life he has weighed everything by a money standard. He has judged all public measures by the cash that was in them."[13]

In response to Ross's attack, Pomeroy wrote an open letter to him, which Ross published on January 12, 1872. Pomeroy confirmed Ross's assertion that he, Pomeroy, had been relatively poor only eleven years before. Said Pomeroy, "To this I reply that 'eleven years ago I was comparatively poor' and that I am so today. But it was only 'comparatively' then. Lands that I then owned have formed the basis of all the property I now own. Then they were of little worth—now valuable." Pomeroy went on to say that the estate of three million was a "delusion and a falsehood." In denying all of Ross's accusations, he proposed that if Ross, or anyone else for that matter, would assume his "legal obligations," he would turn over his landholdings, "bank stock, railroad stock, government bonds, State and county bonds, and vast possessions in lands, all for seventy-five thousand dollars. Now if you believe a word you have written, or any one else believes it, here is an opportunity to test your faith—and I shall stand to this offer."[14]

In the same January 12 issue Ross responded to Pomeroy's letter of denial. Ross charged Pomeroy with taking donated money from the 1860 Kansas Relief Society to buy land from the destitute farmers he was charged with helping. Ross had defended Pomeroy in 1860 when he was widely accused of the same pilfering of funds, believing Pomeroy to be innocent of the charges circulating at that time.[15] Now Ross had a very different perception of Pomeroy's role with the Kansas Relief Society. He called Pomeroy a reprobate who was "lost to all sense of compassion for the sufferings of those helpless ones—regardless of the sacredness of the trust confided to him by a benevolent public."[16]

Ross went on to answer Pomeroy's offer to sell all his investments for $75,000. "Perhaps he has no more than that in his own name, probably not that. The man who would accept his offer would likely get cheated. But if he will turn over all that other persons are holding for him, we will let him keep what he has in his own name." It may be supposed that the effectiveness of Ross's attack on Pomeroy was abated somewhat by the remoteness of Coffeyville, but other Kansas papers repeated the articles, and even the *Chicago Tribune* picked up on the exchange between the two, favoring Ross's side of the story.[17]

There was a topic of greater importance to the people of Kansas in 1871, the corruption and vote buying in the election of Senator Caldwell. It was widely accepted that bribery had been pervasive in the 1871 senatorial race in Kansas and that Caldwell had bought his way into office. For Ross to make the public aware of illicit activities by Senator Pomeroy added fuel to the fire. Ross probably did not anticipate that when the state legislature met in January 1872 it would establish a joint committee of the two houses to investigate bribery in the election of Caldwell the year before. He would also not have anticipated that such an investigation would extend to the senatorial elections of 1867, raising questions about Ross's own relationship to the infamous Perry Fuller.

During late January and February the Kansas Legislature carried out the investigation, calling several dozen witnesses, at least twenty-four of whom were strongly suspected of taking bribes. Only a small amount of the committee's time was taken up with the 1867 election; their primary interest was in January of 1871 when corruption was widely known to be at its worst. Not surprisingly, witness after witness denied having any involvement in impropriety in the 1867 election, but most had heard of vote buying either with money or political favors.[18] The picture that emerged included smoke-filled hotel suites with envelopes of cash, banks opening their doors late at night, and surreptitious encounters. The committee released its findings on February 23. One week later *Ross's Paper* printed the findings (not including testimony, which ran hundreds of pages). Although the senatorial election of 1867 was a minor part of the investigation, as we saw in chapter 11, there was enough testimony taken about that election for the committee to arrive at the finding that "a large sum of money was used and attempted to be used in bribing and attempting to bribe and influence the members of the Legislature to secure the election of S. C. Pomeroy, E. G. Ross and Thomas Carney, by Pomeroy, Thomas Carney, Perry Fuller and others in their employ."[19] The release of these findings had to devastate Ross, even though he was not specifically charged. In the weeks that followed, it appeared that his life was in turmoil.

Five hundred bound copies of the report were released later in March, and some of them were sent to the United States Senate. Ross, who in recent weeks had so aggressively attacked Pomeroy, was now linked to him by virtue of the circumstances of the 1867 elections that had returned both men to the Senate. Ross did not immediately comment on the possible implications of the committee's charges against Pomeroy, Perry Fuller, and others beyond a short article in the March 1 edition of *Ross's Paper* condemning "the condition of rottenness" that had existed in Kansas "for years" and urging reform.[20]

With the report of the joint Kansas committee circulating, Senator Oliver H. P. T. Morton from the Committee on Privileges and Elections introduced a resolution in the Senate on May 11 to investigate the elections of both Pomeroy in 1867 and Caldwell in 1871.[21] The election of 1867 was the first to be investigated. Among the people called to Washington to testify at the Pomeroy hearings was Edmund Ross. Under oath Ross stated that Pomeroy had told him the election had cost him $30,000, but Ross could not say what the money was used for. Ross also admitted that Perry Fuller had used an unspecified sum to pay for one vote for him, Ross, and also one for Pomeroy, but he stated that he did not have prior knowledge of Fuller's action. Ross also testified that he did not directly bribe anyone, nor did he have any arrangement with anyone to engage in bribery on his behalf. Ross could not provide any factual information that would result in Pomeroy's ouster from the Senate.[22] After two weeks of testimony beginning on May 21, Pomeroy was cleared of any wrongdoing; the evidence against him was either hearsay or inconclusive. Of course, Ross was already out of office. Caldwell did not fare as well. His investigation would involve more extensive testimony and considerably more time and was therefore postponed until January.

It is worth noting that Ross was not in Coffeyville on March 1, the day the Kansas legislative findings appeared in *Ross's Paper*. One would guess that Arthur took over for his father, or perhaps they had another employee by that time. A short editorial in the same issue explained that Ross had been gone for three weeks on a trip to Lawrence to sell his home and a tract of land and had become seriously ill for ten days. An apology was made for missing one issue, on February 23. The editorial also suggested that the sale of Ross's Lawrence property would provide the money he needed to make additions to the paper's printing equipment.

Although Ross had been implicated in the bribery scandal of 1867, he did not relent in his attacks on Pomeroy. Perhaps the most damaging column by Ross about Pomeroy came on March 16 when Ross reproduced a letter allegedly written by Pomeroy in 1862. Lillian Leis reported that William Ross had the letter in his possession and shared it with Edmund.[23] The letter was written to William when he was still an agent for the Pottawatomie Indians. Pomeroy's letter proposed that he and William skim profits from a supply program under William's control, sharing it with two other men.

William apparently refused to be a part of the scheme, and the matter simply died. William, however, kept the letter, and Ross printed it in his Coffeyville paper. Two sentences from the letter summarize its meaning without ambiguity. "Mr. J. K. Tappan of New York will take hold and furnish a splendid lot of Goods—provided he gets the license to sell exclusively on the Reserve at St. Mary' Mission. . . . You and I through our two friends are to have 1/2 of the Profits—And Tappan and Clark the other half—and Tappan to do all the business And we have nothing to do, only to take our share of the profits at each payment."[24]

Although Pomeroy ignored the article and reprint of the letter in *Ross's Paper*, other newspapers in Kansas reproduced the article and letter, and it was eventually reproduced in the *New York Sun* in facsimile form with an accompanying editorial. *Sun* editor Charles A. Dana commented that the "letter would give the public 'an exact idea of Pomeroy's handwriting,' while the contents of the letter would 'afford an equally faithful view of Pomeroy's moral nature.'" When he could no longer ignore the negative publicity, Pomeroy denied he ever wrote the letter and then claimed that it was a forgery written by Edward Clark, a former member of the Washington law firm Stewart, Stevens and Clark. Clark later claimed, at an anti-Pomeroy rally, that he had been given $2,000 by Pomeroy to sign a confession that he had written the letter, but Clark, with a change of heart, both exhibited the money and denied ever writing the letter or signing it with Pomeroy's name.[25] Martha Caldwell's scholarly article in the *Kansas Historical Quarterly* in 1944 undertook to determine whether Pomeroy's letter to William Ross was genuine or fake. Ms. Caldwell reproduced copies of the original letter, given to the Kansas Historical Society by Lillian Ross Leis, and a sample of Pomeroy's handwriting known to be his, for comparison. While it looks certain that the original is genuine, she leaves us to decide for ourselves about its authenticity.[26]

By March Ross had a small two-story building moved from the old town of Coffeyville to a new area near the railroad tracks, a distance of about a mile. It appears that Ross and his son Arthur may have comprised the entire staff of the paper. Ross's plan was to set up household on the second floor of the new building and have Lillian come to Coffeyville with his six-year-old son Kay. Lillian would keep house, cook, keep the books for the paper, and take care of Kay. Meanwhile Pitt was to stay in Lawrence with Fannie and the two youngest daughters. As soon as a proper house could be built, the family would be reunited once again, this time in Coffeyville. That was the plan, but it never happened. On April 14 a tornado tore through the area, taking out much of the town including a hotel and utterly destroying Ross's new building. "Even the elements of the air seemed to have it in for me," he wrote. "The cyclone struck me and scattered my building and printing office and material for miles over the prairie—utterly destroying building, press and everything that was destructible—leaving me stunned and bruised, on the ground a considerable distance from where my building had stood—and my last dollar gone."[27]

Both Ross and Arthur were in the building at the time. Leis says that her father was thrown through a window as the building lifted, and he was deposited in the middle of the street where a banker named E. B. Ethridge came to his aid. He was unconscious and had facial cuts but was otherwise all right. Arthur was in the back of the building and was thrown against the press when one of the walls came down. The press, which was destroyed, may have saved Arthur's life by keeping the wall from completely falling on him. If there was a silver lining to the incident, it was that Lillian and Kay had not arrived yet. Newspapers throughout Kansas commented on the disaster. The *Kansas Daily Commonwealth* stated, "Only a short time ago he put in a new press, and the day before the storm paid half the purchase money on the building."[28] The *Atchison Patriot* reported that the "building was torn into kindling wood, the type all scattered and lost, and the press broken into twenty pieces. . . . the public spirited citizens of the plucky town of Coffeyville propose to put up a new building for Mr. Ross, and his friends in Lawrence intend to raise funds to set him on his feet again."[29]

The donations Ross received encouraged him to begin the process of reestablishing *Ross's Paper*. No doubt one donation in particular, $200 from Senator Lyman Trumbull of Illinois, one of the recusant seven, meant a great deal.[30] It would take the better part of three months before the paper reappeared.

Publication of *Ross's Paper* resumed on June 14, but it appears Ross had considerable difficulty making a go of it. One source reported that in July Ross sold out to E. W. Perry, who took what was left of *Ross's Paper* and absorbed it into the *Coffeyville Circulation*.[31] That sale may have taken place, but not in July as the source reported. The last edition of *Ross's Paper* appears to have been October 21, 1872, less than a year after the paper was founded. Ross probably ceased publication in Coffeyville because it was not profitable and because he was operating with less than adequate equipment. Once again he moved back to Lawrence.

During the weeks leading up to the January 1873 session of the Kansas Legislature, when Pomeroy's U.S. Senate seat was up for renewal, Ross made another attempt at newspaper publication with the *Evening Paper* in Lawrence. The Pomeroy–William Ross letter was reproduced again in the *Evening Paper*, the obvious reason being to discredit Pomeroy on the eve of the 1873 legislative assembly. Ross's new venture failed after just three issues. All three issues of the *Evening Paper* were dominated by a reproduction of Pomeroy's infamous letter. This time the letter was not typeset but reproduced in facsimile form and turned ninety degrees on the page to allow for maximum-size reproduction across two pages. The headline accompanying the letter was "The modus operandi of a Senatorial-Indian Steal—How some Senators are made millionaires on Senatorial salaries of $5,000 a year."[32] Pomeroy threatened Ross with a libel suit for first publishing the letter, but Ross boldly reprinted it anyway. That the *Evening Paper* did not last beyond the legislative session of 1873 might lead one to speculate that it was primarily a vehicle for Ross to put an end to Pomeroy's career, but Leis says the *Evening Paper* was a sincere effort by her father to start another newspaper, one that failed rather quickly, leaving Ross almost completely dependent on job work for income.[33] There was little doubt that Ross had done considerable damage to Pomeroy's reputation, but Pomeroy was still confident that he could easily buy enough votes to retain his Senate seat. In attempting to do so, he put an end to his own career.

The events of January 1873 have been reported by many sources in the intervening years, but Edward Winslow Martin (real name James Dabney McCabe) in his book *Behind the Scenes in Washington*, written and published in 1873, provides a contemporaneous account. McCabe/Martin writes that Kansas senator A. M. York, who detested the vote buying that was so common in his state, and who equally detested Senator Pomeroy, approached Pomeroy with an offer to vote for him for a price. This appears to have been a setup hatched by a number of legislators opposed to Pomeroy, with York offering to be the one to call on Pomeroy at his hotel. In consideration for his vote, Pomeroy agreed to pay York $8,000: $2,000 that very night, $5,000 the next day, and an additional $1,000 after his vote was cast. On the day of balloting, just before voting was to commence, Senator York asked to be recognized by the Speaker and, when he was, walked to the front of the chamber to the Speaker's desk and presented two envelopes, one containing $2,000 from the night before and another containing $5,000 from earlier that morning. While the money was being counted,

York explained his encounters with Pomeroy and asked that the money be used to finance an investigation into the senator's activities. When the voting for Pomeroy's seat ensued, John Ingalls received 118 votes of the 132 cast, while Pomeroy received none.[34] Later, another committee of the Kansas Legislature did investigate Pomeroy's activities and found him guilty of bribery and corruption. However, a select committee of the United States Senate, apparently in an attempt to protect its own members, ruled that the investigation in Kansas was only an attempt to defeat Pomeroy for reelection. While he avoided criminal charges, Pomeroy remained unelected, his career at an end. After living some years in Washington, Pomeroy returned to Massachusetts, where he lived until his death on August 27, 1891.[35]

Pomeroy's reputation was further damaged when Mark Twain co-authored, with Charles Dudley Warner, *The Gilded Age: A Tale of Today*, a fictional commentary on American society published in 1873, in which Pomeroy was thinly disguised as the character Abner Dilworthy, a corrupt United States senator. The book characterized Congress as predominantly self-serving, with a minority of its members honorable men, while the majority protected each other when accused of unethical behavior. Dilworthy's downfall comes when his attempt to bribe a state senator backfires in precisely the way that Pomeroy was exposed by Kansas senator A. M. York.[36] But perhaps no assessment of Pomeroy was more scathing than a long *New York Tribune* editorial cited by McCabe/Martin: "Who would have imagined it possible for any Senator to have shown so brutal a contempt for public intelligence and virtue as to go to Kansas, while the State and country were all alive with indignation over the man-traffic of Caldwell, and attempt to buy another legislature? Yet this is what Senator Pomeroy seems to have done. He had no other means of working. He saw his hold on the State was weakening. His popularity was gone. He was without those personal qualities which attract men. His career in the Senate had been marked by nothing but a participation in a series of enormous jobs—by which many men of his kind prospered, and none of them were grateful. His only weapon was his money. He had enough of that, acquired in many ways, and he went to work to use it in the old manner. He had no more sagacity than to go into the open market for votes, and at the very moment when the Caldwell case was throwing a broad shaft of light into all such shady places."[37]

On January 7, 1873, Senator Morton's Committee on Privileges and Elections continued its investigation of the senatorial elections in Kansas by asking for $10,000 to defray the expenses of investigating Senator Caldwell's election in 1871.[38] Some of the testimony in the Caldwell investigation was hearsay, just as it was in the Pomeroy hearings, but not all of it. The most damaging came from Thomas Carney, who admitted to taking $15,000 from Caldwell's people to stay out of the race. Ironically, it was during these same weeks that Pomeroy tried shamelessly to buy his own re-election in Kansas. With the Caldwell investigation completed, on February 17 Morton's committee submitted a one-sentence resolution: "Resolved, That Alexander Caldwell was not duly and legally elected to a seat in the Senate of the United States by the legislature of the State of Kansas."[39] It was a polite and gentlemanly way of ending the senatorial career of Alexander Caldwell after less than two years on the job.

McCabe/Martin quoted the *New York Tribune* in regard to Caldwell's ouster from the Senate. The *Tribune* editorial, paraphrasing the Senate committee, seems rather kind to a man as worldly as Caldwell, who you would think was totally aware of the illegalities regarding his election. Looking back 150 years, it is hard to judge, but if Caldwell was a "novice in politics" and deserving of consideration, so too was Edmund Ross in 1867. Perhaps Ross was even more deserving of consideration. In the following quote from the *New York Tribune*, substitute "Ross" for "Caldwell" and the circumstances of Ross's 1867 election seem a fair assessment, assuming that Fuller actually did buy votes for Ross and that Fuller did so with Ross's consent: "The Committee remark that while Mr. Caldwell did things to procure his election, which cannot be tolerated by the Senate, they believe that he was as much sinned against as sinning. He was a novice in politics, and evidently in the hands of men who encouraged him in the belief that Senatorial elections in Kansas were carried by the use of money."[40]

CHAPTER SEVENTEEN

LIBERALS VERSUS RADICALS

Shifting Alignments

The South is now solidly Democratic—lost entirely and forever to the Republican party because it did not use its power with sense or mercy.

—Ross, *Lawrence Evening Standard*, April 23, 1877

⌐ THE EARLY 1870S WERE among the most difficult of years for Edmund Ross. Ross did not easily release the anger he felt from poor treatment by fellow Kansans for his vote to acquit Andrew Johnson. His anger was understandable. Seemingly few Kansas Republicans ever understood why Ross voted as he did. There seemed to be a universal belief that Ross, and other senators, were obliged to follow the dictates of their constituents regardless of the senator's intimate understanding of the issues and his responsibility, in the case of an impeachment trial, to be an impartial judge. Ross believed himself to be a good senator, who had done his job to the best of his ability, and he believed that the system of government of Adams, Jefferson, and other founders—the system that now allowed the likes of Pomeroy to remain in office while it rejected him—was seriously deteriorating. The integrity of the system was only as good as the men running it. Furthermore, he could not recover the life he knew before his Senate years. It was not just a matter of finding a job or getting himself reestablished in business. That was hard enough. He also endured the scorn of many people who had once held him in high esteem.

In the 1870s Ross would make the perhaps inevitable step of leaving the Republican Party altogether, transitioning to the Liberal Republican movement, and ultimately becoming a Democrat and the Democratic Party nominee for governor of Kansas. It would be a mistake, however, to assume that Ross left the Republican Party solely out of bitterness. He had good reasons to be unhappy with the party, and so did a significant number of other Republicans in all parts of the country. Political observers recognized the Grant administration and both houses of Congress as the models for the political corruption parodied in Mark Twain's 1873 book *The Gilded Age.*

Widespread disaffection among Republicans led to the emergence of the Liberal Republican Party in 1872. Kansas Liberals organized a state convention on April 10 to elect Liberal delegates to a national May 1 meeting in Cincinnati. Edmund G. Ross was listed among the twenty-eight organizers of the Kansas meeting.[1] The April 12 issue of *Ross's Paper*, published just a day after the state convention, gave a brief summary of the meeting and promised to provide a complete report on April 19. Unfortunately, April 14 was the date of the tornado that destroyed Ross's building and press and put *Ross's Paper* out of business for a number of months to come. As a result, his participation in the Liberal Republican movement was greatly curtailed by the attention he needed to give to his personal situation. Moreover, the impact of any anticorruption arguments Ross may have made at this time was weakened by his implication in bribery charges related to the election of 1867. Absent the tornado and the election scandal, he likely would have been more active in the Liberal Republican movement, even on the national level.

Early founders and leaders of the new movement included Senator Lyman Trumbull of Illinois, one of Ross's fellow recusants in the Johnson trial. Trumbull was thirteen years older than Ross, had a superb education at the Colchester Academy in Connecticut, studied law in Georgia, and practiced law in Chicago. Among his public offices were membership in the Illinois Supreme Court and twelve years' service as a United States senator. Trumbull first won his Senate seat when Abraham Lincoln withdrew from consideration, encouraging his followers to vote for Trumbull when it became apparent that he, Lincoln, would not win.[2] Referring to Trumbull's prominence among Liberal Republicans in 1872 and his possible candidacy for president, his biographer Ralph J. Roske wrote that "Trumbull had captured the imagination of an influential national group, including the Mayor of St. Louis, his former senatorial colleague Ross of Kansas, the California superintendent of public instruction," and other political figures.[3]

The Liberal Republican movement became more than that; it was, in fact, a serious third party. There were a number of excellent Liberal candidates for president including Trumbull; David Davis, a Lincoln-appointed Supreme Court justice; Charles Francis Adams, son of John Quincy Adams; Chief Justice Salmon P. Chase; Governor B. Gratz Brown of Missouri; and Horace Greeley, editor of the popular *New York Tribune*. Although Trumbull made a good showing at the convention, after three days of balloting Horace Greeley emerged as the choice of the convention. Trumbull campaigned vigorously for Greeley throughout the North. Ross, who was struggling to survive and get his newspaper back in operation, did what he could in Kansas.[4]

While the Liberal Republican Party platform and candidates were established in May, the Democratic Party did not hold its convention until early July. The Democrats were still reeling from the war years and Reconstruction, their reputation in shatters and the party badly in need of new leadership and a new image.[5] Both the Liberal Republicans and the Democrats had little chance of beating the powerful and well-organized Republican Party. In spite of strong opposition by a minority of Democrats, the party voted to join forces with the Liberal Republicans and accept the Liberal platform and candidates. Knowing that the odds of actually winning against Grant were extraordinarily long, Greeley's campaign manager convinced him to accept the nomination of the Democratic Party. Thus Horace Greeley became a Democratic ally although he had spent his career vilifying Democrats. The new alliance demonstrated both a significant shift in the Democratic Party and a need for a sizeable number of Republicans to reestablish their roots.

During the campaign, Ross did manage to get away to participate in a major rally in Kansas City. As reported in the *Kansas City Times* on July 10, "an immense crowd had assembled at the Old Court-House" in Kansas City where the "Greeley guns had begun to boom." Ross delivered one of the speeches at the rally, a rather long and critical look at the Grant administration, where Ross warned that it should be rare "for any one party to be entrusted with the conduct of the Government for more than a single Presidential term of four years." Ross granted the importance of a second term for Lincoln, deeming it unsafe to change administrations during the war, but he believed that most Americans saw the wisdom "to periodically relegate the administration of the functions of the government. . . . More than all else, is this conviction due to the fact that all parties are prone, naturally to corruption—that in the nature of parties, as of man, the possession of power begets a love of its prerogatives, and a long continuance of its exercise weakens the sense of responsibility to the sources from which it is derived."[6]

Ross, like Trumbull, was particularly unhappy with Grant's failure to follow up on a campaign promise to reform the civil service. Ross supported the Liberal Party resolution "to inaugurate a thorough and effective reform of the civil service that shall put a stop to the shameless abuse of official patronage." As already noted, Ross and the Liberal Party were also in favor of an amendment to change the term of office for president to a single term. Ross did an effective job of combining arguments for both issues. "There is but one way that this country will ever secure a thorough and salutary Civil Service Reform. That is to put it beyond the power of the President by making him ineligible for a second term to use the offices of the country as a political engine for his reelection."[7]

The election results were clear from early in the campaign. Grant won in a landslide, with Greeley carrying only six states, two southern and four border states. Although difficult times were just around the corner for most Americans, the economy was still reasonably strong in 1872, and voters saw little need for a change in administration. Additionally, Grant continued to attract votes based on his Civil War record, while the Democratic Party was still viewed as "unreconstructed."[8] Greeley was devastated by the loss. By the end of November, his health seriously deteriorated, his spirit crushed by the recent loss of his wife and the election, he died even before the electoral votes were counted.

For Ross, 1872 had been the low point of his life. Publicly implicated in the voting scandal of 1867 and having suffered the destruction of his building and press and the loss of *Ross's Paper* along with the accompanying financial hardships, he returned to Lawrence to begin again. As we saw in chapter 16, he failed to make a go of the *Evening Paper* in Lawrence, the paper folding after just three issues.

After the demise of the *Evening Paper*, Ross entered into an association with a J. T. Stevens in early 1873. The Ross-Stevens partnership acquired ownership of the *Spirit of Kansas*, a newspaper founded by Rev. Isaac S. Kalloch. It was a farm and family paper, the official organ of the State Grange. The newspaper office was on the third floor of Frazer Hall. Lillian Ross Leis's notes about the *Spirit of Kansas* are rather confusing, but it appears that Arthur was the compositor, Pitt was the pressman, and she kept the books. Ross himself was editor, foreman, and in charge of job printing, while Stevens was the business manager. Leis also tells us that the walk from their house on the outskirts of town to the office was a long one. The fact that they had to walk is indicative of Ross's precarious financial situation. Apparently

Ross's attempt to sell his house in February 1872 did not work out. However, Leis writes that in September 1873 her father secured a house for the family in downtown Lawrence near the office. Although the walk to the paper was much improved, Ross's health appears to have been a problem. An article appeared in the June 24, 1874, issue of the *Spirit of Kansas* expressing regret that Ross was giving up editorship of the paper but saying he would continue as head of the job-printing department.[9] Stevens assumed editorial responsibility.

By the fall of 1874 Ross and his sons were working for T. D. Thacher, publisher of the *Lawrence Journal*, with Ross as foreman in charge of printing. There was an element of solidarity involved in this relationship, since Thacher, like Ross, detested the union. Ross remained there until October 1875 when, in partnership with J. V. Skiff, he purchased the *Standard*, a paper that had been around for about two and a half years. By October 1876 Ross was the sole owner of the *Standard*; it would become Ross's longest-running publication.[10] The first issue of the *Standard* under Ross's ownership included happy news of the marriage of Lillian Ross to George Leis, a Lawrence pharmacist, and tragic news of the death of Wood Neff in a railroad accident. Neff was the son-in-law of John Speer. "This is a severe affliction to Mr. Speer and his estimable family, and added to those that have preceded it." The previous deaths that Ross refers to were the two sons killed in the infamous raid of 1863 by William Quantrill and his men.[11]

Making a success of a newspaper between the years 1873 and 1879 was not easy, given the long and deep economic depression that dominated those years. It was a period of serious hard times throughout the world, considered by some scholars the real Great Depression. Ross managed to keep the *Standard* alive by, among other things, cutting the physical size to 10 × 14 inches, just a four-page, four-column paper that sold for three cents a copy or fifteen cents per week. A January 1877 article on the front page of the *Standard* acknowledged a *Lawrence Journal* article complimenting the *Standard* for doing what was necessary to continue publication. Ross was happy to say "the *Journal* has our thanks for its kindly notice of the *Standard* this morning and the assurance of our reciprocation of its good wishes."[12] Typically, during those bad months, advertising by Lawrence merchants was scant but partially made up for by patent medicine companies advertising such things as headache cures, stomach bitters, carbolic tablets, baldness cures, and an illustrated guide for the "married and marriageable on the mysteries of the sexual system." A rather large ad for Pond's

Extract advised its use for accidents, bruises, contusions, cuts, sprains, burns, scalds, boils, felons, corns, varicose veins, bleeding from any cause, female weaknesses, kidney disease, all kinds of ulcerations to which ladies are subject, and the list goes on.

While Ross enjoyed cordial relations with others in his business, like T. D. Thacher at the *Journal*, some newspapers still could not let go of Ross's 1868 vote and were determined not to let their readers forget either. Surely the worst of those journalists was D. R. Anthony of the *Leavenworth Times*. Anthony, brother of women's rights advocate Susan B. Anthony, had been emotionally caught up in his disapproval of Ross since Ross refused to vote as Anthony and "1,000 others" demanded at the time of the impeachment trial. In Anthony's newspaper, Ross was always referred to as "little Ross." Ross often ignored Anthony, but in January 1877 he drew the line. Although the reason for a trip Ross made to Topeka was business, not politics, Anthony accused Ross in writing of being in the capital that month to see if there was any chance the legislature would consider him for another term as United States senator. It was not enough for Anthony to point out in writing that Ross had no chance; he renewed the emotionally charged character assassination, which became too much for Ross to ignore. So he republished Anthony's words on the front page of his own paper: "Ross was first known as a fourth-rate printer, then as a stupid editor; afterwards he was associated with John Speer, and was appointed Senator. . . . With a big stove pipe hat on his little head he started for Washington. Andrew Johnson was at that time accidental President. Ross was Perry Fuller's Senator. Fuller bought the votes that elected him, and why shouldn't he belong to the man who paid for him? . . . Ross' term expired; Fuller expired and Ross was dead; and yet this man Ross, who is no bigger than a pint bottle, thinks he stands a show for Senator."[13]

Ross apologized to his readers for writing about matters purely personal and offered a short rebuttal. Calling Anthony's words "excessively ludicrous," he answered the assertion:

> Now as to being a "fourth rate printer," and a "stupid editor," we have nothing to say, except that the pot shouldn't call the kettle black, but as for his disquisition on size, that is too much. We insist that we are fully up to regulation height—5 feet 7 ½. But we would infinitely prefer to be "no bigger than a pint bottle," than to be as big as a big blackguard editor of the *Times*, with a soul like

D. R. Anthony's, shriveled, shrunk and crime stained till it has about as much semblance of humanity and decency as a hyena has to a white robed angel. As for his tirade about Andy Johnson, Perry Fuller, and the election ten years ago, etc., Anthony simply repeats his own foul slanders of that time. He was very mad then, and has very successfully "nursed his wrath to keep it warm," during all these changing years, while people who had more sense and less cussedness have come to far different conclusions.[14]

In early February Ross almost doubled the size of the *Standard* to the five-column format it had had three months earlier. The name also was slightly changed to the *Evening Standard*. Advertising by local merchants gradually picked up, just as Ross had predicted, and continued to improve during that spring and summer. Ross seems to have recovered his pre-senatorial life. He was content for the first time since leaving the Senate; life apparently was good. Arthur was his business manager, and Pitt was doing well handling the job-printing end of the business. In a front-page article Ross proclaimed: "All we have or are is here, and all we expect ever to have or to be. Kansas and Lawrence constitute the center of our aspirations and hopes. Our ambition is to build up here a newspaper that shall be a credit to the town and to the state."[15] Although the worldwide depression would continue for another two years, with an estimated loss of some $12 billion as of April 1877, the *Evening Standard* reflected a much improving economy in Lawrence, with at least twenty-one local advertisements and the usual spread of ads for patent medicines about equal in number to local ads in the same issue.[16]

The following day, April 18, Ross demonstrated his pledge to publish a newspaper that looked as objectively as possible at the issues when he wrote a highly complimentary article about President Rutherford B. Hayes, who had only been in office for about a month. Ross had been a Samuel J. Tilden supporter in the 1876 election, the controversial election in which Tilden carried the popular vote of the nation but lost the electoral vote by a margin of just one. Once in office, the outlook for the Hayes administration, in Ross's opinion, was very promising. Hayes ordered the removal of federal troops from South Carolina on April 10 and indicated his intention to withdraw troops from Louisiana as the *Evening Standard* went to press on April 18. Ross had for some years supported removal of federal troops from the South, believing that Reconstruction should not go on indefinitely, that "the nation should be at peace with itself, that it may enter upon a new era of better fraternal relations and assured commercial prosperity."[17] Ross would find much to like about Hayes. The new president pledged to remain in office for only one term, ordered civil servants not to participate in political activities and even fired future president Chester Alan Arthur for doing so, supported temperance with a ban on liquor in the White House, conspicuously restored transparency and dignity to the presidency, and worked at reforming the civil service and reestablishing harmony between northern and southern states—all issues that Ross had written about.[18]

On Monday, April 23, Ross enlarged the *Evening Standard* again, making it six columns wide. The *Standard* in its various manifestations under Ross (the *Lawrence Standard*, the *Evening Standard*, the *Democratic Standard*, and others) dealt with local, national, and even international news. On the local and state level Ross reported and commented on political, social, and economic issues. Lawrence residents could count on news about local people, churches, civic groups, merchants, farmers, travelers and upcoming events. For such a small-town paper, the news Ross featured on the national level was particularly good. Because of his background and continuing interest in Congress and the White House, his commentary, beyond reporting information, was sophisticated and detailed. Ross did what he had always done with his newspapers: he picked issues that he expounded on relentlessly until they were either resolved or beyond hope of solution. There were probably few sources anywhere that were more detailed and better stated with regard to the demonetization of silver and the arguments for reestablishing silver coinage, nor for explanation of the concept of a national paper currency as the only full legal tender for payment of all debts both public and private. Regularly, in the years 1876 to 1879, the *Standard* featured a report with commentary on one or the other of these issues. Ross clearly sided with both Democrats and the Greenback Party.

By the spring of 1878 the *Standard* had moved into new and larger quarters and added H. C. Burnett to the staff. Burnett's job was strictly reportorial. He assisted Ross in gathering news, but Ross remained on the masthead as the sole editor. Pitt's job expanded to the business side of the *Standard*, but Arthur is not mentioned in a late March article about changes at the paper.[19] By the following spring Burnett's name appeared on the masthead as an associate editor with a statement that the paper was issued every afternoon at four except Sunday and at a price of ten cents per week, a reduction from fifteen cents per week in 1876.[20] A statement in the paper at the end of

May 1879 indicated that "more copies of the *Evening Standard* are circulated in this city every day, than any other daily paper published in Lawrence; and more copies of the weekly edition of the *Standard* are printed and circulated every week, than any other paper in Lawrence."[21]

Ross made a name for himself in the Democratic Party. His newspaper had excellent circulation and had grown to be one of the two most successful Democratic papers in the state. With this exposure and the insightful way Ross expressed himself, he became an important political figure, whether this was his intention or not. In August 1880, at Topeka, Ross was elected by the Democratic Party to be their candidate for governor. The Honorable Martin Van Buren Bennett of Cherokee County gave the nominating speech. Like most nominating speeches, it was somewhat over the top in expressing Ross's accomplishments and was accompanied by "prolonged cheering."[22] Other speeches endorsing Ross followed until a delegate from Clay County was forced to stop speaking by the exuberant crowd. A motion to make the nomination unanimous was made, voted on, and carried.[23] It was a proud moment for Ross, who in ten years had come from a low point in his career to a new high, not only enjoying political status but having recaptured success as a newspaper publisher and editor. However, Ross's hopes for victory could not have been high. He certainly recognized that, as a Democrat, he faced a deficit of tens of thousands of votes to the much more dominant Republican Party.

In the same issue of the *Atchison Patriot* that reported Ross's nomination, another small article reported that ex-senator Lyman Trumbull of Illinois had been selected as the Democratic candidate for governor of his state.[24] Like Kansas, Illinois was a Republican stronghold, and like Ross, Trumbull didn't stand much of a chance. Both Illinois and Kansas Democrats would have benefited from a fusion with the Greenback Party, but Trumbull was opposed to the soft-money beliefs of the Greenbackers, who as a result supported Republicans instead.[25] Ross, on the other hand, had a long record of supporting the Greenback platform, but Republican Greenbackers in Kansas preferred to run their own candidate for governor.

Campaigning was exhausting. In about five weeks, from late September through October, Ross campaigned constantly throughout Kansas, visiting all parts of the state.[26] Getting the candidate's name and the platform before citizens of various communities involved some serious planning on the part of local party leaders. At a rally for Ross at Emporia on October 13, the largest hall in the city was hired, but the turnout was so great that only half the people who showed up were able to gain admittance. The rally included fireworks, with several brass bands led by the Knights Templar Band of Emporia. Emotions ran high as the line of march to the hall was attacked by opponents with "a shower of stones, brick-bats and eggs, to the mortification of all the decent people of Emporia."[27]

It is worth knowing what Ross said at the rally and safe to assume that his speech on October 13 at Emporia was the same he gave ten nights later at Junction City, Kansas. It took three full columns of the *Democratic Standard* to reproduce a mere synopsis of his speech. He explained that southerners had gradually become accustomed to semi-military rule, which had weakened civil administration to the point that people accepted "military authority in civic affairs." He then showed how this "militaristic concept of administration" was creeping into law in all states. For example, an 1872 law had been passed that authorized the president to further authorize local authorities to surround polling places at their discretion to protect voters— a law that had the potential to control elections with military force.[28]

It was a curious speech for both its subject matter and its tone. It had a scholarly quality that one might expect on a university campus, but it was, in fact, a stump speech to an audience composed mainly of farmers and small-town merchants. The audience surely expected to hear something different from a candidate for governor. They must have been curious to know what this man Ross was going to do to make their lives better in Kansas. It would seem that although Ross desired to return to political life, he was fundamentally still not a politician; he seemingly lacked the instincts of Jim Lane, whose speeches fired up his audiences with strong emotions.

These stump speeches were very important for getting people out to vote, and people attended these rallies in great numbers. Besides stump speeches, there weren't many other ways to reach the voting public. Candidates had to rely heavily on newspaper endorsements, and with most newspapers favoring the Republicans, Ross was at a disadvantage. Some newspaper editors, those who had detested Ross since his famous 1868 vote, took delight in renewing their contempt. Sol Miller of the *Kansas Chief*, the man who had once implied a romantic relationship between Ross and Vinnie Ream, called Ross "the man despised above all others by Kansas Republicans."[29] When a fusion with the Greenback Party still appeared possible for Democrats, D. R. Anthony of the *Leavenworth Times* suggested that Democrats "might want to take five minutes to cut Mr. Ross' head off."[30] Anthony was suggesting that Charles Robinson, the first Free-State Kansas governor, might be a more acceptable candidate to the Greenbacks and Democrats, but Anthony's imagery was suggestive of his deep hatred of Ross and foreshadowed a violent incident that was little more than half a year away. Still, there were a number of Republican papers that did endorse Ross.

In the midst of the campaign Ross, his associate, and at least one of his sons decided to move their newspaper from Lawrence to Leavenworth. It is a reasonable guess that, as good as life was in Lawrence, the family was still struggling to get by and did not see much hope for improvement. The plan to make this move likely had been in place for some time before Ross was nominated. Leis reported that Ross had the opportunity to buy the *Leavenworth Press*.[31] Ross probably believed that the heavier concentration of Democrats in Leavenworth would improve circulation of his paper, but the move put him in direct competition with D. R. Anthony, whose Republican-affiliated *Leavenworth Times* dominated the newspaper business there. The city-to-city move could not have come at a worse time. With Ross on the road campaigning, the move and continued publication of the paper was left to Pitt and H. C. Burnett. The name was also changed from the *Evening Standard* to the *Democratic Standard*, although Ross was careful not to let his newspaper become an advertisement for his candidacy.

The *Standard* became a source of news both pro and con for Ross, other candidates and Democratic issues. Even some news people who disliked Ross admired him for the balanced approach of the *Democratic Standard*. In the end both Ross and his friend Trumbull in Illinois sustained sound defeats. Ross received 63,557 votes to incumbent governor St. John's 115,144 and Greenback candidate Vrooman's 20,183.[32] It was unlikely that any Democratic candidate could have won in Kansas or Illinois, but nonetheless Ross managed to poll 4,500 votes more than the Democratic presidential ticket. For Ross the defeat was not a waste of time, although he would not truly appreciate that fact for a few more years. His efforts on behalf of the Democratic Party would pay major dividends when Grover Cleveland was elected president in 1884.

Until Ross moved to Leavenworth, there had not been any face-to-face confrontations between Ross and his chief nemesis D. R. Anthony. However, living in the same town was bound to find the two in each other's presence on occasion, especially since Anthony, in addition to publishing the *Leavenworth Times*, was also the postmaster. Ross made frequent trips to the post office, since he relied upon postal dispatches for news originating outside of Leavenworth. In early May 1881 the *Democratic Standard* reported on a confrontation between Ross and Anthony, the report probably written by one of the *Standard's* staff members. The account alleged that on the previous Saturday Ross was on his way to the post office when he encountered D. R. Anthony, who called Ross a "g——d d——d dirty dog." Ross was said to have replied, "Mr. Anthony, I'll allow you to say whatever you please; it makes no difference to me what you say." When Ross continued on his way, Anthony struck him with a heavy cane, but Ross had a cane also and defended himself, each man striking the other several times. The two parted voluntarily.[33]

The absolute truth of the confrontation will never be known, since apparently there were no witnesses, but Anthony did have a reputation for angry outbursts. At a trial in 1878, Leavenworth judge Samuel D. Lecompte testified that "he knew D. R. Anthony for the last eighteen years, and that he was abusive, tyrannical, libelous and a terror to the community."[34] Knowing Anthony's reputation, Ross's family and friends encouraged him to carry a revolver, which he refused to do. Arthur and Pitt did arm themselves, and Arthur sent word to Anthony that another attack on his father would be the last of his, Anthony's, life.[35]

From the summer of 1881 to the summer of 1882, Ross's spirits declined. Anthony's attack likely had something to do with it, but that was not the whole story. The paper had probably not done as well as Ross expected, and he surely was weary of facing the daily grind without some reward on the horizon. He may have been regretting ever moving from Lawrence, where his life was much simpler, where he felt at peace with the world and knew genuine happiness with his family. It was not surprising that on the first Saturday of March the front page of the *Standard* carried an announcement that the ownership of the paper was transferred from Ross to a group of prominent Leavenworth businessmen. Ross stayed on as the editor and as a member of the board of directors.[36]

Ross apparently had stayed in touch with friends who left Kansas for New Mexico. The future there was bright, the Santa Fe Railroad having finally reached Albuquerque, a town that would become the major railroad center in that territory. During the summer Ross received an invitation from David B. Emmert, along with a railroad pass, to attend the Territorial Fair in Albuquerque in October. Leis remembered, "As his health was not satisfactory and the strain mentally had been strenuous the family persuaded him to accept. He looked weary. I know for he came to my home on his way west, just for a brief call."[37]

In mid-September 1882 there was a front-page announcement that Ross was turning over editorship of the paper to H. C. Burnett. Burnett's first commentary as the editor was a column that praised his boss of five years. There was a sadness to his praise, with Ross leaving for an uncertain future, and it ended with two sentences that suggested Ross's depressed state of mind. "He may not get his reward this side of paradise, but it is sure to come sometime. He will be remembered and honored by all who have been associated with him and know what kind of stuff he is made of."[38]

The family, and even Ross himself, may have believed the end of his career was at hand, but Ross was only fifty-six years old. He still had nearly a third of his adult life ahead of him, and he was about to embark on an adventure entirely different from anything he had ever known. He would become one of the most important men in a territory as foreign as any in the United States.

CHAPTER EIGHTEEN

ALBUQUERQUE

It was a great eager, happy throng of people—men, women and children of every station and degree of life as it is found in Albuquerque, crowded on the platform waiting to give a cordial welcome to Governor Ross, and in the very spontaneity of the tribute to let him feel how general is the satisfaction felt by the people among whom he has made his home.

—*Albuquerque Morning Journal*, June 17, 1885

WHEN EDMUND ROSS STEPPED off the train in Albuquerque in October 1882, he discovered an emerging town with buildings scattered about in various stages of construction, mostly wood framed, some built with brick, a few with adobe, and none more than two years old. Tents occupied some lots. Building materials off-loaded from freight cars were piled up everywhere along Front Street waiting to be toted off for use in some construction project. The town looked a lot like others in the emerging West. This was not one of the exotic communities of lore he might have expected, one of the places established by early Spanish settlers. That part of Albuquerque was a mile and a half west and out of sight from the makeshift train depot. Had Ross somehow been magically dropped onto this same spot only three years earlier, he would have seen nothing but empty semi-desert land, no railroad and no town. In the distance he perhaps would have seen smoke rising from a few chimneys or an American flag flying unusually high in the town plaza.[1] At several times during the day, he would have heard the distant bells from the Church of San Felipe Neri, but he would have had to walk the better part of two miles to get to the town. As he moved closer, he would have seen rude adobe homes and a few commercial establishments—a small steam-powered gristmill, for example. The plaza itself, with its 121-foot flagpole and horses and buggies of various descriptions, would have been busy with people patronizing one of several mercantile stores, open-air markets, a post office, and a newly opened bank. The dominant feature of the plaza was San Felipe Neri with its massive adobe walls and humble fixtures.

Had Ross asked for directions to a hotel or to the mercantile establishment of his old Kansas friend Elias Stover, he would likely have run into a language problem. Spanish was the dominant language, and if one lived in this town, speaking Spanish would have been essential prior to 1880. South, but mostly north from the plaza, stretching many miles along the Rio Grande, Ross would have discovered a number of smaller *placitas*, little plazas each with its own adobe chapel and with clusters of farms and ranchland nearby. The entire mid–Rio Grande valley was rich with farmland irrigated from a series of ancient acequias, ditches that carried not just river water but natural fertilizer that made it possible for farmers to produce excellent crops as long as drought or flooding did not interfere. Unfortunately, such natural calamities were not uncommon, adding to the difficulty of life. Farming and ranching dominated the economy. Retail commerce was modest, and industry was essentially nonexistent. All of that would change with the coming of the railroad in the spring of 1880.

Albuquerque was selected by railroad planners to be a major center for the repair and maintenance of anything associated with the railroad, including facilities for the total overhaul of engines as well as a major staging location for the further expansion of rail lines to the south and west. Once the infrastructure—the shops, a roundhouse, passenger and freight depots, and a foundry, all a coordinated effort of the Atchison, Topeka and Santa Fe and the Atlantic and Pacific—were complete, the regular workforce would consist of more than one thousand men. By placing the freight and passenger depots and other facilities more than a mile and a half from the old town plaza, the railroad was ensuring the growth of a whole new town adjacent to the rail yards, a town that emerged with astonishing speed. The town directory of 1883, a directory that excluded the old town, already included at least 1,800 entries and was 79 pages long. Commercial establishments advertising in the directory included a furniture dealer, a piano and organ retailer, a lumber yard, a watch dealer, an undertaker, a ladies' emporium, an insurance agency, several restaurants, an opera house, and, of serious interest to Edmund Ross, three daily newspapers. Having essentially two towns with the same name right next to each other, and with such radically different cultures, made for a kind of municipal schizophrenia, each town and culture not completely understanding the other.

There was nothing quaint about the new town, and although the future looked bright, New Albuquerque in 1882 was quintessential Wild West. C. M. Chase, editor of the *Vermont Union*, who came west in late 1881 and wrote a series of articles about western territories, described Albuquerque as a town with great promise. However, Chase further described New Albuquerque as a place seriously lacking in social maturity. "The saloons, with three to ten gambling tables each, are in the lead, and the ring of bottles, the rattle of high ball, the click of billiards and the shake of dice, accompanied by the roundest and loudest profanity, fill the air. Set down in Vermont any of the business streets of Albuquerque for just one evening, and the Governor, with all his staff and all the Sheriffs, would take to the woods, under the impression that hell had broke loose, and that any attempt at legal restraint would be suicidal."[2]

For the first five years New Albuquerque was not incorporated into a separate community; a committee of businessmen simply hired marshals, often of questionable character, to keep law and order. One of the first such marshals was Milt Yarberry, who summarily executed a man named Charles Campbell who was innocently walking down the street on his way home from work in the rail yards. Campbell had been mistakenly accused of firing a weapon in a saloon. Yarberry, who was even gleeful at dispensing his idea of justice, was arrested by the county sheriff, was tried for murder, and became the first and only New Mexico lawman to receive the death penalty.[3]

It was this atmosphere that Edmund Ross found when he arrived in Albuquerque. He likely stayed at the Armijo House, the largest hotel at the time. Ross was invited to Albuquerque by David B. Emmert, a former newspaper publisher in Kansas. By 1882 Emmert was an insurance and real estate agent in Albuquerque, and, along with other business leaders, he was interested in promoting the town and enticing as many influential people as possible to come to the Territorial Fair with the hope of interesting them in investing in and taking up residence in New Albuquerque.[4]

Before boarding the train for Albuquerque, Ross would have corresponded with at least three men. One was Elias Stover, a former lieutenant governor of Kansas and a key member of the investigating committee that looked into the bribery scandal in the 1867 senatorial election in Kansas. Stover, who was known to be friendly with Ross, was now a merchant in

Albuquerque's old town. There were two likely newspaper editors who would have been interested in Ross and to whom he would have written. One was William S. Burke, the editor of the *Albuquerque Morning Journal* and the former editor, oddly enough, of D. R. Anthony's *Leavenworth Times* during the years before Ross moved to Leavenworth.[5] Burke may have wanted Ross on the *Morning Journal* staff, but Ross was by then a dedicated Democrat and the *Morning Journal* was staunchly Republican. The other newspaper contact was J. G. Albright, publisher of the *Albuquerque Daily Democrat*, the only Democratic daily newspaper in the territory. It is distinctly possible, if not probable, that Ross knew Albright when both men lived in Kansas. Certainly Albright knew who Ross was. Albright and his wife had come to New Mexico in 1880, first settling in Santa Fe, where Albright published the *Santa Fe Democrat* while his wife pursued her career as a photographer operating Albright Art Parlors. Not long before Ross arrived in Albuquerque, the Albrights moved both of their businesses there. The first issue of the *Albuquerque Daily Democrat* was published in the month Ross arrived, suggesting the possibility that Ross was on the staff of the Albuquerque paper from day one.

If Ross was on the staff from the start, no fanfare was made about it, but a careful reading of the *Daily Democrat* makes clear that Ross was indeed writing for the paper in the first couple of months. In one editorial, the anonymous writer recounted how the Atchison, Topeka and Santa Fe got its start.[6] The article told of how four men from Topeka made a trip to Atchison to meet with other interested parties and how they slept out under the stars, took three days of rations with them, and drank river water. Three of the men are named, with the fourth identified only as "the writer." Of course we know that "the writer" was Ross. References that Ross later makes to his early years in Albuquerque also suggest that he spent considerable time at the printer's case. The first mention of Ross in any Albuquerque paper was on October 22. It was a single sentence in a story about a Democratic rally held on a street corner. Oddly, the story appeared in the *Journal* and not the newspaper where Ross worked. The first time Ross was specifically identified in the *Daily Democrat* was on December 30, 1882, when the paper ran an article about a party of six men who were invited to see the progress of railroad work west of Albuquerque and new mining operations in the Arizona Territory. The men on the trip with Ross were sumptuously entertained by the general superintendent of the Atlantic and Pacific, the company building the rail line west. Interestingly, other members of the party included Ross's friends the merchant Elias Stover and William Burke of the *Journal*.[7]

In his early months in Albuquerque, Ross kept a low profile while learning about this town that was so different from any other in his experience. Writing for the *Democrat* was a good situation for observing the town and its people and assessing his opportunities. Ross's relationship with Albright is something of a mystery. In the long run they were friendly but perhaps not close. Ross had a closer relationship with William Burke in spite of their political differences. Just what Ross was up to in his first year in Albuquerque is not easily determined. There is little extant correspondence with Fannie and, as we have seen, only the slightest mention of Ross in any newspaper. In the 1883 *Albuquerque Directory* Ross is listed as editor of the *Democrat* and Albright as editor and manager, but no address is given for Ross. It is a fair guess that he stayed in a rooming house or a hotel that would give him a long-term rate. He appears to have been maintaining his friendship with Stover and Burke and trying to get himself involved in a situation that would provide respectable income.

With Ross in Albuquerque, the family was in a state of flux. Arthur had departed Leavenworth a year before his father; he had unspecified health problems and sought relief by going to California with a friend. Pitt returned to Lawrence, where he probably began to learn a new trade as a surveyor and where he met Marie Clementine Wilson (Clemie), the woman who would become his wife. As we already know, Lillian, now Mrs. George Leis, was in Lawrence, the wife of a successful wholesale and retail druggist. Meanwhile, it is a good guess that Fannie spent several months wrapping up the family affairs in Leavenworth. Until Ross could be sure of a stable situation in Albuquerque or elsewhere, there was no way he could hope to reestablish a home base for his family. Sometime in 1883, and without a house to live in, Fannie, Eddie, and young Fannie moved in with Lillian and her husband in Lawrence, while Kay moved in with Pitt and his bride. Just when Ross decided to make Albuquerque the new family home is unclear, but the chances are this decision did not come much before the fall of 1883. The family circumstances suggest that Ross's financial condition was precarious, although he must have been optimistic about the future. In the fall of 1883, Ross could not have imagined the possibility that within a year and a half he would become the territorial governor.

In a letter to Fannie on February 6, 1883, Ross said that he was ending his work at the newspaper to pursue opportunities in a mining venture.[8]

The real reason for leaving may have had to do with Ross receiving a very poor salary or the failure of Albright to make payroll. In a small town like Albuquerque, a newspaper would have been a considerable struggle, and salaries were necessarily modest. The mining industry, on the other hand, seemed very promising, with both the *Democrat* and especially the *Journal* promoting the potential to make a fortune in mining. Stories in both papers talked about the future of mines in places as close as the Sandia Mountains just east of Albuquerque or a little farther north in the hills surrounding the small town of Cerrillos. The Cerrillos area was believed to be rich with gold, silver, copper, and both anthracite and bituminous coal; in fact, the predictions about Cerrillos and the area surrounding it proved to be at least partially correct. The town of Madrid, just south of Cerrillos, would become a major coal-producing community. But the place that appeared to offer the greatest potential in 1883, or so the *Journal* would have us believe, was the small community of Copper City located about seventy-five miles northwest of Albuquerque in the hills bordering the Jemez Mountains. It was probably mining in Copper City that Ross was referring to in his February 6 letter to Fannie.

Among the articles about mining in the Albuquerque papers was a long front-page story in the *Journal* by a Professor Paul Langhammer who energetically promoted Copper City. "It cannot fail that capital will be attracted by the immense riches stored away in the mineral deposits of the surrounding mountains." If such a statement seems reasonable for an unabashed promoter, others in the article, such as one describing Albuquerque's future in association with Copper City, were pure hyperbole: "Hundreds of towering chimneys of furnaces and factories will arise and darken the clear atmosphere with volumes of smoke as sign-posts of industry and stepping-stones to wealth. The brand of copper ingots of unrivaled pure metal will be known all over the world and find a ready market."[9] Langhammer's credentials as a professor were questionable at best, but anyone who could excite the residents of a town with the idea that their community would have hundreds of industrial chimneys and a darkened sky, and that this was a good thing, was a master salesman.

Copper City quickly grew to have a population of about five hundred people, with a school, a hotel, miscellaneous stores, and, of course, a variety of saloons.[10] Beginning in 1883, Copper City even had its own post office. The problem for this fledgling community, besides the probability that the mineral wealth was exaggerated, was its location in the foothills of the Jemez

Mountains. Transporting the heavy equipment needed for the serious mining of ore, and the transport of ore to smelters, pretty well dictated a rail line connecting Copper City with places like Albuquerque where copper ore could be processed. At least, such a rail line is what the *Journal* was proposing and aggressively promoting. Langhammer's optimistic article put the matter bluntly: "The railroad must and will come, and soon too, and with it a new era of wealth and affluence for this immediate vicinity and also for the rest of the Territory." In August 1883 the Albuquerque, Copper City and Colorado Company was formed to establish a narrow-gauge rail line to Copper City. A board of directors included Ross, recently of the *Democrat*, and Burke from the *Journal*.[11] Copper City's promise was greatly exaggerated, and the entire scheme, including the rail line, was never realized. As quickly as the town grew, it also died. By 1890 the post office was closed, and the town disappeared. Today there is no trace of Copper City left.

It is possible that Ross had a small sum of money saved from the sale of the *Standard* in Leavenworth and may have used some of it for investments in New Mexico. On the other hand, Ross may have had no money to invest, the more likely possibility, but he was valuable to companies that would find it impressive to show a former United States senator on their boards. Ross was also a man of considerable administrative ability, and he could point to his experience in being one of the founders of the Atchison, Topeka and Santa Fe Railroad. He was readily welcomed into the circle of businessmen in Albuquerque who were planning a network of narrow-gauge rail lines to mining camps throughout New Mexico, the line to Copper City to be a part of the system. A front-page article in the *Albuquerque Morning Journal* in mid-July 1883 described the proposed system in detail but gave no information about who the investors were. The company hired Ross as a vice president and financial agent.[12] He probably was not paid much and may have been compensated with stock in the company. It was an ambitious plan that involved some seven hundred miles of track spreading out in five directions from Albuquerque. If the company did nothing else, it may have provided some income for Ross for a time as he sought investors in New York City. Ross was successful in establishing a working relationship with a New York firm, J. Van Brimmer and Company, that assured Ross they could both find the necessary investors and supervise construction. However, by the time contracts were ready to be executed, Ross was governor of New Mexico and had been replaced on the board by A. W. Cleland, an Albuquerque bookkeeper. It appears that contracts went unsigned, and the rail system was never built. By late 1883 Ross also had been hired by the Atlantic and Pacific Railroad to lobby Congress for land that the A&P needed for expansion. The two rail assignments meant an extended trip for Ross to New York and Washington beginning in November 1883.

Since Ross was to be in Washington, the town fathers of Albuquerque also hired him—presumably paying him for his lengthy efforts—to follow up on an 1881 petition to Congress to get the Albuquerque Land Grant of 1706, some four leagues of land or 17,713 acres, certified under United States law. Clarification was especially important because the original Spanish document, the *instrumento de fundición*, describing the town grant, was hopelessly lost, and thus properties within the granted land lacked clear titles. The surveyor general for the territory had recommended confirmation of the grant based on an abundance of sound circumstantial evidence, but Congress had not yet acted. There was an urgent need for Ross to get Congress to act, since two former soldiers were attempting to establish a soldiers' homestead on part of the grant that appeared to be unclaimed. The two men through their lawyers presented a strong case in Congress, citing the lack of any formal, written grant. Ross's appeal and counterarguments were impressive and are preserved in a document he authored titled "The Albuquerque Town Grant, Its Character and History."[13] Getting the grant certified demonstrated the cumbersome nature of clearing Spanish and Mexican land grants under United States law, a circumstance that only intensified the widespread fraud and corruption in New Mexico. The Albuquerque grant was not finally and absolutely established until 1901, twenty years after the initial appeal.[14] Ross's experience with the Albuquerque grant would lead him to try to change the manner of adjudicating grants, a major issue during his term as governor.

There are inevitable uncertainties in re-creating the life of people who lived generations ago. For example, we don't know precisely when Ross bought his first house in Albuquerque, but the summer or fall of 1883 is the likely time frame, with the address being somewhere on Railroad Avenue, the road that ran from the old town plaza to the railroad yards. In fact, Ross may not have owned the house but merely rented it. Lillian Leis tells us that the house was located near that of Elias Stover, which would put it in the old town.[15] Ross had anticipated that his stay in New York and Washington would be lengthy and so arranged for his son Arthur to come to Albuquerque from California to live in the house and keep an eye on things and perhaps give consideration to making Albuquerque his home.

On his return trip to Albuquerque from Washington in the summer of 1884, Ross stopped in Lawrence to collect Fannie and his two youngest children and the family belongings. He must have been confident about his future in Albuquerque and probably felt uneasy about imposing on Lillian and her husband and Pitt and his wife any longer than necessary. Leis tells us that Eddie, then in her late teens, remained in Lawrence, probably attending the University of Kansas, and that she was employed as a bookkeeper at the Leis drugstore. Kay and young Fannie would accompany Edmund and Fannie to Albuquerque.

Although Ross had part of his family together again, he still did not have a steady source of income. References in several newspaper articles in later years reported Ross having to work "at the case" in Albuquerque. Ross himself reported that he frequently worked typesetting at the *Journal*. An El Paso journalist wrote that he often saw Ross working at the *Journal* office as a "sub" through the long nights and for a mere pittance. "He scorned the idea of asking for assistance or recognition, but even in the midst of his deepest poverty was always recognized by the better element of Albuquerque as a man of superior probity."[16] Although Ross did work for Burke during parts of 1883 and 1884, it also appears that he maintained his friendship with Albright at the *Daily Democrat*. Ross worked at the case to supplement other income sources and would have to be characterized as a kind of freelance agent marketing his administrative, political, printing, and journalistic skills wherever he could until a permanent position with a steady income materialized.

Whether Ross did any writing for the *Journal* is difficult to determine for the simple reason that only in rare instances were writers credited. There is a chance Ross did pen articles for the *Journal* that did not contradict his Democratic views, but never with a byline. Burke, Ross, and other Albuquerque businessmen agreed that the territorial legislature was corrupt or incompetent. Ross's method of expressing his critical opinions about the legislature was to write letters to the editor of the *Journal*. In a couple of letters Ross picked apart the legislature, saying that their results and proceedings were either fraudulent, illegal, or incompetent. Typical of these missives was a September 3 letter pointing out that both the Democratic and Republican Parties in New Mexico had platforms that censured the legislature: "Very many of the measures it pretended to enact into law were conceived in venality and prompted by a desire to plunder the people for personal gain."[17] Ross used the letter-to-the-editor method several times in the summer of 1884, establishing an adversarial role with the territorial legislature without yet having any clear idea of what might lie ahead for him.

Grover Cleveland was not elected president until November 1884, and, in fact, his chances during the campaign were considered to be slim. So Ross could not have been entertaining serious thoughts of being appointed territorial governor. However, Ross must have believed that his letters to the *Journal* would lead to something, even if he was not sure what that might be. He was concerned over the corruption that he and others observed in Santa Fe and publicly demonstrated that concern for the city and future state that he now considered to be his home. His natural inclination was to be a journalist; he could not turn off his need to be involved, nor did he wish to, and so was mostly biding his time working at various jobs until the right situation developed. In the meantime, letters to the editor had to suffice. Ross's various activities did not go unnoticed by Albuquerque leaders, who were forming strong positive opinions about him.

Of serious concern to Ross, Burke, and Stover was statehood for New Mexico, which had been a territory for nearly forty years. Closely related to the statehood issue was education. A territory without public schools was unlikely to be voted into the Union by Congress. Practically every territorial governor since 1851 had urged the New Mexico legislature to establish a public school system, but to no avail. With the failure by the territorial government and by Albuquerque's Bernalillo County to establish a public school system, Burke and Ross in 1883 had written a bill that they submitted to the United States Congress to establish a school system for New Mexico to be exclusively run by the federal government, thus bypassing the territorial legislative assembly.[18] The bill never made it out of committee, but that did not discourage the two men from continuing to fight for an educational system in New Mexico. In 1884 Bernalillo County managed to get an office of public instruction started, and by that fall Burke, because of his efforts to bring educational opportunities to the city, was chosen as the superintendent of public instruction, leaving his job with the *Journal*.[19] It is significant that the creation of the county system was aided by Ross when he persuaded Congress to specify that part of the Albuquerque Town Grant must be designated for educational use.[20]

At about the same time that things were changing for Burke, there was a curious short article in the *Journal* that read in part: "On Monday, the first day of September, *The Evening Democrat* passes from control of J. G. Albright into the hands of the democratic central committee. It is understood that Ex-senator E. G. Ross will have control of the editorial department of the paper. Mr. Albright retains control of the job office and receives $800 for a four months lease of the paper."[21] It may have been Ross's letters to the editor of the *Journal* that caught the eye of the Democratic committee, which believed that Ross was just the man for the job. It was an election year, and the *Democrat* became the official voice of the Democratic Party in New Mexico. Possibly Albright was not doing an effective job of promoting Democratic issues and the party committee knew Ross would be more effective. If Ross did edit the paper beginning in September, the role was assumed very quietly. The editorial page in each issue simply read, "The *Daily Democrat* by J. G. Albright." It is possible that Ross handled the editing without credit. There was a similar situation earlier in the summer of 1884 at the *Journal* when that paper was leased out to a J. H. Gardner. During Gardner's short tenure, no editor for the *Journal* was listed, either. Of course, it is also possible that Ross declined to edit the *Democrat*, though that seems unlikely unless he was expected to do it without compensation.

Ross's thoughts about becoming territorial governor probably surfaced in November or shortly before. An interesting article that appeared in the *Deming Headlight* in 1893 describes the November 1884 night when Grover Cleveland was elected to the presidency and suggests that by that time Edmund Ross was considered a candidate for the job. In the article, an unnamed Republican lawyer tells of how he and Ross sat in the attic of the *Journal* until the early hours of the morning. One gets the picture of a couple of men chatting in a dark room lit by several oil lamps. The Republican attorney's impressions of Ross are worth citing: "It would be a platitude to say that he has the courage of his convictions, so I will put it this way: he has an intelligent knowledge of American history and the nation's institutions, gleaned more from actual experience than from any other source. In other words, he is a thinking man. He is liberal, broad and American, and has advanced ideas. He is mentally way above that coward attribute of small politicians,—the fool desire to please present passing public prejudice. To put it this way, he is something of a Cleveland himself. That is a good deal for a Republican to say about a man, isn't it? Well, I know what I am talking about. I sat in the attic of the old Journal building here in Albuquerque election evening in 1884, with old man Ross. We were both waiting with opposite hopes and fears."[22] The Republican lawyer was speaking only for himself, but he might as well have been speaking for many Republicans, as respect for Ross was widespread in Albuquerque.

Cleveland and Ross were alike to the extent that both men were reformers with strong reputations for honesty. At the national level, corruption was rampant in Washington, and the idea of a reformer in the White House was appealing to most Americans. During the campaign Republicans managed to discover that Cleveland possibly fathered a child in Buffalo, New York, as a young man. Cleveland indeed helped support a child, but that he actually fathered a child could not be proven. The mere possibility that he was the father led Cleveland to assume responsibility, and he made no attempt to deny the story. In November Cleveland won the election by a margin of just a quarter of one percent of the popular vote over James G. Blaine, the Republican candidate. Cleveland became the first Democrat to win the White House since 1856 and would be the only Democrat to do so until 1912.[23]

In New Mexico it was clear to most Democrats and a fair number of Republicans that self-serving politicians from both parties, but especially Republicans, dominated the judicial, legislative, and, to a degree, executive branches of the territory through a series of corrupt associations—rings—controlled by a blatant group in the capital popularly known as the Santa Fe Ring. From the time that New Mexico became a part of the United States in 1846, corruption had flourished. The possibility of confronting the so-called Ring in Santa Fe as territorial governor was just the kind of challenge that appealed to Ross and, for that matter, to the town leaders in Albuquerque, most of whom were new to New Mexico and disappointed by what they observed in Santa Fe.

Leading up to his decision to seek the governorship, Ross had been a vocal supporter of fellow Democrat Antonio Joseph, who was New Mexico's territorial delegate to Congress. However, as Ross became more and more familiar with territorial politics, he was deeply disappointed to learn that Joseph and even C. H. Gildersleeve, the chairman of the Democratic Party in New Mexico, were allied with the Ring.[24] Both Joseph and Gildersleeve worked behind the scenes in Washington to secure the defeat of Ross as a candidate for governor, knowing that he would be a serious thorn in their sides.[25] Ross and Joseph would eventually gain respect for each other and, in the long run, worked effectively together in the interests of New Mexico.

President Cleveland was sworn into office on March 4, 1885. Edmund Ross was in Washington for the inauguration and, in fact, had been there since early February, ready to present his case for being named territorial governor. Such an appointment was not of immediate importance to Cleveland, given the multitude of other issues facing a new president; Ross knew that there would be some weeks of waiting, but the weeks must have seemed interminable. Ross submitted his formal request to the secretary of the interior. By April 6, when the president had not yet taken any action, a group of thirty Albuquerque Democrats took the initiative to write to President Cleveland stating their reasons for supporting Ross for the job. Among the signers was J. G. Albright, Ross's former employer. It was a letter that expressed the widely held confidence that the people of Albuquerque had in Ross. At the same time, the letter expressed opposition to Judge L. S. Trimble, also of Albuquerque, based on his association with the Santa Fe Ring.[26]

While Ross could feel good about his acceptance in Albuquerque, the same widespread confidence did not exist in Santa Fe, either because people there knew nothing about him or because they knew him to be a threat to the established way of doing things. By April 30, when Ross had still heard nothing from the president, and knowing that a number of other candidates were vying for the job, Ross wrote a long letter to Cleveland, a draft of which is extant, reminding the president of the support he, Ross, enjoyed in New Mexico. He pointed out that he had the endorsement of numerous active and influential businessmen on signed petitions, along with newspaper endorsements of both political parties. Most important, Ross emphasized the goal he had for New Mexico. "I hope, as governor of New Mexico, to become instrumental in the correction of glaring abuses that have become [a] chronic theme and which only a vigorous system of administration can rectify."[27]

By May 13 the White House was still silent, with the anxiety level in some quarters of New Mexico growing. The *Journal* ran a short editorial expressing frustration with the process. "Meanwhile Mr. Cleveland, who feels none of the aches and pains of an expectant office seeker whose hopes are deferred from day to day and whose hotel bills are growing at an alarming rate with no salary coming in to meet them, keeps remarkably cool and imperturbable under the tremendous New Mexico pressure, and is evidently in no hurry to take the candidates off the rack."[28] On May 20 Burke, perhaps worrying that Cleveland was not committed to Ross, wrote a letter to the president stressing that he, a Republican and former editor of the territory's leading Republican paper along with "a large number of Republican papers," favored Ross.[29] At long last, on May 26 the *Journal* was able to announce that Ross was Cleveland's choice.

Ross's return to New Mexico was not immediate. There were meetings with the president, the secretary of the interior, and other heads of executive departments. Ross apparently arranged with Governor Lionel A. Sheldon, whom he was replacing, to have the swearing-in take place at daybreak on June 15. It is not surprising that Ross chose to avoid the fanfare of a traditional noisy inauguration. Such pomp did not fit with his quiet nature, nor did the consumption of liquor, almost demanded by such an occasion, conform to his temperance principles. In Lawrence Ross stayed a night or two with his daughter and her family while the town fathers planned a celebration that included the city band serenading him at Lillian's house and escorting him to the Opera House, where an enthusiastic crowd of Kansans were present to congratulate him and to hear him speak. Both Lillian, with her two children, and Pitt accompanied their father back to New Mexico.[30] At the town of Las Vegas—the stop along the old Santa Fe Trail where during the Mexican-American War the territory of New Mexico was first claimed by the United States—they were met by newly appointed New Mexico chief justice William A. Vincent and other prominent citizens, who accompanied Ross to Santa Fe. Ross's lack of anticipation of any ceremonial aspect to the official swearing-in is indicated by the fact that his children and grandchildren stayed on the train and went directly to Albuquerque, where they were met by Fannie and the other siblings, none of whom attended a ceremony that Ross had believed would be a brief, quiet affair.

Ross's train did not arrive in Santa Fe until 1:40 in the morning, only hours before the swearing-in, and so he had only a vague idea of the preparations made for that event. Even before sunrise cannons were fired at Fort Marcy just north of the governor's mansion, waking up most of the residents of the town. In dramatic fashion the *Santa Fe New Mexican* reported the events of June 15 in a long article the following day. "The cannons strained their iron-bound throats; the dawn of the day saw fifty American flags playing whiplash in the fresh morning breeze; the 13th U.S. Infantry band discoursed martial music 'neath the rich foliage in the city plaza, and a little Spartan band of half a hundred democrats and republicans, all aggressive young citizens imbued in the keenest sense with patriotic enthusiasm, flocked in and out of the historic executive palace to welcome and congratulate Governor Edmund G. Ross and shake hands with Chief Justice Vincent, and chat with the numerous prominent citizens who constituted themselves a committee of welcome."[31]

Ross, who appeared to be overwhelmed by the reception, had expected to be sworn in and then board the next train for Albuquerque. It was clear that there was more to this than he realized. He decided he could not possibly leave the capital as planned and wired ahead that he would be delayed until the next day. Indeed his day was filled with activities. After breakfast, Ross and Chief Justice Vincent, along with a group of civilians and army officers, were escorted to Fort Marcy, where they were entertained by the post commander and his wife. As they entered the grounds, a seventeen-gun artillery salute was fired. By late morning Ross was greeted by a great many Santa Feans at the Palace of the Governors and was afterward escorted to historic places in the capital, places that he had never seen. At eight o'clock in the evening members of the GAR post in Santa Fe assembled at their hall and marched to the Palace Hotel, where Ross was staying. Their fife and drum corps no doubt caught the attention of the people of Santa Fe, who by eight thirty filled the street in the front of the hotel on Washington Street. If that were not enough, the 15th Infantry Band led a second large group of people to the hotel, and for an hour and a half there was music and speech making. As the *Santa Fe New Mexican* reported it, the event was nonpolitical, with every class of society discernible.[32]

Although Ross was truly touched by the festivities in Santa Fe, his arrival back in Albuquerque may have meant even more to him. He reportedly was welcomed by the largest single gathering of people in Albuquerque's history.

It was a great eager, happy throng of people—men, women and children of every station and degree of life as it is found in Albuquerque, crowded on the platform waiting to give a cordial welcome to Governor Ross, and in the very spontaneity of the tribute to let him feel how general is the satisfaction felt by the people among whom he has made his home. . . . The train was on time and when the locomotive whistled for Albuquerque, hundreds of necks were craned forward as though the owners of the necks felt sure that Governor Ross was sitting on the pilot of the engine and could best be viewed while in that conspicuous attitude. Chief Howe and policeman Bowen were kept busy keeping small boys off the track and preserving a passageway from the edge of the platform to the carriage in waiting. . . . An archway had been erected on the platform, spanning the space between the iron railings surrounding the little parks, and on the arch was the inscription, "Welcome to Our Governor." Three large silk banners helped to give effect to the scene. As the train rolled up, the Washington Band struck up a lively air, and when the familiar features of Governor Ross appeared at the door of the car all semblance of order was destroyed and people rushed for the platform. . . . The governor hurried across the platform and took his seat in the carriage . . . preceded by the Washington Band and followed by a great crowd of people, some on foot, some on horseback and some in vehicles, then started up Railroad Avenue with the band playing a martial air. The sidewalks on the avenue were thronged with people, and the middle of the street dotted thickly with them.[33]

The Ross family was given time to eat dinner at their home before a seven o'clock reception was scheduled at the Grant Opera House at Third and Railroad Avenue. Sometime before seven the band began to entertain the gathering crowd in the front of the building. The opera house was literally a large meeting hall with a stage and a seating capacity of about one thousand people located on the second floor of the A. A. Grant Building. Well before Ross was escorted into the room, every seat was filled, and every space for standing was occupied. There were speeches, of course, and even the playing of an original composition called "The Governor Ross March." Harvey Fergusson, an Albuquerque attorney, made the longest of the speeches, recounting Ross's career with special emphasis on Ross's courageous acquittal vote in 1868. When Ross spoke, his remarks were frequently interrupted by loud applause and cheering. It was not a formal speech, nor was it especially long. "Albuquerque is my home and I expect it to be my home as long as I live, [Loud applause] and I shall never lose an opportunity to advance its proper and material interests. . . . I am very much pleased at the reception you have given me this evening. It is more than I could have expected and more than I bargained for, and you must not be surprised if it is a little too much for me. It is impossible for me to give adequate expression to the feelings of my heart. . . . after seventeen years of poverty and obscurity this vindication is worth a thousand times more to me than would be all the offices of the territory rolled into one and offered to me."[34]

More than what was said, it was the events of that day that were the real message. Ross had endeared himself to a community in a way he may never have thought possible. The audience was made up of working men and women in their everyday clothes who recognized Edmund Ross as one of them—a man who, like them, opposed the self-serving politicians in Santa Fe and who intended to do something about that.

If June 16 was the night for the working class to honor Ross, the night of July 22 was reserved for the elite. It was on this night that the newly completed San Felipe Hotel was opened for the first time. It was a grand hotel by western standards and, if you could believe the *Journal*, a grand hotel by eastern standards as well. "The visitor finds himself in a spacious hall way which leads directly to the rotunda, and reaching this, it is difficult for him to realize that he is away out here in the far west, for everything around him is indicative of the hotel palaces of Chicago."[35] It was a night for evening dress and a lavish banquet for 186 "important" people seated at six long tables with "glittering silver, glass and chinaware." Four spectacular chandeliers provided brilliant light, and an orchestra played the "*Très Jolie Waltz*" as guests took their seats. Ross and his wife, who were given the privilege of being the first guests to sign the hotel register, had never experienced anything like this. The *Journal* article about the event, which covered most of the front page of the paper the following day, declared: "It was a scene to stimulate a reporter's pencil to the point of paralysis and make him go off to some lonely place and commit suicide because he couldn't do justice to the occasion." Perhaps the most insightful sentences in the article described Ross himself: "In all that great company the quiet little man with the genial smile and the honest, manly clear cut features who answers to the name of Edmund G. Ross, governor of New Mexico, was perhaps the most unpretending and unobtrusive, and one not familiar with the governor would not have supposed that the great occasion was specially intended to do honor to him. He moved easily among the crowds of gentlemen in the rotunda and corridors with a cordial greeting for all and with none of the 'I am governor of New Mexico' style about him."[36]

Again, it was not what was said during the speeches that night; the event itself told the story. Of the names on the guest list only six were Hispanic, and two of those were Armijos from the wealthiest of Old Albuquerque families. Some of the guests, particularly some from Santa Fe, whose intentions may have been honorable and their presence at the banquet not just a matter of being seen at an important function, would be enemies of Ross in the coming months and years. They would discover—if they didn't already know—that the quiet, genial little man with gray hair would be as fierce a political opponent as they had ever encountered.

CHAPTER NINETEEN

UNDERSTANDING NEW MEXICO

Out of such consideration, I could have done no more than to have
exiled myself to this kingdom, at the ends of the earth and remote
beyond compare.
                    —Don Diego de Vargas to his son-in-law, April 9, 1692

⌁ TWO CENTURIES AFTER THE Pueblo Revolt of 1680, the land that Don
Diego de Vargas reconquered could still be considered "remote."[1] But with
the railroad reaching New Mexico in the first few years of the 1880s, the territory rapidly emerged from its isolated past. Historian Howard R. Lamar
described New Mexico as "dramatically behind the rest of the country
in income, education, population, economic opportunity, and political
standards." The reformers that Grover Cleveland brought into his administration in 1885 believed New Mexico was badly in need of "a radical reconstruction of its economy and politics."[2] Cleveland, the first Democrat to be
elected president after the Civil War, ran on a platform of reform, and to
that end—given Edmund G. Ross's exceptionally strong support from the
Albuquerque business community—he appointed Ross to serve as territorial governor. At the same time Cleveland appointed George Washington
Julian as surveyor general of New Mexico. Both men had been active in
the abolitionist movement and were equally determined to bring change to
New Mexico and to purge its government of corrupt officials.[3]

The story of Edmund G. Ross's tenure as territorial governor cannot
be properly told without some knowledge of why New Mexico was unique
and seriously lagging behind much of the country. Indeed, picking up on

any aspect of New Mexico history in the late nineteenth century, without a basic understanding for its very old past, would offer only a fragmentary understanding of the land and peoples of New Mexico. Among the territories, New Mexico was unique mainly because it evolved in isolation not just from the United States but even from Spain and Mexico in previous decades and centuries.

The first permanent European settlers to join the aboriginal people of the area came in 1598, led by the conquistador Don Juan de Oñate. Settlers were led to believe that life, in reasonable time, could be fashioned into something akin to life in the better social stratum of New Spain (Mexico). Grants of land were an incentive, along with the promise of good conditions for farming, with natives to do much of the work, and access to untapped mineral wealth. Spanish titles, coveted by men of that era, occasionally were given as an inducement. It was assumed that what could not readily be provided in New Mexico would be brought in by wagon train from New Spain. However, life was not nearly so easy; the distance for traders and government supply trains was great and the travel dangerous. Because New Mexico was found to have so little to offer in the way of resources or products and no navigable rivers or seaports, the settlers were poorly and infrequently supported by the viceroyalty.

New Mexico's Spanish settlers, those who managed to survive the early years, did so partly by their wits and with the help of the Pueblo Indians whose communities and farms, mostly along the banks of the Rio Grande and its tributaries, were established even centuries before the Spanish arrived. When the settlers did not easily adapt to their new and often harsh circumstances, they demanded much of the Pueblo people including their labor, their food, and other essentials. Franciscan friars who came with the settlers had the mission of converting the natives to Christianity. In the process they too demanded much of the Puebloans to help support their daily needs and to build their churches.

In time the difficulty of living in semi-arid New Mexico became something of an equalizer. The Spanish settlers had to do without much they formerly took for granted. They learned to live without milled lumber, and the windows of their modest homes were left unglazed. As clothing wore out, buckskin became a common substitute for cloth. Tools of any kind were hard to come by and sometimes were fashioned from otherwise useless armor. Anything made of metal was worth its weight in gold. Adobe and some stone were pretty much the only building materials. Although shortages of nearly everything were a reality, perhaps the most serious shortage of all was knowledge of life outside New Mexico's ill-defined borders. Schools and libraries did not exist. There was little regular contact with the rest of the world. Communities, when established in California and Texas, were hundreds of miles away, difficult to reach across the vast and arid terrain controlled by hostile nomadic tribes. As generations folded one into another, traditions, language, and even the Catholic religion evolved uniquely, or in some respects did not evolve much at all, while the rest of the world did.[4]

Among the earliest buildings was an impressive two-story adobe structure in Santa Fe, New Mexico's only city for more than a hundred years. The building housed the central government of the northern province of New Spain. Construction began on the building in 1610, making it what is believed to be the oldest public building in the United States. The building would become known as the Palace of the Governors, the home of nearly all future governors including Edmund Ross.[5]

By 1798 Spanish settlers, still in essential isolation, could look back on two hundred years of history in New Mexico largely unaware of the establishment and early decades of development of the United States far to the east. New Mexico continued to be a Spanish colony until 1821, when Mexico declared its independence from Spain. But even under Mexican rule, New Mexico remained little more than a remote province of minor importance.

Simultaneously with Mexican independence, the Santa Fe Trail got its start initiating trade between the United States and Mexico. For the first time, wagon trains of goods reached Santa Fe after two months or more of arduous travel from St. Louis. By the 1840s the trips were more common and the goods flowing into New Mexico more plentiful, but the amount was still slight compared with what the railroad would eventually bring. In the summer of 1846, with the United States flexing its doctrine of Manifest Destiny, and in the midst of war with Mexico, the U.S. Army of the West made its way across the Santa Fe Trail to claim New Mexico as a possession of the United States.

General Stephen Kearny made promises to the citizens of New Mexico, beginning in the town of Las Vegas, where he stood on a rooftop next to the plaza to speak to the people gathered. Of the promises, three were most important: The United States would not interfere with long-established property rights granted under Spanish and Mexican rule. Religious practices, whatever they might be, were the right of citizens. And Kearny's army was there to provide protection from Indian raids on communities, farms, and ranches. "The Apaches and Navajos come down from the mountains and carry off your sheep, and even your women whenever they please. My government will correct all this. It will keep off the Indians, protect you and your persons and property: and I repeat again, will protect you in your religion."[6]

A few days later, with the Army of the West occupying Santa Fe, Kearny, at the Palace of the Governors, presented Juan Bautista Vigil y Alarid, representing the people of New Mexico, with a formal proclamation announcing that New Mexican people were no longer citizens of Mexico.[7] The flag of the United States was raised over the plaza for the first time.

American newcomers, who began to arrive in greater numbers after the Kearny conquest, and especially after 1850, when New Mexico officially was made a United States territory, were astonished by what they experienced. Life in New Mexico was vastly different from any other place they had known, and it was often perceived as primitive. Books, articles, government reports, memoirs, and stories of life in New Mexico were carried back to the states by travelers whose accounts created a lasting and mostly negative impression of a strange and remote territory.

W. W. H. Davis, who was sent to New Mexico to be the United States attorney for the territory, kept a journal of his experiences during the three years he was there. He published his observations in a book, *El Gringo: New Mexico and Her People*, in 1857. Davis reported that education in New Mexico was "at a very low ebb," with illiteracy a more serious problem than in any other American territory, and declared that the "fearful amount of ignorance among the people is enough to make us question the propriety of intrusting them with the power to make their own laws."[8]

Because the book was widely distributed, and his reputation respected, it contributed to the poor reputation of New Mexico in the states and in Congress. Thirty years after the publication of *El Gringo*, during Edmund Ross's third year as territorial governor, Davis's book was quoted verbatim by members of the House Committee on Territories who were arguing against New Mexico statehood. "The standard of female chastity is deplorably low . . . prostitution is carried on to a fearful extent, and it is quite common for parents to sell their own daughters to gratify the lust of the purchasers, thus making a profit from their own and their children's shame. . . . It is the custom of married men to support a wife and mistress at the same time, and but too frequently the wife has also her male friend. . . . Such practices are indulged by three-fourths of the married population. . . . The people of New Mexico are extremely superstitious, and which prevails to a greater or lesser degree among all classes, the intelligent as well as the most ignorant."[9]

Ross was astonished by the use of the Davis quotations by House members nearly thirty years after publication. To counter what he considered shocking ignorance, he prepared a memorial to be read at an open session of Congress on March 27, 1888. Ross believed the findings were pure prejudice and a gross exaggeration of conditions in New Mexico. He believed that the Davis quotations were practically the only reason New Mexico was denied statehood.

Ross may have convincingly defended New Mexico in regard to these prejudicial statements, but what he could not deny was the failure of the people to establish schools even when every territorial governor had encouraged every legislature to do so. The best he could do was cite a statistic that purported to show that illiteracy in New Mexico had declined by 20 percent in recent years. Ross's efforts notwithstanding, New Mexico had to wait another twenty-four years before achieving statehood in 1912.

Davis's book is important but should be read with the writer's biases in mind. Davis did correctly observe that isolation is what caused New Mexico to be the impoverished place it was in the 1850s. "There is no country protected by our flag and subject to our laws so little known to the people of the United States as the territory of New Mexico. Its very position precludes an intimate intercourse with other sections of the Union, and serves to lock up knowledge of the country within its own limits."[10]

There is more to add to the statehood story. The subcommittee considering New Mexico statehood also considered the annual reports of former governors Lew Wallace and Lionel Sheldon, both of whom had commented on the primitive state of agriculture in New Mexico. Ironically, given that Ross badly wanted statehood during his watch, the subcommittee also considered Ross's report of corruption in the legislative assembly and included the negative observations of all three governors in making their recommendation to deny statehood.[11]

Colonel Edwin Vose Sumner began his tour of duty as commander of the army in New Mexico in July 1851. For a time Sumner also administered civilian affairs when James S. Calhoun, New Mexico's first territorial governor, became seriously ill and left the territory in May 1852. On May 27 Sumner wrote a long letter to the secretary of war expressing his honest belief that the United States should give New Mexico back to the "Mexicans and Indians": "With all the economy that can be used, and exertions in agriculture and the like, so long as we hold this country, as we do now, it must be a very heavy burden to us; and there never can be the slightest return for all this outlay—not even in meliorating the condition of the people; for this distribution of public money makes them more idle and worthless. There is no possibility of any change for the better. Twenty—fifty years hence—this territory will be precisely the same as it is now. There can never be an inducement for any class of our people to come here whose example would improve this people. Speculators, adventurers, and the like, are all that will come, and their example is pernicious rather than beneficial."[12]

Sumner did not seem to understand why New Mexico was lagging in development compared with other parts of the country. He apparently believed New Mexicans were hopelessly lazy and ignorant; it was their own fault they lived as they did. But like Davis's memoirs, Sumner's words should not be discounted completely. He did foresee the negative effect to be brought by speculators, a self-serving breed of people whose influence and actions would play an important role in New Mexico history in the not-so-distant future. What Sumner did not and likely could not see was the impact that the railroad would have. Beginning in 1879, the rail lines would bring to New Mexico the very class of people he did not think could ever be induced to come, people like Edmund Ross. They came by the thousands. They were people who had, or planned to have, families. They were community builders who wanted the towns they settled in to be at least as livable as the towns they left behind. They were concerned about politics and the elected officials who affected their lives. For Ross the newcomers comprised a true constituency of citizens who supported him and opposed the self-serving powerbrokers in Santa Fe.

Historian Thomas E. Chávez commented on the difference in cultural influence between the newcomers from the East and the people of New Mexico. American roots were English, God fearing, and Protestant with a strong Puritan ethic. Their mindset was steeped in individualism, with the belief that hard work and dedication to a moral goal would lead one to the good life, which might even include material success. New Mexicans, by contrast, were a product of Catholic Spain with a strong measure of Native American influence. Chávez sees them as "less individualistic and more inclusive." Morality did not lead to material rewards. The reward for leading a good life was eternal.[13] The perceptions of newcomers, like Davis and

Sumner, were influenced by their world, which included a belief in Manifest Destiny and often an insensitivity to other cultures.

To be sure, Edmund Ross was a man who emerged from the American Protestant ethic, but rooted deep within him was also an abolitionist view of life. He had a built-in compassion for people who were poor, ill educated, and victimized by those who would rationalize their right to take advantage of the less privileged. Ross would see the likes of Samuel Pomeroy over and over again in the speculators who dominated politics in New Mexico, wealthy men who probably believed that they were being rightfully rewarded for their initiative.

Property ownership for both New Mexicans and the new settlers from the Midwest and the East was important, but the concept of land ownership was different for the two groups. New Mexicans generally prized property for its usefulness, for farming or livestock grazing, and as their principal form of wealth to be passed on to future generations. To Americans, land was often no more than a commodity, a way of acquiring wealth. In early 1880, three Albuquerque men—Franz Huning, William Hazeldine, and Elias Stover—bought up a sizeable acreage of land, long held by local families, east of the town plaza. The land was quietly purchased on behalf of the Santa Fe Railroad at a "modest" price, in advance of the railroad actually reaching the area, and probably for no more than a few dollars per acre.[14] About half of the land was used for the railroad yards, while the other half was subdivided into hundreds of future town lots and sold off at huge profits both for the railroad and for Huning, Hazeldine, and Stover. The land is now downtown Albuquerque.

The most serious land grabbing by newcomers would come from the settlement of land grants under United States law. New Mexicans had been promised continued ownership of their property both in the declaration of General Kearny in 1846 and in the formal treaty of Guadalupe Hidalgo in 1848. However, New Mexicans would find that attaining fulfillment of the promise required considerable effort on their part. In addition to at least some fluency in English and written proof of ownership, which they often did not have, a knowledge of the American system of land patents was needed, a concept totally foreign to New Mexicans. A lawyer to plead their case was always necessary, and that, of course, took money—or, in lieu of money, giving up some of their land, sometimes as much as half, in payment for legal services.

By the time Edmund Ross became governor, the lawyers and the businessmen associated with them, men who coveted huge tracts of land, would dominate business, ranching, mining, and government throughout the territory. Their massive landholdings, one close to 2 million acres, were acquired through manipulations of the law that were at the very least questionable. These were the speculators that Colonel Sumner had warned would soon come to the territory.

There is a poignant footnote to the 1888 story of Ross's hopes for New Mexico statehood. Twice before, in 1874 and 1876, New Mexico had narrowly missed becoming a state. In 1888 more than a decade had passed; New Mexico's population had dramatically increased, and the two rail lines that now traversed the territory had put an emphatic end to New Mexico's isolation. To Ross, the chance that New Mexico would "make it" this time was very good indeed.

Ross had a vision for New Mexico which he repeated often during his tenure in office but never with greater enthusiasm than in a letter to H. C. Burnett, director of immigration for New Mexico, on February 24. Ross was in Washington, D.C., at the time and had learned that day that New Mexico was to be nominated for possible statehood. He believed that statehood would bring the entrepreneurs who could not fail to see the great potential in the new state. Statehood in Ross's words would "put the new state on the high road to prosperity."[15]

Ross could foresee that statehood would also bring the funds necessary to control devastating floods in the valleys by storing irrigation water from mountain runoff in reservoirs to be available for future irrigation needs. Ross had been raised in a farming family and believed farming would always be the backbone of the economy in New Mexico. He was sure farming could flourish as never before with statehood. But it was not to be, not in 1888 at least. As disappointed as Ross was about the failure of statehood, it was only the first of two devastating blows. The next would be the defeat of his plan to deal with New Mexico's land grant problems.

CHAPTER TWENTY

GOVERNOR ROSS AND THE COURT OF PRIVATE LAND CLAIMS

What we especially desire as machinery for the adjudication of these matters is a separate, independent judiciary, for the time being disconnected in every way from the current courts of justice, a tribunal that shall devote its entire time and effort to this single purpose, and be in its fullest sense a court of equity, authorized and competent to take entire jurisdiction of all the complicated phases of this most extraordinary condition of affairs. No other tribunal can successfully grapple with it.

—New Mexico territorial governor Edmund G. Ross, testifying before the House Committee on Territories, January 11, 1888

Every calculation based on experience elsewhere fails in New Mexico.

—New Mexico territorial governor Lew Wallace, April 29, 1881

⌒ LEW WALLACE'S OBSERVATION about New Mexico was at the same time humorous and, although cynical, mixed with a degree of truth. New Mexico was a unique place with problems unlike those of any other state or territory. While Wallace could throw up his hands at New Mexico's problems and at the end of his term move on to challenges elsewhere, New Mexico was Edmund Ross's home; as territorial governor, all problems were a serious matter to him. Lew Wallace dedicated part of his time in New Mexico (1878–1881) to the completion of his novel *Ben-Hur.* Ross's immediate predecessor, Governor Lionel Sheldon (1881–1885), who came to New Mexico from Louisiana, had a casual attitude toward governing, believing that the territory pretty much ran on its own.[1] Other than a respectable amount of time with his family, Ross devoted all of his energies to his work as governor.

Lillian Ross Leis describes her father's evenings as frequently taken up with informal calls from guests who would drop by the Palace of the Governors. He would visit with them "in a carefree manner and enjoy it, but work again after their departure." His routine was to work until midnight and often until three.[2] No doubt many of Ross's evening visitors combined business and pleasure. One can easily imagine George W. Julian, the surveyor general for New Mexico, dropping in for an after-hours discussion on a range of issues relating to land grant problems. Ross's and Julian's careers were similar to the extent that both had been abolitionists and Republicans (Julian had served six terms in the United States House as a representative from Indiana), then active leaders of the Liberal Republican Party, and both ultimately became Democrats. Although they maintained a friendly relationship, Ross and Julian did not always see eye to eye.

Julian, who was ten years older than Ross and a trained lawyer, indicated that he had at first turned down President Cleveland's request to help sort out the land grant problems at the core of corruption in New Mexico. Julian claimed that President Cleveland had offered him his pick of being named governor or surveyor general, advising that the surveyor general was the more important job. Julian's journal and letters to Cleveland, however, show that actually he solicited the job of governor and was happy to settle for the surveyor general position.[3] Perhaps because he was older with more formal education, Julian thought of himself as superior to Ross. At the time he took the job, Julian's health was poor, and his financial circumstances were marginal. Although he may at first have thought that life in distant New Mexico, dealing with notorious territorial politicians, would be bad for him, he took the job hoping Santa Fe's reputedly healthful climate would help him regain his vitality.[4]

Julian arrived to begin his job in Santa Fe on July 22, 1885, the day when Ross was being feted at the San Felipe Hotel in Albuquerque.[5] It was the intention of Albuquerque leaders to honor their fellow resident and celebrate the opening of their lavish new hotel, but some of the guests who rode the train down from Santa Fe saw the event as an opportunity to curry favor with the new governor. New Mexico's reputation for corruption and land fraud was widely known. It was no secret that President Cleveland expected Ross and Julian to break up the elite groups who had accumulated massive land holdings including vast acreage that belonged in the public domain. Speculators who were believed to have fraudulently manipulated the law were put on notice with the Ross and Julian appointments; but so were Ross and Julian being alerted to the entrenched power of the loose association of men in Santa Fe who had come to be known as the Santa Fe Ring.

In his July 22 speech in Albuquerque, as Julian was unpacking his suitcases in Santa Fe, Ross made it clear to the movers and shakers before him that he was governor of all the people in New Mexico and would not give preference to any one group. In his own dignified way, which the occasion called for, Ross singled out the cattle industry for its superior professional "organization and with its manifest advantages," meaning that cattle barons had extraordinary influence with all agencies of government. However, continued Ross, "The executive, by virtue of his position, is the conservator of all, the arbiter between all, and the friend of all, to whom all have the same right of appeal, whose duty it is under the law to protect each against infringements from all."[6]

It was Ross's way of telling the men before him that he could not be intimidated by any group, particularly the cattle industry. Indeed, by 1885 cattle ranching had become New Mexico's largest industry, with expansion accelerated by the Atchison, Topeka and Santa Fe and Southern Pacific railroads, which often carried more cattle than any other kind of freight. In 1880 there were an estimated 347,000 head of cattle in New Mexico, and 1,630,000 by 1890.[7]

Ross foresaw, perhaps naïvely given the semi-arid climate, that much of New Mexico would be "studded with small farms, and our markets supplied with an ample store of food, the product of New Mexican growth and manufacture." He believed the day would come, "and it is not very distant, [when] the immense land grants, and the great cattle and sheep ranches must give way to the small farmer."[8] It did not take an expert to recognize that farming was then far more modest than it could be and would probably see a great deal of expansion in the coming decades. Six years before Ross, Lew Wallace observed that "agriculture in New Mexico is yet in its primitive condition. The wooden plow of the Mexican fathers holds preference with the majority of farmers. . . . Iron piping will then take the place of the open acequias, and the area of planting will be vastly increased."[9]

Ross was required to submit his first report on the state of affairs in New Mexico in October 1885. This was rather short notice for a new governor who had little time to assess territorial conditions. Under the circumstances Ross does a more than fair job and gives the lion's share of the space in his report to land problems, but he mentions nothing about Surveyor General Julian. Julian would need a considerable amount of time to do a thorough job of evaluating the work of former surveyors general and to render his opinion about the system of adjudicating land grants. That Ross would show preference for land grant problems in his report is not surprising, given the orders he and Julian received from President Cleveland to find a fix for the problems caused by New Mexico's land-grabbing "rings."

Although Ross did not have the wealth of factual evidence that Julian would provide in the coming months, he did demonstrate a grasp of the problems related to land grants. In the report it is clear Ross understood the fundamental promise of the United States to New Mexican residents. "As a rule the lands actually occupied are held by an unimpeachable tenure, having been handed down from generation to generation . . . which leads them to suppose that there is no necessity for a public record for their holdings or a formal patent from the government."[10]

Ross is referring in this part of his report to several thousand small landholdings, few of which were ever formally titled by the Spanish or Mexican government but which were nevertheless recognized as valid. The Treaty of Guadalupe Hidalgo required the United States to also recognize these holdings as valid and to patent them according to United States law. The size of the properties may have been as small as five acres and rarely more than forty. When Ross and Julian came into office, it was thirty-one years since the office of surveyor general was established, and not only had New Mexicans with small properties failed to seek perfect title, but the surveyors general had also neglected to pay attention to these small holdings. The very large grants were the real problem that consumed their time.

Generally land grants, both Spanish and Mexican, fell into two categories: private grants to individuals and community grants to a group of individuals. Both private and community grants were an inexpensive way for the Spanish and Mexican governments to encourage and expand settlement. Private grants were awarded for a variety of reasons—recognition of public service rendered, for example—or simply because the individual applying would be helping to further establish Spanish or Mexican presence. Community grants to groups were large and included relatively small individual grants to members of the larger grant plus common areas owned collectively and available to all members. Common areas were for pasturing of livestock, woodcutting, and other collective activities. Individuals were free to sell their private land, but collectively owned community property could never be sold; at least, that was the intention under Spanish and Mexican jurisdiction.[11] There were two other categories of land grants closely related to community grants: town grants and grants to Pueblo Indian tribes.

The land grant problem with which the Cleveland administration was most concerned—and which it was Ross's and Julian's mission to fix—was the enlargement of grants far beyond the size initially claimed. In his 1885 annual report Ross cites an unnamed case in Rio Arriba County where the claimant stated he believed the grant to be 184,000 acres, a huge piece of land in itself. However, after the surveyor general and Congress validated the grant and the claim was then surveyed, it was found to be 472,000 acres. The difference between the two figures—288,000 acres—was believed to be a fraudulent increase in the size of the grant; that is, what was believed to be the theft of 288,000 acres of land in the public domain. Ross also cited a claim for 300 acres in Santa Fe County that grew to be 23,000 acres.

Ross expressed the opinion in his report that the practice of "enlarging the boundaries of bona fide grants" was so common "that public faith in large grant titles has largely diminished" and, in turn, a lack of faith in the validity of titles discouraged would-be investors in New Mexico land.[12] This same opinion about the unwillingness of investors to buy land in New Mexico was cited by Governor Sheldon before Ross and by Governor L. Bradford Prince after Ross, all of whom considered this barrier to settlement and agricultural development to be a serious problem.

The surveyor general system designed to evaluate land claims in New Mexico was established in 1854 and was, from its inception, a less than adequate way of dealing with claims. The idea was to have the surveyor general listen to, hold hearings on, and evaluate claims in his office and to make recommendations to the United States Congress, which had the authority of certifying the validity of a claim and eventually, after the land was surveyed, issuing patents. It was an absurdly difficult task for one man, and it was fraught with the potential for serious mischief.

The problem for landholders in proving ownership under United States law was the need to provide some kind of written proof to the surveyor general, preferably a deed. But written proof, of any kind, frequently could not be produced even in the case of communities. A public record for grants before 1680 was either destroyed during the Pueblo Revolt or perhaps never existed, and numerous holders of grants from the eighteenth and early nineteenth century likewise lacked written documentation of ownership. This was true for the community of Albuquerque, which could not produce any documentation showing that it had been recognized as a validly established community in 1706.[13] Ownership under generations-old New Mexico custom was often no more than the tacit recognition that the people who lived on and worked certain land were indeed the owners.

Congress restricted the surveyor general in several important ways. For a time he was prohibited from inspecting properties in advance of rendering a judgment or from authorizing the surveying of a property until after certification by Congress.[14] Once the claim was approved by Congress, the actual survey could be carried out without restriction. Field surveyors were paid by the size of the grant being surveyed and often were accompanied by the party or parties making the claim. It was to the advantage of surveyor and claimant alike to enlarge the grant, resulting in greatly exaggerated claims that encompassed massive amounts of land that would normally have been public domain. Hearing claims was only one of the responsibilities of the surveyor general. His other major responsibility was to represent the United States to assure that publicly owned land was protected. If George Julian's evaluation was correct, the surveyor general system was a spectacular failure. In evaluating this system, historian and attorney Malcolm Ebright declared that "the surveyor general was merely a passive agent of the government, and the procedure before his office was not really an adjudication at all."[15]

In his 1885 report, Ross suggested that New Mexico's surveyor general be replaced by a three-member commission, much like the California commission system, established in 1851, that had certified a high percentage of claims in that state over the space of three years. Congress had been motivated to authorize the California commission to quickly and efficiently settle claims because of that state's high-profile gold mining and its long seacoast with potential for ever-increasing international trade. Landlocked New Mexico, a mere territory, with little to recommend it and with numerous negative reports about its people and their strange customs, corrupt government, and nonexistent educational system, was not given the same attention by Congress. Ross was willing to acknowledge that the California commission was flawed, but it was far better than the system used in New Mexico. The alternative of settling claims in the court system, Ross submitted, would "result in the eviction of hundreds, if not thousands, of honest occupants and claimants through the costs of litigation, a class of claimants, too, who the United States is bound by solemn treaty stipulation to protect."[16]

Ross persuaded New Mexico's congressional delegate, Antonio Joseph, to sponsor a bill to establish the commission system for New Mexico.[17]

Governor Lionel Sheldon, in his annual report the previous year, also mentioned the need for Congress to do something to change the method of adjudicating land grants and suggested a commission as the most expedient way to handle the problem, but he went into very little detail. Sheldon's suggestion is confined to a short paragraph, where Ross's remarks, even in the early months of his time in office, covered two and a half pages of the report. Lew Wallace mentioned the problem of land grants in only a single sentence of his 1879 report, pointing out that the large grants were a hindrance to the development of agriculture.[18]

By the time of his 1886 report, Ross was armed with more detailed information supplied by Julian, to whom he gives credit for work that was "careful, laborious and intelligent." The second annual report by Ross repeated his plea for Congress to do something to correct the surveyor general system in New Mexico. The report included the observation that "many thousands of acres of public lands are still enclosed by private fences and otherwise held in great cattle ranges, to the exclusion of small farmers." Additionally, "many grants have been thus absorbed into great cattle ranches, merely for the purpose of getting control of water courses and springs, and to thus keep out settlers and small herds; and in others, the lands have been thus stolen for purely speculative purposes."[19]

Although Ross was governor, George Julian was directly responsible to William Sparks, the General Land Office commissioner in Washington, from whom he received his instructions and to whom he issued his reports. Julian, of course, shared his findings with Ross, whose instructions from the president were to break the hold of the Santa Fe Ring on the affairs of New Mexico. For Ross this meant doing his part to bring equity to the adjudication of land grant claims in addition to dealing with the myriad other problems all governors faced. Ross relied upon Julian's findings as he considered his recommendations to Interior Secretary L.Q.C. Lamar.

George Julian made sure his findings were made public. He published partial results of his work in the July 1887 issue of the prominent periodical the *North American Review* in an article titled "Land-Stealing in New Mexico." The controversial article ran fifteen pages and impressively documented fraudulent activity on the part of claimants and likely on the part of some, if not most, of the surveyors general who preceded him. Julian began the article with a description of the scope of land grants, explaining that the grants amounted to about 24,000 square miles, "being equal in extent to the land surface of the four states of Rhode Island, Connecticut, New

Hampshire and Vermont."[20] The sheer size of the grants was beyond the experience of Washington officials and contributed to the belief that much of public domain land was being taken illegally. Julian set out to prove this was, indeed, the case.

Julian went on to explain the great responsibilities and power of the surveyor general and to argue that the job was best suited for a first-rate lawyer who was incorruptible, since he had the authority to pass on titles to these vast land claims that "no court in the Union had any authority to review." Surveyors general were poorly paid, and thus "competent and fit men" were unwilling to accept the work, and those who did frequently were corruptible, at least in Julian's assessment. Of the men who held the job before him, only one or two, according to Julian, were lawyers.[21]

To support his findings, Julian's article examined thirteen claims that were still awaiting initial approval in Congress. In each case Julian showed how land grants were embellished to absurd proportions. A typical example was the alleged Ignacio Cháves grant, a claim of four leagues or 17,712 acres. Julian could find "no evidence that the conditions of the grant were ever complied with, or of the existence of any heirs or legal representatives of the grantee. The grant, however, was pronounced valid by the Surveyor-General at the time, and the survey subsequently made the tract fifteen miles from north to south and twenty-two from east to west, containing an area of 243,036 acres, or nearly 380 square miles."[22]

He also reported that 49 claims already had reached the patenting stage with Congress and that 24 of those claims had actually been patented, with 2 rejected, thus leaving 23 pending. Of all the 62 claims reported in his article, Julian estimated that there were nearly 9 million acres of land taken illegally from the public domain. Unfortunately, Julian believed the lands already patented were now beyond legal reach unless fraud could be proven.[23]

Julian did not hesitate to name those he believed guilty of fraud, including former United States senator Stephen W. Dorsey, prominent Republicans Stephen Elkins and Thomas Catron, and even fellow Democrat C. H. Gildersleeve. His strident public description of these men was perhaps ill advised: "They have hovered over the territory like a pestilence. To a fearful extent they have dominated governors, judges, district attorneys, legislatures, surveyors-general and their deputies, marshals, treasurers, county commissioners, and the controlling business interests of the people. They have confounded political distinctions and subordinated everything to the greed for land."[24] Ross may or may not have agreed with Julian's assessment, but given the fact that Ross had to deal with these men on a broad range of issues, it seems unlikely he would have encouraged Julian to publicly express his opinions in this manner. On the other hand, perhaps Ross had read Julian's article before publication and believed that Julian could be the lightning rod without there being harm to his own ability to run the affairs of the territory. If that was the case, the plan backfired. In the words of historian Howard R. Lamar, "Julian took the view that truly Draconian measures must be employed. . . . Much of the intense bitterness over Ross's administration, therefore, was actually caused by Julian's ruthless scrutiny of land records and his scathing reports to Washington."[25] Though probably there were times when Ross was in closer agreement with the Santa Fe power brokers than with Julian, Ross and Julian would always be regarded as two of a kind, and Ross's place in New Mexico history would suffer because of their close affiliation.

Ross and Julian could not agree on a solution to New Mexico's land problems. Julian believed the commission idea, supported by Ross, was little better than the surveyor general program: "The commission was composed of men of ability and character, but under the malign influence of land-stealing experts the most shameful raids upon public domain were made [in California] through fabricated grants and fraudulent surveys."[26] Julian eventually won Ross over to this opinion. However, Ross could not see much value in Julian's solution, which was to have the secretary of the interior act on the recommendations of the surveyor general in place of Congress, since Congress was so slow to act. The secretary of the interior, Ross felt, was in no better position than Congress to make the necessary complex evaluations. The secretary was already burdened with a heavy agenda and would be delegating the basic work to his subordinates, people who sat in offices two thousand miles from New Mexico. What the two men did agree on was that the core of the problem was Congress and its inability or unwillingness to find a better way to resolve land grant problems.

Ross expressed his frustration with Congress in September 1887 in his third annual report, but interestingly, while Julian might have left readers of his *North American Review* article with the idea that he found nothing but fraud in New Mexico, Ross pointed out that "the investigations of the surveyor-general have shown that a considerable proportion of these grants are meritorious and ought to be confirmed, in accordance with treaty obligations." He went on to deplore the inability of the two houses of Congress to agree on action going forward. As it was, there had been little action on New

Mexico claims in the 1880s. The one bright spot that Ross could point to in his report was the adoption by the House of Representatives of a commission system much as he had proposed it in October 1885. The Senate, however, passed a quite different bill, sponsored by Senator George F. Edmunds of Vermont, to refer all land claims to the district court system. Both Ross and Julian could see nothing but a dead end with claims in district court. In Julian's words, the Senate bill should be titled "an act to postpone indefinitely the settlement of all titles to Spanish and Mexican grants."[27] In Ross's words, "The man is not born who would see the end."[28]

Ross decided to take matters into his own hands and began to organize a delegation of New Mexicans to travel to Washington with him to seek a settlement between the two houses. On November 14 he wrote to Senator Daniel W. Voorhees of Indiana seeking his advice on timing. Should he bring his delegation to Washington early in the coming congressional session or wait until later? He explained, "I have a Bill proposed, which combines the best features of both the Bills that have heretofore passed, one in the Senate and the other in the House but failed of concurrence."[29] Voorhees strongly encouraged an early arrival: "Nothing can be lost by promptitude and much might be by delay."[30]

On January 11, 1888, Ross addressed the House Committee on Territories speaking in support of a proposed bill for the settlement of land grants in New Mexico. Ross took his time making sure the committee understood the background of New Mexican land grants: "Their grants were held under special concessions to individuals or communities, or by general laws for colonization or town building, and by right of possession. . . . Their ownership was universally recognized, and the indefinite nature and lack of minute description of boundaries was of small moment in a country whose population was so sparse that there was ample room for all and land was practically valueless." He explained the difference between individual and community grants and the differences between claims, of which he identified four distinct classes, "each demanding recognition and each hedged about by complications and intricacies peculiar to it, which nothing short of patient and rigid judicial investigation by a tribunal vested with all the powers of a court of equity can clear away. . . . What we especially desire as machinery for the adjudication of these matters is a separate, independent judiciary, for the time being disconnected in every way from the current courts of justice, a tribunal that shall devote its entire time and effort to this single purpose, and be in its fullest sense a court of equity, authorized and competent to take entire jurisdiction of all the complicated phases of this most extraordinary condition of affairs. No other tribunal can successfully grapple with it."[31]

Ross was formally proposing, for the first time, a court of private land claims. It would be a temporary court that would consider nothing but land claims, and when its job was done, it would disband. It was an excellent compromise between House and Senate bills. Whether Ross can be credited totally with the concept of an independent court is hard to say. There was at least one other New Mexico resident suggesting something similar. Oddly, it was the powerful land speculator Stephen W. Dorsey, who published an article in the *North American Review* answering Julian's charges from earlier in the year. In his article Dorsey suggested the possibility of an independent court to rule on land claims. Dorsey's article appeared in October 1887 during the time Ross was organizing his contingent to go to Washington.[32] Ross's letter to Senator Voorhees leaves open the possibility that the idea originated with someone else. In the letter Ross does not take absolute credit for the idea of a new court. However, what is beyond dispute is that it was Ross who organized the delegation and took it to Washington, and it was Ross who convincingly spoke to Congress at length and with clarity.

Ross remained in Washington to monitor the progress of the bill for a total of four months. On February 11, 1888, he appeared before the House Committee on Private Land Claims to propose an amendment to the bill that would require the court to conduct its business in the territory where the claim was being made. Ross believed this was imperative, since many of the claimants were poor people who would find it impossible to travel to Washington and who had no paperwork to prove ownership. Ross again was recognizing that, in addition to the massive land grants that garnered most of the attention, there were thousands of small claims, in the ten-to-forty-acre range, for which claimants had no documentation but could bring witnesses to establish their ownership: "We have a conspicuous illustration of the value and the need of localizing the processes of the courts, to the end that they shall see and know that justice is done to all, and that a beneficent government is not despoiled."[33] The defense of those who were threatened by people with power, wealth, and superior knowledge was a recurring theme with Ross. He detested people who used that power to overwhelm with impunity.

It was in this period that statehood for New Mexico was under consideration in Congress. Although Ross's hopes of statehood quickly faded, he was still hopeful that the land claim bill would pass both houses of Congress. A major problem for Ross came from George Julian, who attacked the Court of Private Land Claims in a letter released to New Mexico territorial newspapers.[34] One newspaper (apparently the *Santa Fe Herald*) commented: "There is good reason to believe that the House bill would have passed on the 31st of March and the whole subject been now in Committee of Conference, had not the time allowed for its discussion been consumed by opposition inspired by the Surveyor General of New Mexico."[35] The article further indicated that the House and the Senate were working on bills that were very similar. It was likely these differences could easily have been resolved.

It was not until July that the Court of Private Land Claims was approved by the House of Representatives. A July 30 letter from Antonio Joseph to Ross in New Mexico offered warm congratulations to Ross for his "untiring and faithful services over a period of months" in getting the bill passed in the House. Joseph also was impressed with the fact that Ross had spent those months in Washington "at your own personal expense." In addition Joseph said he believed that the Senate "Ransom bill" would soon pass and that a joint committee would correct the differences between the two bills. He had high hopes that "some measure for our relief will be passed before adjournment."[36] The letter reveals the strong working relationship Ross and Joseph had established during the three previous years. It was not merely a note of routine congratulations; it was a heartfelt letter of admiration. It would appear that Ross and Joseph had a better working relationship than Ross and Julian in spite of Joseph's opposition to Ross's appointment in the spring of 1885.

When no progress seemed to be coming from the Senate by August, Ross exchanged letters with Senator William M. Stewart of Nevada hoping to understand the inaction of the Senate. Stewart wrote on September 10, "I did not mean to have you infer from my letter of the 25th that there was any affirmative opposition to the land court bill on the part of any Democratic Senator, but the trouble is their want of interest and their inaction in regard to it."[37] Stephen Elkins, the former New Mexico delegate to Congress, a reputed member of the Santa Fe Ring and former partner of Thomas Catron, was reported to have expressed the opinion that there would soon be a new administration in Washington and that the passage of the CPLC bill should be delayed to ensure that a Republican president would appoint the judges to the new court and to prevent Cleveland from having that opportunity.[38] Ross would not have given up, but in November, as Elkins apparently predicted, Republican Benjamin Harrison defeated President Grover Cleveland even though Cleveland won the popular vote by a small margin. Ross would have only six months left in office.

Historians sometimes overlook the good that politicians and others do. Two of the most often quoted New Mexico historians, writing near the end of the territorial years, say little about Ross and his attempts to find a better solution for resolving land grant problems. L. Bradford Prince, the man who would replace Ross in the Palace of the Governors, would later in his life write a number of books on New Mexico history including his *Concise History of New Mexico*, published in 1912. Prince would mention nothing about Ross's efforts to have a court of private land claims established, while at the same time he wrote about his own successful attempt two years after Ross was out of office. Prince reported how he as governor organized a group of New Mexico residents to travel with him to Washington to be with him as he advocated for the court system that Ross, in fact, had proposed.[39] Prince took full credit for getting the Court of Private Land Claims through Congress, without acknowledging the fact that his predecessor, Edmund Ross, had proposed the same tribunal and demonstrated the method for inducing Congress to act.

Probably the most highly regarded New Mexico historian writing during the earliest years of the twentieth century was Ralph Emerson Twitchell. He gives details of Prince's efforts to establish a committee to accompany him to Washington to speak on behalf of the bill and of how the Court of Private Land Claims finally became law in 1891. Like Prince, he makes no mention of Ross's identical efforts in 1888. In fact, Twitchell even gives the retiring president of the New Mexico Bar Association credit for suggesting the idea for a court of private land claims in 1890.[40] Surely Twitchell knew better about the origins of the land claims court; he was a lawyer and had been active in New Mexico politics since 1884. He was a Republican whose bias against the Ross administration was emphatic. He especially detested George Julian, who he said was "steeped in prejudice against New Mexico and its people and their property rights. . . . Not content with officially passing upon the matters coming regularly before him, for strictly partisan purposes, [Julian] saw fit to use his name and office in a vain attempt to destroy the titles to land grants in New Mexico. . . . The pernicious influence of this political mountebank was far reaching in the eastern states of the union."[41] Twitchell could find little of value in Ross's administration, but at least he did not attack Ross on the personal level as he did Julian.

Other New Mexico historians have relied upon the work of Prince and Twitchell, men whose reputations as historians are respected. Knowledge of when the Court of Private Land Claims was created may be all that is important to a historian, and it is certainly true that the court was established in 1891, after Ross was out of office. Victor Westphall, writing in 1983, gives his account of the Court of Private Land Claims: "Edward F. Hobart replaced Julian on September 7, 1889 and served until August 2, 1893. During this time he witnessed the creation of the Court of Private Land Claims, established for the purpose of settling land grants in New Mexico. Hobart's greatest contribution to the territory as its surveyor general was in the field of small-holding claims."[42] Again no mention of Ross, even in regard to Ross's efforts on behalf of small landholders.

During the thirteen years the Court of Private Land Claims met, it examined (among others) twelve of the thirteen unsettled claims cited by Julian in his *North American Review* article (one was never submitted). Five were rejected by the court, and seven were partially approved. What initially was claimed to be more than 3 million acres of land was certified by the court at 117,640 acres, only 3 percent of what was sought.[43]

Edmund Ross could be justifiably proud of lobbying as hard as he did for the Court of Private Land Claims, regardless of the lack of recognition he received for his efforts. During his tenure it was not Ross's function to personally evaluate individual land claims; it was his job to seek a solution for the land claim quagmire, and in that respect he did a superb job.

It is doubtful that any scholar would defend the surveyor general system as the best way of resolving land claims in New Mexico. The Court of Private Land Claims surely was superior, and it is unlikely a better system could have been found. However, there are scholars who argue that the resolution of land claims by the court resulted in vast acreage being unjustly withheld from private ownership. In all, the court adjudicated 282 large claims (plus several thousand small claims), an aggregate total of more than 20 million acres, with only about 2 million acres confirmed.[44] If claimants were unjustly denied title by the court, it was not because the fundamental concept of the court was wrong but because the United States government was intent on keeping as much of the land as possible in the public domain.

CHAPTER TWENTY-ONE

THE SANTA FE RING AND THE
TERRITORIAL LEGISLATURE

The despotic rulers of Europe and Asia hate it [freedom of expression] for it is their implacable enemy. The political schemer hates it, for it is sure to bring his schemes to light and him to disgrace. The criminal hates it, for it is worse than a sleuthhound upon his track. The ignorant hates it, for it shames his ignorance. All men who live otherwise than in the broad, open light of day, and are ashamed that the world may know their acts, hate the press and pray for libel laws like this.

—Edmund G. Ross, territorial governor, vetoing the Libel Law,

January 28, 1889

IN MARCH 1887, when Ross had been in office for nearly two years, he wrote to a friend, John O'Grady, in St. Louis, Missouri. The letter appears to be in response to an inquiry by O'Grady about the general condition of affairs in New Mexico. Ross's reply ran to sixteen pages. It was essentially an elaborate description of the Santa Fe Ring, that infamous alliance of politicians, lawyers, and businessmen, and the influence of the Ring on the territorial legislature.

The O'Grady letter is unlike others written about conditions in New Mexico during that era. Ross does not place native New Mexicans at the heart of the territory's problems; on the contrary, he sees them as victims. "The curse of the territory is rings. Many years ago a few sharp, shrewd Americans came here, discovered a number of small Mexican and Spanish Grants—purchased them at nominal prices—learned the Spanish language—ingratiated themselves into favor with the Mexican people, proceeded to enlarge the Grants they had purchased, and to manufacture at will, titles to still others, and to secure therefore Congressional recognition."[1] Howard Lamar's research showed that eventually 80 percent of Spanish land grants would fall into the hands of American lawyers and their clients, with thirty-four of the claimants holding more than 100,000 acres each.[2]

Ross named two men in the O'Grady letter, "Elkins and Catron," without mentioning their first names. Both men would have been familiar to O'Grady, since both were from Missouri and both had widely established reputations by 1887. Stephen Benton Elkins (b. 1841) and Thomas Benton Catron (b. 1840) were the sons of men who greatly admired Senator Thomas Hart Benton and who coincidentally gave their sons the same middle name in honor of the famous Missouri senator.[3] Catron biographer Victor Westphall makes it clear that although the two names were linked for most of their lives, their relationship was "an alliance of convenience that was often stormy and almost never more than cordial."[4] Early political differences prior to the Civil War were the first test of their friendship, Elkins declaring his allegiance to the North while Catron sided with the South. Both men served as officers during the Civil War but on opposite sides.

After an early release from duty, and estranged from his family—they were ardent South sympathizers—Elkins found it wise to seek his future elsewhere. New Mexico was a logical choice, with regular wagon trains departing for Santa Fe from Missouri. Elkins quickly became fluent in Spanish and established himself in legal practice in Santa Fe before the end of the war. He maintained regular correspondence with a fiancée in Wellington, Missouri. In June 1866 he was married in Missouri and, with his bride, found himself, apparently by coincidence, on the same wagon train to New Mexico with Thomas Catron.[5] The weeks that it took to make the trek to Santa Fe brought Elkins and Catron together again. They rediscovered their mutual interest in law, and, although it would not happen directly, they would become partners, albeit for only a little more than two years, between January 1874 and May 1876.[6] Elkins also convinced Catron to become a Republican in a territory heavily dominated by Republicans. As Westphall observed, "while both enjoyed politics, the political career of each was motivated to a degree by the part politics could play in developing their respective economic empires."[7]

Elkins was New Mexico's territorial delegate to Congress from 1873 to 1877, a political position that meant that he spent nearly all of his time in Washington. Although Elkins and Catron were no longer law partners after May 1876, they continued to be business associates and worked closely with each other for many years, using the mail and occasional personal visits.

With this arrangement it was possible for Elkins to continue his association with the Ring. In 1878 Elkins opened a law office in Washington, D.C., and in 1879 he moved the office to New York City, all the while maintaining his rapport with congressional leaders and various members of the administration. Elkins apparently never resumed residence in New Mexico, no doubt realizing that his hope of becoming a United States senator from New Mexico was unrealistic. His personal and professional interest in the territory remained strong and his influence on land claim settlements impressive. During his time as the New Mexico delegate, seven large grants were patented with Elkins's assistance. Of the seven, his associate Catron was directly involved in five. Sixteen more claims were patented by Congress between 1878 and 1883, and Elkins apparently was involved in all of them either as a direct legal representative of the claimants or using his influence on their behalf with the General Land Office or with Congress. Of the sixteen cases, Catron was an active party to ten.[8]

Others who had an apparently friendly association with the Ring would follow Elkins as New Mexico delegates, including Democrat Antonio Joseph, who would occupy that post during the entire four years of Ross's tenure as territorial governor.[9] By the late 1880s Elkins had settled in West Virginia. In 1895 he realized his dream of being a senator, representing the state of West Virginia in the United States Senate until his death in 1911.

Catron remained in New Mexico, probably amassing more land than any single person in United States history to that time. William Keleher reported that in 1896 Catron owned fractional interests in thirty-one land grants and additionally owned 1,076,711 acres outright.[10] In 1894 the *Santa Fe New Mexican* estimated that Catron owned nearly 2 million acres and was part owner or attorney for an additional 4 million.[11] Like Elkins, Catron would become a United States senator, New Mexico's first, in 1912.

Elkins and Catron were and are controversial figures in New Mexico history. To Ross they were the "principal originators and manipulators" of the Land Grant Ring. Beside land schemes, Elkins and Catron were heavily involved in banking, mining, and cattle ranching and held politically appointed or elected positions during most years of their post–Civil War lives.

There were dozens of other lawyers and land speculators in late-nineteenth-century New Mexico. Ross told O'Grady that there was "an average of one lawyer to every ten Americans."[12] But to Ross, Elkins and Catron were the first lawyers to pursue massive landholdings, especially Catron, who was the leader of the Land Grant Ring and the senior partner in the largest law firm in New Mexico. In his O'Grady letter, Ross went on to explain that "from the Land Grant Ring grew others as the opportunities for speculation and plunder were developed. Cattle Rings, Public Land Stealing Rings, Mining Rings, Treasury Rings and rings of almost every description grew up, till the affairs of the territory came to be run almost exclusively in the interest and for the benefit of combinations organized and headed by a few long headed, ambitious and unscrupulous Americans attracted hither by the golden opportunities for power and plunder."[13]

It was widely believed that the rings consolidated their power in the commercial and political center of the territory, Santa Fe, and that the lesser rings answered to a controlling group known as the Santa Fe Ring. Whether such a highly organized ring actually existed is at least debatable. Certainly there was no formal organization that called itself the Santa Fe Ring. However, political power concentrated in the hands of relatively few men was a reality. They were mostly Republicans in a country that had been dominated by Republicans for twenty-five years. Some Democrats were also affiliated with the Ring, including the New Mexico Democratic chairman, C. H. Gildersleeve. What Democratic Ring members had in common with their Republican cohorts was a quest for land and wealth. With the election of Grover Cleveland, Edmund Ross would be the first Democratic territorial governor after the Civil War and the first to oppose the entrenched political establishment in Santa Fe, an establishment whose recognized leader was Thomas Benton Catron. To Ross the Santa Fe Ring was quite real. He told O'Grady that "the Ring dictated at will the legislation and general conduct of the affairs of the Territory, with branches here and there in the lesser towns but all subservient to the Central head. For years its rule was imperious and unquestioned. It elected legislatures and Delegates to Congress. It had the ear of the administration at Washington and could build up and pull down men at its pleasure. Whoever dared to oppose its purposes or methods was purchased or intimidated into silence, or killed, unless he escaped by flight."[14]

New Mexico Supreme Court rulings were not immune to Ring influences. At the time President Cleveland appointed Ross to serve as territorial governor, he also appointed New Mexico resident and Democrat William A. Vincent to be the New Mexico territorial chief justice. Only a few months later, in October 1885, Cleveland fired Vincent, who by then had appointed former United States senator and influential Ring member Stephen W. Dorsey to a five-man commission to select the grand and petit jurors who would hear cases possibly of interest to or involving Dorsey or other land speculators. Dorsey had moved to New Mexico from Arkansas and had become a successful cattle rancher with a major spread of land in Colfax County and an interest in adding even more acreage.[15] His reputation had been tarnished by his involvement in the infamous "star route" mail fraud scheme of 1881. Vincent, although he was removed from office by the president, was rewarded a year later for his dedication to the Ring when he was elected president of the New Mexico Bar Association.

Ross told O'Grady that the bar was essentially a "close corporation" controlled by the Santa Fe Ring.[16] Every bill under consideration by the legislature, according to historian Victor Westphall, was first reviewed by the bar association and without bar approval did not pass. The bar association thus controlled the legislature on behalf of the Ring.[17] Ross described the relationship between the bar and the legislature in a similar manner. "It is a matter of public notoriety that a given number of copies of every printed bill was immediately upon being printed, and previous to any action being had, forwarded by a page to a corresponding number of these outside gentlemen [bar association members], for their examination and sanction or rejection."[18]

Ross's immediate problem upon taking office was to assemble his own team, a problem that was complicated by an 1880 territorial court ruling that made the jobs of incumbents in the territorial office secure for two years. Ross's immediate predecessor, Lionel Sheldon, a Republican friendly with Santa Fe Ring members, appointed a group of fellow Republicans to high-level jobs just before leaving office. Thus for two years Ross was compelled to work with men not of his choosing.[19] On August 24, 1885, Ross wrote a six-page letter to United States Attorney General A. H. Garland hoping for some solution to his dilemma. "I am surrounded by subordinate officials appointed by my predecessor, Republican in politics, of that class of politicians who inaugurated and sustained the obnoxious practices that have obtained here for the past twenty years and of course antagonistic to the methods of reform and better government, politically and economical, that I desire to establish. The laws of the territory are such that there is doubt of my power to remove them, even under charges of malfeasance and misfeasance in office."[20]

Ross had the freedom to appoint his own personal secretary, and for that position he chose his son Arthur who stayed on the job for about a year. Arthur's health continued to be a concern; he returned to California briefly and came back with a new bride but did not resume his previous job at the Palace of the Governors.[21] Ross kept the personal secretary job in the family, however, by hiring his daughter Eddie, who would remain with him for the duration of his term. Ross also arranged for his son Pitt to be responsible for field surveying, working directly for George Julian. These appointments were nepotism, of course, but they were also a way for Ross to ensure that not all important jobs were controlled by Ring members.

There appeared to be nothing Ross could do about appointments to most major positions, but he was determined nonetheless to do what he could. The most difficult appointee for Ross was territorial attorney general William Breeden, a powerful member of the Santa Fe Ring who was also founder and chairman of the Republican Party in New Mexico and Thomas Catron's law partner. Breeden served as attorney general throughout the years of the Sheldon administration, and Sheldon, perhaps because he was unfamiliar with New Mexico, essentially allowed Breeden to run the government.[22] Ross, in his determination to break the hold of the Ring on his administration, fired Breeden in much the same way that Andrew Johnson had once fired Edwin Stanton, hoping to test the validity of the New Mexico tenure law in the courts. Breeden publicly and cynically fired back at Ross in a Santa Fe newspaper. Ross then wrote a public letter to Breeden on November 24, 1885, explaining his reasons for firing him. "As to the 'cause' for your suspension . . . you were suspended for drunkenness, licentiousness, gambling and misfeasance, malfeasance and nonfeasance in office: crimes which ought not to be tolerated in a public official. As a public office is a public trust, so a public official is a public exemplar. No man who habitually infracts the laws of sobriety or decency is fit for public trust. . . . As you deemed it proper to furnish the press with a copy of your communication, to which this is an answer, I trust you will pardon me for taking the same liberty."[23]

Ultimately Ross's attempt to fire Breeden failed when the territorial Supreme Court ruled in favor of Breeden, who then continued to serve with Ross for the remainder of his term.[24] It is easy to imagine how awkward the situation was, since Breeden's office was in the Palace of the Governors adjacent to Ross's office and family living quarters. Furthermore, Ross had to find a civilized way of working with Breeden on a regular basis.

The other major appointee challenged by Ross, this time successfully, was territorial treasurer Antonio Ortiz y Salazar. Ross charged Ortiz y Salazar with speculating in territorial warrants, accusing him of preferential treatment of Ring members at a loss of some $500,000 to New Mexico residents. He also accused him of mismanaging funds for the construction of a new territorial penitentiary. When Ortiz y Salazar refused to relinquish his office to Bernard Seligman, the man Ross chose to replace him, Ross wrote a lengthy open letter to the newspaper.[25] Ortiz y Salazar did not challenge Ross or attempt to respond in print.

Especially after the Breeden incident, Ring opposition to Edmund Ross was unrelenting. Some Santa Fe residents under the influence of the Ring were, in Ross's words, "bitterly hostile" while other territorial communities, Albuquerque residents in particular, strongly favored Ross. After Breeden there was a stepped-up attempt to have the president withdraw Ross's name and, failing that, to have the Senate reject the Ross nomination. Although Ross tells O'Grady that confirmation of his appointment was "practically unanimous" in the Senate,[26] it is also true that his appointment was held up for an entire year, during which time an accumulation of accusations piled up with the subcommittee reviewing his appointment.[27] Ross served on a provisional basis until May 1866.

One of Ross's major contributions in office came from confronting the legislative assembly head on, especially when the legislature was self-serving. Ross vetoed legislation either because it violated the organic laws of the federal or territorial government or because it was clearly meant to establish favoritism or unfair advantage for one segment of the population to the detriment of another. Ross knew a thing or two about the way legislatures were supposed to work, and he knew the law pertaining to territories.

As we have seen, practically no bills were passed without the approval of the bar association, a group that blatantly interfered with the legislature. On the other hand, Ross proved to be equally troublesome for legislators and Ring members during the twenty-seventh session (winter 1886–1887), the first of the two sessions held during his tenure as governor. Ross had the power to veto, which he did regularly during the two sessions. In his O'Grady letter he stated, "I found it necessary to defeat, by direct and pocket vetoes, twenty-five percent of all the measures that passed the two Houses, many of them absolutely vicious, and all of them of questionable character."[28] Ross stated that considerable money was spent to secure passage of several of the bills during the twenty-seventh legislature. Although there was a Republican majority in both houses, Ross controlled enough votes to stop the passage of veto overrides, which required a two-thirds vote in both houses. In that session only a single bill was passed over Ross's veto. Ross told O'Grady that he derived much satisfaction from defeating "vicious" legislation. He also said he was enclosing a pamphlet explaining his 1887 vetoes.

The pamphlet Ross referred to was titled *Seven Vetoes*.[29] One of the vetoes involved the desire of some residents of the city of Socorro to unincorporate the community. The makeup of the twelve-man Legislative Council (the territorial equivalent of a senate) was six Republicans, five Democrats, and one unaffiliated member named Candelario Garcia, a Socorro resident. The Republicans promised Garcia a special bill to unincorporate Socorro, assuming that he therefore would align himself with the Republicans who were trying to achieve enough voting power to override Ross vetoes.[30] When the Socorro bill hit Ross's desk, he vetoed it with a thorough explanation. "That its effect is purely local and in no sense general, makes this a local and special measure, and therefore repugnant to the law of Congress prohibiting local and special legislation."[31] Furthermore, the General Incorporation Act of 1884, under which Socorro was incorporated—and which was upheld by the New Mexico Supreme Court—provided the means for a city to unincorporate.[32] Even if special legislation were a possibility, it would have been unnecessary, and therefore Ross's veto was justified. Of course, the actual motive of the Council did not go unnoticed by Ross. Ross's understanding of the law and his ability to cite specifics is impressive in all of his vetoes. The extent to which he could rely upon his attorney general is unclear.

One of the other bills examined in the pamphlet was the Torts Bill. Ross described the act as a "very little bill . . . in a very innocent guise." He went on to say, however, that "there was never before presented to the consideration of a legislative body a proposition more replete with iniquitous results, or that embraced in the same space a wider scope of mischievous consequences to the poor people of New Mexico." Ross pointed out that if it should become law it would "entirely revolutionize the practice and rules of evidence now in force in the Courts . . . that it put upon the defendant, instead of the complainant, or accuser, the burden of proof of ownership or of innocence. That this Bill is a cunningly devised scheme of robbery and directed mainly to the eviction of the occupants of this class of land grants for the benefit of doubtful claimants, is apparent from a careful examination by any one at all familiar with the prevailing conditions of land tenure in this territory."[33]

Another of the 1887 bills that Ross vetoed was known as an act creating the County of Logan. This was an attempt by the legislature to divide Grant County in two, but, as Ross pointed out, the new county would take about two-thirds of the territory of Grant County and with that about fourteen-fifteenths of the railroad taxable property. The two principal communities in Grant County were Deming in the south and Silver City in the north. Civic leaders from Deming lobbied the legislature to divide the county in two.[34] But as Ross was quick to note, "Taken altogether it is the boldest and baldest scheme of plunder that has so far characterized this session of the Legislative Assembly; equaled only in that respect by the instrumentalities which have been employed to secure its passage."[35] When Ross vetoed the bill, a collection of Deming residents hanged and burned him in effigy,[36] ironic since Ross would, before too many years, become the editor of the *Deming Headlight* newspaper.

Ross believed that those who supported his vetoes in 1887 did so "in the face of threats and bribes that, if taken, would have made them rich." He was confident, with some justification, that "the rule of corrupt rings is broken—a victory for decent government." He was premature with his prediction, but indeed he did prevail with the 1887 assembly. "Hence the howl that is now going up for my removal. All the thieving, plundering rings are combining in a last desperate effort for my overthrow and thereby the return of the good old days when they could rule and rob at will."[37]

Republican delegates to the Twenty-eighth Legislative Assembly in the winter of 1888–1889 could approach their work with a strong sense of confidence. By then Ross was in his last days in office, and Republicans could count 8 seats on the Council to only 4 Democrats, while they controlled the House 15 to 9. They had managed to do this with a number of dubious elections the previous fall. Howard Lamar notes: "The election of a new legislature was accompanied by evidence of such blatant frauds at the polls that Ross appealed to Washington for legal aid to prevent the defeated candidates from contesting the election and thus hampering the legislature."[38] Ross did not want any delays with the legislative process that would keep him from leaving his mark on the proceedings. He had only months left in office. Ironically, this meant that Republicans had enough control to defeat his vetoes even though some of them had been fraudulently elected. Once again Ross liberally used the veto with well-reasoned justification but with a certain futility. Of the Twenty-eighth Legislature, historian Ralph Emerson Twitchell, a contemporary of Ross's, wrote, "One hundred and forty-five laws were passed. . . . Governor Ross used his veto power on nearly every measure, but in each instance the power of the republican leaders was brought to play and the vetoes were not sustained."[39]

Twitchell, a Republican who had been friendly with Ring members during his career, wrote with disdain about Ross's term. His observation about Ross's use of the veto during the Twenty-eighth Legislature would lead his readers to believe that Ross vetoed nearly 145 bills. The truth was far from that, although Ross used the veto more often than any previous governor. On February 28, 1889, Eddie Ross wrote to her sister Lillie during the short breaks she had from serving her father during the last night of the legislative session. She told of a wager in the office that there would be a total of 25 vetoes; she herself had predicted 24, and in the end the total was 23.[40] Like Twitchell, L. Bradford Prince made it sound as if Ross disapproved the great majority of bills, citing the fact that Ross had approved only 47.[41] That left a total of 75 bills on which he took no action at all, the implication being that he chose to pocket veto those bills, realizing they would become law even though he disapproved of them. According to Ross, the majority of the bills were of a routine nature and some "were of a class of measures that rendered it immaterial whether they became laws or not."[42]

Like the 7 veto messages of the Twenty-seventh Legislature, all 23 written vetoes of the Twenty-eighth were subsequently typeset and made available to the public.[43] The vetoes were well reasoned and clearly written. The vetoes cited violations of the United States Constitution or the New Mexico territorial constitution or the self-serving nature of legislation designed to benefit few people at the expense of many. While Ross's vetoes were soundly reasoned, Twitchell and Prince did not give reasoned objections to Ross's vetoes but merely implied that Ross was reckless and was doing serious harm by vetoing so much legislation. In fact, the opposite was true. Perhaps for the first time the governor was standing up to the power brokers in Santa Fe and was doing it with a true constituency of citizens who had rallied to Ross's support when the president was making his choice for governor. In the years after Ross, Ring control of the legislature would diminish. With the expansion of communities along the route of the AT&SF, the influx of newcomers to New Mexico was dramatic and the demand for reformed government even stronger.

Republican members of the Twenty-eighth Assembly did their best to maintain control of government in New Mexico with a bill commonly referred to as the solicitor general bill or "An act with reference to the offices of Solicitor General and District Attorneys." The bill abolished the territorial attorney general position and established the new post of solicitor general with virtually the same job description. The obvious purpose was to make it impossible for Ross to appoint an attorney general who could remain in office after October 1, 1889, the date when the new solicitor general post would become active. The new governor therefore would not be burdened with a Democratic attorney general for two years, as Ross had been with the Republican Breeden. The bill would also make it the responsibility of the Legislative Council to appoint district attorneys rather than having those appointments made by the governor. In both cases, the legislature was plainly in violation of Article IV of the United States Constitution, which reserves to Congress the power to make rules and regulations controlling territorial government organization, but nevertheless the bill passed into law over Ross's veto.[44]

Another of the bills that made it to Ross's desk was the Libel Law or "An act to define the offense of libel and affix punishment therefore." It was a law that attempted to "make it a crime to publish information on a political candidate's physical, mental or moral record."[45] It was specifically aimed at control of the press in New Mexico. The subject of libel especially was one to which Ross had given great thought during his career as a newspaper editor and publisher. His veto message ran to four pages. It was a veritable dissertation meant to educate the lawmakers of the territory. Libel, it said, "has been defined as a censorious or ridiculous writing, picture or sign, made with a malicious or mischievous intent. . . . Libel may be punished criminally by indictment, also by action for damages. . . . In some ages of the world the penalty for libel has been death, in England at one time by the loss of the tongue. But in the advanced civilization of today, and of this country, where one of the paramount purposes of the law is conservation of personal right and the freedom of the individual, the rule has come to prevail that 'the jury shall have the right to determine the law and the fact under the direction of the court, as in other criminal cases.'"[46] Ross continued his treatise by quoting the organic law of the territory of New Mexico. "Every citizen shall be at liberty to speak, write or publish his opinion on every subject, being responsible for the abuse of that privilege, and no law shall be passed curtailing the liberty of speech or the press." Ross saw in Ring members and their allies an attempt to stifle free expression, and in vetoing the Libel Act he compared them, by implication, with despots, political schemers, criminals, and the ignorant of society. "All men who live otherwise than in the broad, open light of day, and are ashamed that the world may know their acts, hate the press and pray for libel laws like this."[47] In spite of his eloquence and sound reasoning, his veto was not sustained.

On February 12, 1889, Ross vetoed a bill titled "An act to prevent women from entering saloons for the purpose of drinking therein." Ross, although a temperance advocate, believed the bill also prohibited women from working in saloons, the real intent of the bill, and thus made it more difficult for them to earn an honest livelihood. "This bill . . . presupposes that women are something less than rational beings as compared to men. . . . no law should be permitted that seeks or has the effect to circumscribe her independence or diminish her power of self reliance. . . . Any vocation that is honest and honorable to men is also equally honest and honorable to women, and any that is dishonorable to women is equally dishonorable to men."[48]

Of the bills that Ross "returned without executive approval," the most blatantly unconstitutional bill, designed to benefit just two cases from one law firm, was a bill to amend procedures in the territorial Supreme Court. The bill was an amendment to a bill that would favor the law firm of Catron, Knaebel and Clancy, and no other firm, by allowing the Catron lawyers to introduce new evidence in support of their clients in two appeals to the Supreme Court. Not only would the new evidence not have been allowed under the previous act to which this was an amendment, but it was also in violation of the prohibition of special legislation imposed by the United States Congress. Ross concluded his thorough, four-page veto message with "Few of us enjoy the extraordinary advantage of having laws passed for our special benefit, to say nothing of participating in their passage ourselves."[49] Thomas Catron served on the territorial Legislative Council during that session. This bill was so clearly unconstitutional that the legislature had no choice but to sustain the veto.

The greatest disappointment to Ross was the failure of the Twenty-eighth Legislative Assembly to pass an adequate school law. Eddie Ross, in her letter to her sister Lillian, explained that the big fight of the evening of February 28 was the dispute over a school law. "There is great excitement over it—that is if I can judge from those who are hurrying in and out of the office."[50] Howard Lamar described the problem: "It was evident that Spanish-American members, having grown used to the territorial system, displayed no great interest in admission to the Union. . . . The statehood men were caught in a dilemma. If they were successful in passing the school bill, the Spanish-Americans would not vote to call a constitutional convention. If they did not establish schools, Congress would not admit them."[51] The school bill and a call for a constitutional convention were two items where Ross and his adversaries agreed. The school bill failed yet again, but the constitutional convention bill passed both houses.[52]

The school bill was introduced to the Twenty-eighth Legislature by a Ross supporter, Russell A. Kistler of Las Vegas. Ross had strongly endorsed the bill in his message to the legislature, writing that there was "great need of reform in the public school system. . . . Among the most important of these needs is the creation of the office of territorial superintendent of instruction. Our present system is in need of a head, from which the entire system, throughout the territory, shall take direction and management, to insure coherency and effectiveness."[53] The territory would be divided into districts, and taxation money collected within each district would be used for school construction in that district. The bill also called for persons of lawful age, both male and female, to be eligible to vote on all education issues.

Ross, who had fought for an education bill since his earliest days in New Mexico, despaired over the inability of the legislature to pass the school law. The need for a territory-wide educational system was evident from statistics cited by Ross. Of the more than 109,000 people in the territory, 57,000 were illiterate. Of 44,000 school-age children, only 12,000 received any kind of education.[54]

Eddie kept adding bits and pieces to her letter to Lillian as she was able to find time that night. She described the tension and workload in her father's office adjacent to the legislative chambers in the new capitol building. She told Lillian that her friend Kate was married that evening while she, Eddie, had to stay at the capitol building to transcribe veto messages from Ross to the Council and House chambers. Then she injected into the letter, "Judge Sloan has just come in and reports the [education] bill 'killed'—which will be a hard blow to the territory."[55]

The hour was late and snow had been falling since three o'clock: "Very disagreeable out of doors," in Eddie's words. It had probably taken more than eight hours for Eddie to find enough quiet moments to complete her letter to Lillian. At ten-fifteen Eddie remarked, "Have just taken in my last messages, two to the House and three to the Senate and draw a long sigh of relief." Her next sentence reads, "After twelve and all over—am waiting now for father and Mr. Ashenfelter to be ready to go home—most everybody has left." Her last sentence may offer a clue to the way Ross evaluated bills from a legal standpoint. He could not completely trust his own attorney general and yet he surely needed the advice of a lawyer who was at least somewhat familiar with territorial and federal law. Singleton M. Ashenfelter, Ross's nephew by marriage and a former U.S. district attorney for New Mexico, had been appointed by Ross to serve as district attorney in the Third Territorial District in 1885. It is not unreasonable to assume that Ashenfelter, whose home was in Silver City, would have been Ross's principal legal advisor during the legislative session.

It is hard to imagine Ross returning to the Palace of the Governors, after a long and difficult day and night spent in confrontation with the legislature, and just retiring. It is probable that Ashenfelter was a houseguest and that, on their return sometime after midnight, the two men sat by a fire in the parlor to discuss the day's events. It is also possible that after a time Ashenfelter excused himself and turned in while Ross found paper and pen to compose an open letter to the people of New Mexico, the letter that was released later that day. Ross simply did not give up, even though he had scant time left in office. The letter, dated March 1, appeared in newspapers throughout the territory during the following days.

> The twenty-eighth legislative assembly has refused to give you an adequate school law. . . . The result is most disgraceful to New Mexico, and coming at this particular juncture, in the face of our pending application for statehood, is apt to have a most disastrous influence upon our future.
>
> I believe the intelligent, progressive people of New Mexico have the remedy largely in their own hands. Let us at once call public meetings in every town in the territory to memorialize congress, circulate petitions and write our friends at the national capital, praying congress to grant us now, the non-sectarian public law, which the national government has been under a moral obligation to give New Mexico ever since the treaty of Guadalupe Hidalgo. Let us demonstrate that the great mass of our people fully appreciate the value of public schools and the necessity of general attendance thereat.
>
> Let us go to work then, and work unitedly in an appeal to congress for the relief that our own lawmakers have denied us. . . . They have denied us the enjoyment of our most basic right. . . . They have sown the wind. Let them reap the whirlwind.[56]

Ross's proposal was similar to the bill he and his friend and fellow newspaper editor William Burke had tried unsuccessfully to introduce to

Congress in 1883.[57] Soon to be out of office, Ross was unable to provide the leadership needed to rally the people of the territory, but his high-profile push for a school bill may have made a difference after all: two years later the Twenty-ninth Legislature did pass essentially the same education bill that the Twenty-eighth voted down.

Ross did have the satisfaction of seeing the legislature pass a serious financial reform bill introduced by Henry L. Waldo. Ross had spoken at length about the bill in his general and special messages at the beginning of the session. Although his message is preserved in the permanent record, few Republicans if any attended the joint session to hear Ross in person.[58] The bill included a revamping of the system to identify all taxable lands and to levy taxes in an equitable manner, making county treasurers responsible for collections. The bill also called for the payment of territorial debts with cash, largely eliminating the warrant system that had been so badly abused by territorial treasurer Antonio Ortiz y Salazar.[59] Ross's December 29 message had also stated that there were as many insane people as there were convicts in the territory and proposed that funding be made available for an insane asylum as well as additional funding for "a school and asylum for the deaf, dumb and blind unfortunates of the territory." The asylum for the insane was approved.

The greatest satisfaction that Ross experienced that February of 1889 was the establishment of a university, a school of mines, and an agricultural college. Ross had pushed especially hard for the Twenty-eighth Legislative Assembly to establish the agricultural college, reminding them that a congressional act of 1887 provided $15,000 for an agricultural experiment station to any state or territory with a college to teach agriculture. To his delight the Twenty-eighth Legislature established all three schools: the New Mexico College of Agriculture and Mechanic Arts at Las Cruces, the New Mexico School of Mines at Socorro, and the University of New Mexico at Albuquerque.

Probably no territorial governor had ever put as much energy into the job. Certainly the two months during which the Twenty-eighth Legislative Assembly met were exhausting. Beyond dealing with politicians who wanted him gone and who must have felt highly satisfied to override his vetoes, Ross, who would soon move out of the Palace of the Governors, had the profound disappointment of not realizing his fondest dreams for New Mexico. A sound educational system, statehood, and the Court of Private Land Claims all seemed within reach during his tenure but were unfortunately no closer. As historian Howard Lamar pointed out, it would be Ross's successor, L. Bradford Prince, whom historians remember for programs originated by Ross.[60]

Edmund Ross represented a new breed of businessmen who quickly asserted themselves in territorial affairs. In particular, Albuquerque businessmen included manufacturers, a wide range of retail and wholesale merchants, skilled craftsmen, and professional people of all stripes, people who had actively supported Ross although a good number were Republicans. The arrival of the AT&SF railroad with its concurrent investment in the Albuquerque community, as well as the town's central location, made a move to Albuquerque by large numbers of newcomers a more logical choice than other New Mexico towns. The rise of a new economic and commercial center in Albuquerque, accompanied by rapid population growth, put a very real scare into the entrenched power brokers in Santa Fe. During the 1884–1885 legislative session, Albuquerque businessmen lobbied hard, and almost successfully, to have the capital moved to Albuquerque.[61] There was bitter rivalry between the two communities, and a good part of the dislike for Ross's administration in Santa Fe resulted from the fact that Albuquerque was Ross's permanent residence—not to mention, of course, that he was also a Cleveland Democrat.

To a significant extent Ross was responsible for the less than fair picture of his administration. He had never completely learned to be a successful politician. He was uncompromising and could be difficult to deal with. He did not have a politician's seemingly natural ability to engage others who held a different point of view and to disarm them by listening to their opinions. Many of his adversaries might have been allies had he approached them with an open mind, just as Antonio Joseph proved to be a true asset to his administration. Ross had announced at the beginning of his tenure: "I expect to have to do some pretty hard hitting, and fellow citizens when I begin to hit, I will hit hard."[62] It was not an approach designed to win people over, people you had to deal with on a regular basis. He may have been too quick to categorize people. That was the danger of perceiving much of New Mexico to be made up of rings. Certainly a considerable percentage of people believed to be associated with the Ring were excessively greedy and not hesitant to do what it took to line their pockets without consideration of who was harmed in the process. Other high-profile people were only loosely associated with the so-called Ring. Had Ross been more successful in finding common ground with many of the people he perceived to be enemies, he might have enjoyed greater success and today be remembered for much of what Bradford Prince is given credit for.

Leaving the Palace of the Governors was difficult for Ross. Loss of power is only part of the story. Ross loved that old building. After the new four-story capitol was completed in 1887, Ross continued to keep an office in the palace, adjacent to his family living quarters, even though a more elaborate office was provided for him in the new building. Ross had a fondness for adobe structures, and the palace, being adjacent to the old Santa Fe plaza, appealed to him. Except in winter, he kept the outside doors open to the wide hallway next to his office, especially when there were band concerts in the plaza—a nearly daily occurrence during warm months—so he could hear the music.[63] Fannie mentions the frequent concerts also. As she was writing a letter to a nephew in April 1887, she heard the band begin to play and explained that she was stopping so she could listen undistracted.[64] When Ross needed a break, he would often sit in one of several chairs under the long portico that ran the length of the palace facing the plaza and smoke a cigar. He would greet passersby, people who often took a seat next to him. Sometimes the conversations would attract a sizeable, friendly crowd.[65]

Probably the only time he regretted living in the ancient structure was when a family friend, a Mrs. Warner, would ring the bell in the morning with a group of tourists. Because Ross always worked late each night, often well past midnight, he also tended to sleep later than most people, rising each day at about eight. Mrs. Warner promised her tourists that they would see the room where Lew Wallace had written *Ben-Hur*. Unfortunately, it was also the room where Edmund and Fannie slept. Other curious visitors would also enter from time to time, ambling through the various rooms set aside for the Ross family. Such inconsiderate visits were not welcomed. At a reasonable hour, requests to see the family chambers were always approved.

At the request of the new governor and with the approval of President Benjamin Harrison, Ross remained on the job longer than expected to accommodate Governor Prince's arrangements to have friends attend his inauguration. Leis tells us that in spite of political differences, Ross and Prince were friendly. Edmund's and Fannie's personal belongings had been packed up and sent to Albuquerque, where Fannie had already moved. Eddie and young Fannie, who had come from Kansas with Lillian for a visit, remained in the palace with their father for a time, but soon they too left for Albuquerque. Alone then in the palace, Ross contemplated his situation with genuine worry. He lived strictly on his salary and had little if any savings. At age sixty-three his future was uncertain. His major comfort was his family. All of his children were then in New Mexico for the first time and, as fate would have it, for the last time. Lillian and young Fannie would soon return to Kansas; Arthur remained for a few years until his enterprise running an egg and poultry business failed, and he moved back to California; Pitt pursued his carrier as a surveyor in Albuquerque; Eddie married an Albuquerque photographer; and Kay managed a ranch not far from Albuquerque.

CHAPTER TWENTY-TWO

THE FINAL YEARS

I'll be a bigger man dead than I have ever been alive.
—Ross, winter of 1906–1907

At the reception they told me he enjoyed the music, applauding heartily, but as to the congratulatory speeches he comprehended little, for his own gratification the turning point of the tide of public opinion had come too late.
—Lillian Ross Leis, "Memoirs of Edmund G. Ross, Part Three"

⌒ IN AUGUST 1889 an article appeared in the *New York Times* titled "Ross's Varying Fortune." It was well written, without a byline, seemingly by someone who knew Edmund Ross well and who thought highly of him. The article had a Topeka dateline of August 17. The writer commented: "Kansas Republicans with long memories are discussing with evident relish the fact that Edmund G. Ross, late Governor of New-Mexico, is now a common printer in the office of a Santa Fé newspaper." The implication was that such a job was demeaning for a former United States senator and territorial governor, and there was therefore delight in knowing he was having to labor in such a manner. The writer, however, was quick to point out that Ross had "frequently told his Washington associates that he would be found at the case when his Senatorial duties were over." He did not see any loss of dignity in his job; to him it was honest labor.[1]

Lillian Ross Leis confirms that after leaving office her father did work at a Santa Fe newspaper, which she identifies as the *Santa Fe New Mexican*—although given that paper's editorial policy, which was strictly Republican, the *Santa Fe Herald* would seem to have been the more logical place for Ross. What additionally made the *New Mexican* an unlikely employer was Max Frost. Frost was part owner, publisher, and editor of the *New Mexican* in late-nineteenth-century New Mexico and an archenemy of the Ross administration. Frost's newspaper was not only Republican, it was a voice of the Santa Fe Ring, and Frost himself was an important investor in land grant schemes. He also had served for a time as the territorial land regis-ter and was charged with fraudulent activity in connection with the job. George Julian had preferred the charges. Frost was tried and found guilty, but the conviction was later overturned.[2]

Although Ross had once worked for the Republican *Albuquerque Journal*, a stint with the Republican *Santa Fe New Mexican* would be quite another matter. Ross's working for the *New Mexican* remains a possibility, and it must be said that Ross and Frost did find common ground when it came to promoting statehood in 1888. If the *New Mexican* was Ross's only offer of employment, although not what he might have desired, he may have swallowed his pride a bit just to stay in Santa Fe, the political power center of the territory. Ross was, after all, a leading Democrat, and he probably wanted to keep a high profile in Democratic circles in Santa Fe while seeing what other opportunities might open for him. It is probably correct that wherever Ross worked, it was a job "at the case," not an editorial position, and at most Ross would have worked at a Santa Fe paper for a only few months.

In August 1889 Singleton Ashenfelter of Silver City wrote to let Ross know that his purchase of the *Deming Headlight* newspaper was complete and to offer Ross editorship of the paper at one hundred dollars per month. The letter has an apologetic tone to it. The one hundred dollar salary was less than half what Ross had earned as governor, but Ashenfelter promised his salary "would increase in proportion as the business warranted."[3] The letter was sent to Ross in Santa Fe, suggesting that Ross was at the time employed there. Deming was a small but promising town near New Mexico's southern border. The AT&SF and the Southern Pacific met at Deming, a surprisingly thriving community. A second letter sent later in August indicated that Ross would arrive in Deming on a Friday or Saturday at the end of the month.[4] The first edition of the *Headlight* with Ross as editor was dated September 7, 1889. Although Santa Fe was the real power center of New Mexico, Ross saw that as editor of the *Headlight* he had a platform for expressing himself and that his commentaries very likely would be carried in other New Mexico papers.

Although there is no evidence to show that Ross applied for work at an Albuquerque paper, it seems as if he would have. There may not have been an editorial position in Albuquerque or a paper that showed the same financial promise as the *Headlight*. A job in Albuquerque would have allowed Ross to develop the property he and the family referred to as "the ranch." The property was acquired through the Homestead Act with a "soldier's claim" exemption for Civil War veterans. In 1886 Ross was alerted to the property by George Albright, the brother of his former employer at the *Morning and Evening Democrat* in Albuquerque.[5] The land, about four miles south of town, originally owned by the A&P Railroad, had been forfeited and then made available through an act of Congress. Ross shared a section of land with three other men, including Albright, each getting 160 acres. On his father's share of the land, Pitt Ross built the required structure (a minimum of 12 × 14 feet) in which a member of the immediate family had to live for a period of time each year to fulfill homesteading requirements. With Ross as governor, Fannie apparently lived in the house for at least part of the required time. Fannie referred to it as their "shanty," which was a good description. Later Arthur would build a small house on the property as well and take responsibility for cultivating the land, which was rather barren, without trees or shrubbery of any decent size. There appears to have been an irrigation ditch on the property, evidence of which is still there today.

At some point during Ross's time as governor, Pitt and Arthur rented an adobe house, large enough for the entire family, supposedly next to the claim. Leis describes it as "roomy, having been built by an American family for a country home. A wide hall the length of the building—double glass doors at each end."[6] Leis's recollection is that after her father left the governor's office and the *Deming Headlight* and was living back in Albuquerque, he could walk a short distance to the shanty, where he would write and keep a small library. Pitt also rented an adobe house at 920 Barelas Road, which was much closer to town, only a short walk to the business district of Albuquerque.[7] This probably happened in 1893. City directories at that time did not provide information on residents living outside the new town limits, and the Barelas house was just beyond the limit.

Fannie probably lived with Pitt and his wife Clemie during the spring and summer of 1889, up to the time that Ross took the editorship of the *Headlight* in Deming. The family's "shanty" would eventually be enlarged by adding what appears to be a kitchen. The ranch property was finally patented in Ross's name on January 26, 1896.[8] The property became an important family gathering place. Group photos show the family assembled at the shanty even after Fannie's death in 1899. There are few family group photos taken anywhere else. One exception is a picture of the family gathered for the marriage of Eddie to William Cobb in 1891. The wedding photo could have been shot in either the Barelas house near town or the rented adobe home near the ranch.

The *Deming Headlight* proved to be a good move for Ross. In the first issue, with his name atop the editorial page, he expressed a surprising point of view: he was now opposed to statehood. Ross was still distraught from the beating he took dealing with the Twenty-eighth Legislature. He believed the legislature was "unable to get together a trustworthy body of lawmakers." It was apparent to him that "if a state government were organized, it would inevitably be controlled by the corrupt ring of politicians who have already done so much to bring evil fame upon New Mexico." He believed taxation would increase with statehood but "in the hands of the scoundrels who loom up as guiding the present movement, it would be financially ruinous." He saw that statehood would bring an "incompetent and venal judiciary." Capable attorneys would not work for the salaries the new state could afford to pay, and therefore "inferior men would pollute even the present political atmosphere."[9]

One month later Ross responded to territorial newspapers that had expressed surprise that he could so adamantly support statehood less than two years before and now be opposed to it. In his article of October 12 Ross recounted the legislation he had vetoed during the Twenty-eighth Legislature, highlighting the greed and dishonesty that he perceived during the session, a session that took place in the months that intervened since he spoke in favor of statehood. He concluded: "When the people shall have forever buried out of sight the gang that perpetuated these infamies, New Mexico will be ready for statehood, but not so long as they are above ground and sustained as they have always been by the National party to which they belong. . . . We desire statehood as earnestly as anybody in New Mexico, now as ever, but prefer to wait till there can be no further danger from this source."[10]

The fall of 1890 was an off-year in national politics, but an important year in New Mexico. Two major events dominated the *Headlight*: the October 7 vote to accept or reject a state constitution, whose framers believed it would improve New Mexico's chances for statehood, and the election in November of delegates to the Territorial House of Representatives and the Council. Ross opposed passage of the constitution, believing there were major flaws. In a detailed critique, Ross demonstrated how the constitution would give unbalanced power to the legislature. There could be an override to a governor's veto with a minority of votes, since the constitution would require only the concurrence of two-thirds of the legislators present and voting, rather than two-thirds of the total legislature. The document also would make it possible for the House of Representatives to suspend a governor without a hearing if they found him to be at odds with them during a legislative session.[11] The convention that drew up and amended the constitution beginning in the previous year was dominated by owners of land grants (and their lawyers), whose total holdings were believed to be near 10 million acres.[12] The *Headlight* and other newspapers no doubt played a major role in defeating the proposed constitution on October 7.

In his campaign for the defeat of Republicans at the polls on November 4, Ross believed the "campaign was well begun by the signal defeat of the late Constitution in that it was an entering wedge to the destruction and burial of the infamous ring of pestiferous, self-seeking and brainy scoundrels that for a quarter of a century has sucked the life-blood of the body politic."[13] In a turnaround from the Twenty-eighth Legislature, in the Twenty-ninth the Democrats controlled the House of Representatives and had a much stronger presence in the Council.

With the Twenty-ninth Legislature in the early days of its 1890–1891 session, New Mexico Democrats held what was described as a reception and donation party at the Palace Hotel, at which Ross was a guest of honor. "Donation" probably meant that money was being collected for Edmund and Fannie. The event drew a large gathering for an elaborate dinner where Ross was seated in a prominent place. This came as a complete surprise to him. "He was dumbfounded, and when Judge Burus, speaker of the House, stepped up and presented him with a large and richly carved gold headed cane as a testimonial of the affectionate regard from his friends, his sturdy and Democratic heart overflowed at his eyes."[14] Leis incorrectly remembers 1897 as the year of the banquet when her father was given the gold-headed cane, but she probably correctly recalls someone saying the cane was given to him "as it had been some time since he had received a caning." The remark, in a lighthearted way, referred to the 1881 incident when D. R. Anthony, editor of the *Leavenworth Times*, attacked Ross with his cane on a Kansas street.[15]

What delighted Ross most about the Twenty-ninth Legislature was passage of the school bill on February 5—the bill that Ross considered "the one vastly above all others in importance." The Paulin School Bill passed the House unanimously and the Council without amendment in spite of repeated attempts by Thomas Catron to alter the bill. Later, in early March,

Ross would again find vindication for his efforts as governor with the establishment of the Court of Private Land Claims by the United States Congress.
Ross graciously congratulated Antonio Joseph for his years of labor on
behalf of the bill and for the "delegations [that] have visited Washington
and ably supplemented his efforts."[16]

Ross worked at the *Headlight* for more than three years, but it is unlikely
there was any real promise of a lucrative future for him in Deming. He and
Fannie moved back to Albuquerque in 1893. Ross had probably hoped they
would be returning to Santa Fe. In the 1892 presidential election, Grover
Cleveland went head-to-head with Benjamin Harrison for the second
time, and this time Cleveland won decisively and regained the presidency
for another four years. A more than willing candidate for another term
as governor, Ross had reason to believe his chances were very good. He
had wide support from many territorial newspapers and had a fair amount
of backing from party members. However, William Taylor Thornton, who
had been elected the first mayor of Santa Fe in 1891, was also endorsed by
many Democrats and even some Republicans. Thornton had been a New
Mexico resident since 1877, had a well-known law firm in Santa Fe, was a
successful investor in mining ventures, and had a reputation for promoting
New Mexico in the states.[17] There were other factors that favored Thornton:
He was seventeen years younger than Ross—only fifty when he became
governor—and he was a dynamic and outgoing leader, as contrasted with
Ross, who in his daughter's words "greatly disliked ostentation where he
was concerned."[18] An important factor was Cleveland's pledge not to reap-
point prior appointees except in particular instances.[19] Ross's last day at the
Headlight fell within the same week that Cleveland was sworn in for his
second term. Ross apparently was ready to move on in any case, no longer
wanting to remain in Deming. He would eventually return to Santa Fe, but
not as governor.

While still working at the *Headlight*, Ross was asked by *Scribner's
Magazine* to write an article about the Andrew Johnson impeachment,
which he agreed to do.[20] When published, the article ran five pages. It contained Ross's reasonable interpretation of the facts, with heavy emphasis on
the drama leading up to the historic vote on May 16, 1868. Consistent with
his years as a journalist, Ross wrote in the third person until the story inevitably led to his own vote. "Conscious that I was at the moment the focus
of all eyes, and conscious also of the far reaching effect, especially upon
myself, of the vote I was about to give, it is something more than a simile to

say that I almost literally looked down into my open grave."[21] Although his prose style was effusive and somewhat melodramatic, his description of the trial was accurate. The *Scribner's* article may have been a kind of catalyst serving to make him aware that his recollections about territorial Kansas and his time in the Senate were valuable or at least interesting to others. With the move back to Albuquerque, Ross began to write about his past experiences in Kansas and Washington while either staying with Pitt and his wife Clemie or living in the "shanty."

Although Ross did not get a second chance at being governor, he did return to Santa Fe when, in 1895, he was made secretary of the Bureau of Immigration. The job provided income Ross badly needed, but it was not a great salary, certainly no larger than Ashenfelter had paid him in Deming. From Governor Thornton's perspective, Ross was the perfect man for the job. As a former governor and a longtime advocate for the Bureau of Immigration, he was well suited to the task of attracting business and industry to the territory. It is a good guess that Ross lived away from his family while working in Santa Fe, no doubt making frequent trips to Albuquerque to be with Fannie. Ross was in Santa Fe for part of 1895, all of 1896, and part of 1897, and, while living alone in Santa Fe, he was able to devote some part his time and energies to work beyond his duties at the immigration job.

Perhaps there were friends who read the *Scribner's* article who encouraged Ross to write a full account of the impeachment, or perhaps the idea was his. Whatever prompted him to undertake the project, he did not act until two years after the original article appeared. While still living in Albuquerque in mid-1894, Ross wrote to his old friend Thomas Ewing Jr. about the possibility of writing an impeachment history. Ewing's response was thoughtful and encouraging. He also offered to assist Ross in any manner he could and reassured him that "I have not the slightest doubt that the proper man to write the history of the impeachment of Andrew Johnson is yourself. I think the subject will attract more attention coming from you than from anyone else, and that it is due to yourself and your family that the whole subject should be presented without any withholding of fact, and, of course, without any perversion of fact, so that the public, who can now consider the matter dispassionately, will judge the actors as they deserve to be judged."[22]

Ross managed to complete his *History of the Impeachment of Andrew Johnson, President of the United States*, and probably to supervise its printing at the New Mexican Printing Company in Santa Fe, in 1896. A United

States senator from New York, David B. Hill, wrote the preface. With nearly thirty years having passed since the impeachment, Hill (along with Ewing and others) believed the general public knew little of the impeachment, and yet, wrote Hill, "it was one of the most important and critical events, involving possibly the greatest consequences, in the entire history of the country."[23] To characterize the impeachment in such terms may seem like hyperbole, given that the trial took place just three years after the end of the Civil War; but the Johnson impeachment was, in fact, a serious, dangerous, and unique threat to constitutional stability in the United States.

Departing from the *Scribner's* article, Ross chose to write the book-length account of the impeachment without the drama used in a commercial magazine. His goal was to report the facts as they unfolded in 1868 as honestly as he could. He saw this as an important contribution to history, an honest report by one of the key participants in the Johnson trial. While part of the book could be considered objective reporting, most of it is told from his point of view, and bias is unavoidable. Perhaps most surprisingly for twenty-first-century readers is Ross's commentary on President Johnson, who today is poorly regarded by most historians.

Although Ross had been an outspoken critic of Johnson as a newspaper editor in Kansas in the year before his appointment to the United States Senate and even in his first year as a senator, by 1896 he believed Johnson had tried to carry out President Lincoln's plans for Reconstruction, his take on Johnson being decidedly positive. He willingly admitted that Johnson's obstinate nature made it difficult for him to find common ground with the Congress, but he had come to believe that Johnson was doing his best to deal with equally obstinate Radical Republicans.

Using the third-person voice in the book made it awkward for Ross to describe his own role in the impeachment trial: "Mr. Ross of Kansas, was the fifth Republican Senator to vote 'Not Guilty.' Representing an intensely Radical constituency—entering the Senate but a few months after the close of a three years enlistment in the Union Army and not unnaturally imbued with the extreme partisan views and prejudices against Mr. Johnson then prevailing . . . he had sworn to judge the defendant not by his political or personal prejudices, but by the facts elicited in the investigation. In his judgment those facts did not sustain the charge."[24] Although Ross described himself at the time of the impeachment as "not unnaturally imbued with the extreme partisan views and prejudice against Mr. Johnson," it is clear that by the time of the impeachment vote he had become much more of a moderate. Regardless of what his political thinking was at the time, it can be said that Ross and his fellow "recusants" registered their "not guilty" votes with more objectivity than nearly all the other Republicans.

With the heavy pressure on Ross to vote "guilty" in the Johnson trial; with the harsh treatment of his fellow Republicans following the May 16 vote; with the self-serving greed Ross witnessed by a good many of his colleagues, in particular Samuel Pomeroy; with his loss of patronage influence at the hands of President Grant; with the way some Kansans would not let him forget his vote—with all of this, Ross became a resentful and, at times, even an angry man and eventually a Democrat. It is not surprising that in 1896 Ross had a positive take on Johnson and a strongly negative view of Radical Republicans. Regardless of how modern historians may see President Johnson's time in office, Ross presents a clear, convincing, and not inconsistent indictment of the politically motivated impeachment proceedings in Congress.

It must also be said that Ross's 1896 understanding of Johnson is not different from that of other historians of his time. In the preface to *Reconstruction: America's Unfinished Revolution*, historian Eric Foner describes the changing interpretation of Reconstruction since the early twentieth century. In part Foner observes William Dunning's take on the administration of Andrew Johnson. Dunning (1857–1922) was a professor at Columbia University whose specialty was the Johnson impeachment and Reconstruction. Foner summarizes Dunning's understanding of Johnson: "Abraham Lincoln had embarked on a course of sectional reconciliation, and during Presidential Reconstruction (1865–1867) his successor, Andrew Johnson, attempted to carry out Lincoln's magnanimous policies. Johnson's efforts were opposed and eventually thwarted by the Radical Republicans in Congress."[25] Dunning and Ross had a nearly identical take on Johnson.

Ironically, Ross's 1865–1866 editorials critical of President Johnson are consistent with modern, negative interpretations of Johnson's tenure in office. Ross had been outraged by Johnson's sympathetic view of "black codes" and his vetoes of the Freedmen's Bureau renewal bill and the Civil Rights bill. He was openly critical on the Senate floor of the president's opposition to the Fourteenth Amendment. What seems to be true of Ross's late-in-life view of President Johnson is that his anger with Radical Republicans trumped his former negative perception of Johnson.

It would seem remarkable that Ross managed to write *The History of the Impeachment of Andrew Johnson*, work at the Immigration Bureau, and also, in 1895, complete and/or release for publication four essays. However, it is likely that he wrote the essays, or at least had them outlined, between the end of his time in Deming and the start of his position with the Bureau of Immigration. The first of these essays was an eight-page pamphlet, an almost poetic account of Kansans who struggled to make their territory a free state in the 1850s. The essay was called *The Pilgrim and the Cavalier in Kansas*. It was not meant to be an historical account as much as a tribute and remembrance of those who, with great sacrifice, stood against the spread of slavery beyond the South. Ross took great care to make every word count. "On its solution hung the gravest and grandest problem that ever confronted the philosopher, the humanitarian or the statesman—whether the great Republic should thenceforth be the home and citadel of freedom or the kennel of the slave. It was on the plains of Kansas that this most masterful of all the issues that ever arose to vex the politics of the world was fought to a finish, and freedom triumphed."[26]

Ross also did two articles for the *Forum* magazine in 1895. The July issue included a more detailed, ten-page description of the Johnson impeachment titled "A Previous Era of Popular Madness and Its Lessons." Ross traced the origins of the trouble that caused such bitterness within Congress that it would be led to enact articles of impeachment, and stressed the frenzy of public sentiment as it affected members of both houses. A second article for the *Forum*, "Political Leaders of the Reconstruction Period," is an interesting and valuable description of the key members of Congress, the president, and members of the cabinet as Ross remembered them. It is a unique, although biased, estimation of twenty or more key men who served during Ross's years in the Senate.

One other article appeared in 1895, in the *North American Review*. "The Future of the Arid West" was a long, somewhat rambling essay that spoke of the importance of people owning their own homes and land. As governor, Ross had a vision for New Mexico, no doubt influenced by memories of his own parents, farmers who raised fourteen children. Ross viewed farming as an inevitable and necessary part of New Mexico's future. He probably believed that more of New Mexico could be farmed than was the case, but he was not wrong that much more could be done to improve farming.

Ross was impressed with the simplicity of the New Mexican acequias, which he believed should continue to be at the core of irrigation expansion. While others had written about and begun work on improved irrigation along New Mexico's larger rivers,[27] Ross believed more could be done to improve irrigation along the tributaries. He proposed a system that would divert excess water from streams and arroyos during times of heavy runoff from the mountains. The water would be diverted downstream to a series of reservoirs where it could be stored for future irrigation needs. He envisioned that these diversion "piers" would have the dual advantage of conserving water and preventing the serious flooding that frequently plagued New Mexico farmers and townspeople.[28]

While at the Bureau of Immigration, Ross certainly recognized that the job would probably end with the next presidential election. He would deal with that eventuality when the time came; that was news he could anticipate. But on January 20, 1897, while still on the job in Santa Fe, Ross was jolted by the news that his son Arthur had died in Ventura, California. Arthur had often been ill during his brief life; he was only forty-three years old. It was a crushing blow for both Edmund and Fannie, whose children all meant so much to them, but the loss of Arthur may have been particularly difficult for Edmund. Arthur had worked closely with his father during much of his adult life.

Within a few months of Arthur's death, when the presidency was once again in the hands of a Republican, William McKinley, both Thornton and Ross were replaced. There are hints, and in some cases frankness, in Ross's letters that he was concerned about having enough income for him and Fannie to survive independently. A letter from Ross to Fannie, who was staying with friends in Mesilla Park near Las Cruces, broke the news. The letter also revealed that Ross believed he could not afford to remain unemployed for long. "I have some rather unpleasant news for you today—though not unmixed, for now that I have been suspended here, I will be able to spend more time with you hereafter. . . . How soon that will be, no one knows yet, but very likely in a few weeks. Then I shall go down to the Ranch for a short time and then down to you—probably to stay for some weeks— not very long, for I must get to work somewhere soon."[29]

Another letter from Santa Fe was sent to his daughter Lillian in Colorado one month later. This letter also suggests his need for income. "It had been so long since I heard from you or about you, that I supposed you had gone back to Lawrence. . . . I would go up to see you were it possible, but it is not, so regrets are useless.[30] I expect to leave here and go back to Albuquerque in the course of a week or ten days. I shall go down to Albuquerque then for a few days and then down to Mesilla Park, where Mother is for a while. Beyond that I have nothing in view now, but am pretty sure that something will turn up for me before many months."[31] Though Ross hoped to find paying work, it is doubtful he was ever employed again.

Another letter to Fannie was dated April 19 and sent from Albuquerque. It contains a good deal of information about their situation, with Ross trying to put a positive spin on it. The letter indicates that Ross was living in the shanty and never made the trip to Mesilla Park. The adobe house near the shanty (Ross referred to the shanty as a "cabin") may no longer have been available to them. The distance to Pitt's house on Barelas Road would have been about three miles. Ross would rely on Pitt either to come out to the cabin to bring him food and other essentials or to give him a ride to town. When Pitt did not come out to the ranch, Ross would have had to walk the distance. Ross assumed he and Fannie would live in the shanty, an enormous difference in lifestyle from the Palace of the Governors and surely a poorer arrangement than their home in Deming. The house when first built was not more than 300 square feet, and even when enlarged, it probably did not exceed 600 square feet. Ross rightly predicted that Clemie would never hear of them living in the shanty. Still it became Ross's place to live until Fannie returned. Edmund and Fannie then lived with Pitt and Clemie until Fannie's death in 1899, when the shanty again became Ross's place to live for a few years.[32]

As if there had not been enough bad news for Fannie and Edmund in 1897, they also learned of the death of an infant grandson, Edmund Ross Miles, the son of their youngest daughter, Fannie, who was then living in Silver City, New Mexico. Just the year before, young Fannie and her husband had lost their first child, Simpson Holstein Miles.

At Fannie's request ("mother wrote pathetically"), Lillian gathered together as much of the family as she could to celebrate the forty-ninth wedding anniversary of her parents in October 1897.[33] "We agreed to call it the 'Golden Wedding' as we felt we would not be all together on the exact date [1898]. We were at brother Pitt's house then, father and mother living with them, sister Eddie and her family from Albuquerque, Kay from twenty-five miles away where he was in charge of a ranch. Mother had insisted on his [Edmund] wearing a broadcloth suit he seldom wore, not a business one, and a silk hat. We [Lillian and her father] had walked out into the meadow and gathered a large bouquet of wild flowers, which he showed me saying, 'This is for mother.' It was an enjoyable day though we missed the absent ones."[34]

Fannie's request that the family gather for a reunion indicates that she knew her time was short. Lillian's prediction that a celebration the next year might not be possible proved to be correct. It would appear that Lillian did not return for the actual fiftieth anniversary, but she did return for the fifty-first on October 15, 1899, with the knowledge that her mother's life would soon end. The celebration must have been a sad one; Fannie died on November 12, 1899. Leis writes very little about her mother's death except to say, "Father said to me, 'it is all right,' but he was broken." Ross, Pitt, Lillian, and Eddie were at her bedside. She was buried at the Fairview Cemetery in Albuquerque. Leis tells of how she chose to linger at the graveside as the carriages disappeared down the hill; a friend of her father's stayed by her side.[35]

Possibly as early as 1897, Ross began a rewrite of his *History of the Impeachment of Andrew Johnson*. He may have been urged to write this version in the first person, to make it more readable, and to reveal more about the impact of the trial on his life and on his family. Leis remembered that "he had a desk in the small house [the shanty] and would come every day, where it was quiet and he had his books." She recalled that "one day he said to me as he rose from his chair, 'there, that is finished.' He placed all in order, placed something on top of the manuscript, it was a high one, and smiled with relief. It was ready for a typewriter, but is just as he left it."[36] The new version was never published. Later Ross tried writing additional articles, one in particular for *Harper's Magazine*, but because his memory was beginning to fail him and there were frequent repetitions, the article was never submitted.[37]

After the turn of the century Ross probably did not live alone at the shanty for too many years and perhaps only months. Both his eyesight and hearing were failing. Pitt and Clemie moved him back again to the house on Barelas Road. The house was on a couple of acres of land with fruit trees and other established vegetation. Even in the first decade of the twentieth century it was already an old adobe, which suited Ross perfectly; he loved the house. Leis writes that he would go "strolling among the trees and flowering shrubs, beneath the sweeping boughs of a Tamarack tree where several chairs could be placed." He took long walks and sawed firewood for exercise, and although his right arm bothered him from an injury during the war, Leis says that "he persisted and enjoyed having some special task. . . . He would carry in an armful, fill up the stove in the wide hall, draw his chair before it and watch the glow with great satisfaction."[38]

Pitt's business as a surveyor was a success in a quickly growing town and territory where there was a constant need for his services. Whatever the reason—Leis believed it was the encroachment of the nearby railroad shops—in about 1905 Pitt built a new house on West Railroad Avenue

(Central Avenue after 1908). This was a substantial two-story brick house situated alongside other homes of successful businessmen. Leis says that Pitt built it especially for his father's "convenience and pleasure, but he was loath to leave the old place."[39]

When it came time for her father to move, Lillian came from Kansas to help sort his belongings, books, letters, newspapers, and miscellaneous documents, an accumulation he had amassed over many years. Ross recognized that his *Annals of Congress* and *Congressional Globes* were volumes he would never use again; they were boxed and put into storage. As far as his papers were concerned, he told her to "take anything you want." She packed a trunk of documents to take with her back to Kansas. The one item that did concern him was his yet-to-be-typed manuscript; he asked her to take special care with it. The final day in the old Barelas house was a hard one for Ross. With his books and papers packed up, out of his sight forever, leaving the house for a modern new home was like severing himself irretrievably from his past. Leis recalled the night: "When the family was ready for us on the last day, I took father to the new home. We were the last to leave the old adobe, which he had grown so fond of. It was dark but some one was waiting to lock the glass doors as we departed along the flower bordered path to the gate, from where we gazed back at the dim outline of the house. But with all our diplomacy he was greatly agitated after our arrival. The house was lighted—Sister Clemie at the door to welcome home and supper waiting. His new room, conveniently located down stairs, with his own furnishings all around. I said, 'This is so much nicer than the old place.' 'Yes,' he said, his voice trembling, 'but I am used to it.'"[40]

Ross turned eighty in December 1906. His birthday was celebrated by the family with a dinner on December seventh, and on the twenty-ninth of the same month there was a combination holiday and twenty-fifth wedding anniversary celebration for Pitt and Clemie. The house was filled with people, many of them questioning Ross about the politics of former years. Leis writes that he insisted on standing with the other men, leaning against his cane. He was in his element and enjoyed the attention.

Although he adjusted to life in the new house, his health continued to decline, and he was failing noticeably. He had pain in his chest, and was under a doctor's care. When she was in town, Leis remembered making sure he wore a muffler snugly wound around his neck and chest to protect him from cold when he went out to walk. His children either walked with him or watched carefully to be sure he returned safely.

In March Ross had a most unusual visitor from Kansas, a man whose eccentricities were so bizarre and widely known that the family did not take the announcement of his intention to arrive with any seriousness. Earlier in life he was known as (brevet) General Hugh Cameron, a Civil War officer who served with the Second Kansas Cavalry, in the same unit in which Ross's brother George served and the same unit commanded by Samuel Crawford, the man who appointed Ross to replace Senator Jim Lane.

In his post-military years Cameron was remembered for his inordinately long white hair and beard and for the strange way he lived. He built a shack on an old stone foundation next to a ravine near Lawrence. Outside the shack he kept a ladder propped against a tree at the top of which was a tree house where he apparently lived much of the time. He wore an old military uniform with brass buttons and, when it was cold, wrapped himself in an army blanket as he walked about town. During his occasional trips into Lawrence for supplies, his unusual appearance and odd lifestyle earned him the name the Kansas Hermit. There is no explanation of his unusual lifestyle, but New Mexico historian Marc Simmons believes Cameron lived in this odd manner, in a tree house, as a protest for the disgraceful way Kansans had treated his old friend Edmund Ross. According to Simmons, Cameron announced he would withdraw from society until Kansans repented and freely "admitted they had done their senator wrong."[41] Others believed it was an "unrequited love affair" when, after his death, a packet of love letters written by Cameron was found returned to him unopened by Mary Phelps, the sister of a Missouri governor.[42]

Whatever his reason for living as he did, it is true that Cameron spent a matter of weeks, and probably months, arranging for prominent older Kansans, who remembered the Johnson impeachment years, to write letters to Ross recognizing him for his wisdom in voting to acquit President Johnson. Cameron announced that he planned a pilgrimage to Albuquerque to make it plain to Ross that he had indeed been vindicated by the people of Kansas. The *Albuquerque Morning Journal* noted that Cameron arrived (on March 10) with "a grip full of letters, newspaper clippings and other documents."[43] In an article the day before, the *Journal* reported that "almost every newspaper in the west has announced his unique pilgrimage,"[44] many people assuming he would walk the distance to Albuquerque. Letters from the Kansas governor, lieutenant governor, and speaker of the House were among the tributes to Ross. Cameron's arrangements included a resolution by the Kansas Legislature in which, even in a formal document, Cameron is referred to as the Hermit. "Resolve that we commend and approve of the Hermit's mission in conveying to the Honorable Edmund Gibson Ross the most universal approval of his vote which saved the State and Nation from disgrace and that we send to him our cordial invitation to return to the state and enjoy the distinction brought about by said vote." One of the letters that Cameron carried to Albuquerque was from William H. Carruth, a history professor at the Kansas University, who wrote: "It has not been said often enough that in the best judgment of the present day, Senator Ross voted wisely, and that an incalculable calamity would have befallen the nation had he not cast the vote for which his fellow citizens execrated and even threatened him. It goes hard for us to admit that he was wiser than the majority of us."[45]

The Hermit proved to be more important than Ross's family expected. The *Journal* did stories practically every day of the Hermit's week-long visit, and Ross was photographed with Cameron and his old friend Elias Stover as they rode through town on successive days in both a horse-drawn carriage and a modern horseless one. Among their destinations was a public reception for Ross and the Hermit. Leis believed her father "enjoyed the music, applauding heartily, but as to the congratulatory speeches he comprehended little, for his own gratification the turning point of the tide of public opinion had come too late." Leis also wrote that while she was spending quiet time with her father during that winter, he told her, "I'll be a bigger man dead than I have ever been living." The statement was an expression of disappointment that certain of his achievements were not as widely acknowledged as he had hoped, but there was also implicit hope that in the future his accomplishments would be more widely recognized.

Leis was critical of the brief excursions that were made on very cold days during the Hermit's visit. "These trips were entirely unnecessary and, I feel, hastened his death. Also, going out at night, unusual and fatiguing."[46] But even if the Cameron visit did shorten Ross's life by a matter of days, it is hard to imagine that Ross would have traded those days for the recognition he felt and believed he had earned. Ross died of pneumonia at eleven on the morning of May 8, 1907. A few days later the *Journal* reported: "All Albuquerque was represented yesterday at the funeral services of the late Senator Edmund G. Ross, held in the First Presbyterian Church. The church was crowded with friends and admirers of the former New Mexico governor. . . . No more impressive tribute has been paid to a public man in New Mexico."[47]

In 1956 John F. Kennedy described Ross's grave as "lonely" and Ross a man "forgotten and unknown." On May 10, 1907, this was hardly the case. Ross was escorted to the Fairview Cemetery by members of the Grand Army of the Republic and hundreds of mourners who made the long, dusty trek to the highland area east of town, some on foot, others in carriages. His grave was separated from Fannie's by five or six feet, presumably to accommodate what was expected to be a large group of mourners. Final prayers were recited by the Reverend Hugh A. Cooper, and when the rite of burial was complete, just as it was for Fannie, the mourners formed an impromptu procession and began the return trip across the mesa, back to town. It is true that the gravesite quickly became a lonely place later that day, with Edmund and Fannie lying next to each other.

During the first half of the twentieth century, Ross's notoriety faded until Kennedy wrote *Profiles in Courage*, including his name with those of John Quincy Adams, Daniel Webster, Thomas Hart Benton, Sam Houston, L. Q. C. Lamar, George Norris, and Robert Taft. But Kennedy, as well as Ross's modern critics who questioned the courage of Ross's 1868 impeachment vote, focused only on Ross's role in the Johnson impeachment.

Ross was much more than just a junior senator who in 1868 found himself face-to-face with a dilemma to which, for him personally, there was no satisfactory answer. As a young father in 1856 he could have stayed in Milwaukee, where he would likely have become a successful printer and journalist, but chose instead to lead a wagon train of abolitionists and Free-Staters into primitive early Kansas. No one would have faulted him had he not volunteered to serve in the Civil War, leaving his wife and children to risk his life in a cause that others in like circumstances chose to avoid. Perhaps in 1871 a lesser man would have chosen to move to a state where he was not detested by so many of the people, instead of standing by his principles and becoming, in 1880, the Democratic candidate for governor of Kansas. In New Mexico he could have been a governor who chose to find favor with power brokers and perhaps acquired the wealth that always eluded him. Instead, he stayed true to the principles that had always guided him, and he died a poor man but a man who, generations later, is still admired for the courage of his convictions.

NOTES

Chapter One

1. Legler, "Rescue of Joshua Glover"; see also Wisconsin Local History Network, "Ripon's Booth War."

2. Legler, "Rescue of Joshua Glover."

3. Leis, "Memoirs," 7–8. Lillian Ross Leis's "memoirs" of her father were never published. They were written in three parts, a total of about eighty typewritten pages. The first two parts were provided to me by family members. Part 3 was found at the New Mexico State Archives, with Governor Ross's papers. Edward Bumgardner in his book *The Life of Edmund G. Ross* made use of the first two parts.

4. Ableman v. Booth, 62 U.S. 506 (1858). See supreme.justia.com/cases/federal/us/62/506.case.html.

5. Legler, "Rescue of Joshua Glover."

6. Leis, "Memoirs," 8.

7. Ibid., 2.

8. Harrington, *Edmund G. Ross*, 20.

9. Leis, "Memoirs," 4; Bumgardner, *Life of Edmund G. Ross*, 16.

10. Ross's great-grandson Edmund "Ned" Ross, a Lutheran minister and later an Episcopalian minister in Albuquerque, said in an interview that he believed Ross was a Unitarian in his adult years, although he could not be certain.

11. Sandusky Library, "The Underground Railroad in Sandusky."

12. Leis, "Memoirs," 3–4.

13. Ibid. The text of Ross's capital punishment speech can be found in Arthur Elliot Harrington's biography, *Edmund G. Ross*, appendix B. The term "working at the case" is a reference to the printing shop's job case, a drawer divided into many small compartments for the various moveable metal letters and ligatures used in typesetting in the nineteenth century. The case compartments were arranged by frequency of use and included both capital letters, found in the upper part of the case, and "lower case" type, giving rise to terms still in use today.

14. Fannie Lathrop to George Lathrop, December 10, 1846, Edmund G. Ross Collection, 1856–1907, Kansas State Historical Society, Topeka (hereafter Ross Collection, Topeka).

15. Harrington, *Edmund G. Ross*, 99–100.

16. Ibid.

17. Leis, "Memoirs," 5–6.

18. Roberts, *Cholera of 1849*.

Chapter Two

1. Leis, "Memoirs," 8.

2. Ibid., 9.

3. Fugitive Slave Act of 1850, see *A Century of Lawmaking*, Statutes, 31st Cong., 1st sess., 462–65.

4. Kennedy, *Profiles in Courage*, 61–62.

5. McPherson, *Battle Cry of Freedom*, 70–77.

6. Etcheson, "Great Principle of Self-Government," 54.

7. Ibid., 55.

8. Leis, "Memoirs," 9.

9. Johnson, "Emigrant Aid Company," 121.

10. Bumgardner, *Life of Edmund G. Ross*, 21.

11. Leis, "Memoirs," 9.

12. Robinson, *Kansas*, 89. Although Robinson does not refer to William Ross by name, she does refer to him as Mr. R., and the other members of his party make it clear the "R" is William Ross. See also Leis, "Memoirs . . . Part Two," 1–3.

13. Ibid., 89.

14. Etcheson, "Great Principle of Self-Government," 59–60.

15. William W. Ross to Edmund Ross, January 10, 1856, in possession of Ross descendants, reproduced in Leis, "Memoirs . . . Part Two," 4–5.

16. Bumgardner, *Life of Edmund G. Ross*, 24.

17. The article goes on to name the twenty-four adults in the party but not the twenty-six children. John Rastall, at the time sixteen years old, probably was one of the unnamed eight children listed as traveling with Ross.

18. Leis, "Memoirs . . . Part Two," 8–9.

19. Ross, "Reminiscence of the Kansas Conflict."

20. Leis, "Memoirs," 10.

Chapter Three

1. Leis, "Memoirs . . . Part Two," 12.

2. Cutler, *History of the State of Kansas*, "Jackson County," part 5.

3. Bumgardner, *Life of Edmund G. Ross*, 39.

4. Leis, "Memoirs . . . Part Two," 8.

5. Ibid., 7.

6. Ross's portfolio today is in possession of his descendants in Albuquerque.

7. Leis, "Memoirs . . . Part Two," 11.

8. Ibid., 10.

9. The 1854 poem by Whittier, a Quaker and fervent abolitionist, is partially reproduced in Cordley, *History of Lawrence*, chap. 1.

10. Cutler, *History of the State of Kansas*, "Jackson County," part 5.

11. See note 15 to chapter 2.

12. Langsdorf, "S. C. Pomeroy," 227–29.

13. Cutler, *History of the State of Kansas*, "Territorial History," part 36.

14. Collins, *Jim Lane*, 72; see also Speer, *Life of Gen. James H. Lane*. Both sources provide good information on Lane.

15. Lewis, "The Man the Historians Forgot," 85–86.

16. Etcheson, *Bleeding Kansas*, 93.

17. Ibid., 97.

18. S. N. Wood was the man who had co-owned the *Kansas Tribune* with John Speer when William Ross arrived in Kansas in September 1855. Wood apparently sold his interest to Ross in December of that same year.

19. Etcheson, *Bleeding Kansas*, 100–102.

20. Free-State governor Charles Robinson, getting early word that he would be arrested, left Kansas with his wife Sara to seek support in Washington from Republicans. Because two of the three congressional investigators were Republicans, Robinson was given a summary of the testimony taken by the committee. At Lexington, Missouri, Robinson was arrested, but Sara Robinson continued to Washington, carrying the findings of the congressional committee concealed in her clothing. Robinson would remain in prison until early September.

21. Robinson, *Kansas*, chap. 15.

22. Ibid., chap. 16.

23. Etcheson, *Bleeding Kansas*, 104–5.

24. See note 13.

25. Sumner, "The Crime Against Kansas," 144.

26. Etcheson, *Bleeding Kansas*, 109–10.

27. Robinson, *Kansas*, chap. 23.

28. Ibid., chap. 22.

29. Etcheson, *Bleeding Kansas*, 116.

30. Leis, "Memoirs . . . Part Two," 13.

31. Ibid.

32. Ibid.

33. Edmund G. Ross discharge document provided by Ross's descendants.

34. Cutler, *History of the State of Kansas*, "Territorial History," part 43.

35. Ibid., "Territorial History," part 39.

36. Watts, "How Bloody Was Bleeding Kansas?" 12.

37. Bumgardner, *Life of Edmund G. Ross*, 33–34.

38. Ross, *Reminiscence of the Kansas Conflict*.

39. Root, "First Day's Battle at Hickory Point," 32.

40. Bumgardner, *Life of Edmund G. Ross*, 37–38.

41. Root, "First Day's Battle at Hickory Point," 49.

42. Leis, "Memoirs . . . Part Two," 15.

43. Bumgardner, *Life of Edmund G. Ross*, 37.

44. Watts, "How Bloody Was Bleeding Kansas?" 124.

Chapter Four

1. Etcheson, *Bleeding Kansas*, 131–33.

2. Free-State Army discharge paper in possession of Ross descendants.

3. Leis, "Memoirs . . . Part Two," 14.

4. *Kansas Tribune*, August 1, 1857.

5. *Kansas Tribune*, February 2, 1857.

6. The *Kansas Tribune* was first published in Lawrence in October 1854 under the name *Kansas Pioneer*. The name was changed to *Tribune* in January 1855. The *Herald of Freedom*, a paper sponsored by the New England Emigrant Aid Company, also began publication in Lawrence in October 1854 and continued to be published until 1859, with the exception of a brief period after the Sack of Lawrence in 1856. Several other Free-State papers emerged in this era, but nearly all closed after a short time. The *Tribune* and the *Herald of Freedom* remained active longer than other Free-State papers during the territorial period. Shortly after the Ross brothers suspended publication of the *Tribune* in 1858, John Speer, the original founder, resumed its publication in Lawrence. Edmund Ross would again edit the *Tribune* from late 1865 to late July 1866 in partnership with Speer.

7. Leis, "Memoirs . . . Part Two," 16.

8. *Kansas Tribune*, November 7, 1857.

9. In Ewing's reference to "the Tribune" it is unclear whether he is referring to the *Kansas Tribune* or some other publication, possibly the *New York Tribune*.

10. Thomas Ewing Sr. to Thomas Ewing Jr., July 23, 1857, unbound correspondence, 1856–1908, Ewing Collection, Kansas State Historical Society, Topeka (hereafter Ewing Collection).

11. *Kansas Tribune*, September 19, 1857.

12. Etcheson, *Bleeding Kansas*, 153–55.

13. *Kansas Tribune*, November 7, 1857.

14. Etcheson, *Bleeding Kansas*, 156.

15. *Kansas Tribune*, November 21, 1857.

16. Etcheson, *Bleeding Kansas*, 156.

17. *Kansas Tribune*, November 28, 1857.

18. Etcheson, *Bleeding Kansas*, 157.

19. Ponce, "Pledges and Principles," 78.

20. *Kansas Tribune*, December 26, 1857.

21. Etcheson, *Bleeding Kansas*, 163–64; see also Smith, *Thomas Ewing, Jr.*, 53–65.

22. Smith, *Thomas Ewing, Jr.*, 56–57.

23. *Kansas Tribune*, January 2, 1858.

24. Ponce, "Pledges and Principles," 78.

25. Etcheson, *Bleeding Kansas*, 165; Smith, *Thomas Ewing, Jr.*, 59–60.

26. Ponce, "Pledges and Principles," 76. Ponce's essay is recommended for its thorough discussion of the relationship between Walker and Buchanan and the influence of Free-Staters on Walker and Stanton.

27. *Kansas Tribune*, March 27, 1858.

28. Etcheson, *Bleeding Kansas*, 177.

29. Ibid., 174.

30. *Kansas Tribune*, May 8, 1858.

31. Ibid.

32. The *Kansas News*, later known as the *Emporia News*, also a Free-State paper, remained in operation from June 1857 until October 1862. Preston Plumb, who would serve with Ross during the Civil War and who would later be a United States senator from Kansas, founded and edited that paper.

33. *Kansas Tribune*, April 25, 1857.

34. *Kansas Tribune*, April 18, 1858.

35. Leis, "Memoirs . . . Part Two," 16, 17.

36. Ibid., 15.

37. Ibid., 16.

38. Socolofsky, "Kansas in 1876," 3. Although Socolofsky's article describes farm life in 1876, life for the Rosses was surely not different in 1858. The Ross home was indeed small and temporary, with Ross intending to build a much larger home.

39. Leis, "Memoirs . . . Part Two," 17.

40. Ibid., 19.

41. See the Kansas State Historical Society web page kshs.org/wyandotte-constitutional-convention-bibliography/17148 for a comprehensive list of articles and documents relating to the subject.

42. The reader should note that much of the history of Kansas in this era is not covered in this chapter. As this work is a biography, I have tried to focus on the aspects of the Bleeding Kansas period that directly involved Edmund Ross. Consequently, many significant events are not discussed here. I encourage readers to pursue territorial Kansas histories. In particular I recommend *Bleeding Kansas* by Nicole Etcheson, whose work is often cited in this book. It would be a mistake, for example, to think that violence ended in 1856. Indeed, it continued, albeit in a much less pervasive form. The violence mostly came from extremists on both sides of the slavery issue, but the Ross brothers did not take part in these incidents. Jim Lane killed his neighbor in May of 1858 over a simple land dispute but was acquitted on a self-defense plea, and John Brown went on to make history at Harper's Ferry, taking along with him John Henry Kagi, who worked for the Ross brothers at the *Tribune* in 1857.

Chapter Five

1. Leis, "Memoirs . . . Part Two," 20.

2. Etcheson, *Bleeding Kansas*, 205.

3. Ibid., 206.

4. *Kansas State Record*, November 5, 1859.

5. *Kansas State Record*, December 24, 1859.

6. Ibid.

7. Malin, "Dust Storms," 133.

8. *Kansas State Record*, November 17, 1860.

9. Crawford, *Kansas in the Sixties*, 7–8. Apparently Crawford did not consider Ross to be a part of any fraud. The high esteem in which he held Ross led him to appoint Ross to the United States Senate in 1866.

10. *Kansas State Record*, December 1, 1860.

11. Cutler, *History of the State of Kansas*, "Era of Peace," part 2.

12. Snell and Wilson, "Atchison, Topeka and Santa Fe," 114.

13. Ibid.; see also Ross, *Albuquerque Daily Democrat*, December 22, 1882.

14. *Kansas State Record*, September 22, 1860.

15. Cutler, *History of the State of Kansas*, "Era of Peace," part 2.

16. *Kansas State Record,* October 20, 1860.

17. Ibid.

18. Cutler, *History of the State of Kansas*, "Era of Peace," part 2.

19. *Kansas State Record*, October 13, 1860.

20. *Kansas State Record*, June 1, 1861.

21. Ibid.

22. *Kansas State Record*, February 16, 1861.

23. *Kansas State Record*, March 2, 1861.

24. *Kansas State Record*, October 12, 1861.

25. There is actually some uncertainty about Eddie's given name. Edmundie appears to be correct, but at least one descendant believes the given name was Edwina.

26. Leis, "Memoirs . . . Part Two," 21.

27. "Eleventh Regiment Kansas Volunteer Infantry."

Chapter Six

1. Hamilton, "A Colonel of Kansas," 282–83; see also Scott, "Fighting Printers," 4.

2. Hamilton, "A Colonel of Kansas," 283, 285.

3. Connelley, *Life of Preston B. Plumb*, 107. It is worth noting that both Ross and Plumb would, at different times, share the honor of being United States senators from Kansas. Plumb was a senator from 1877 to 1891.

4. Hamilton, "A Colonel of Kansas," 283, 285.

5. "Eleventh Regiment Kansas Volunteer Infantry," 2; see also Scott, "Fighting Printers."

6. Scott, "Fighting Printers," 3; see also Cutler, *History of the State of Kansas*, "Military Record," part 12.

7. Ross to Fannie, October 4, 1862, Ross Collection, Topeka.

8. "Eleventh Regiment Kansas Volunteer Infantry," 3; see also Ross to Fannie, October 25, 1862, Ross Collection, Topeka.

9. William also served in the militia but apparently did not participate in any battles.

10. Ross to Fannie, October 25, 1862, Ross Collection, Topeka.

11. Connelley, *Life of Preston B. Plumb*, 109–10.

12. Ross to Fannie, November 30, 1862, Ross Collection, Topeka.

13. Ibid.

14. Ross to Fannie, December 1, 1862, Ross Collection, Topeka.

15. Scott, "Fighting Printers," 13.

16. Ibid., 22. The Scott paper cited here is the most thorough and balanced discussion of the *Buck and Ball*. The Connelley biography of Major Plumb also contains a short chapter on the *Buck and Ball*, possibly giving Plumb more credit than he actually earned. John Howard Kitts's diary of the Civil War is the only firsthand account of the *Buck and Ball* other than Ross's two-sentence description to his wife.

17. Scott, "Fighting Printers," 20.

18. Shea, *Fields of Blood*, 124–25.

19. Ross to Fannie, December 12, 1862, Ross Collection, Topeka.

20. Shea, *Fields of Blood*, 230.

21. Scott, "Fighting Printers," 21.

22. Crawford, *Kansas in the Sixties*, 84.

23. "Eleventh Regiment Kansas Volunteer Infantry," 6.

24. Ross to Fannie, December 12, 1862, Ross Collection, Topeka.

25. Ibid.

26. "Eleventh Regiment Kansas Volunteer Infantry," 6–7. For a detailed description see Shea, *Fields of Blood*, 274–81.

27. "Eleventh Regiment Kansas Volunteer Infantry," 7.

28. Connelley, *Life of Preston B. Plumb*, 142–43.

29. Leis, "Memoirs . . . Part Two," 23–24.

30. Ibid., 24–25.

31. *Kansas Tribune*, August 13, 1863. As noted in the text, Ross's men are described as passing through the town rather than leaving town. This seems consistent with Leis's story, since the men would have had to pass through the town from their "west of the town" bivouac.

32. Smith, *Thomas Ewing, Jr.*, 192.

33. Foote, *The Civil War*, 2:704–5.

34. Ibid.

35. Connelley, *Life of Preston B. Plumb*, 152.

36. Foote, *The Civil War*, 704. The murdered recruits mentioned by Foote may have been men whom Ross had signed up for duty with a new cavalry regiment and who had not yet been officially assigned to a unit. Foote mentions the 14th Cavalry, but this regiment was not activated until later in 1863.

37. Ibid.

38. *Kansas State Journal*, October 8, 1863.

39. Ross to Fannie, September 17, 1863, Ross Collection, Topeka.

40. Leis, "Memoirs . . . Part Two," 26.

41. Ibid., 27–28.

42. Ibid., 27–29.

43. *Kansas Tribune*, February 27, 1864.

44. *Kansas Tribune*, January 14, 1864.

45. "Eleventh Regiment Kansas Volunteer Infantry," 8–9.

46. Ewing was forced to retreat with his 1,400-man army from Fort Davidson toward St. Louis. The details of General Price's march through Missouri and a part of Kansas are complex and beyond the scope of this biography. In the bibliography please see books by Samuel Crawford, William Connelley, Ronald Smith, and Albert Castel for more detailed accounts. Also see the history of the Eleventh

Kansas Regiment, available online through the Kansas State Historical Society, plus soldiers' personal recollections contained in *Tales of Kansas in the Civil War*, drawn from the Society's publications.

47. Crawford, *Kansas in the Sixties*, 146.

48. Connelley, *Life of Preston B. Plumb*, 181–82.

49. Ibid., 185.

50. Crawford, *Kansas in the Sixties*, 146.

51. Hamilton, "A Colonel of Kansas," 285–86.

52. Ibid.; Connelley, *Life of Preston B. Plumb*, 186.

53. Crawford, *Kansas in the Sixties*, 146–47.

54. "Eleventh Regiment Kansas Volunteer Infantry," 19.

55. Crawford, *Kansas in the Sixties*, 236.

56. Smith, *Thomas Ewing, Jr.*, 246.

57. "Eleventh Regiment Kansas Volunteer Infantry," 21.

58. Connelley, *Life of Preston B. Plumb*, 192.

59. Leis, "Memoirs . . . Part Two," 31.

60. Ibid., 32.

61. Ibid.

62. Hamilton, "A Colonel of Kansas," 287–88.

63. Leis, "Memoirs . . . Part Two," 32.

Chapter Seven

1. Ross to Fannie, May 10, 1865, Ross Collection, Topeka.

2. *Kansas Tribune*, September 15, 1855.

3. Leis, "Memoirs . . . Part Two," 32.

4. *Kansas Daily Tribune*, November 11, 1865; see also *Kansas Weekly Tribune* of March 15, 1866, where Speer describes the business arrangement with Ross, citing Ross as the regular editor of the paper.

5. Leis, "Memoirs . . . Part Two," 32–33.

6. "The Negro Question," *Kansas Weekly Tribune*, August 10, 1865.

7. *Kansas Tribune*, January 4, 1866.

8. Ibid.

9. Editorial, *Kansas State Record*, March 16, 1861.

10. Etcheson, *Bleeding Kansas*, 75; see also Collins, *Jim Lane*, 44–47, 59–64, for Lane's views.

Chapter Eight

1. Ross, *History of the Impeachment*, 15; see also Randall and Donald, *Civil War and Reconstruction*, 561–62.

2. Ross, *History of the Impeachment*, 18–19.

3. An excellent discussion of these matters can be found in McKitrick, *Andrew Johnson and Reconstruction*, chapters 5 and 6.

4. Foner, *Reconstruction*, 184.

5. Randall and Donald, *Civil War and Reconstruction*, 560–63.

6. Simpson, *The Reconstruction Presidents*, 70.

7. Randall and Donald, *Civil War and Reconstruction*, 559.

8. Ibid., 576–78.

9. *Kansas Tribune*, February 22, 1866.

10. Civil Rights Act of 1866: see *A Century of Lawmaking*, Statutes, 39th Cong., 1st sess., April 9, 1866.

11. *Kansas Tribune*, April 12, 1866.

12. *Kansas Tribune*, April 14, 1866.

13. *Kansas Tribune*, April 19, 1866.

14. The only instance of Edmund Ross running for public office other than for governor in 1880 was in February 1866 when he was persuaded to run for mayor of Lawrence by the Friends of Temperance. One week later on March 6 he lost the election by about 100 votes out of nearly 900 cast. It is also interesting to note that the February 27, 1866, issue of the *Tribune* reported that his brother William was taking a yearlong leave of absence from his job as mayor of Topeka, apparently for health reasons.

Chapter 9

1. Crawford, *Kansas in the Sixties*, 235.

2. Telegraphed statement from the *St. Louis Post Dispatch*, reprinted in the *Kansas Weekly Tribune*, July 5, 1866.

3. Ibid.

4. Crawford, *Kansas in the Sixties*, 235, citing an article in the *Leavenworth Conservative*.

5. *Kansas Tribune*, July 8, 1866.

6. "The Cause of Suicide," *New York Tribune*, July 2, 1866, reprinted in the *Kansas Tribune*, July 10, 1866.

7. Lewis, "The Man the Historians Forgot," 102.

8. Ibid.

9. Leis, "Memoirs . . . Part Two," 35.

10. *Kansas Daily Tribune*, July 11, 1866.

11. Plummer, "Crawford's Appointment," 147.

12. Leis, "Memoirs . . . Part Two," 34.

13. Ibid.

14. Plummer, "Crawford's Appointment," 148.

15. Crawford, *Kansas in the Sixties*, 236–37.

16. Leis, "Memoirs . . . Part Two," 35.

17. *Kansas Tribune*, July 21, 1866.

18. Ibid.

19. Leis, "Memoirs . . . Part Two," 35.

20. Ibid., 35–36.

Chapter Ten

1. *Congressional Globe*, 39th Cong., 2d sess., 213.

2. Ibid.

3. Trefousse, *Impeachment of a President*, 5, citing Charles Nordhoff letter to W. C. Bryant, February 2, 1867, Bryant-Godwin Collection, New York Public Library; see also Foner, *Reconstruction*, 180.

4. Simpson, *The Reconstruction Presidents*, 94.

5. Andrew Johnson, annual message to Congress, December 3, 1866, *Congressional Globe*, 39th Cong., 2d sess., Appendix, 1.

6. Simpson, *The Reconstruction Presidents*, 107–9.

7. Randall and Donald, *Civil War and Reconstruction*, 591.

8. Joint Resolution S.R. 152, Committee on Reconstruction, December 19, 1866, *Congressional Globe*, 39th Cong., 2d sess., 211.

9. McKitrick, *Andrew Johnson and Reconstruction*, 474–76.

10. Hebert, *Modern Maine*, 204.

11. By coincidence, Ross's daughter Eddie would marry William Cobb, a nephew of William Pitt Fessenden. They would name their son Edmund Fessenden Cobb, in honor of both E. G. Ross and the Fessenden name. Young Edmund Cobb would grow up to be a western movie star who appeared in more than five hundred films between 1912 and 1966.

12. Ross, handwritten vita, Ross Collection, Topeka. This five-page document bears the notation "32422" on the first page.

13. *Congressional Globe*, 39th Cong., 2d sess., 212.

14. Ibid.

15. Abraham Lincoln, April 11, 1865; text at historyplace.com/lincoln/reconst.htm, quoted with slight variations in Ross, *History of the Impeachment*, 18.

16. Ross, *History of the Impeachment*, 18.

17. Excellent and fairly concise descriptions of the Fourteenth Amendment can be found in Randall and Donald, *Civil War and Reconstruction*, 580–85, and in McKitrick, *Andrew Johnson and Reconstruction*, 326–63.

18. See, for example, Representative Thaddeus Stevens, speaking to the Joint Committee on Reconstruction, January 3, 1867, *Congressional Globe*, 39th Cong., 2d sess., 251.

19. McKitrick, *Andrew Johnson and Reconstruction*, 476n67.

20. Stevens to the Joint Committee on Reconstruction, 251.

21. The Fortieth Congress convened in a special session the day after the Thirty-ninth adjourned.

22. Randall and Donald, *Civil War and Reconstruction*, 598–99.

23. Ibid., 595; see also 596–600 for a description of how the Reconstruction Acts played out during the first year after passage. An excellent description of the debate leading to passage of the Reconstruction Act can be found in McKitrick's *Andrew Johnson and Reconstruction*, 476–85. Also note that a fourth Reconstruction Act was enacted in March 1868, a full year after passage of the first act. The fourth act eliminated the requirement of a majority of all voters to pass a new constitution in seceded states, changing the law to a majority of voters taking part in constitutional referendums.

Chapter Eleven

1. The *Journal of the Senate* shows Ross still voting on January 10 but not after that date until February 1; see *A Century of Lawmaking*, Senate Journal, 39th Cong., 2d sess., 84–193.

2. Bumgardner, *Life of Edmund G. Ross*, 163–65.

3. Kansas Territorial Legislature, *Report of the Joint Committee of Investigation*, 244–45. Note that Clarke, who had been the Kansas representative to Congress, failed in his bid for reelection in 1869 and was running for the Senate seat vacated by Ross.

4. Crawford, *Kansas in the Sixties*, 346–47.

5. Kansas Territorial Legislature, *Report of the Joint Committee of Investigation*, 239–40.

6. Ibid., 243.

7. Ross to Andrew Johnson, June 23, 1868, Andrew Johnson Papers, Library of Congress; see also Plummer, "Profile in Courage?" 41.

8. Barker, "Perry Fuller," 1.

9. Ibid., 3.

10. Litteer, *Perry Fuller*, 10. This work contains a significant number of errors and should be used with caution. It is probably reliable for establishing a date for Fuller to be in Baldwin. There are no footnotes to indicate sources.

11. Sherwood, *A Labor of Love*, 21–22; see also Harold E. Miner to F. E. Blackburn, July 31, 1954, Kansas State Historical Society, Topeka, filed under BB, MSS, Fuller.

12. Sherwood, *A Labor of Love*, 22.

13. Miner and Unrau, *End of Indian Kansas*, 64–65.

14. *Ross's Paper*, March 1, 1872, 49.

15. Ibid.

16. Note that Ross's senatorial term ended a little more than a year before his appearance before the Committee on Privileges and Elections.

17. See testimony before the Senate Committee on Privileges and Elections (investigating the Kansas senatorial elections of 1867 and 1871), May 27, 1872, *Congressional Globe*, 42nd Cong., 2d sess., Appendix: entire testimony, 606–26, Ross testimony, 617–19.

18. The election of Alexander Caldwell to replace Edmund Ross and his dismissal from the Senate a year later is covered in chapter 16.

19. See chapter 14 for further discussion of Ross's "Fuller" letter and of other letters to Johnson from Ross.

20. "Seizure of Goods in Transit to Kansas—Attachment Against Fuller," *New York Times*, September 4, 1869.

21. "Ex-Collector Perry Fuller in Court," *New York Times*, September 26, 1869, reprinted from *New-Orleans Bee*, September 21, 1869.

22. Miner to Blackburn (see note 11).

Chapter Twelve

1. Ross, *History of the Impeachment*, 57.

2. Benedict, *Impeachment and Trial*, 47.

3. Ibid., 48.

4. Ross, *History of the Impeachment*, 57–58.

5. *A Century of Lawmaking*, Senate Journal, 39th Cong., 2d sess., 216.

6. Ross, *History of the Impeachment*, 62, quoting President Johnson's objections to the Tenure of Office Act.

7. *A Century of Lawmaking*, Senate Journal, 40th Cong., 2d sess., 419.

8. *Congressional Globe*, 41st Cong., 1st sess., 241. The Tenure of Office Act was repealed in 1887 during the Democratic administration of Grover Cleveland.

9. Ross, *History of the Impeachment*, 63–64; see also Trefousse, *Impeachment of a President*, 79, and Hearn, *Impeachment of Andrew Johnson*, 118.

10. Benedict, *Impeachment and Trial*, 53–54; Trefousse, *Impeachment of a President*, 72–73.

11. Trefousse, *Impeachment of a President*, 81, citing Stanton letter to Johnson, August 5, 1867.

12. Ibid., 82.

13. Ibid., 85–97.

14. *Congressional Globe*, 40th Cong., 2d sess., Appendix, 1–4.

15. Ibid., 2–3.

16. Trefousse, *Impeachment of a President*, 55–58.

17. Ross, *History of the Impeachment*, 53.

18. Randall and Donald, *Civil War and Reconstruction*, 602–3; see also Ross, *History of the Impeachment*, 46–53, for a more detailed exposition.

19. *A Century of Lawmaking*, Senate Executive Journal, 40th Cong., 2d sess., 96.

20. Benedict, *Impeachment and Trial*, 95.

21. *A Century of Lawmaking*, Senate Executive Journal, 40th Cong., 2d sess., 128.

22. Ibid., 129.

23. Ibid., 130. Three other senators (Grimes, Henderson, and Van Winkle) who would vote with Ross to acquit the president in May also abstained from voting on the Doolittle amendment; see Benedict, *Impeachment and Trial*, 99.

24. Trefousse, *Impeachment of a President*, 125–28; Benedict, *Impeachment and Trial*, 96–99.

25. McKitrick, *Andrew Johnson and Reconstruction*, 504.

26. Trefousse, *Impeachment of a President*, 131–34; see also McKitrick, *Andrew Johnson and Reconstruction*, 504–5.

27. Trefousse, *Impeachment of a President*, 135–36.

28. *A Century of Lawmaking*, Senate Executive Journal, 40th Cong., 2d sess., 170–72.

29. Ross, *History of the Impeachment*, 66n.

30. Ibid., 67.

31. McKitrick, *Andrew Johnson and Reconstruction*, 505n32.

32. Ibid., 507.

33. *Kansas State Record*, March 4, 1868.

34. Although Ross was appointed to the job in July 1866, he did not really become active until December.

35. There appears to be no extant correspondence between Ross and Ewing Jr. prior to the impeachment trial. Since they were living in the same town, there probably was little reason for written correspondence, but at least two letters written by Ewing to General John McDowell, one on August 29, 1867, and another dated October 1867, reveal his friendly relationship with Ross; see Ewing Collection, MSS 570.

Chapter Thirteen

1. Ross, *History of the Impeachment*, 126–28; Trefousse, *Impeachment of a President*, 138.

2. Benedict, *Impeachment and Trial*, 113; Trefousse, *Impeachment of a President*, 138–39; Ross, *History of the Impeachment*, 83.

3. Ross, *History of the Impeachment*, 83–84.

4. Hearn, *Impeachment of Andrew Johnson*, 166.

5. Benedict, *Impeachment and Trial*, 115–16.

6. Ross, *History of the Impeachment*, 105–26.

7. Ibid., 114–16; Sherman testimony, *Congressional Globe*, 40th Cong., 2d sess., Supplement: Trial of Andrew Johnson, 158–60.

8. Ross, *History of the Impeachment*, 125.

9. Ibid., 133.

10. Ibid., 129–33.

11. Dewitt, *Impeachment and Trial*, 543–44.

12. Ross, quoted in "Ex-Senator Ross's Own Story of the Johnson Impeachment Trial," *Kansas City Star*, May 17, 1903.

13. Dewitt, *Impeachment and Trial*, 539.

14. For Pomeroy's testimony see United States Congress, House Select Committee, "Raising of Money to be Used in Impeachment," 30–32; for Ross's speech see *Congressional Globe*, 40th Cong., 2d sess., 4515–16.

15. Dewitt, *Impeachment and Trial*, 533.

16. Jellison, *Fessenden of Maine*, 244–45.

17. *Congressional Globe*, 40th Cong., 2d sess., 4515–16.

18. *Congressional Globe*, 40th Cong., 2d sess., 2599.

19. *Congressional Globe*, 40th Cong., 2d sess., 4516.

20. Stewart, *Impeached*, 269.

21. Sherwood, *A Labor of Love*, 23, 31–36, 37–45. Ream's statue of Lincoln is still in the Capitol.

22. Interview with General Dan Sickles attributed to the *Chicago Record* and printed in the *Boston Daily Globe*, November 1, 1896; see also Sherwood, *A Labor of Love*, 96, citing Swanberg, *Sickles the Incredible*, 299–301, and *New York Sun*, October 25, 1896.

23. Plummer, "Profile in Courage?" 37.

24. Ross, "The Impeachment Trial," 521.

25. There were multiple closing arguments that took days to present. Evarts's closing argument alone, for the defense, lasted fourteen hours and spanned four days (see Hearn, *Impeachment of Andrew Johnson*, 193). It is not the intention of this biography to give a detailed account of the impeachment proceedings. However, one important difference between the prosecution and defense, regarding the president's legal responsibilities, was revealed in arguments offered by Stevens for the House managers and by Stanbery for the president.

26. *Congressional Globe*, 40th Cong., 2d sess., Supplement: Trial of Andrew Johnson, 321.

27. Ibid., 373.

28. Benedict, *Impeachment and Trial*, 137–38, citing Browning, *Diary*, 2:195 (May 5, 1868); Richardson, *Messages and Papers of the Presidents*, 6:632.

29. Kennedy, *Profiles in Courage*, 126–27.

30. "Impeachment, Final Vote in the Senate on the Eleventh Article," *New York Times*, May 16, 1868.

31. Some accounts describe Grimes rising to his feet with great difficulty.

32. See note 30.

33. Ross, "The Impeachment Trial," 524.

34. Plummer, "Profile in Courage?" 36 and n21; Welles, *Diary*, 3:358. Plummer identifies Senators Morgan, Sprague, and Nye as inclined to vote "not guilty." Welles claimed Senators Anthony, Corbett, and Cole as hopeful "not guilty" voters. See also Roske, *His Own Counsel*, 149–50.

35. *Congressional Globe*, 40th Cong., 2d sess., 4516.

36. Ibid. See also the full text of United States Congress, House Select Committee, "Raising of Money to be Used in Impeachment." Other than Pomeroy's testimony, there is comparatively little about Ross in the report and certainly nothing damaging about Ross. There is a great deal about Perry Fuller and his efforts to raise money for the defense of the president.

37. Welles, *Diary*, 3:362.

38. Dewitt, *Impeachment and Trial*, 573–74.

39. Ibid., 575.

40. "Ross's Varying Fortune, From Case to Senate and Back Again," *New York Times*, August 18, 1889, reprinted from the *Leavenworth Conservative*, August 17, 1889.

41. *Leavenworth Daily Conservative*, May 17, 1868.

42. Leis, "Memoirs . . . Part Two," 37–38.

43. Bumgardner, *Life of Edmund G. Ross*, 89.

44. Leis, "Memoirs . . . Part Two," 36.

45. *Congressional Globe*, 40th Cong., 2d sess., 2599.

46. *Congressional Globe*, 40th Cong., 2d sess., 4515, 4517.

47. Dewitt, *Impeachment and Trial*, 548–49.

Chapter Fourteen

1. *Congressional Globe*, 40th Cong., 2d sess., 2599.

2. Ibid.

3. Ibid.

4. Ibid.

5. Heitzman, "Reaction of the Kansas Press," 43–60.

6. Kennedy, *Profiles in Courage*, 128.

7. McCabe, *Behind the Scenes in Washington*, 456.

8. Taylor, "Business and Political Career of Thomas Ewing, Jr.," 185–88.

9. *Congressional Globe*, 40th Cong., 2d sess., 4515.

10. Berwanger, "Ross and the Impeachment," 239.

11. Plummer, "Profile in Courage?" 33.

12. Berwanger, "Ross and the Impeachment," 239.

13. Report from H. C. Whitney to editor Prouty, cited in Berwanger, "Ross and the Impeachment," 239.

14. Taylor, "Business and Political Career of Thomas Ewing, Jr.," 186–87.

15. Ross to Andrew Johnson, June 6, 1868, Andrew Johnson Papers, Library of Congress.

16. Ross to Andrew Johnson, June 23, 1868, Johnson Papers.

17. Welles, *Diary*, 3:39.

18. See chapter 11 for a detailed account of the 1867 elections of both Ross and Pomeroy.

19. Ross to Andrew Johnson, July 1, 1868, Johnson Papers.

20. Ross to Andrew Johnson, July 10, 1868, Johnson Papers.

21. Benedict, *Impeachment and Trial*, 137–38, citing Browning, *Diary* 2:195 (May 5, 1868); Richardson, *Messages and Papers of the Presidents*, 6:632.

22. Bumgardner, *Life of Edmund G. Ross*, 78.

23. Dewitt, *Impeachment and Trial*, 569–70.

24. *Congressional Globe*, 40th Cong., 2d sess., 4513.

25. Ibid., 4516.

26. Ibid., 4514.

27. Ibid.

28. McCabe, *Behind the Scenes in Washington*, 455.

29. Sherwood, *A Labor of Love*, 98–99.

30. *Congressional Globe*, 40th Cong., 2d sess., 2676.

31. See *Thaddeus Stevens, Champion of Freedom*, 5.

32. Whitney to Ross, January 19, 1869, Ross Collection, Topeka.

33. Leis, "Memoirs . . . Part Two," 36–37.

Chapter Fifteen

1. Ross to Fannie, from Cane Hill, Arkansas, December 12, 1862, Ross Collection, Topeka.

2. Snell and Wilson, "Atchison, Topeka and Santa Fe," part 2.

3. Leis, "Memoirs . . . Part Two," 38–39.

4. Ibid., 40–41.

5. McCabe, *Behind the Scenes in Washington*, 92.

6. Leis, "Memoirs . . . Part Two," 40.

7. *Congressional Globe*, 40th Cong., 3d sess., 982.

8. Ibid.

9. Ibid., 983.

10. Roske, *His Own Counsel*, 154.

11. *Congressional Globe*, 40th Cong., 3d sess., 984.

12. *Congressional Globe*, 41st Cong., 1st sess., 241.

13. Leis, "Memoirs . . . Part Two," 41.

14. McCabe, *Behind the Scenes in Washington*, 145–46.

15. Leis, "Memoirs . . . Part Two," 41.

16. *Congressional Globe*, 41st Cong., 1st sess., 731, quoting "A Speck of War at the White House," *New York Herald*, April 13, 1869.

17. *Congressional Globe*, 41st Cong., 1st sess., 732.

18. Ibid.

19. Ibid.

20. See *Congressional Globe*, 40th Cong., 1st sess., 750, 751; see also Jellison, *Fessenden of Maine*, 222–23.

21. *Congressional Globe*, 41st Cong., 1st sess., 732–33.

22. McCabe, *Behind the Scenes in Washington*, 456.

23. Ross to Fannie, June 2, 1869, Ross Collection, Topeka.

24. Leis, "Memoirs . . . Part Two," 43.

25. Ross to Fannie, December 15, 1869, Ross Collection, Topeka.

26. Ross to Fannie, December 29, 1869, Ross Collection, Topeka.

27. "Impeachment Trial," *Kansas State Record*, January 5, 1870.

28. The name of the school that Lillian was attending is not recorded in any Ross family document, but the chances are good it was in Chicago, since Ross mentions in his letter that he hopes to be able to meet Lillian in Chicago on the way home.

29. Ross to Fannie, March 6, 1870, Ross Collection, Topeka.

30. Ibid.

31. Ross to Fannie, March 7, 1870, Ross Collection, Topeka.

32. Ross to Fannie, March 28, 1870, Ross Collection, Topeka.

33. Ross to Fannie, April 4, 1870, Ross Collection, Topeka.

34. Ross to Fannie, April 19, 1870, Ross Collection, Topeka.

35. Ross, handwritten vita (see note 12 to chapter 10).

Chapter Sixteen

1. LaForte, "Gilded Age Senator," 237.

2. Ibid., 250.

3. Ibid., 240.

4. Ross to Pitt Ross, March 8, 1871, Ross Collection, Topeka.

5. Ross to Fannie, March 12, 1871, Ross Collection, Topeka.

6. Ross to Fannie, March 17, 1871, Ross Collection, Topeka.

7. Ross to Fannie, July 24, 1871, Ross Collection, Topeka.

8. Leis, "Memoirs . . . Part Two," 43–44.

9. *Ross's Paper*, December 22, 1871.

10. Ibid.

11. Grove, "The Man Who Saved Andrew Johnson," 11. Based on an interview with Ross, the piece was not published until 1910.

12. *Ross's Paper*, December 22, 1871.

13. *New York Tribune* editorial, quoted in McCabe, *Behind the Scenes in Washington*, 184.

14. Samuel Pomeroy, "Open Letter to Edmund Ross," *Ross's Paper*, January 12, 1872.

15. For Pomeroy's role in administering drought relief funds, see chapter 5.

16. *Ross's Paper*, January 12, 1872. In addition to Pomeroy's houses in Washington and Boston and his ranch in Kansas, Ross further claimed that Pomeroy had two hundred lots in the town of Neodesha and owned half the town of Augusta, half the town of Concordia, a hundred town lots and several quarter sections of land around the city of Ottawa, 90,000 acres of Pottawatomie land, and 40,000 to 50,000 acres of Kickapoo Indian land, in addition to 23,000 acres of Kickapoo land that he had sold to a Swedish company for seven dollars per acre after acquiring them for a dollar an acre.

17. *Ross's Paper*, February 2, 1972.

18. Kansas Territorial Legislature, *Report of the Joint Committee of Investigation*; see also chapter 11.

19. *Ross's Paper*, March 1, 1872, 49.

20. Ibid. Readers are urged to see the full text of the article in chapter 11, which deals at length with the 1867 election.

21. See *A Century of Lawmaking*, Senate Journal, 42d Cong., 2d sess., 714.

22. See chapter 11 for a more detailed account of Ross's testimony before the United States Senate Committee on Privileges and Elections.

23. Leis, "Memoirs . . . Part Two," 46.

24. Caldwell, "Pomeroy's 'Ross Letter,'" 463–65.

25. Ibid. 466–70; see also McCabe, *Behind the Scenes in Washington*, 176.

26. Caldwell, "Pomeroy's 'Ross Letter.'"

27. Ross, handwritten vita (see note 12 to chapter 10), 4.

28. Heitzman, "Reaction of the Kansas Press," 9, citing *Kansas Daily Commonwealth*, April 17, 1872.

29. *Atchison Patriot*, April 23, 1872.

30. White, *Life of Lyman Trumbull*, 322.

31. Heitzman, "Reaction of the Kansas Press," 10.

32. *Evening Paper*, January 20, 1873.

33. Leis, "Memoirs . . . Part Two," 47–48.

34. McCabe, *Behind the Scenes in Washington*, 173–84.

35. Caldwell, "Pomeroy's 'Ross Letter,'" 470.

36. Twain and Warner, *The Gilded Age*, 518–19; LaForte, "Gilded Age Senator," 234.

37. McCabe, *Behind the Scenes in Washington*, 182–83, citing the *New York Tribune* with unspecified date.

38. *A Century of Lawmaking*, Senate Journal, 42d Cong., 3d sess., 111.

39. Ibid., 382.

40. McCabe, *Behind the Scenes in Washington*, 188.

Chapter Seventeen

1. *Ross's Paper*, March 8, 1872; see also Cutler, *History of the State of Kansas*, "Legislative and Political Annals," part 3, 1872.

2. White, *Life of Lyman Trumbull*, 44–45.

3. Roske, *His Own Counsel*, 161.

4. Ibid., 163–67; White, *Life of Lyman Trumbull*, 386–87.

5. Earle Dudley Ross, *The Liberal Republican Movement*, 67–69.

6. *Ross's Paper*, July 19, 1872, 98.

7. Ibid.

8. Earle Dudley Ross, *The Liberal Republican Movement*, 190–91.

9. *Spirit of Kansas*, June 24, 1874, 4.

10. Leis, "Memoirs . . . Part Two," 49–50; Heitzman, "Reaction of the Kansas Press," 10–11.

11. *Lawrence Standard*, October 8, 1876; see also chapter 6 with reference to Quantrill's raid.

12. *Lawrence Standard*, January 11, 1877.

13. *Lawrence Standard*, January 23, 1877.

14. Ibid.

15. *Lawrence Evening Standard*, February 12, 1877, 1.

16. *Lawrence Evening Standard*, April 17, 1877, 1, reporting on the depth of the depression.

17. *Lawrence Evening Standard*, April 18, 1877.

18. Miller Center, "American President: Rutherford B. Hayes."

19. *Lawrence Evening Standard*, March 29, 1878.

20. *Lawrence Evening Standard*, April 10, 1879.

21. *Lawrence Evening Standard*, May 30, 1879.

22. *Atchison Patriot*, August 28, 1880. The *Atchison Patriot* may have been the one Kansas Democratic newspaper that had a larger circulation than the *Lawrence Standard*.

23. Heitzman, "Reaction of the Kansas Press," 80.

24. *Atchison Patriot*, August 28, 1880.

25. Roske, *His Own Counsel*, 170.

26. Heitzman, "Reaction of the Kansas Press," 94–95.

27. *Leavenworth Democratic Standard*, October 20, 1880.

28. *Leavenworth Democratic Standard*, October 27, 1880.

29. Heitzman, "Reaction of the Kansas Press," 81–82, quoting the *Kansas Chief*, September 2, 1880.

30. *Leavenworth Times*, August 29, 1880.

31. Leis, "Memoirs . . . Part Two," 50.

32. Heitzman, "Reaction of the Kansas Press," 96.

33. *Leavenworth Democratic Standard*, May 3, 1881.

34. "A Black Record," *Leavenworth Democratic Standard*, January 1, 1882.

35. Leis, "Memoirs . . . Part Two," 51.

36. *Leavenworth Democratic Standard*, March 4, 1882.

37. Leis, "Memoirs . . . Part Two," 51–52; for David B. Emmert, see *Albuquerque City Directory* 1883, 49.

38. *Leavenworth Democratic Standard*, September 15, 1882.

Chapter Eighteen

1. Between 1846 and 1867 various army companies were garrisoned at Albuquerque. During that time an unusually tall (121-foot) flagpole was erected in the plaza used by the army for military formations.

2. Chase, *Editor's Run*, 137–43. Chase's discourse on Albuquerque is well written and appears to be an unbiased assessment of the town. In addition to being printed in booklet form, Chase's articles apparently were serialized in the *Vermont Union*, a newspaper that Chase edited.

3. Simmons, *Albuquerque: A Narrative History*, 288–89.

4. *Collections of the Kansas State Historical Society* 12 (1912): 449n; Leis, "Memoirs . . . Part Two," 51.

5. Anderson, *History of New Mexico*, 1:470.

6. *Albuquerque Daily Democrat*, December 22, 1882; see also chapter 5.

7. *Albuquerque Daily Democrat*, December 30, 1882.

8. Ross to Fannie, February 6, 1883, cited in Lamar, "Edmund G. Ross," 181. The letter is no longer in the files of the New Mexico State Archives.

9. *Albuquerque Morning Journal*, February 18, 1883. Langhammer was identified in *The World's Industrial and Cotton Centennial Exposition, New Orleans, 1884–1885* by Herbert S. Fairall as a U.S. commissioner and professor promoting various industries in New Mexico at the New Orleans Exposition.

10. See "Copper City," ghosttowns.com/states/nm/coppercity.html.

11. Rebard, "Social History of Albuquerque," 13.

12. Lamar, "Edward G. Ross," 183n19; see also J. Van Brimmer and Co. to Ross, August 12, 1886, and W. H. Rohrer and W. M. Riley to A. W. Cleland, September 23 and 25, 1886, Governor Edmund Ross Papers, 1885–1889, New Mexico State Archives, Santa Fe (hereafter Ross Papers, Santa Fe).

13. Ross, "The Albuquerque Town Grant, Its Character and History," MSS 496 BC, Edmund G. Ross Papers, 1865–1907, University of New Mexico Center for Southwest Research, Albuquerque (hereafter Ross Papers, Albuquerque).

14. An excellent summary of the Albuquerque grant can be found in Bowden, "Private Land Claims in the Southwest," 1681–94.

15. Leis, "Memoirs . . . Part Three," 1.

16. *Santa Fe Herald*, June 23, 1888, reprinted from the *El Paso Tribune*.

17. Ross, letter to the editor, *Albuquerque Morning Journal*, September 3, 1884; see also his letter to the *Journal* on August 6, 1884.

18. Lamar, "Edmund G. Ross," 183–84. It seems likely that the Ross-Burke educational bill was submitted to Congress during the months when Ross was in Washington, November 1883 through early summer 1884.

19. As of September 6, 1884, Burke's name had disappeared from the editorial page of the *Journal*.

20. Lamar, "Edmund G. Ross," 184n24.

21. *Albuquerque Morning Journal*, August 29, 1884.

22. *Deming Headlight*, March 4, 1893, reprinted from the *Albuquerque Times*, date unknown.

23. Note that Cleveland served two terms that were separated by the single term of Benjamin Harrison.

24. Lamar, *The Far Southwest*, 157.

25. Lamar, "Edmund G. Ross," 187.

26. Democratic Leaders of Albuquerque to Grover Cleveland, April 6, 1885, Ross Papers, Santa Fe.

27. Ross to Grover Cleveland, April 30, 1885, Ross Papers, Santa Fe.

28. *Albuquerque Morning Journal*, May 13, 1885.

29. Burke to Grover Cleveland, May 20, 1885, Ross Papers, Santa Fe.

30. Leis, "Memoirs . . . Part Three," 3.

31. *Santa Fe New Mexican Review*, June 16, 1885.

32. Ibid.

33. *Albuquerque Morning Journal*, June 17, 1885.

34. Ibid.

35. *Albuquerque Morning Journal*, July 23, 1885.

36. Ibid.

Chapter Nineteen

1. Kessell, *Remote Beyond Compare*, xiv.

2. Lamar, *The Far Southwest*, 146.

3. Ibid.

4. For a description of daily life in colonial New Mexico, see Simmons, *Coronado's Land*. For a description of the colonial Spanish era from the perspective of Pueblo Indians, see Sando, *The Pueblo Indians*. For an excellent summary of colonial New Mexico history, see Chávez, *New Mexico Past and Future*. For a deeper understanding of relations between Pueblo people and Spaniards, see Kessell, *Pueblos, Spaniards, and the Kingdom of New Mexico*.

5. Shishkin, *The Palace of the Governors*.

6. Stephen Watts Kearny, speaking to the people of Las Vegas, New Mexico, August 15, 1846. The full text of the speech is preserved in a plaque in the town plaza, where the speech was given.

7. For the Kearny Proclamation, see Keleher, *Turmoil in New Mexico*, 15–16.

8. Davis, *El Gringo*, 193.

9. Ross, "Memorial in Behalf of the Bill for the Admission of New Mexico to Statehood," Ross Papers, Santa Fe, reprinted in *Santa Fe Herald*, April 21, 1888; see also Davis, *El Gringo*, 221–25.

10. Davis, *El Gringo*, 57.

11. Prince, *New Mexico's Struggle for Statehood*, 40–41.

12. Quoted in Keleher, *Turmoil in New Mexico*, 61–62.

13. Chávez, *New Mexico*, 122–23.

14. Simmons, *Albuquerque: A Narrative History*, 218.

15. Ross to H. C. Burnett, February 24, 1888, Ross Papers, Santa Fe. This H. C. Burnett is likely to be the same man who was Ross's assistant editor in Leavenworth, Kansas, and, it would appear, followed Ross to New Mexico.

Chapter Twenty

1. Lamar, *The Far Southwest*, 132.

2. Leis, "Memoirs . . . Part Three," 11.

3. Schiller, "George W. Julian," part 1 (April 2010).

4. Julian, "Land-Stealing in New Mexico," 17.

5. See chapter 18 for an account of the July 22 banquet.

6. Ross, banquet speech, July 22, 1885, Ross Collection, Topeka.

7. Lamar, *The Far Southwest*, 154.

8. See note 6.

9. Wallace, *Report of the Governor . . . 1879*, 1.

10. Ross, *Report of the Governor . . . 1885*, 4.

11. Westphall, *Mercedes Reales*, 9–10, citing McBride, *Land Systems of Mexico*, 107–8.

12. Ross, *Report of the Governor . . . 1885*, 4–5.

13. Westphall, *Mercedes Reales*, 19–20. A court decision in 1892 decided Albuquerque and Santa Fe were validly established town grants, but the decision was later nullified. It took an act of Congress in 1902 to certify the grants. See chapter 18 for Ross's efforts to settle Albuquerque's claim for validation.

14. Although this prohibition against surveying before congressional approval may have been established early on, later reports by Surveyor General Julian indicate that surveying prior to congressional approval did take place some of the time.

15. Ebright, *Land Grants and Lawsuits*, 39. Most of the information in this book concerning land grants and the surveyor general comes from Ebright, 21–45.

16. Ross, *Report of the Governor . . . 1885*, 5.

17. Lamar, *The Far Southwest*, 160, citing letters from Joseph to Ross on May 31 and July 19, 1886.

18. Wallace, *Report of the Governor . . . 1879*, 4.

19. Ross, *Report of the Governor . . . 1886*, 5–9.

20. Julian, "Land-Stealing in New Mexico," 17.

21. Ibid., 18.

22. Ibid., 21–22.

23. Ibid., 23–24.

24. Ibid., 28.

25. Lamar, *The Far Southwest*, 159.

26. Julian, "Land-Stealing in New Mexico," 29.

27. Ibid., 30.

28. Ross, address to the House Committee on Territories, January 11, 1888, Ross Papers, Santa Fe.

29. Ross to Voorhees, November 14, 1887, Ross Papers, Santa Fe.

30. Voorhees to Ross, undated, Ross Papers, Santa Fe.

31. See note 28.

32. Dorsey, "Land Stealing in New Mexico," 404.

33. Ross, argument before the House Committee on Private Land Claims, February 11, 1888, Ross Papers, Santa Fe.

34. Julian, "The Surveyor General and the Land Grant Titles," letter released to territorial newspapers, reprinted in an undated cutting, likely from the *Santa Fe Herald*, in Ross Papers, reel 101, no. 650, Santa Fe.

35. Commentary accompanying Julian's letter (see note 34).

36. Joseph to Ross, July 30, 1888, Ross Papers, Santa Fe.

37. Stewart to Ross, September 10, 1888, Ross Papers, Santa Fe.

38. *Santa Fe Herald*, September 10, 1888.

39. Prince, *Concise History of New Mexico*, 208–9.

40. Twitchell, *Leading Facts*, 2:463–65.

41. Ibid., 2:462.

42. Westphall, *Mercedes Reales*, 105.

43. Ibid., 133.

44. Schiller, "George W. Julian," part 4 (July 2010). In addition to his four-part series in the *La Jicarita News* examining the role of George Julian as surveyor general in New Mexico, see Schiller's paper "The History and Adjudication of the Antonio Chávez Grant"; see also Twitchell, *Leading Facts*, 2:463–65.

Chapter Twenty-One

1. Ross to John O'Grady, March 26, 1887, Ross Papers, Santa Fe, 1.

2. Lamar, *The Far Southwest*, 131, citing Herbert O. Brayer.

3. Interestingly, Edmund G. Ross would one day be included with Thomas Hart Benton and six other senators in John F. Kennedy's *Profiles in Courage*.

4. Westphall, *Thomas Benton Catron*, 7.

5. Ibid., 21.

6. Ibid., 399.

7. Ibid., 25.

8. Westphall, *Mercedes Reales*, 157–58.

9. Although Antonio Joseph was thought to be a Ring member, his working relationship with Ross appears to have been excellent. See chapter 20.

10. Keleher, *The Fabulous Frontier*, 130.

11. Lamar, *The Far Southwest*, 131.

12. Ross to John O'Grady, 5.

13. Ibid., 3, 4.

14. Ibid., 5–6.

15. "The President Indignant; He Suspends Chief-Justice Vincent, of New Mexico," *New York Times*, October 15, 1885; see also Keleher, *The Maxwell Land Grant*, 137–38.

16. Ross to John O'Grady, 5.

17. Westphall, *Thomas Benton Catron*, 201; see also Twitchell, *Leading Facts*, 2:501.

18. Ross to John O'Grady, 9.

19. Westphall, *Thomas Benton Catron*, 200.

20. Draft, Ross to A. H. Garland, August 24, 1885, Ross Papers, Santa Fe.

21. Leis, "Memoirs . . . Part Three," 10. Family papers in Albuquerque indicate the bride was Mabel Lucy Griswald.

22. Lamar, *The Far Southwest*, 132–33, 140–41.

23. Ross to William Breeden, November 24, 1885, Ross Papers, Santa Fe.

24. Westphall, *Thomas Benton Catron*, 200–201.

25. Ross to Antonio Ortiz y Salazar, July 28, 1886, Ross Papers, Santa Fe.

26. Ross to John O'Grady, 7–8.

27. Senators M. C. Butler and Charles Manderson to Ross, March 2, 1886, Ross Papers, Santa Fe.

28. Ross to John O'Grady, 11. Note that page 10 is missing; either there is no page 10 or the letter is not numbered correctly.

29. Ross, *Seven Vetoes*. A copy is in the Ross Papers, Santa Fe.

30. Ross to Secretary of the Interior L. Q. C. Lamar, [January 1887], Ross Papers, Santa Fe.

31. "The Socorro Disincorporation Bill," January 20, 1887, in Ross, *Seven Vetoes*, 1.

32. See Board of Co. Com'rs of Socorro Co. v. Leavitt and others, January 8, 1887, in New Mexico Supreme Court, *Reports*, 4:74–78, online at books.google.com/books?id=p_sDAAAAYAAJ.

33. "The Torts Bill," February 24, 1887, in Ross, *Seven Vetoes*, 9.

34. "Opposing Logan County," *Santa Fe Weekly New Mexican*, January 13, 1887.

35. "The Logan County Bill," February 21, 1887, in Ross, *Seven Vetoes*, 7.

36. *Silver City Enterprise*, March 4, 1887.

37. Ross to John O'Grady, 13, 14.

38. Lamar, "Edmund G. Ross," 203–4.

39. Twitchell, *Leading Facts*, 2:501.

40. Eddie Ross to Lillian Ross Leis, February 28, 1889, Ross Papers, Santa Fe.

41. Prince, *Concise History of New Mexico*, 205–6.

42. "About Executive Vetoes and Vicious Legislation," *Deming Headlight*, January 21, 1893. The article indicates there were 87 bills that became law when Ross did not act on them within three days. If Prince was right about Ross approving 47 bills, then the number Ross did not act upon was 75.

43. All messages from Ross to the Twenty-eighth Legislative Assembly, including his veto messages, are bundled in the printed file *General and Special Messages of Governor Ross to the 28th Legislative Assembly*, Ross Papers, Santa Fe. Ross's papers as governor are all on microfilm at the New Mexico State Library, which adjoins the archives. *General and Special Messages . . . to the 28th Assembly* are on roll 102 beginning at frame 220. The date on the heading is wrong: it should be December 28, 1888, but the typesetter has it as 1889.

44. Veto dated February 13, 1889, in Ross, *Vetoes of the 28th Legislative Assembly*, 51. See also United States Constitution, Article IV, Section 3: "The Congress shall have Power to dispose of and make needful Rules and Regulations Respecting the territory or other Property belonging to the United States."

45. Shane, "Edmund G. Ross: Governor of New Mexico."

46. Veto dated January 28, 1889, in Ross, *Vetoes of the 28th Legislative Assembly*, 32.

47. Ibid., 35–36.

48. Veto dated February 12, 1889, in Ross, *Vetoes of the 28th Legislative Assembly*, 47–48.

49. Veto dated February 28, 1889, in Ross, *Vetoes of the 28th Legislative Assembly*, 80–83.

50. See note 40.

51. Lamar, *The Far Southwest*, 162.

52. Lamar, "Edmund G. Ross," 205.

53. Ross, *General and Special Messages . . . to the 28th Legislative Assembly*, entry for December 29, 1888, 11. Note that the published messages were incorrectly dated 1889.

54. Lamar, *The Far Southwest*, 162, citing figures used by Ross in a March 31, 1890, pamphlet, *Public Schools and Statehood for New Mexico*.

55. See note 40.

56. Ross, "Address to the People of New Mexico," March 1, 1889, Ross Papers, Santa Fe.

57. See chapter 18 regarding the Ross and Burke proposal to the United States Congress to have the federal government finance and run a public school system in New Mexico.

58. *Santa Fe Daily Sun*, January 1, 1891.

59. See note 53; see also Lamar, "Edmund G. Ross," 205–6.

60. Lamar, "Edmund G. Ross," 206.

61. Simmons, *Albuquerque: A Narrative History*, 231–32.

62. "Welcome Home," *Albuquerque Morning Journal*, June 17, 1885.

63. Leis, "Memoirs . . . Part Three," 6.

64. Fannie Ross to a nephew named Charles, April 24, 1887, Ross Collection, Topeka.

65. Leis, "Memoirs . . . Part Three," 6.

Chapter Twenty-Two

1. "Ross's Varying Fortune," *New York Times*, August 18, 1889.

2. Lamar, *The Far Southwest*, 159.

3. Ashenfelter to Ross, August 10, 1889, Ross Papers, Santa Fe.

4. Ashenfelter to Ross, August 25, 1889, Ross Papers, Santa Fe.

5. George Albright to Ross, July 9, 1886, Ross Papers, Santa Fe; see also Leis, "Memoirs . . . Part Three," 10.

6. Leis, "Memoirs . . . Part Three," 12.

7. Lillian Leis was writing several decades after her father's death, and her recollections are not always accurate, especially in part 3, which seems to have been written later than the first two parts. Her memories of where and when her brother Pitt and her mother and father lived are not always reliable. Leis's memory of the adobe house adjacent to the "ranch" may be wrong; she may be confusing it with the home on Barelas Road. I have chosen to assume she is right about there being two adobe houses over a period of years. Even if she is wrong, it is of little consequence. Probably Pitt and his wife were living on Barelas Road by sometime in 1893.

8. Homestead Certificate No. 1719, January 22, 1896, Bureau of Land Management, Santa Fe, New Mexico.

9. *Deming Headlight*, September 7, 1889.

10. *Deming Headlight*, October 12, 1889. Statehood was not achieved until January 1912, five years after Ross's death.

11. *Deming Headlight*, October 4, 1890.

12. Ibid.

13. *Deming Headlight*, October 25, 1890.

14. *Deming Headlight*, reprinted from the *Santa Fe Sun*, January 10, 1891.

15. Leis, "Memoirs . . . Part Three," 20; see also chapter 17 for an account of the Anthony incident.

16. "Land Court Bill Passed," *Deming Headlight*, March 7, 1891.

17. See New Mexico Office of the State Historian, "Thornton, William Taylor."

18. Leis, "Memoirs . . . Part Three," 13.

19. See "The Governorship," *Deming Headlight*, March 25, 1893. The article indicates strong newspaper endorsement both of Ross and of Cleveland's non-reappointment policy.

20. *Scribner's Magazine* to Ross, November 4, 1891, Ross Collection, Topeka. The letter acknowledges that Ross has accepted their invitation to write the Johnson impeachment article.

21. Ross, "The Impeachment Trial," 524.

22. Thomas Ewing Jr. to Ross, July 26, 1894, Ross Collection, Topeka.

23. Ross, *Impeachment of Andrew Johnson*, preface.

24. Ibid., 38–39.

25. Foner, *Reconstruction*, xvii.

26. Ross, *The Pilgrim and the Cavalier*, n.p.

27. See "A Great Irrigation Enterprise," *Deming Headlight*, November 23, 1889.

28. Ross, "Future of the Arid West."

29. Ross to Fannie, March 16, 1897, Ross Papers, Santa Fe.

30. This may have been during a time when Leis was known to have been on an extended vacation in Colorado.

31. Ross to a daughter, probably Lillian, April 10, 1897, Ross Papers, Santa Fe, 7.

32. Ross to Fannie, April 19, 1897, Ross Papers, Santa Fe.

33. Leis may be confused about the year. A picture of Ross, dressed just as she described, was likely shot in 1896. The picture shows the family (without Fannie) gathered at the shanty and includes Arthur, who died in January 1897.

34. Leis, "Memoirs . . . Part Three," 15, 16. Lillian is confused about the dates of her presence in Albuquerque. She is right that the family celebrated the forty-ninth anniversary in October 1897, but she is incorrect that she returned one year later. She would have returned two years later in 1899. Also, Lillian writes of one grandchild who died. She is probably referring to Wilson Ross, the four-year-old son of Pitt and Clemie who died in 1894. She fails to mention the deaths of her sister Fannie's children in 1896 and 1897.

35. *Albuquerque Journal Democrat*, November 14, 1899, reporting the death of Fannie Ross; see also Leis, "Memoirs . . . Part Three," 16.

36. Leis, "Memoirs . . . Part Three," 16. If the manuscript has survived, its location remains a mystery.

37. Ibid., 16.

38. Ibid., 17, 18.

39. Ibid., 18.

40. Ibid., 18–19.

41. Simmons, *Albuquerque: A Narrative History*, 313–14.

42. Rowe, *Wonderful Old Lawrence*, 116–18.

43. *Albuquerque Morning Journal*, March 12, 1907.

44. *Albuquerque Morning Journal*, March 11, 1907.

45. Quoted in Bumgardner, *Life of Edmund G. Ross*, 102–3.

46. Leis, "Memoirs . . . Part Three," 21.

47. *Albuquerque Morning Journal*, May 11, 1907.

BIBLIOGRAPHY

Archival Sources

Andrew Johnson Papers. Library of Congress.

Edmund G. Ross Collection, 1856–1907. Kansas State Historical Society, Topeka.

Edmund G. Ross Papers, 1865–1907. University of New Mexico Center for Southwest Research, Albuquerque.

Ewing Collection. Kansas State Historical Society, Topeka.

Governor Edmund Ross Papers, 1885–1889. New Mexico State Archives, Santa Fe.

Congressional Databases

A Century of Lawmaking for a New Nation: U.S. Congressional Documents and Debates, 1774–1875. Washington, D.C.: Library of Congress, 1998–. memory.loc.gov/ammem/amlaw/lawhome.html. Searchable database with sections containing Statutes and Documents, Journals of Congress, and Debates of Congress including the *Congressional Globe* (1833–1873).

Congressional Globe. See *A Century of Lawmaking.*

Newspapers

For Kansas newspapers, the excellent collection of the Kansas State Historical Society is available on microfilm. For New Mexico newspapers, the New

Mexico State Library adjacent to the state archives has an extensive collection on microfilm. Some are also available at newspaperarchives.com.

Albuquerque Daily Democrat, 1882.

Albuquerque Evening Democrat, 1885.

Albuquerque Journal Democrat, 1899.

Albuquerque Morning Journal, 1883–1885, 1907.

Atchison (KS) Patriot, 1880.

Deming (NM) Headlight, 1889–1891, 1893.

Kansas City Star, 1903.

Kansas City Times, 1872.

Kansas Daily Tribune (Lawrence), 1865. Also *Kansas Weekly Tribune* (Lawrence), 1866.

Kansas State Journal (Lawrence), 1863.

Kansas State Record (Topeka), 1859–1861, 1868, 1870.

Kansas Tribune (Lawrence), 1855, 1863–1866.

Kansas Tribune (Topeka), 1857–1858.

Lawrence (KS) Daily Tribune, 1866.

Lawrence Evening Paper, 1873.

Lawrence Standard, 1876–1877. Also *Lawrence Evening Standard*, 1877–1879, and *Lawrence Democratic Standard*, 1880.

Leavenworth (KS) Daily Conservative, 1868.

Leavenworth Daily Press, 1878.

Leavenworth Democratic Standard, 1880–1882.

Leavenworth Times, 1880.

Milwaukee Sentinel, 1856. Ross Collection, Topeka.

New York Herald, 1869.

New York Sun, 1896.

New York Times, 1866, 1868–1869, 1885, 1888–1889.

New York Tribune, 1866.

Ross's Paper (Coffeyville, KS), 1871–1872.

Santa Fe Daily Sun, 1891.

Santa Fe Herald, 1888.

Santa Fe New Mexican Review, 1885.

Silver City (NM) Enterprise, 1887.

Spirit of Kansas (Lawrence), 1874. Kansas State Historical Society, Topeka.

Other Published Materials

Anderson, George B. *History of New Mexico: Its Resources and People.* Vol 1. Los Angeles: Pacific States, 1907.

Barker, Deborah. "Perry Fuller: Indian Agent, Self-Made Man and White Collar Criminal." Paper presented to the Franklin County Historical Society, April 28, 2012. franklincokshistory.org/wp-content/uploads/2012/07/Perry-Fuller-talk.pdf.

Benedict, Michael Les. *The Impeachment and Trial of Andrew Johnson.* New York: W. W. Norton, 1973.

Berwanger, Eugene H. "Ross and the Impeachment: A New Look at a Critical Vote." *Kansas History* 1 (Winter 1978): 235–42.

Bowden, J. J. "Private Land Claims in the Southwest." 6 vols. Master's thesis, Southern Methodist University, 1969.

Browning, Orville Hickman. *The Diary of Orville Hickman Browning.* Vol. 2. Edited by James G. Randall. Springfield: Trustees of the Illinois State Historical Library, 1933.

Bumgardner, Edward. *The Life of Edmund G. Ross: The Man Whose Vote Saved a President.* Kansas City, MO: Fielding-Turner, 1949.

Caldwell, Martha B. "Pomeroy's 'Ross Letter': Genuine or Forgery?" *Kansas Historical Quarterly* 7 (August 1944): 463–72.

Castel, Albert. *Civil War Kansas: Reaping the Whirlwind.* Lawrence: University Press of Kansas, 1997.

Chase, C. M. *The Editor's Run in New Mexico and Colorado.* 1882. Whitefish, MT: Kessinger, 2010.

Chávez, Thomas E. *New Mexico Past and Future.* Albuquerque: University of New Mexico Press, 2006.

Collins, Robert. *Jim Lane: Scoundrel, Statesman, Kansan.* Gretna, LA: Pelican, 2007.

Connelley, William Elsey. *The Life of Preston B. Plumb.* Chicago: Browne and Howell, 1913.

Cordley, Richard. *A History of Lawrence, Kansas.* Lawrence, 1895. Kansas Collection Books, kancoll.org/books/cordley_history.

Crawford, S. J. *Kansas in the Sixties.* 1911. Ottawa: Kansas Heritage Press, 1994.

Cutler, William G. *History of the State of Kansas.* Chicago: A. T. Andreas, 1883. Kansas Collection Books, kancoll.org/books/cutler.

Davis, W. W. H. *El Gringo: New Mexico and Her People.* 1857. Lincoln: University of Nebraska Press, 1982.

Dean, Virgil W., ed. *Kansas Territorial Reader.* Topeka: Kansas State Historical Society, 2005.

Dewitt, David Miller. *The Impeachment and Trial of Andrew Johnson.* New York: Macmillan, 1903.

Dorsey, Stephen W. "Land Stealing in New Mexico, a Rejoinder." *North American Review* 145 (October 1887): 396–409.

Ebright, Malcolm. *Land Grants and Lawsuits in Northern New Mexico.* Albuquerque: University of New Mexico Press, 1994.

"Eleventh Regiment Kansas Volunteer Infantry." In Cutler, *History of the State of Kansas,* "State History," Military Record, part 12. kancoll.org/books/cutler /sthist/milrec-p12.html.

Etcheson, Nicole. *Bleeding Kansas: Contested Liberty in the Civil War Era.* Lawrence: University Press of Kansas, 2004.

———. "The Great Principle of Self-Government: Popular Sovereignty and Bleeding Kansas." In Dean, *Kansas Territorial Reader,* 53–67.

Foner, Eric. *Reconstruction: America's Unfinished Revolution, 1863–1877.* New York: Harper and Row, 1988.

Foote, Shelby. *The Civil War: A Narrative.* Vol. 2, *Fredericksburg to Meridian.* New York: Random House, 1963.

Goodwin, Doris Kearns. *Team of Rivals: The Political Genius of Abraham Lincoln.* New York: Simon and Schuster, 2005.

Grove, Nettie Thompson. "The Man Who Saved Andrew Johnson." *Taylor-Trotwood Magazine,* May 1910, 3–11. Copy in Ross Collection, Topeka.

Hamilton, Clad. "A Colonel of Kansas." In *Collections of the Kansas State Historical Society* 12 (1912): 282–92. skyways.lib.ks.us/genweb/shawnee /library/KSHSvol12/lindsey.txt. Reprinted in *Tales of Kansas in the Civil War,* 19–28.

Harrington, Arthur Elliot. *Edmund G. Ross: A Man of Courage.* Franklin, TN: Providence House, 1997.

Hearn, Chester G. *The Impeachment of Andrew Johnson.* Jefferson, NC: McFarland, 2000.

Hebert, Richard A. *Modern Maine: Its Historic Background, People, and Resources.* New York: Lewis Historical Publishing, 1951.

Heitzman, Paul R. "The Reaction of the Kansas Press to the Career of Edmund G. Ross, 1856–1907." Master's thesis, University of Kansas, 1953.

Horn, Calvin. *New Mexico's Troubled Years: The Story of the Early Territorial Governors.* Albuquerque, NM: Horn and Wallace, 1963.

Jellison, Charles A. *Fessenden of Maine: Civil War Senator.* Syracuse, NY: Syracuse University Press, 1962.

Johnson, Samuel A. "The Emigrant Aid Company in Kansas." In Dean, *Kansas Territorial Reader*, 120–29.

Julian, George W. "Land-Stealing in New Mexico." *North American Review* 145 (July 1887): 17–32.

Kansas Territorial Legislature. *Report of the Joint Committee of Investigation, Appointed by the Kansas Legislature of 1872*. Topeka, 1872.

Keleher, William A. *The Fabulous Frontier: Twelve New Mexico Items*. Rev. ed. Albuquerque: University of New Mexico Press, 1962.

———. *The Maxwell Land Grant: A New Mexico Item*. 4th ed. Albuquerque: University of New Mexico Press, 1983.

———. *New Mexicans I Knew: Memoirs, 1892–1969*. Albuquerque: University of New Mexico Press, 1983.

———. *Turmoil in New Mexico, 1846–1868*. Santa Fe, NM: Rydal, 1952.

Kennedy, John F. *Profiles in Courage*. 1956. New York: Harper Perennial Classics, 2004.

Kessell, John L. *Pueblos, Spaniards, and the Kingdom of New Mexico*. Norman: University of Oklahoma Press, 2008.

———, ed. *Remote Beyond Compare: The Letters of Don Diego de Vargas to His Family from New Spain and New Mexico, 1675–1706*. Albuquerque: University of New Mexico Press, 1989.

Kitts, John Howard. "The Civil War Diary of John Howard Kitts." In *Collections of the Kansas State Historical Society* 14 (1918): 318–32. Reprinted in *Tales of Kansas in the Civil War*, 49–62.

LaForte, Robert S. "Gilded Age Senator: The Election, Investigation, and Resignation of Alexander Caldwell, 1871–1873." *Kansas History* 21 (Winter 1998–1899), 234–55.

Lamar, Howard R. "Edmund G. Ross as Governor of New Mexico Territory: A Reappraisal." *New Mexico Historical Review* 36 (July 1961): 177–209.

———. *The Far Southwest, 1846–1912*. Rev. ed. Albuquerque: University of New Mexico Press, 2000.

Langsdorf, Edgar. "S. C. Pomeroy and the New England Emigrant Aid Company, 1854–1858 [Part One]." *Kansas Historical Quarterly* 7 (August 1938): 227–45.

Larson, Robert W. *New Mexico's Quest for Statehood, 1846–1912*. Albuquerque: University of New Mexico Press, 1968.

Legler, Henry E. "Rescue of Joshua Glover, a Runaway Slave." 1898. library.wisc.edu/etext/wireader/WER1124.html.

Leis, Lillian Ross. "Memoirs of Edmund G. Ross." In the possession of Ross descendants.

———. "Memoirs of Edmund G. Ross, Part Two." In the possession of Ross descendants.

———. "Memoirs of Edmund G. Ross, Part Three." Governor Edmund Ross Papers, New Mexico State Archives, Santa Fe.

Lewis, Lloyd. "The Man the Historians Forgot." *Kansas Historical Quarterly* 8 (February 1939): 85–103.

Litteer, Loren K. *Perry Fuller: Baldwin's Millionaire Indian Agent.* Topeka: Kansas State Historical Society, 1982.

Magoffin, Susan Shelby. *Down the Santa Fe Trail and into Mexico . . . 1846–1847.* Edited by Stella M. Drumm. New Haven, CT: Yale University Press, 1926.

Malin, James C. "Dust Storms: Part One, 1850 to 1860." *Kansas Historical Quarterly* 14 (May 1946): 129–44.

Martin, Edward Winslow. *See* McCabe, James D.

McBride, George McCutchen. *The Land Systems of Mexico.* New York: American Geographical Society, 1923.

McCabe, James D. [Edward Winslow Martin, pseud.] *Behind the Scenes in Washington.* 1873. New York: Arno, 1974.

McKitrick, Eric L. *Andrew Johnson and Reconstruction.* Chicago: University of Chicago Press, 1960.

Miller Center for Public Affairs, University of Virginia. "American President: Rutherford B. Hayes." millercenter.org/president/hayes.

Miner, H. Craig, and William E. Unrau. *The End of Indian Kansas: A Study of Cultural Revolution, 1854–1871.* Lawrence: Regents Press of Kansas, 1978.

New Mexico Office of the State Historian. "Thornton, William Taylor, 1893–1897." newmexicohistory.org/filedetails_docs.php?fileID=23588.

New Mexico Supreme Court. *Reports of Cases Determined in the Supreme Court of the Territory of New Mexico.* 16 vols. Santa Fe: New Mexican Printing Company, 1881–1912.

Plummer, Mark A. "Governor Crawford's Appointment of Edmund G. Ross to the United States Senate." *Kansas Historical Quarterly* 38 (Summer 1962): 145–53.

———. "Profile in Courage? Edmund G. Ross and the Impeachment Trial." *Midwest Quarterly* 27 (Autumn 1985): 30–48.

Pomeroy, Samuel. "Open Letter to Edmund Ross." *Ross's Paper,* January 12, 1872.

Ponce, Pearl T. "Pledges and Principles: Buchanan, Walker, and Kansas in 1857." In Dean, *Kansas Territorial Reader,* 68–81.

Prince, L. Bradford. *A Concise History of New Mexico.* 2d ed. Cedar Falls, IA: Torch, 1914.

———. *New Mexico's Struggle for Statehood*. 1910. Santa Fe, NM: Sunstone, 2010.

Randall, J. G., and David Donald. *The Civil War and Reconstruction*. 2d ed. Lexington, MA: D. C. Heath, 1961.

Rebard, Bernice Ann. "Social History of Albuquerque, 1880–1885." Master's thesis, University of New Mexico, 1947.

Richardson, James D., ed. *A Compilation of the Messages and Papers of the Presidents*. Vol. 6. Washington, D.C.: Government Printing Office, 1902.

Riddleberger, Patrick W. *George Washington Julian, Radical Republican: A Study in Nineteenth-Century Politics and Reform*. Indianapolis: Indiana Historical Bureau, 1966.

Roberts, Joel. *The Cholera of 1849 and the Opinions of Medical and Other Professional Gentlemen in Regard to Its Origin and Proper Treatment*. Sandusky, OH, 1850. ohiomemory.org/cdm/compoundobject/collection /p267401coll36/id/4048/rec/3.

Robinson, Sara T. L. *Kansas: Its Interior and Exterior Life*. Boston: Crosby, Nichols, 1856.

Root, George A., ed. "The First Day's Battle at Hickory Point: From the Diary and Reminiscences of Samuel James Reader." *Kansas Historical Quarterly* 1 (November 1931): 28–49.

Roske, Ralph J. *His Own Counsel: The Life and Times of Lyman Trumbull*. Reno: University of Nevada Press, 1979.

Ross, Earle Dudley. *The Liberal Republican Movement*. New York: Henry Holt, 1919.

Ross, Edmund G. "The Future of the Arid West." *North American Review* 161 (October 1895): 438–50.

———. *History of the Impeachment of Andrew Johnson, President of the United States*. Santa Fe: New Mexican Printing Company, 1896.

———. "The Impeachment Trial." *Scribner's Magazine* 11 (April 1892): 519–24.

———. *The Pilgrim and the Cavalier in Kansas*. Washington, D.C.: Hayworth, 1895.

———. "Political Leaders of the Reconstruction Period." *Forum* 20 (October 1895): 218–34.

———. "A Previous Era of Popular Madness and Its Lessons." *Forum* 19 (July 1895): 595–605.

———. *A Reminiscence of the Kansas Conflict*. Albuquerque: Albright and Anderson, 1898.

———. *Report of the Governor of New Mexico to the Secretary of the Interior for the Year 1885*. Washington, D.C.: Government Printing Office, 1885. Copy in Governor Ross Collection, New Mexico State Archives, Santa Fe.

———. *Report of the Governor of New Mexico to the Secretary of the Interior for the Year 1886*. Washington, D.C.: Government Printing Office, 1886. Copy in Governor Ross Collection, New Mexico State Archives, Santa Fe.

———. *Seven Vetoes*. Pamphlet. Santa Fe, 1887.

Rowe, Elfriede Fischer. *Wonderful Old Lawrence*. Kansas City, KS: World Company, 1971. Kansas Collection Books, kancoll.org/books/rowe.

Sando, Joe S. *The Pueblo Indians*. San Francisco: Indian Historian Press, 1976.

Sandusky Library. "The Underground Railroad in Sandusky." *Sandusky History*, February 10, 2009. sanduskyhistory.blogspot.com/2009/02/underground-railroad-in-sandusky.html.

Schiller, Mark. "The History and Adjudication of the Antonio Chávez Grant." Paper presented at the University of New Mexico Symposium on Land Grants, January 15, 2010.

———. "Surveyor General George W. Julian: Reformer or Colonial Bureaucrat." *La Jicarita News* (Chamisal, NM) 15, nos. 4–7 (April–July 2010).

Scott, Kim Allen. "The Fighting Printers of Company E, Eleventh Kansas Volunteer Infantry." Johnson, AK: Kinnally Press, 1987.

Shane, Karen Diane. "Edmund G. Ross: Governor of New Mexico, 1885–1869." Master's thesis, University of New Mexico, 1983.

Shea, William L. *Fields of Blood: The Prairie Grove Campaign*. Chapel Hill: University of North Carolina Press, 2009.

Sherwood, Glenn V. *A Labor of Love: The Life and Art of Vinnie Ream*. Hygiene, CO: SunShine Press, 1997.

Shishkin, J. K. *The Palace of the Governors*. Santa Fe: Museum of New Mexico, 1984.

Sides, Hampton. *Blood and Thunder: An Epic of the American West*. New York: Doubleday, 2006.

Simmons, Marc. *Albuquerque: A Narrative History*. Albuquerque: University of New Mexico Press, 1982.

———. *Coronado's Land: Essays on Daily Life in Colonial New Mexico*. Albuquerque: University of New Mexico Press, 1991.

Simpson, Brooks D. *The Reconstruction Presidents*. Lawrence: University Press of Kansas, 1998.

Smith, Ronald D. *Thomas Ewing, Jr.: Frontier Lawyer and Civil War General*. Columbia: University of Missouri Press, 2008.

Snell, Joseph W., and Don W. Wilson. "The Birth of the Atchison, Topeka and Santa Fe Railroad." *Kansas Historical Quarterly* 34 (Summer 1968): 113–42.

Socolofsky, Homer E. "Kansas in 1876." *Kansas Historical Quarterly* 43 (Spring 1977): 1–43.

Speer, John. *Life of Gen. James H. Lane "The Liberator of Kansas."* 2d ed. Garden City, KS: John Speer, 1897.

Stewart, David O. *Impeached: The Trial of President Andrew Johnson and the Fight for Lincoln's Legacy.* New York: Simon & Schuster, 2009.

Sumner, Charles. "The Crime Against Kansas: The Apologies for the Crime; The True Remedy." Speech delivered to the United States Senate, May 19–20, 1856. In *The Works of Charles Sumner*, 4:125–249. Boston: Lee and Shepard, 1870–1873.

Swanberg, W. A. *Sickles the Incredible.* New York: Scribner, 1956.

Tales of Kansas in the Civil War. Tucson, AZ: A Plus Printing, n.d.

Taylor, David Gene. "The Business and Political Career of Thomas Ewing, Jr.: A Study in Frustrated Ambition." PhD diss., University of Kansas, 1970.

Thaddeus Stevens: Champion of Freedom. Harrisburg: Pennsylvania Historical and Museum Commission, 2006. phmc.state.pa.us/ppet/stevens.

Trefousse, Hans L. *Impeachment of a President: Andrew Johnson, the Blacks, and Reconstruction.* 2d ed. New York: Fordham University Press, 1999.

Twain, Mark, and Charles Dudley Warner. *The Gilded Age: A Tale of Today.* Hartford, CT: American Publishing Company, 1874.

Twitchell, Ralph Emerson. *The Leading Facts of New Mexican History.* Vol 2. Cedar Falls, IA: Torch Press, 1912.

United States Congress. House. Select Committee of the Managers of Impeachment. "Raising of Money to be Used in Impeachment." 40th Cong., 2d sess., July 3, 1868. Report no. 75.

Wallace, Lew. *Report of the Governor of New Mexico Made to the Secretary of the Interior for the Year 1879.* Washington, D.C.: Government Printing Office, 1879. Copy in Governor Wallace Papers, New Mexico State Archives, Santa Fe.

Watts, Dale E. "How Bloody Was Bleeding Kansas? Political Killings in Kansas Territory, 1854–1861." *Kansas History* 18 (Summer 1995): 116–29.

Welles, Gideon. *Diary of Gideon Welles, Secretary of the Navy under Lincoln and Johnson.* 1911. Edited by Howard K. Beale. 3 vols. New York: W. W. Norton, 1960.

Westphall, Victor. *Mercedes Reales: Hispanic Land Grants of the Upper Rio Grande Region.* Albuquerque: University of New Mexico Press, 1983.

———. *Thomas Benton Catron and His Era.* Tucson: University of Arizona Press, 1973.

White, Horace. *The Life of Lyman Trumbull.* Boston: Houghton Mifflin, 1913.

Wisconsin Local History Network. "Ripon's Booth War: Aftermath of the Fugitive Slave Act in Wisconsin." 1999. wlhn.org/topics/boothwar/booth_war_intro.htm.

INDEX